INTERNATIONAL CO-OPERATION IN CIVIL AND CRIMINAL MATTERS

International Co-operation in Civil and Criminal Matters

Third Edition

DAVID McCLEAN

CBE, QC (Hon), DCL (Oxon), Hon Litt D (Sheff), FBA
Bencher of Gray's Inn
Emeritus Professor of Law, University of Sheffield
Membre de l'Institut de Droit International
Chancellor of the Diocese of Sheffield

OXFORD
UNIVERSITY PRESS

UNIVERSITY PRESS

Great Clarendon Street, Oxford, OX2 6DP,
United Kingdom

Oxford University Press is a department of the University of Oxford.
It furthers the University's objective of excellence in research, scholarship,
and education by publishing worldwide. Oxford is a registered trade mark of
Oxford University Press in the UK and in certain other countries

First Edition published in 1992

Second Edition published in 2002

Third Edition published in 2012

Impression: 1

British Library Cataloguing in Publication Data

Data available

Library of Congress Cataloging in Publication Data

Data available

ISBN 978–0–19–960206–3

Printed in Great Britain by
CPI Group (UK) Ltd, Croydon, CR0 4YY

Preface

It continues to be the aim of this book to assist lawyers, scholars, administrators, and policy-makers in exploring the legal bases for international co-operation in civil and in criminal matters. The need for such co-operation becomes greater with each passing year as commercial and criminal activity increasingly ignores national boundaries. If civil and commercial disputes are to be properly resolved and international crime properly dealt with, there must be active co-operation between national civil and criminal justice systems. The different history, structure, and content of national legal systems means that it is not easy to devise international arrangements which work effectively. If I offer criticism of some of the international texts, I couple it with admiration at the way in which many problems, once seen as intractable, have been successfully overcome. Although international in focus, this book is written in the United Kingdom and I have sought to trace the implementation of the international instruments in UK law.

In the preface to the last edition, I expressed the hope that we might have reached something of a plateau as the major international instruments were in place. Those words were written during a period of frenetic international activity following the events of September 2001, and it is significant that the outcome was a realization that adequate legal bases for co-operation already existed; no new instruments were needed. But my plateau did not stretch very far. New policies have emerged, sometimes in response to new technology; and the European Union's resolve to build an area of freedom, security, and justice has kept the Brussels printing presses busy.

In the area of civil justice, the established Hague Conventions continue to provide a reliable basis for co-operation, and many of the early controversies as to their interpretation have been resolved. Developments in this area include new practices in taking evidence at a distance, through video-conferencing and similar techniques, and in cross-border mediation.

Crime attracts greater political interest and I lamented in the last edition that the wish to be seen to be 'doing something about crime' led to the adoption of more and more texts which added little to what had gone before. In my judgment that phase has passed; there continue to be many new texts but the developments seem more principled. The major updating of the Commonwealth Scheme in 2011 is of global importance, and the Council of Europe has continued its excellent work in this field, an example being its Convention on Human Trafficking. The EU's decision to emphasize mutual recognition alongside mutual assistance has led to an incremental, and necessarily piecemeal, development which will eventually produce a comprehensive system.

I have had to police the boundaries of this book with some care. It does not deal with the recognition of civil and commercial judgments or with extradition;

although related to my theme, both are major topics well served in the literature. I have, however, included material on the European Arrest Warrant as a part of the EU's programme. To accommodate the new developments, there has been a great deal of re-writing and re-organization, in which I was much helped by the comments of OUP's anonymous reviewers.

I am happy once again to record my appreciation of many enduring and stimulating friendships with others working in this field, especially in the Commonwealth Secretariat and in the Hague Conference.

David McClean

New Year's Day 2012

Contents—Summary

Contents—Detailed

List of Abbreviations

AetD	Actes et Documents
APG	Asian/Pacific Group on Money-Laundering
ATS	amphetamine-type stimulants
CARIN	Camden Assets Recovery Inter-Agency Network
CDD	customer due diligence
CFATF	Caribbean Financial Action Task Force
CICAD	Inter-American Drug Abuse Control Commission
CIDIP	Inter-American Specialized Conference on Private International Law 1971
CIDIP 2	Second Inter-American Specialized Conference on Private International Law 1979
CODEXTER	Committee of Experts on Terrorism
CPR	Civil Procedure Rules
CPT	Committee for the Prevention of Torture and Inhuman or Degrading Treatment or Punishment
EAG	Eurasian Group on combating money laundering and financing of terrorism
e-App	Electronic Apostille Pilot Program
EAW	European Arrest Warrant
EEA	European Economic Area
EEW	European Evidence Warrant
EEJ-NET	European Extrajudicial Network
ESAAMLG	Southern African Anti-Money Laundering Group
FATF	Financial Action Task Force
FIU	financial intelligence unit
FSA	Financial Services Authority
GAFISUD	South American Financial Action Task Force
GEMME	European Association of Judges for Mediation
GIABA	Inter Governmental Action Group against Money Laundering in West Africa
GRECO	Group of States against Corruption
GRETA	Group of Experts on Action against Trafficking in Human Beings
ICPO	International Criminal Police Organization (Interpol)
JHA	Justice and Home Affairs
MENAFATF	Middle East and North Africa Financial Action Task Force
MLAT	Mutual Legal Assistance Treaty
MLRO	money laundering reporting officer
MONEYVAL	Committee of Experts on the Evaluation of Anti-Money Laundering Measures and the Financing of Terrorism
NCCTs	non-co-operative countries or territories
NICS	National Criminal Intelligence Service
OAS	Organization of American States
OECD	Organisation for Economic Co-operation and Development

PC-R-OC	Select Committee of Experts on the Operation of European Conventions in the Penal Field
PPA	Problems Arising from the Practical Application of the European Convention on Mutual Assistance in Criminal Matters
SIENA	Secure Information Exchange Network Application
SOCA	Serious Organised Crime Agency
S-TESTA	Trans European Services for Telematics between Administrations
TREVI	inter-governmental forum for co-operation in combating terrorism, drugs trafficking, and serious crime and public order
UNODC	United Nations Office on Drugs and Crime
WCO	World Customs Organization

Table of Cases

USA

Table of Legislation

Table of Treaties and Conventions

1

Civil Matters: Challenges and Solutions

The scale of the activity that forms the subject matter of this book, international co-operation in civil and criminal matters, has grown quite dramatically in recent years. It increasingly engages the attention of lawyers in private practice, in the offices of corporate legal counsel, and in government service.

The reasons are not difficult to find. They lie in part in technological developments: the growth of ever faster air services for both passengers and freight; the possibilities opened up by electronic fund transfer and by increasingly sophisticated telecommunications. Others are in the political sphere: regional groupings such as the European Union remove barriers to movement of people, goods, and services, and themselves develop extensive legislative or quasi-legislative powers. Others again reflect the sad realities of drug abuse, political violence, and terrorism, and the growth of highly organized international criminal syndicates with resources greater than those of the governments of smaller states.

International co-operation has become a normal and well-accepted feature in both civil and criminal matters; but it was not always so. States were proudly independent and ill-informed about, and so rather suspicious of, other legal systems. There has always been an international dimension to civil litigation, but the rules of private international law, regulating the jurisdiction of a nation's courts and the law they should apply to govern particular issues, developed much later in England than in continental Europe.[1] When the English courts began to formulate such rules, the context was often a case in which the foreign country was in fact Scotland or a British possession overseas, so exposure to the ideas and practices of countries in the civil law tradition was limited. This introductory chapter looks at the obstacles that all this presented to the development of efficient international co-operation, and at some of the ways in which those challenges could be overcome.

I. Differing approaches

In the context of civil proceedings, international co-operation is primarily concerned with the service of documents, 'process' of one sort or another, but also extra-judicial documents of significance, and the taking of evidence. Post-trial assistance, in the form of the enforcement of judgments and orders, is traditionally treated as a (major) topic in its own right. In all these areas, common law and civil law traditions adopt very different approaches.

1. Differing approaches to the service of process

Each country has its own law and practice as to the service of process and other documents issued for use in ordinary, non-international, cases. International discussion of service of process is influenced—and often confused—by the differing assumptions of the participants, each of whom tends to project on to the international plane the familiar features of his or her own national system.

So, in many common law jurisdictions, and in countries such as those in Scandinavia with a similar approach, the responsibility for service rests with the plaintiff or the agents (solicitors, process-servers) whom he employs. There are in fact many exceptions to this proposition. In England, service by the court is now the general rule, the Civil Procedure Rules (CPR) generalizing a practice formerly applicable only to county court process and some Admiralty writs.[2] In the United States' federal courts, summonses in civil actions may be served by a United States Marshal;[3] but service by the plaintiff or his or her agent is nonetheless seen as the

---

[1] See Dicey, Morris and Collins, *The Conflict of Laws* (14th edn, Sweet & Maxwell, 2006), para 1–018 and the material there cited.

[2] CPR, r 6.4.

[3] Federal Rules of Civil Procedure, r 4(2)(c)(3).

common law norm. In English practice 'a document is served personally on an individual by leaving it with that individual';[4] it is not sufficient to leave the document with a relative or an obliging neighbour. Under English practice it is not possible to draw any meaningful distinction between 'formal' or 'informal' service, or between service 'accepted voluntarily' and 'enforced' service.

Normal practice in civil law countries is very different. Originating summonses and equivalent documents will be served by an officer of the court, who may be the clerk to the court (as in Switzerland), or an officer with specific functions including the service of process (such as the *ufficiale giudiziario* in Italy), or in some countries such as France a *huissier de justice*, a process-server appointed by the state authorities but engaged in a professional capacity by the plaintiff. Whatever the precise position of the person effecting service, the activities will typically be closely regulated by legislation, and service by him will be regarded as 'formal'. In some contexts, and particularly where the document to be served originated abroad, an informal mode of service is used; typically the document is passed to a local police station, and is either taken round to the defendant's address or the defendant is invited to call in to collect it. This 'simple delivery' (*remise simple* in French) is referred to in the text of the Hague Convention on Service Abroad of 15 November 1965 as 'delivery to an addressee who accepts it voluntarily'.[5] Readers from a common law background are often puzzled by this, because it looks like the single concept of 'service' with which they are familiar; one has to keep in mind the civil law distinction between more and less solemn modes.

2. Differing approaches to the taking of evidence

The differences between the common law and civil law traditions are important despite the fact that the actual concept of service of process is relatively straightforward. Legal systems may vary enormously in the types of civil claim they will entertain and in the conduct of the proceedings by which claims are adjudicated, yet all but the most primitive of legal systems will know the idea of giving notice to the other party of the making of a claim or of the initiation of a significant step in the resulting proceedings.

In any discussion of international co-operation in the taking of evidence, conceptual differences loom much larger. The subject matter is much more closely related to the actual business of judicial decision-making and so to the ideology and practice of particular systems of civil procedure. Those systems are almost infinitely variable, and merely to categorize a system as within the common law or civil law tradition would conceal important differences. All that can be done here is to identify some of the relevant variables, using what must inevitably be a broad brush in their description.[6]

---

[4] CPR, r 6.5(3)(a).
[5] See p 39.
[6] For a detailed analysis of different systems of civil procedure, see 16 Int Ency Comp L, chaps 1 and 6.

Some of the crucial variables are best identified by posing a single question, in some such form as, 'What happens at the eventual hearing of the case by the trial court?' One possible answer, which might be given where the relevant legal system remains close to the classical approach of the civil law tradition, would be along these lines: 'The court, having reviewed the written minutes containing the evidence as to the facts of the case, hears submissions on behalf of the parties as to the conclusions to be drawn in the light of the applicable law.' Another answer, characteristic of a system within the common law tradition, might be: 'The court hears oral evidence as to the facts from the parties or their witnesses or both, and then hears submissions on behalf of the parties as to the conclusions to be drawn in the light of the applicable law.'

The first answer describes a procedure in which the trial court deals, so far as the facts of the case are concerned, with written material, which will have been assembled and put into a particular form by one or more members of the court's personnel. The preparation of the material may be undertaken by the trial judge, or one of the trial judges, or by another judge or court officer whose primary work consists of such preparation. The material itself may include some original documents and written reports of experts, but will also contain a record, in the form of a deposition or summary, of oral testimony given by witnesses and, in some systems, by the parties. The second answer describes a procedure which relies, in principle, upon oral evidence received at the actual trial, a good deal of importance being attached to the impression that the court forms of the parties and the witnesses as they give their evidence.

This contrast between written and oral procedures is seldom absolute. Many civil law systems find room for oral evidence at the eventual hearing. A common law court will receive some evidence in writing, whether in the form of reports, exhibits, or 'agreed bundles of documents'; a written witness statement stands as a witness's evidence in chief unless the court orders otherwise;[7] but in principle the evidence is 'heard' at the actual trial, the form of which is influenced by the needs of the jury even in those systems, such as the English, where the actual presence of a jury in a civil trial is now quite exceptional. It will be seen that the taking of evidence abroad, which must necessarily be done before the eventual trial and (unless modern techniques such as video recordings are brought into use) be reduced to writing, fits more naturally into the written than into the oral tradition.

The two hypothetical answers also point to another contrast. The common lawyer was able to speak of 'the parties or *their* witnesses'. In that tradition, with very limited exceptions, the witnesses are selected and called by the parties, and examined and cross-examined by the parties or their counsel. To quote a judicial explanation:

Under the civil procedure of the High Court the court does not, in general, exercise any control over the manner in which a party obtains the evidence which he needs to support his case. The court may give him help, certainly; for instance by discovery of documents *inter*

---

[7] For the English practice, see CPR, r 32.5(2).

partes[8] . . . ; by allowing evidence to be obtained or presented at the trial in various ways . . . ; and by the issue of subpoenas[9] . . . Subject, however, to the help of the court in these various ways, the basic principle underlying the preparation and presentation of a party's case in the High Court in England is that it is for that party to obtain and present the evidence which he needs by his own means, provided always that such means are lawful in the country in which they are used.[10]

Civil law systems see these aspects of evidence-gathering as a judicial function. While the parties may proffer the names of witnesses, and may have considerable scope for suggesting questions to be put to the witnesses, the civil law judge typically decides which witnesses to summon, conducts the questioning, and settles the deposition or minute which records the evidence. This means that the taking of evidence, even more emphatically than the service of process, is an exercise of the judicial sovereignty of the state. The taking of evidence within the territory of one state by the authorities of another, or on behalf of the parties to litigation in another state, will be seen as a serious affront to that sovereignty, unless of course official permission is sought and given.

One further distinction needs to be drawn. The hypothetical question posed above spoke of 'the eventual hearing of the case by the trial court'. A common lawyer would almost certainly refer, much more simply, to 'the trial', taking as granted the distinction between the trial itself and 'pre-trial proceedings', between the 'day in court' and the preparatory work done on behalf of the parties. Such language would be quite inappropriate if applied to the typical civil law system. The trial process there must include the various hearings at which evidence is received. Instead of a concentrated 'day in court', which provides a focus for the whole operation, there is a sequence of 'audiences' at which progress is made. It has been said that in the civil law tradition proof-taking 'often resembles a series of isolated pre-trial conferences rather than a concentrated trial',[11] which is helpful but must not be read as suggesting that these earlier stages are merely interlocutory; they are an integral part of the judicial process.

3. Seeking assistance from other states

As between states in the civil law tradition, the service of process or the taking of evidence abroad traditionally required the prior permission of the authorities of the state in which action was to be taken. This involved a formal request, initiated by a court or some related official, transmitted via the diplomatic channel, and ultimately considered by a court or other authority in the state of destination. The document that set out what was required was referred to as a 'letter (or letters) of

---

[8] This is now to be read as referring to the order of disclosure of documents under CPR, Part 31.

[9] Now referred to in the CPR as 'witness summonses'.

[10] *South Carolina Insurance Co v Assurantie Maatschappij 'De Zeven Provincien' NV* [1987] AC 24, 41–2.

[11] Cappelleti and Garth, 16 Int Ency Comp L, chap 1, para 5.

request' or 'letter rogatory'.[12] Letters of request were used in many contexts, including the enforcement of foreign judgments.[13]

Given that in common law states the service of process and the gathering of evidence was essentially for the parties, this procedure was relatively little known in such states. Those English courts whose practice was influenced by civilian ideas, especially the ecclesiastical and admiralty courts, were familiar with letters of request.[14] The ecclesiastical courts used them to transfer jurisdiction in ecclesiastical matters from the courts of one diocese to those of another. Those same courts had jurisdiction in probate matters and in 1755 in *King v Gordon*[15] a novel procedure was adopted, letters of request being sent by the Prerogative Court to the Scottish probate authorities to cite the next of kin, who resided in Scotland, to appear and accept administration, or show cause why they should not. The Scottish authorities did as they were asked, but not every other court was as co-operative: the following year the magistrates of Jersey refused to act on a similar letter of request.[16] The English courts would act on foreign letters of request in similar contexts.[17] The diplomatic channel was always used.[18]

II. Modes of communication

International co-operation necessarily entails communication between individuals or bodies in the two states concerned. The procedures used were once extremely formal and correspondingly slow; the dignity of states seemed to require nothing less. There has been a slow but steady move to greater simplicity, informality, and speed of communication. Layers of bureaucracy have been removed and there has been growing decentralization, so that there can be direct communication from local courts, agencies, or individuals and their counterparts in another state. What follows is an account of the range of forms of procedure which are, or have in the past been, found in national legislation and in practice under international conventions. All are potentially applicable to the service of process and many also to requests for the taking of evidence.

---

[12] The latter term is prevalent in United States usage.

[13] See eg *The Delta v The Erminia Foscolo* (1875–76) LR 1 PD 393 (French judgment given executory force in Italy after a letter of request under the Franco-Sardinian treaty of 1760).

[14] See the learned judgment of Sir Robert Phillimore in *The City of Mecca* (1879–80) LR 5 PD 28.

[15] (1755) 2 Lee 139.

[16] *Le Briton v Le Quesne* (1756) 2 Lee 261.

[17] eg *In the Goods of Luis Bianchi (deceased)* (1859) 1 Sw & Tr 511 (letters of request from the Judge of Orphans of Brazil addressed to 'the Judge of Orphans, or other judicial authorities in England' asking that the property of the deceased in England be delivered to a named person with a view to its distribution under Brazilian law). Cf *Re Sottomaior (A Lunatic)* (1873–74) LR 9 Ch App 677 (lunacy case: court recognized duty to assist the Portuguese court which had requested an examination of the lunatic's state of health but was unable to comply because of possible prejudice to third parties).

[18] eg *Baron de Bildt* (1905) 7 F 899 (petition by the Envoy Extraordinary and Minister Plenipotentiary of His Majesty the King of Sweden and Norway to the Court of St James, to the First Division of the Court of Session under the Foreign Tribunals Evidence Act, 1856).

1. The diplomatic channel

The most venerable and most formal mode of communication is the diplomatic channel. It may lend a certain dignity to the whole transaction but is notoriously slow. This is due to the number of distinct administrative hierarchies whose active co-operation is required, and whose officers frankly have other tasks of much greater priority and interest.[19] Under this procedure, documents emanating from, say, a court or *parquet* in the state of origin are transmitted (perhaps via the Ministry of Justice of that state) to its Foreign Ministry. They are then sent to the Embassy maintained in the state of destination, which conveys them to the Foreign Ministry of that state, which will pass them over to its Ministry of Justice to be sent down to the appropriate court by which evidence is to be taken or the appropriate local agency for service on the addressee. The evidence obtained and any required acknowledgement of due service may have to retrace the whole path.

2. The (direct) consular channel

The service of judicial documents and the taking of evidence are well-recognized consular functions. Their exercise depends very much on the conventions governing consular relations between the states concerned. It may be that the consul for the state of origin can deal in these contexts only with nationals of that state, or with anyone of whatever nationality in the area of responsibility served by the consulate. In some cases, notably where consuls are not in post, these consular functions may actually be performed by diplomatic officers.

3. The indirect consular channel

Many writers treat the diplomatic and (direct) consular channels as part of the customary practice of states. Arguably the indirect consular channel, like the modes of transmission still to be noted, is solely a creature of conventions. The 'indirectness' lies in the fact that the consul does not approach the defendant directly, but the appropriate authority in the state of destination; this will usually be some central government agency, within the Ministry of Justice for example, but local officers can be specified.

4. Ministry of Justice (or central authority) to Ministry of Justice (or central authority)

It is considerably simpler to exclude the relevant foreign ministries and their diplomatic or consular staffs from the process. The administration of justice is a

---

[19] For its use even as between neighbouring countries (France and Germany), see Oberlandesgericht Düsseldorf, 19 October 1984 (3 W 319/84), IPRax 1985, 289 (Asser 4/111); the EU Regulation considered below (see p 54) has changed the practice dramatically.

central concern of a Ministry of Justice, and direct communication between the two Justice Ministries is likely to produce greater understanding and a speedier response. What is essential to this mode is that each country should communicate via some agency of central government located in that part of the state's apparatus which is concerned with the administration of justice. This agency can have a title other than that of Ministry of Justice (for example, Attorney General's Department), or may be located in the courts service or form a specialist bureau. In every case, the agency will communicate with its counterpart in the other country.

5. Competent official to Ministry of Justice (or central authority)

Most of the modes considered so far require the involvement in each state of an agency of central government as well as a court or competent official (*parquet*, etc) at the local level. There is a readily identified 'central government interest' within the state of destination where considerations of sovereignty may be seen to be involved and where some knowledge of the nature of the documents to be served or the evidence sought is necessary if the state of destination is to be sure that its public policy (eg, as to bank secrecy) is not offended. At least in the service of process, the interest of central government of the state of origin is less pressing. There may be real practical advantages in having a central source of expertise; such a source is more likely to send documents in a form, and with accompanying material, required by the state of destination or specified in the applicable bilateral or multilateral convention. If, however, the local officials in the state of origin have access to appropriate procedural guidance, there is no strong reason of principle not to allow them to communicate directly with the Justice Ministry or other central authority of the state of destination. This mode comprises just that procedure.

One theoretical possibility which is thought not to be found in actual practice would be for the plaintiff, in a state of origin which regarded service and evidence-gathering as a matter for the parties to handle, to be allowed to make a direct approach to the Justice Ministry or other central authority of the state of destination. Ministries of Justice are, however, quite properly unwilling to enter into dialogue with private citizens of other states in this context, or to operate an advisory service for foreign lawyers.

6. Court or competent official to court or competent official

The argument supporting mode 5 above can be taken a stage further. Provided the competent local officials in the state of destination have adequate administrative guidance, their Justice Ministry may be content, or even happy, to withdraw from active involvement. This opens the way for direct communication between a judge or appropriate officer (*parquet*, etc) in the state of origin and his or her counterpart in the state of destination.

7. *Huissier de justice* to *huissier de justice*

Where both concerned states have the institution of *huissier de justice* for the service of process, a variant of the last mode is possible. The facts that *huissiers* are appointed or licensed by the state and have a defined role in Codes of Civil Procedure in respect of service enable them to be treated as in a similar position to the competent state officials, and direct communication from *huissier* to *huissier* (who will then act in the state of destination to involve the local *parquet*) can be authorized.

8. Plaintiff to court or competent official

This mode represents the ultimate 'deregulation'. It allows a direct approach by the plaintiff or his or her agent to the court or competent local official in the state of destination, no official of the state of origin being involved.

9. Service by post

In the service of process, the final mode eliminates all official involvement and permits the plaintiff or his agent to send the documents, with some appropriate means of obtaining confirmation of their delivery, by post.

It may be that 'post' will need progressive reinterpretation to include electronic communications, but only the most recent international instruments reflect these newer possibilities. This means that the older conventions requiring the use of the post impose delays which any commercial firm with access to modern technology would not tolerate in its normal practice. More generally, international law-making lags behind technological advances: e-mail and video conferencing are often used by judges where the facilities are available, and many international instruments are coming to seem distinctly old-fashioned.

III. Seeking solutions

Any progress towards more efficient co-operation required discussion and agreement between states. Only then could there be a clearer understanding of the differing approaches of common law and civil law countries and agreement on methods which all could adopt. Only international agreement could facilitate a movement away from the traditional slow formality of communications between states. The twentieth century saw a great deal of progress, largely by means of international conventions negotiated under the auspices of the Hague Conference on Private International Law, which in turn informed regional arrangements in Europe and Latin America.

Every businessman knows that a brief face-to-face meeting or ten minutes conversation by telephone can produce much more progress than months of written exchanges. Every reader of this book will know how easy it is to speak to a colleague, friend, or family member on the other side of the world, even from a mobile phone. It is difficult to realize how different matters were only a few decades ago. In these facts lie the seeds of less formal methods of co-operation, the notions of liaison magistrates and judicial networks, which seek to take a matter forward by means of simple conversations.

1. The Hague Conference

As between the civil law states of continental Europe, both service of process and the taking of evidence were governed partly by practice, partly by a limited number of bilateral conventions; there was no uniformity on matters of detail. Until the end of the nineteenth century, practice amongst the states of Europe as to service of process has been described as being in *un état anarchique*.[20] Efforts to produce a standardized practice were an early priority of the Hague Conference on Private International Law, which was and is still of the first importance in this area.[21]

Its title conceals the fact that it is an inter-governmental organization as significant in its field as, for example, the World Intellectual Property Organization. It first met in 1893 under the leadership of Tobias C M Asser, a notable Dutch scholar, though it was the work of the Italian Pasquale Stanislao Mancini which first promoted the idea of such a meeting. Civil procedure was high on its agenda.

The Conference was originally very much a European, and a civil law, club. The United Kingdom declined an invitation to participate in its first Session. Observers from the UK attended occasionally in the 1920s, but no common law country was a member of the Conference until it was revived after the Second World War, following a long interruption in its activities from 1928. Its present Statute entered into force on 15 July 1955, and declares it to have a permanent character, with the object of 'the progressive unification of the rules of private international law'.[22] The Statute was revised during the Twentieth Session of the Conference in 2005, largely to allow the European Community to become a member as a Regional Economic Integration Organisation,[23] and the opportunity was taken to make other changes to reflect current practice. Despite its international character, the conference continues to function under the supervision of a Commission of State of the Netherlands established by Royal Decree in 1897, and the Netherlands Government bears the costs of the Sessions of the Conference, held generally every four

---

[20] G A L Droz, 'Mémoire sur la Notification des Actes Judiciares et Extrajudiciares à l'Etranger', *AetD(10)*, vol 3, p 15.
[21] See J Offerhaus '*La Conférence de la Haye de droit international privé*' (1959) 16 Annuaire Suisse de droit international 27; M van Hoogstraten, 'The United Kingdom Joins an Uncommon Market: the Hague Conference on Private International Law' (1963) 12 ICLQ 148; for two commentaries from a common law perspective, see J D McClean, 'The Contribution of the Conference de la Haye to the Development of Private International Law in Common Law Countries' in *Recueil des Cours*, vol 223 (1992-II), pp 267–304; J D McClean, 'Common Lawyers and the Hague Conference' in A Borras et al (eds), *E Pluribus Unum: Liber Amicorum Georges Droz* (Kluwer, 1996), pp 205–18.
[22] Statute, art 1. The Statute has a single French-language text.
[23] See Statute, art 3.

years;[24] however, the Member States bear the cost of its Permanent Bureau,[25] the annual budget being approved by their diplomatic representatives in The Hague.[26] The Permanent Bureau works under the direction of the Council on General Affairs and Policy, which considers proposals for the inclusion of items in the work programme of the Conference and decides how they should be handled.[27]

In January 2012 seventy-one states and one regional organization (the EU) had accepted the Statute and so become members of the Conference. Membership is now much more representative of the various legal traditions, with the Russian Federation, China, and a number of Eastern European countries representing the socialist tradition; Australia, Canada, Ireland, New Zealand, the United Kingdom, and the United States from the common law tradition; and South Africa and Sri Lanka those countries influenced by Roman-Dutch legal ideas.[28] There is an increasing number of Latin American members, whose participation was formerly handicapped by the lack of official (or even agreed unofficial) Spanish texts of the conventions, and the absence until 1991 of simultaneous translation into Spanish at Conference meetings.[29] The Permanent Bureau has done much in recent years to emphasize the global nature of the Conference and has paid particular attention to the Latin American region, with other regional activities in Africa, across the Mediterranean, and in the Asia Pacific region. An open-ended meeting of members was held in December 2010 which made proposals for strengthening the work of the Conference.[30] Most of the conventions are open to non-Member States.

The Conference has a regular pattern of work in considering new conventions, though in 2011 no such activities were planned, most of the resources of the Conference being devoted to assisting members in the operation of the existing instruments. A preliminary study of the topic proposed for a new convention prepared within the Permanent Bureau is considered by a Special Commission of experts appointed by, but at that stage not usually under detailed instructions from, governments. This group prepares a Draft Convention, a process usually taking several meetings each of some weeks' duration, for consideration at the next Session of the Conference.

In recent years, the growing size of the Conference has led to groups of states holding 'co-ordination meetings' to adopt common positions on matters under discussion. The European Union was the first to adopt this practice, and Latin American and other groupings have followed. The effect has been to reduce the element of cut-and-thrust in the discussions in plenary sessions, some expert delegates being heard only in the private meetings. Experience during the abortive discussions of a Draft Judgments Convention led to the abandonment

---

[24] Statute, arts 4(6) and 11.
[25] Statute, art 5, which provides for a Secretary-General and four Secretaries.
[26] Statute, art 10.
[27] Statute, art 4.
[28] The Commonwealth Secretariat has had Observer status since 1978.
[29] French alone was used for many years; the first official English text was adopted in 1961.
[30] See Preliminary Document 5 of March 2011, prepared for the 2011 meeting of the Council.

of the practice of voting on specific points, with the aim now being decision by consensus.[31]

The major documents of Special Commissions and the full papers, including minutes, of the Sessions of the Conference are published in the invaluable *Actes et Documents* series and are also made available on the website of the Conference.[32] Each convention is accompanied by a very full Explanatory Report.

The modern Hague Conventions on international co-operation in civil procedure are examined in later chapters, but some account is given now of the way in which the work began to take shape.

2. Early work at The Hague

(a) Service of process

The second session of the Hague Conference on Private International Law held in 1894 agreed a draft Convention on Civil Procedure which was signed on 14 November 1896, the first of four Hague Conventions to deal with service of process.

The 1896 Convention, like each of its successors, selected one mode of assistance as the primary or preferred mode while recognizing others as permissible. Article 1 of the 1896 Convention provided for service at the request of officers of the *ministère public* or of the courts of a Contracting State addressed to the competent authority in the state of destination; the diplomatic channel was to be used for communication from country to country unless direct communication between the relevant authorities of the two states was allowed by bilateral agreement. Article 6 of the Convention also declared that its provisions did not preclude any of the following so far as the laws of the concerned states or conventions entered into between them allowed:

(i) service by post;
(ii) direct approach by the plaintiff to the competent official in the state of destination;
(iii) direct service on the defendant by diplomatic or consular agents of the state of origin.

The 1896 Convention was revised and replaced by a Convention on Civil Procedure of 17 July 1905. The text of the 1905 Convention is much fuller when compared with the terse formulation of its predecessor, and it contains a number of changes of principle.

The first is the selection as the primary or preferred mode of transmission of the indirect consular channel. Article 1 provides that service will be effected in

---

[31] See D McClean, 'The Hague Judgments Project' in J Fawcett (ed), *Reform and Development of Private International Law; Essays in Honour of Sir Peter North* (OUP, 2002), pp 257–71.
[32] Cited in this book as *AetD* followed by the number of the Session; eg *AetD(14)* refers to the *Actes et Documents* of the Fourteenth Session held in 1980.

Contracting States on the request of a consul of the state of origin addressed to an authority designated for the purpose by the state of destination. Nothing is prescribed as to who is entitled to initiate this process; this is left to the law of the state of origin. The authority initiating the request had, however, to be identified in the written request delivered by the consul, which was also to contain information about the parties and the nature of the document to be served and was to be prepared in the language of the state of destination.

The 1905 text gives some flexibility as to the precise method of communication. The use of the diplomatic channel, normal under the 1896 Convention, is not prescribed but an individual Contracting State might insist upon it. The possibility of pairs of states allowing direct communication between their respective authorities, bypassing the consul, is also recognized, as it was in the earlier text.[33]

Another change of principle made in the 1905 text affects article 6, which in 1896 permitted three other modes of service (service by post; direct approach by plaintiff to competent authority; the direct consular mode) only to the extent that the relevant laws or bilateral conventions expressly permitted. In the 1905 text, these other modes have a rather higher status. The text provides that they are available if permitted under a bilateral convention, or, in the absence of a convention, if the state of destination does not object. It provides further that the direct consular channel shall always be available where service is to be effected without any compulsion on a national of the state of origin.[34]

The 1905 Convention was considered at the Sixth Session of the Conference in 1924 when a Protocol was agreed permitting accession by states not represented in 1905[35] and some further work was set in hand which led to the publication in 1929 of a proposed revised Convention.[36] No changes were envisaged in Chapter I dealing with service, and the long intermission in the activities of the Conference prevented any action being taken.

(b) Taking of evidence abroad

Provisions as to the taking of evidence abroad were included in the Civil Procedure Conventions of 1896 and 1905, and in that of 1954, which reproduced the evidence provisions of the 1905 Convention. They are primarily concerned with the use of letters rogatory.

Article 8 of each Convention had the same text which survives, with only minor drafting changes, in the text of the most recent Hague Convention on the topic, that on the Taking of Evidence Abroad of 1970.[37] It provided that in civil or commercial matters a judicial authority of a Contracting State might, in conformity with the provisions of its legislation, communicate by letter rogatory with the

---

[33] See art 1 of each Convention. For the bilateral agreements entered into under each Convention, see J Kosters and F Bellemans, *Les conventions de la Haye de 1902 et 1905* (Nijhoff, 1921), pp 922–72.

[34] 1905 Convention, art 6.

[35] *AetD(6)*, 515–16.

[36] Reproduced in *AetD(7)*, vol 2, p 60ff.

[37] The text forms art 8 of the 1954 Convention, and art 1(1) of the 1970 Convention.

competent authority of another Contracting State in order to request that the latter should, within its jurisdiction, effect either an examination (*un acte d'instruction*) or other judicial acts (*actes judiciaires*). These terms are not further defined; they include taking the evidence of witnesses and of experts, viewing a place, and examining commercial books and records;[38] they do not include any *acte d'execution* such as ordering the return of an abducted child.[39]

The 1896 Convention provided for the use of the diplomatic channel unless the authorities of the states concerned had allowed direct communication between their competent authorities.[40] In the 1905 text, changes were introduced which closely parallel those made in the context of service of process. So, the primary or preferred mode of transmission was the indirect consular channel, from the consul of the requesting state to an authority designated for the purpose by the state addressed; a Contracting State could, however, still insist on the use of the diplomatic channel, and the new Convention did not preclude more direct communication between competent authorities by agreement between the states concerned.[41]

Nothing was said in the early conventions about the contents of the letters rogatory, although from 1905 there was a requirement that letters should be drawn up in, or accompanied by a certified translation into, the language of the requested authority[42] (or another language agreed between the states concerned).[43] The execution of the letters rogatory might be refused only if the authenticity of the document was not established; or if in the requested state its execution was not included within 'the attributes of judicial power';[44] or if the request infringed the sovereignty or security of the requested state.[45] The forms to be followed in executing the request[46] were those of the requested state, but a request that a special form be followed would be complied with provided the form specified were not contrary to the legislation of that state.[47] So, for example, a request that

[38] See the exchanges recorded in *AetD(4)*, p 92.

[39] *Tristany v Astruc*, Cour de cassation, 29 November 1973, Rev crit dip 1974, 690 (noted Couchez) (Asser 2/14).

[40] 1896 Convention, art 9(1).

[41] 1905 Convention, art 9. See Oberlandesgericht Koln, 16 June 1975 (13 W 40/75), NJW 1975, 2349 (Asser 2/14): German courts encouraged to make use of the direct communication available under Dutch–German agreement of 1962.

[42] This usage, identifying the relevant language as that of the requested authority rather than that of the requested State is to be found in each of the Hague Conventions on this subject.

[43] See art 10 in each of the 1905 and 1954 texts.

[44] eg, the ordering of a blood sample in a paternity case held not to be within the attributes of Italian judicial power: Cagliari CA, 29 February 1968, RDIPP, 1968, 461 (Asser 1/17) (applying, *per incuriam*, the 1905 text, which is, however, to the same effect as that of 1954).

[45] 1905 and 1954 Conventions, art 11. There were provisions to the same effect in the 1896 text. A request for evidence as to the relationship between the parties to a paternity case was held by the Milan CA not to threaten the sovereignty or security of Italy: 5 April 1968 (Asser 1/17).

[46] This will apply to matters of procedure (eg, the administration of the oath) but not to questions of the competence of the witness (eg, a spouse): Brussels CA, 18 May 1966, Pas 1967, 87 (Asser 1/16).

[47] 1905 and 1954 Conventions, art 14; again, similar provisions were in the 1896 text.

evidence be taken on oath would be complied with in Switzerland despite the fact that the oath was not used under local procedure.[48]

Finally, article 15 of the 1905 Convention expressly preserved the right of states to take evidence through their diplomatic and consular agents, insofar as consular conventions between the two states permitted, or if the state in which the evidence was to be taken did not object.

3. English bilateralism

No common law country took part in this early work at The Hague, but the 1905 Convention was examined by the Committee on British and Foreign Legal Procedure (the Sumner Committee) in 1918–1919. It advised against accession by the United Kingdom. One reason was political: some parties to the Convention were recent enemies. The two legal reasons were that full adherence would require greater changes in English law than the committee could recommend, and that the Convention was concerned with service via official channels, whereas 'the great need is to obtain facilities for the use of less official channels'.[49] The Committee did stress that there was 'a real desire for improvement'[50] and prepared a draft Convention which provided for service via the consular channel, or by an agent appointed either by a party or by the Court whose process was involved.[51] On the taking of evidence, the report set out three quite different formulations, each permitting a different range of procedures.

The Committee's advice was that bilateral Conventions should be concluded with Allied countries. This advice was accepted and the first such Convention was concluded with France on 2 February 1922. This was followed by twenty-two other conventions, details of which are given in Table 1.1.

Although originally solely bilateral, the UK Conventions have some wider significance. Many of them were extended to territories for the foreign relations of which either the United Kingdom or the other party was responsible. In 1976, Australia, Canada, Fiji, New Zealand, Sri Lanka, and Trinidad and Tobago expressed themselves, in response to a Questionnaire circulated by the Commonwealth Secretariat, as parties to all the Conventions listed in the Table with the exception of that with Israel.[52]

Of the twenty-three states listed in the Table, many are parties to the more recent Hague Conventions which do not involve the abrogation of the earlier bilateral

---

[48] Bezirksgerichtspräsidium Appenzell, 25 October 1976, [1977] SJZ 141. Cf Roermond, 16 March 1972 (Asser 1/18), where a Dutch court had omitted to ask the German court to administer the oath. See also Oberlandesgericht Stuttgart, 13 February 1968 (1 V A 3/67) (Asser 1/15) (art 14 should be given a liberal interpretation; evidence provided for Austrian application for the maintenance of a child despite possible inadmissibility of evidence sought under German law).

[49] Report, Cmd 251, para 44.

[50] Ibid, para 43.

[51] Ibid, Appendix B.

[52] There were minor variations in the listings: Fiji excluded Hungary; New Zealand listed Iceland, *semble* within the scope of the UK–Denmark Convention.

Table 1.1 United Kingdom Bilateral Conventions

Reference	Other party	Date signed	Service modes	Evidence modes
127 LNTS 167	Austria	31 March 1931	1 2 3 4 6	1 2* 3*
24 LNTS 91	Belgium	21 June 1922	1 2 3 6 7	1 2* 3*
48 LNTS 425	Czechoslovakia	11 November 1924	1 2 5 6	1 2
139 LNTS 9	Denmark	29 November 1932	1 2*3*4* 6 7 8	1 2* 3*
132 LNTS 231	Estonia	22 December 1931	1 2 3 4 6 8	1 2 3
149 LNTS 131	Finland	11 August 1933	1 2 3 4 6	1 2* 3*
10 LNTS 448	France	2 February 1922	1 2	1 2*
90 LNTS 287	Germany	20 March 1928	1 2* 3*4* 6 7	1 2* n
185 LNTS 113	Greece	27 February 1936	1 2 3 4 6 8	1 2* 3*
170 LNTS 51	Hungary	25 September 1935	1 2* 6*	1 2* n
176 LNTS 229	Iraq	25 July 1935	1 2	1 2*
630 UNTS 189	Israel	5 July 1966	1 2 6 8	1 2 3
131 LNTS 79	Italy	17 December 1930	1 2 3¶ 4¶ 7	1 2 3
201 LNTS 37	Latvia	23 August 1939	1 2 3 4 6 8	1 2* 3*
169 LNTS 373	Lithuania	24 April 1934	1 2 3 4 6 8	1 2 3
140 LNTS 287	Netherlands	31 May 1932	1 2 3 4 6 7	1 2* 3*
123 LNTS 343	Norway	30 January 1931	1 2 3 4 6	1 2* 3*
131 LNTS 19	Poland	26 August 1931	1 2 3 4 6 8	1 3
129 LNTS 417	Portugal	9 July 1931	1 2*3*4* 6 8	1 2* 3*
101 LNTS 375	Spain	27 June 1929	1 2 3 4 6 7 8	1 2* 3*
114 LNTS 9	Sweden	28 August 1930	1 2 3 4 6	1 2* 3*
141 LNTS 225	Turkey	28 November 1931	1 2* 6*	1 2* n
181 LNTS 241	Yugoslavia	27 February 1936	1 2 6	1 2*

Key to service modes:

* = not permitted on nationals of the foreign country (or in the case of the Turkish Convention, permitted only on subjects of the country of origin).

¶ = the agent in Italy must be a Notary Public or an Advocate.

1 = by the judicial authority.

2 = by a diplomatic agent or consular officer.

3 = by agent appointed by the tribunal of the requesting state.

4 = by agent appointed by party.

5 = by solicitor or notary of the country where service effected appointed by the requesting authority or a party.

6 = by post.

7 = by persons concerned, directly through competent officials of the country in which the document is to be served.

8 = by any other mode not illegal in the country where service is to be effected.

Key to evidence procedures:

1 = Letters of request

2 = Consular agent

3 = Other special examiner

Note: The procedures indicated are those available in the case of requests originating from England; the Conventions sometimes make more generous provision in respect of the taking of evidence in England.

Limitations

* = Measures of compulsion not to be used

n = Only to take evidence of British nationals

Conventions but have in practice largely superseded them so far as the United Kingdom is concerned. Even more are EU Member States and so subject to under Regulation 1393/2007 on service and Regulation No 1206/2001 on the taking of evidence, considered below;[53] but they do not prevent the Member States from maintaining other agreements compatible with the Regulation, and some of these bilateral Conventions are sometimes relied upon.[54]

In addition to these United Kingdom bilateral conventions, there was a very large number of bilateral arrangements between states, many of whom were parties to the 1905 Hague Convention, regulating procedures and providing for other modes of communication; the Hague Conference Permanent Bureau listed over fifty such arrangements known to it in 1967.[55]

4. Resumed work at The Hague

The revived Hague Conference on Private International Law renewed the Civil Procedure Convention in 1954, but a full revision was not undertaken until 1964. In that year Chapter I, dealing with Service of Process, was revised to become the Hague Service Convention of 1965.[56] The revision of Chapter II on Evidence followed and was completed at the Eleventh Session of the Conference in October 1968. They are considered in detail below.[57]

5. Liaison magistrates and judicial networks

The work of the Hague Conference has traditionally been, and remains substantially, devoted to resolving the problems inherent in international co-operation by the negotiation of binding conventions. One effect of its Special Commission meetings, which bring together officials involved in the day-to-day operation of the Hague Conventions, has been a growing realization of the value of face-to-face contact. Conversations on the margins of Hague meetings have often cleared up misunderstandings or eased the handling of particular cases.

(a) Liaison magistrates

In the 1990s a number of countries appointed 'liaison magistrates', sometimes based in their home country and sometimes in a foreign centre with whose courts and authorities there was a great deal of 'trade'. These appointments were sometimes made with international crime as the focus, but the handling of civil matters,

---

[53] See pp 54–60 and 104–111.
[54] See Regulation 1393/2007, art 20 and Regulation 1206/2001, art 24(2) and *Debt Collection London Ltd v SK Slavia Praha-Fotbal AS* [2009] EWHC 2726 (QB) (service in Czech Republic under UK–Czechoslovak bilateral). The UK–Italy bilateral was relied on in *Molins plc v GD SpA* [2001] ILPr 9.
[55] *AetD*(11), vol 4, pp 19–20.
[56] See p 27 et seq.
[57] See p 27 ff and 73 ff.

including family cases, also benefited from this approach. In 1996 the European Union provided a formalized framework for the exchange of liaison magistrates in a Joint Action.[58] This provided guidelines for the posting or the exchange of magistrates (in the civil law sense, which includes judges) or officials with special expertise in judicial co-operation procedures as between Member States, on the basis of bilateral or multilateral arrangements. The main aim of creating a framework for the exchange of liaison magistrates was declared to be to increase the speed and effectiveness of judicial co-operation and to promote the pooling of information on the legal and judicial systems of the Member States and to improve their operation.[59] The Joint Action defined the functions of liaison magistrates as normally including any activity designed to encourage and accelerate all forms of judicial co-operation in criminal and, where appropriate, civil matters, in particular by establishing direct links with the competent departments and judicial authorities of the host state. If the two states so agreed, liaison magistrates could also undertake any activity connected with handling the exchange of information and statistics designed to promote mutual understanding of the legal systems and legal databases of the states concerned and to further relations between the legal professions of each of those states.[60]

(b) Judicial networks

Two years later, further steps were taken to enable appropriate direct contacts between judicial authorities and other authorities responsible for judicial action against forms of serious crime. This took the form of a further Joint Action which created a European Judicial Network.[61] The idea was essentially to decentralize international co-operation by enabling those concerned with particular cases to communicate directly and without going through intermediaries in national agencies. This Network was concerned solely with criminal matters and its operation and development is described elsewhere in this book.[62]

In 2001, the Council decided to extend the concept of judicial network to civil and commercial matters.[63] A separate Network was created, though rather confusingly it was also named the European Judicial Network, albeit with the addition of the words 'in civil and commercial matters'.[64]

---

[58] Joint Action of 22 April 1996 adopted by the Council on the basis of art K.3 of the Treaty on European Union, concerning a framework for the exchange of liaison magistrates to improve judicial co-operation between the Member States of the European Union, OJ L 105/1, 27.4.1996.
[59] Joint Action, art 1.
[60] Joint Action, art 2.
[61] Joint Action of 29 June 1998 adopted by the Council on the basis of art K.3 of the Treaty on European Union, on the creation of a European Judicial Network, OJ L 191/4, 7.7.1998.
[62] See p 167.
[63] Council Decision 2001/470/EC of 28 May 2001 establishing a European Judicial Network in civil and commercial matters. Other European networks of judicial organizations or judges also exist, eg the European Network of Councils for the Judiciary, the European Network of Supreme Judicial Courts, and the European Judicial Training Network.
[64] Council Decision, art 1.

The Network as originally established was composed of:

(a) a contact point designated by each Member State,[65] or when local circumstances so require a 'limited number' of contact points;[66]

(b) central bodies and central authorities provided for in Community instruments, instruments of international law to which the Member States are parties, or rules of domestic law in the area of judicial co-operation in civil and commercial matters;

(c) the liaison magistrates to whom the Joint Action of 22 April 1996 applies, where they have responsibilities in co-operation in civil and commercial matters; and

(d) any other appropriate judicial or administrative authority with responsibilities for judicial co-operation in civil and commercial matters whose membership of the Network is considered to be useful by the Member State to which it belongs.

The Council Decision of 2001 identifies a number of tasks the Network is to carry out. It is to further judicial co-operation between the Member States in civil and commercial matters, and this includes devising, progressively establishing, and updating an information system for the members of the Network. It seeks to ensure the smooth operation of the effective and practical application of EU instruments or conventions in force between two or more Member States and more generally of procedures having a cross-border impact and the facilitation of requests for judicial co-operation between the Member States, in particular where no Community or international instrument is applicable. It is to devise, progressively establish, and maintain an information system for the public on judicial co-operation in civil and commercial matters in the EU, relevant EU and international instruments, and the domestic law of the Member States, with particular reference to access to justice.[67]

Meetings of the contact points are to be held at least once each half year.[68] The purpose of the periodic meetings of contact points is declared to be to enable the contact points to get to know each other and exchange experience, in particular as regards the operation of the Network; to provide a platform for discussion of practical and legal problems encountered by the Member States in the course of judicial co-operation, with particular reference to the application of measures adopted by the EU; and to identify best practices in judicial co-operation in civil and commercial matters and ensure that relevant information is disseminated within the Network.[69] Meetings can be held to address specific issues, and in the

[65] Denmark is not a Member State for this purpose: Council Decision, art 1(2); but may be represented at Network meetings: art 11a (1) as inserted by Decision 568/2009.

[66] See Council Decision, art 2(2). Detailed provisions as to the duties of contact points and their relationship to other relevant authorities are in arts 5–8.

[67] See the rather convoluted art 3 of the Council Decision, which was amended in detail by Decision 568/2009.

[68] Council Decision, art 9(1).

[69] Council Decision, art 10, which also identifies the meetings' role in connection with the information systems.

early years much time was in fact spent on the information systems, which are the subject of detailed provisions in Title III of the Decision.[70]

Considerable information on the nature and working of the Network is contained in the first Commission Report on the subject, published in 2006.[71] In October 2005 the network comprised 424 members in four categories: the contact points (93 members); the central authorities provided for in EU instruments and international agreements (159 members); the liaison magistrates (13 members); and other judicial or administrative authorities with responsibilities for judicial co-operation (159 members). The Commission noted that all contact points had modern communications facilities, but rarely enjoyed a sufficient complement of supporting staff. Some contact points had other functions and so were only partially at the disposal of the Network.

The Network has a confidential system for information exchanges between members, a 'Circa' intranet managed by the Commission, but its usage was fairly low. Much more successful was the Network's website with information on international, EU, and national law on twenty legal topics. There is also a 'European Judicial Atlas', with the details of the courts and authorities responsible for implementing a variety of EU instruments (including those dealing with the service of documents, obtaining evidence abroad, and access to justice).

Article 19(2) of the Council Decision envisaged as future developments direct public access to the contact points of the Network, access to and involvement of the legal professions in its activities (for example by giving their representative bodies direct access to the contact points), and links with the European Extrajudicial Network for the settlement of consumer disputes (EEJ-NET).[72] In fact this Network was merged in January 2005 with the former network of European Consumer Centres to form the ECC-Net network enabling consumers to obtain information and assistance direct from a single contact point in each Member State.

On the basis of the 2006 Report, the Commission proposed a revision of the Council Decision, and this led to the adoption of an amending Decision in 2009, the amendments taking effect in January 2011.[73] This added a new category of members of the Network, 'professional associations representing, at national level in the Member States, legal practitioners directly involved in the application of Community and international instruments concerning judicial cooperation in civil and commercial matters'.[74] It also provided for closer links with national judiciaries: if the designated contact point is not a judge, the Member State concerned

---

[70] Council Decision, art 11.

[71] Report from the Commission to the Council, the European Parliament and the European Economic and Social Committee on the application of Council Decision 2001/470/EC establishing a European Judicial Network in civil and commercial matters, COM(2006) 203 final, 16.5.2006.

[72] See Council Resolution 2000/C 155/01 of 25 May 2000 on a Community-wide network of national bodies for the extra-judicial settlement of consumer disputes.

[73] Decision No 568/2009/EC of the European Parliament and of the Council of 18 June 2009 amending Council Decision 2001/470/EC establishing a European Judicial Network in civil and commercial matters, OJ L 168/35, 30.6.2009.

[74] Council Decision, art 2(1)(e) and 2(4A) both as inserted by Decision 568/2009. The scope of this provision is described in Recital (12) to the latter Decision, referring to 'lawyers, solicitors,

must provide for effective liaison with the national judiciary, and to facilitate this a Member State may designate a judge to support this function, that judge being a member of the Network. Member States are now obliged to ensure that the contact points have sufficient and appropriate facilities in terms of staff, resources, and modern means of communication adequately to fulfil their tasks.[75] A new time-line provision requires contact points to respond to all requests submitted to them without delay and at the latest within fifteen days of receipt. If a contact point cannot reply to a request within that time limit, it must inform the maker of the request briefly of this fact, indicating how much time it considers that it will need to reply, but this period is not, as a rule, to exceed thirty days.[76] Finally, a new task was added. In cases in which the law of another Member State is applicable, the courts or authorities responsible for the matter may apply to the Network for information on the content of that law.[77]

It remains to be seen whether the development of judicial networks and the growing use of electronic means of communication including video-conferencing will render the current conventions and arrangements seem as dated as the very first Hague Conventions. The following chapters examine the current arrangements in service of process, taking evidence, and other areas of co-operation.

---

barristers, notaries and bailiffs directly involved in the application of Community and international instruments concerning civil justice'.

[75] Council Decision, art 2(2a) as inserted by Decision 568/2009.
[76] Council Decision, art 8(1) as substituted by Decision 568/2009.
[77] Council Decision, art 3(2)(b) as substituted by Decision 568/2009.

2

Service of Process

I. Introduction

The issues examined in this chapter may at first sight appear quite straightforward. Primus, a resident of state A, believes that he has a good claim against Secundus, who lives in state B. Secundus does not acknowledge the rightness of the claim, so Primus must go to court. He will prefer to go to his own courts in state A, assuming they have jurisdiction. Justice requires that Secundus be given proper notice of the fact that litigation is pending against him, of the nature of the case, and of the date by which action on his part is required; and that this notice be given promptly and in time for the defence to be adequately prepared. How these requirements of justice are given practical effect is the subject of this chapter.

It might be thought that this was essentially a matter for the internal law of state A, the forum state. As a matter of doctrine, procedural matters are governed by the *lex fori*. The court will look to its own law to determine whether there has been good service, sufficient in many common law systems to found jurisdiction; the same law will identify the steps required to set running the time which must elapse before a default judgment can be entered; and the same law will, in some countries, apply to determine whether service was so defective that a default judgment must be set aside. This, however, is to ignore the legal and practical interests of state B, the country in which the defendant is to be found.

Whatever method of service is used, the object is the giving of information to the defendant. It must involve some acts being done in state B, over which the law of that state may properly exercise a measure of control. That control might be exercised on the basis of considerations of sovereignty: as noted in the previous chapter, some countries in the civil law tradition see service of process as an act of state, an exercise of its judicial power, and are reluctant to permit within their borders an expression of the sovereignty of another state. In Switzerland, for example, service on behalf of the plaintiff of foreign process without the permission of the Swiss authorities appears to be an offence punishable by imprisonment (and even, theoretically, solitary confinement and hard labour).[1] Or control might be exercised in the interests of defendants, seeking to ensure that if they are to be proceeded against abroad information reaches them with the speed and security that the use of official channels is supposed (probably quite unrealistically) to guarantee. In the hypothetical example with which I began, ultimately it may well fall to the authorities of state B to enforce the judgment against Secundus and his assets. Compliance with the procedural rules of the *lex fori* will not ensure that enforcement, for state B may impose its own requirements and is likely to scrutinize default judgments with particular care.[2] So international agreement and co-operation is in this field not merely an ideal but a practical necessity for effective justice.

---

[1] Swiss Penal Code, art 271, the scope of which was examined, with a review of relevant authorities, in the English High Court in *Ferrarini SpA v Magnol Shipping Co Inc, The Sky One* [1988] 1 Lloyd's Rep 238 (affd CA, ibid.).

[2] See, eg, Oberlandesgericht Frankfurt (20 W 154/90), 21 February 1991, [1991] RIW 587 (English writ purportedly served in Germany by post, a mode of service then unacceptable under German law; default judgment given in England refused recognition in Germany); Supreme Court of Portugal, 10 November 1993 (Asser 5/369) (English writ served by plaintiff's lawyer; valid by *lex fori* but resulting judgment not recognized in Portugal, such service not being allowed by the Convention). It may well be held immaterial that the defendant had actual knowledge of the contents of the document: Bundesgerichtshof (XII ZB 64/91), 2 December 1992, NJW 1993, 598 (Asser 5/359) (US divorce papers sent by courier to Germany without any translation: nullity of service not cured by

1. Factors to be considered

The form which is taken by international assistance in the service of process depends upon a number of necessarily interrelated factors. International discussion is eased if they are distinguished as far as possible.

The first issue concerns the *initiation of international action within the state of origin*.[3] The law of that state, as *lex fori*, will prescribe any special procedures to be followed where service is to be effected abroad. Where the common law approach of treating service as a matter for the plaintiff prevails, there are usually few special requirements. The leave of the court or of some other official agency may be required,[4] and official assistance may be available to those who choose to avail themselves of it; but no special steps to initiate the actual business of service abroad will be mandatory. The *lex fori* will be satisfied by proof that the plaintiff has secured the service of the documents on the defendant abroad, either by taking them personally or (much more usually) by employing an agent.

The more formal civil law tradition requires international service to be initiated by specified officials.[5] Action may be required by the court itself, the court issuing a Letter of Request asking either a foreign court or another competent authority in the state of destination to assist in having the documents served; this practice is particularly entrenched in Latin America. In many other countries the initiating steps will be taken by an officer attached to the court. Taking the French system as an example, the *huissier de justice* engaged by the plaintiff will deliver the documents to the *ministère public*; this is a body of officers attached to the court and primarily responsible for the public prosecution function in the criminal jurisdiction, and customarily and conveniently referred to as the *parquet* (which literally means 'the well of the court' where these officers used to be placed). The *parquet* is responsible for the onward transmission of the documents via central government agencies. The law may allow the *huissier* himself, given a *huissier*'s semi-official position, to initiate contact with the competent authorities (or a brother *huissier*) in the state of destination, or may (as has French law since 1966[6]) require the *huissier* to take informal steps such as the use of the post to supplement the official service initiated by the *parquet*.

The second issue is in a sense the counterpart of the first, for it concerns *the proper addressee in the state of destination*. The law of that state as to the service of

---

respondent's actual receipt of documents); *Wohnungsbaugesellschaft mbH v Flyvholm* (Danish Sup Ct, 5 August 1999) (201/1999), [1999] UfR 1775 (process served in Denmark without required translation; German default judgment refused recognition despite the defendant having made written representations to German court).

[3] In this chapter, except where a direct quotation is made from a legal text, the countries concerned will be referred to as 'the state of origin' and 'the state of destination'.

[4] As under CPR, r 6.36 (service out of the jurisdiction).

[5] Detailed information about the practice in individual countries can be found (for EU Member States) on the website of the European Judicial Network; and (for States Parties to the Hague Convention) in the *Practical Handbook on the Hague Service Convention*, published by the Permanent Bureau of the Hague Conference.

[6] See now NCPC, art 686 as substituted by Decret 85–1330.

documents originating abroad may permit documents to be sent directly to the defendant without the use of any local official acting as intermediary, or it may insist on the documents passing through, for example, the court having jurisdiction at the defendant's place of residence, the *parquet* attached to that court, or a *huissier* practising in the relevant area.

The third issue is *the precise mode of service* on the defendant, and in particular whether it is service in solemn form or 'simple delivery'. The various means of communication found in international practice were examined in the previous chapter.

II. International Conventions

An account has already been given of some of the early work of the Hague Conference in civil procedure. The activities of the Conference at its Seventh Session in 1951 led to the signature of a new Convention on Civil Procedure of 1 March 1954, but its substantive provisions are almost identical with those of 1905. There is a certain irony about the events leading up to the 1954 Convention. The British Government had proposed to the Council of Europe that it should examine a range of questions including that of service of process abroad, which the United Kingdom had hitherto included in its bilateral civil procedure conventions. In response, the Netherlands Government drew attention to the past work and impending revival of the Hague Conference. The Council of Europe stayed its hand, and the Seventh Session of the Conference found that by making two small amendments to the service provisions of the 1905 text (the definition of '*autorité compétente*' in article 2, so as to include solicitors; an addition to article 3 providing for the supply of two copies of the document to be served) the Hague text could be made entirely acceptable to the British Government. In the event, the United Kingdom never acceded to the Convention.[7]

A more radical review of the system for service abroad had to await the Tenth Session of the Conference in 1964. It was prompted by a memorandum from the *Union Internationale des Huissiers de Justice et Officiers Judiciaires* which reviewed current practice and suggested the introduction of a new mode of service involving direct communication between a *huissier de justice* in the country of origin and a similar officer in the country of service. That particular proposal was of interest only to the limited number of countries that have *huissiers de justice*, and when the issue was raised in the Hague Conference in 1960 the British delegate, Professor Graveson, expressed the traditional preference of the British Government for bilateral conventions,[8] but the topic attracted more general interest and it was decided to re-examine the whole range of possibilities.

---

[7] These events can be traced in *AetD(7)*, vol 1, pp 274–84 and 293–310. Ireland had also raised the issue in the Council of Europe but was not represented at The Hague.

[8] *AetD(9)*, vol 1, p 171.

1. The Hague Convention of 15 November 1965

A draft Convention was prepared by a Special Commission of the Hague Conference in February 1964[9] and agreed by the 10th Session of the Conference in the
following October.[10]

The starting points for the revision of the existing Conventions of 1905 and
1954 were dissatisfaction with the indirect consular channel, as being inappropriate
in current conditions, and concern that the non-obligatory nature of the channels
provided for in the existing text enabled some countries to make use of the system
of *notification au parquet* to which increasing exception was being taken. This latter
system, which was then available in at least some cases in Belgium, France, Greece,
Italy, and the Netherlands,[11] allows legally effective service on a defendant resident
abroad to be made by leaving the relevant document at the office of the *parquet* in
the forum state. Although the *parquet* was then expected to take steps to bring the
document to the attention of the defendant, service was already complete and time
began to run for various purposes regardless of the date upon which the defendant
received actual notice of the proceedings. The principal changes introduced in
response to these points were:

(a) the introduction of a new preferred mode, service through a designated
Central Authority in each Contracting State, using prescribed forms and
procedures;

(b) the giving of some obligatory quality to the new Convention;

(c) the addition of 'guarantees' to safeguard the position of defendants who
remained in ignorance of the proceedings being taken against them.

2. Scope of the Convention

The Convention applies 'in all cases, in civil and commercial matters, where there is
occasion to transmit a judicial or extra-judicial document[12] for service abroad'.[13]

---

[9] See *AetD(10)*, vol 3, pp 65–73 (preliminary draft, with English translation at pp 112–19) and
74–111 (explanatory report).

[10] See *AetD(10)*, vol 3, pp 141–331 (minutes and working documents of the Third Commission),
335–81 (plenary session, final text, and explanatory report).

[11] *AetD(10)*, vol 3, p 75.

[12] Despite the breadth of this phrase, there is a tendency for courts to treat the Convention as
applying only to documents initiating proceedings: Oberlandesgericht München, 30 December 1986,
7 W 3138/86 (Asser 4/94); *Chabert v Bacquie* 694 So. 2d 805 (Fla App, 1997); *Securities and Exchange
Commission v Credit Bancorp Ltd* (SDNY, 2011). Contrast a decision of the Italian Corte di Cassazione, 19 November 1993, no 11446, Rivdir.int.privproc. 1994, 833 (Asser 5/354), holding that a
witness summons was a 'judicial document' and that it was wrong to limit the scope of that phrase.

[13] Convention, art 1. 'Service' is used in the English text to translate two terms, *signification* and
notification in the French. In a number of continental systems, and in Scotland, the former implies
service by an officer of the court or *huissier*, the latter having a wider meaning; see the discussion in
AetD(10), vol 3, pp 165–7 and R H Graveson, 'The Tenth Session of the Hague Conference on Private
International Law' (1965) 14 ICLQ 528, 539.

This provision was the product of long debate, focusing on its obligatory character ('in all cases') and on the meaning of 'civil and commercial'.

(a) Obligatory character

The authors of the Convention were never quite of one mind as to the obligatory quality they wished to give their text, and it took many years after the coming into effect of the Convention for some measure of agreement to emerge. It is clear that if there is occasion to serve documents abroad, the modes of transmission and the 'guarantees' of the Convention apply universally. Unfortunately, this does not address the question of in which cases such service is required; it does not, read strictly, touch those provisions of the law of the state of origin which allow valid service by *notification au parquet*. This issue was of concern to the Rapporteur, Mr Taborda Ferreira of Portugal, who expressed his anxieties in his commentary on the preliminary draft.[14] The issue was not discussed in depth at the Tenth Session of the Conference, but the Rapporteur felt able to declare, in a passage set in capital letters, that the 'authentic interpretation of the Commission' favoured its obligatory application.[15]

What remained controversial was the precise meaning of this supposed obligatory character. It is clear that where service is required to be effected in a Contracting State, the provisions of the Convention, as given effect in national law or as a self-executing Treaty, will prevail over the general law as to service of process. So US courts have declared invalid service which met the requirements of state law or of the Federal Rules of Civil Procedure but which did not meet the terms of the Convention,[16] and a Netherlands court has refused to grant *exequatur* to a Belgian judgment granted after service which complied with Belgian law but not the Convention's requirements.[17] On the other hand, the Hague Convention deals with a limited issue, that of service abroad; it does not affect the rules as to the extent of the jurisdiction of the courts of a particular state,[18] the rules of the forum court as to which documents are required to be served,[19] nor the time limits set for procedural steps under that law.[20]

Between these areas of relative clarity lies the case where the procedural law of the forum recognizes some action within the jurisdiction as legally sufficient to constitute service on a defendant who is actually resident abroad. This includes the procedure of *notification au parquet* to which the authors of the Convention took

---

[14] *AetD(10)*, vol 3, p 81.

[15] Ibid, p 367.

[16] See, eg, *Vorhees v Fischer & Krecke GmbH* 697 F 2d 574 (4th Cir, 1983); *Kaduta v Hosofai* 608 P 2d 68 (Ariz App, 1980); *Weight v Kawasaki Heavy Industries Ltd* 597 F Supp 1082 (ED Va, 1984); *Cipolla v Picard Porsche Audi Inc* 496 A 2d 130 (RI, 1985); *Bowers v Wurzburg* 519 SE 2d 148 (WVa, 1999).

[17] Arrondissementsrechtbank Breda, 15 October 1979 (Asser 2/173).

[18] *DeJames v Magnificence Carriers Inc* 654 F 2d 280 (3rd Cir, 1981).

[19] *Re v Breezey Point Lumber Co* 460 NYS 2d 264 (NY Sup Ct 1983).

[20] *Breyer v Total-Belgique SA* (Luxembourg CA, 21 January 1981), [1983] Pas Lux 374, [1985] 2 CMLR 328 (Asser 3/134); see Droz, Rev crit dip, 1981, 708.

such exception, or even a device such as that once recognized in the English ecclesiastical courts of affixing citation of a foreign resident 'upon one of the columns of the Royal Exchange, or in front of some other well-known building, in a place of public resort, which merchants are in the daily habit of frequenting or passing by'.[21] Luxembourg, Netherlands, and US courts have addressed the matter, and the judgments reveal the reality of these fears.

The Luxembourg case concerned a notice of appeal from the decision of a lower court, required by the *lex fori* to be given within fifteen days of the date of the judgment. Notice was given within that time limit by '*exploit*' of a *huissier* acting for the appellant and a copy posted at the door of the courthouse. Another copy was sent to a Belgian *huissier* who delivered it to the Belgian respondent twenty days after the date of the judgment. The Court held that this amounted to good service in accordance with the Convention (read with a Belgium–Luxembourg agreement made under the 1954 Hague Convention) but also that service of the notice of appeal was validly completed by the posting of the notice as required by internal Luxembourg law.[22]

The Netherlands *Hoge Raad* (Supreme Court) considered a not dissimilar case in 1986, that of *Segers and Rufa BV v Mabanaft GmbH*.[23] For the purposes of proceedings before the appeal court in The Hague, the respondent had 'elected domicile' at the office of its attorney in that city. A summons relating to the further appeal to the *Hoge Raad* was served at that office in accordance with an amendment to the Netherlands Code of Civil Procedure introduced in 1985.[24] The *Hoge Raad* held that the point as to the cases in which there was 'occasion to transmit a . . . document for service abroad' was entirely left to the domestic law of the state of origin of the documents. On the other hand, given the importance the Netherlands attached to the Convention, the 1985 amendment was interpreted as not displacing the application of the Convention, and so the requirements of article 15 had to be complied with.

The US cases are in one sense less threatening to the policy of the Convention, in that typically they do involve the actual delivery of the relevant document rather than some notional equivalent such as publication at the courthouse door. But in another sense they raise a much more serious issue, one likely to arise in many jurisdictions whenever the defendant is not an individual but a corporation or some other form of association; and it will be recognized that a very great proportion of

<hr />

[21] Oughton's *Ordo Judiciorum* (1728); see the translation in Law, *Forms of Ecclesiastical Law*, 2nd edn, 1844, p 93.

[22] *Breyer v Total-Belgique SA* (Luxembourg CA, 21 January 1981), [1983] Pas Lux 374, [1985] 2 CMLR 328 (Asser 3/134). See to the same effect *Van Opdorp v Compagnie Belge d'Assurance Crédit* (Luxembourg CA, 6 December 1989), [1991] ILPr 316, [1990] Pas Lux 358; *Treuhand & rechtpraxis Ulrich Diener-Hafner AG v Füchsl* (Cour de cassation, 31 January 1991), [1991] Pas Lux 131.

[23] (27 June 1986), NJ 1986, 764. See to similar effect, *Nieuwersteegv Colonia Versicherungs AG* (Hoge Raad, 2 February 1996), NJ 1997, 128 (Asser 5/357).

[24] Code of Civil Procedure, art 407(5), introduced by a Law of 3 July 1985 (Stb 384). See also a Greek case where a judgment was delivered to the public prosecutor for service on a party resident abroad; the time for an appeal to be brought began to run immediately: *Nikoloudos v Nikoloudos* (Greek Supreme Court, 11 March 2004), [2006] ILPr 21.

international litigation does involve corporate defendants. In this type of case, the nearest equivalent to direct personal service on an individual defendant would be service at the registered office or 'seat' of a company, or at the principal place of business of some other type of business association, on a senior executive of the company or association. Many jurisdictions have taken the view that to insist on such service would unfairly disadvantage potential plaintiffs, and have provided that where an enterprise based abroad does business within the jurisdiction, service may be effected at some business address there without the need to serve any document abroad. If there is no 'occasion to transmit a . . . document for service abroad', then the Convention does not apply.

So, in England the Civil Procedure Rules allow service on a company by a range of methods specified in the Rules and also by further methods permitted under the Companies Act 2006.[25] Under the Rules, service on a company or other corporation may be by personal service, leaving it with a person holding a senior position within the company or corporation;[26] at the business address of a solicitor within the jurisdiction or any other European Economic Area (EEA) state acting for the company or at any other address, where in each case the claimant has been told in writing that service may be effected there;[27] or, in the case of a company registered outside England and Wales, any place of business of the company within the jurisdiction.[28] Under the companies legislation, an overseas company, one incorporated outside the United Kingdom,[29] that opens a UK establishment is required to register certain particulars including a service address for each of its directors and for its secretary.[30] A document may be served on such an overseas company by leaving it at, or sending it by post to, the registered address of any person resident in the United Kingdom who is authorized to accept service of documents on the company's behalf, or, if there is no such person or if any such person refuses service or service cannot for any other reason be effected, by leaving it at or sending by post to any place of business of the company in the United Kingdom.[31] A document may also be served on a director, secretary, or permanent representative of such a company by leaving it at, or sending it by post to, the person's registered address.[32]

Many legal systems have procedures of this general type. It may be that a distinction can be drawn between two different groups of provisions. In one there is something that can almost be regarded as 'submission to service': the registration of an address for service, the express appointment of an agent, the 'election of domicile' at a lawyer's office. This element is lacking in another group of cases, where nothing turns on any prior act of the potential defendant

---

[25] CPR, r 6.3(2).
[26] CPR, r 6.5(3)(b). 'Senior position' is explained in PD 6A.
[27] CPR, rr 6.7, 6.8.
[28] CPR, r 6.9(2).
[29] Companies Act 2006, s 1044.
[30] Companies Act 2006, s 1046; Overseas Companies Regulations 2009, SI 2009/1801, reg 6.
[31] Companies Act 2006, s 1139(2).
[32] Companies Act 2006, s 1140(2); Overseas Companies Regulations 2009, reg 75.

but rather on the delivery of the document to the official of the forum state or its publication at some prescribed place. The practical significance of this distinction is that in the first group of cases there is a greater likelihood of the necessary information being passed rapidly to the defendant, and that will in turn meet the objective of the Convention's authors and also the standards set by 'due process' tests. But these distinctions and considerations were not expressly addressed in the Convention's negotiating process and so do not feature explicitly in its text.

The whole question was examined by the US Supreme Court in 1988, in *Volksvagenwerk AG v Schlunk*,[33] something of a *cause célèbre*. The case arose out of a fatal road accident in Illinois, the plaintiff's parents having been killed as a result of a head-on collision between their Volkswagen Rabbit and another vehicle. Proceedings were commenced against Volkswagen of America (VWoA), a New Jersey corporation which did business in Illinois and had a registered address for service there. Subsequently the plaintiff sought to join the German parent company, Volkswagen AG (VWAG) as co-defendant, alleging design defects in the car. Service was effected in Illinois on VWoA 'as Agent for' VWAG. VWAG moved that service be quashed, arguing that VWoA was not its agent for service, and that an attempt to serve process on an agent in Illinois violated the Hague Convention. The Appellate Court of Illinois, affirming the decision at first instance, rejected both arguments,[34] holding that VWoA was agent by operation of law as an 'involuntary agent' under a well-established doctrine in the law of Illinois, and that the Convention was inapplicable to service effected within the borders of the United States. This decision provoked a remarkably hostile response from foreign governments, and those of four Contracting States to the Convention addressed notes of protest to the United States Government. The German Government declared that the decision ignored the 'mandatory character' of the Convention, producing effects similar to those of *notification au parquet*. Similar protests were made by Japan, France, and the United Kingdom, the last-named making the additional point that the uniformity which had been the hope of the authors of the Convention would be frustrated if it were subject to the inconsistencies between the service rules of fifty different States.[35]

Nonetheless the US Supreme Court affirmed the decision. The court took the view, supported by an *amicus* brief by the US Solicitor General, that:

Service of process refers to a formal delivery of documents that is legally sufficient to charge the defendant with notice of a pending action . . . The legal sufficiency of a formal delivery of documents must be measured against some standard. The Convention does not prescribe a standard, so we almost necessarily must refer to the internal law of the forum state.[36]

However, the Court went out of its way to spell out the advantages of using the machinery of the Convention:

[33] 486 US 694 (1988).
[34] 503 NE 2d 1045 (Ill App, 1986).
[35] See the *amicus curiae* brief filed by the United States in the Supreme Court proceedings.
[36] 486 US 694 (1988), at p 700.

The Convention provides simple and certain means by which to serve process on a foreign national. Those who eschew its procedures risk discovering that the forum's internal law required transmittal of documents for service abroad, and that the Convention therefore provided the exclusive means of valid service. In addition, parties that comply with the Convention ultimately may find it easier to enforce their judgments abroad.

Three members of the Supreme Court, Justices Brennan, Marshall, and Blackmun, joined in a concurring opinion, rejecting the view of the majority that each forum had, in effect, complete freedom to decide when the Convention should control; it was 'implausible' that that represented the intention of the drafters of the Convention. The three Justices found that the Convention embodied a substantive standard, directed at the purpose of the Convention, which was seen as being to ensure timely notice to the defendant. There was, in other words, an unarticulated 'due process' requirement in the Convention, against which the law of a forum state could be measured. On the particular facts of the case, service on a wholly owned, closely controlled subsidiary was reasonably calculated to secure timely notice to the parent company, and so to meet the United States' version of due process.

What are the implications of the decision for practices such as *notification au parquet* and service upon a state official, in the US typically a Secretary of State? The United States' *amicus* brief tried, unconvincingly, to demonstrate that both these forms of procedure should be regarded, and had been by the drafters of the Convention, as forms of 'service abroad'. If this argument has any substance, it lies in the fact that service on an involuntary agent attracts no legal as opposed to practical requirement that there be any supplemental transmission of information to the defendant abroad, whereas supplemental transmission of the actual documents served is required to be effected by the *huissier* initiating *notification au parquet* and by a Secretary of State on whom documents are served under the similar US practice. The Supreme Court held that 'the only transmittal to which the Convention applies is a transmittal abroad that is required as a necessary part of service'.[37] Subsequent decisions in lower courts have held that where the relevant State law requires the Secretary of State or similar official to send the documents or one copy of them abroad to a foreign party, and service is not regarded as complete until that is done, the Hague Convention does apply and pre-empts State law.[38]

The matter has been repeatedly discussed at Special Commissions of the Hague Conference held to review the operation of the Convention, and both the meetings in 2003 and 2009 accepted that the Convention had 'a non-mandatory but exclusive character'. More fully:

The language [of art 1] 'where there is occasion to transmit' is understood as meaning that the Service Convention is non-mandatory in the sense that it is a matter for the *lex fori* to determine whether a document must be transmitted for service abroad. The use of the word 'shall' is understood as meaning that the Service Convention is exclusive, in the sense that

---

[37] Ibid, at 697.
[38] *Bowers v Wurzburg* 519 SE 2d 148 (WVa, 1999); *Knapp v Yamaha Motor Corp* 60 F Supp 2d 566 (SD WVa, 1999); *Davies v Jobs & Adverts Online GmbH* 94 F Supp 2d 719 (ED Va, 2000); *Man Ferrostaal Inc v M/V Vindonissa* (SD Tex, 2009).

once the law of the forum has determined that a document must be transmitted abroad for service, the channels of transmission expressly available or otherwise permitted under the Hague Service Convention are the *only* channels that may be used.[39]

(b) Civil and commercial matters

The Convention applies to 'civil and commercial matters'. This phrase has appeared in Hague Conventions since 1896, in many bilateral civil procedure conventions including those entered into by the United Kingdom, in other multilateral conventions,[40] and, outside the area of civil procedure, in many EU instruments such as the Brussels Convention on jurisdiction and the enforcement of judgments in civil and commercial matters 1968,[41] and in Council Regulation 44/2001 which replaced it. Discussion of the phrase at The Hague is something of a hardy perennial, because of the evident fascination of different methods of categorizing legal rules, and the issue arises in the context of the taking of evidence abroad as well as in the present context.[42] A common law country will usually interpret the phrase to include almost anything which is not a criminal matter, but civil lawyers use a larger number of categories and take differing views on the relationship of administrative or public law matters, fiscal cases, or those including questions of personal status, to the categories of 'civil' and 'commercial'. All are agreed, however, that it is the nature of the 'matter' which is important, and it was recognized early in the history of the Hague Conventions on Civil Procedure that some civil or commercial matters could arise in the context of an administrative jurisdiction.

It is well recognized that these differences in styles of legal thinking do exist, and the Convention is interpreted in practice in such a way that its objectives will be secured despite those differences. If a document is regarded as within the 'civil and commercial' field in its country of origin, it will be served by the authorities in other Contracting States.[43] In many cases, the state of destination will either accept the classification of the state of origin, or waive any right it may have to reject the document under article 4, or simply serve the document as an act of goodwill even if the Convention is regarded as not strictly applicable. One exception to this statement was the attitude taken by the Bavarian Central Authority in the late 1980s in connection with product liability cases in the courts of the United States.

---

[39] Preliminary Document 10 for the Special Commission of 2009, para 6.

[40] Eg, the Inter-American Convention on Letters Rogatory 1975, art 2: see p 63.

[41] On the phrase in this context, where it is given an 'independent' meaning, not necessarily following that of any national law, see Case 29/76 *LTU GmbH & Co KG v Eurocontrol* [1976] ECR 1541, [1977] 1 CMLR 88; Dicey, Morris and Collins, *The Conflict of Laws* (14th edn, 2006), paras 11–024 ff.

[42] See pp 88–91.

[43] Where service is effected by a means not involving the authorities of the state of destination (eg by post under art 10(a)) the characterization of the *lex fori* will inevitably prevail. See also art 13, expressly prohibiting a refusal to serve based on the ground that the internal law of the state of destination would not permit the action on which the application was based: eg a class action, as to which see Oberlandesgericht Frankfurt, 21 March 1991 (20 VA 2/91), RIW 1991, 417 (Asser 5/358). On art 13, see further p 41.

Where the plaintiff claimed punitive damages as well as compensation, the request
for service was refused on the basis that this was a claim for a penalty and not a civil
claim. The Bavarian position was repudiated by the German Federal authorities
and when the matter was finally tested in the courts was held incorrect.[44] However,
the Frankfurt Oberlandesgericht held that an attempt to obtain damages for a
conspiracy to defraud the US Government, although a civil action in the US courts,
was outside the category of 'civil and commercial'.[45]

A generous interpretation aids both plaintiffs, who may need to have service
effected before proceeding to judgment, and defendants, who can benefit from
knowledge of pending proceedings. The state of destination, by serving a document, does not commit itself to recognize any judgment the plaintiff may ultimately obtain: for service facilitates proceedings and does not guarantee that their
outcome will be recognized. For these reasons, the uncertainty about the scope of
'civil and commercial matters' does not have the serious implications it has in the
context of the taking of evidence for use abroad. It was, therefore, a little surprising
that a Special Commission of the Hague Conference in April 1989 took a rather
conservative position on the matter. Largely at the prompting of the Swiss representative, Professor Volken, who raised the issue as one of principle (Switzerland,
not being a party to the Convention, had no actual practical experience), the
Commission considered it desirable that the words 'civil or commercial matters'
should be interpreted in an 'autonomous' manner, without reference exclusively to
the law either of the state of origin or of the state of destination, or to both laws
cumulatively. This interpretation should be common both to the Service and to the
Evidence Convention.[46] The Commission did, however, recognize a diversity of
practice, a freedom to adopt a broad reading of the phrase, and an 'historical
evolution' which treated the Convention as applicable to at least some of the topics
in the grey area between public and private law: bankruptcy, insurance, and
employment, but not tax matters.[47] It may be that growing co-operation between
states in respect of tax, and indeed criminal, matters will reduce the importance of
this whole issue.

(c) The case of the unknown address

During the meeting of the Special Commission which prepared the preliminary
draft of the Convention there was considerable, but inconclusive, discussion of the

---

[44] Oberlandesgericht München, 9 May 1989 (9 VA 3/89), IPRax 1990, 175 (Asser 5/352);
Bayerische Motorenwerke v State of Bavaria (Oberlandesgericht München, 15 July 1992 (9 VA
1/92)), [1994] ILPr 7, RIW 1993, 70 (Asser 5/353) (where the compensatory damages were US
$4,000 and the punitive damages US$4million); *Re The Service of An American Writ in a Claim for
Punitive Damages* (Bundesverfassungsgericht, 7 December 1994 (I BvR 1279/94)), [1997] ILPr 325,
NJW 1995, 649 (Asser 5/359).
[45] Oberlandesgericht Frankfurt am Main (3 December 2009) (50 E/2—93/09); see *United States ex
rel Bunk v Birkart Globistics GmbH & Co* (ED Va, 2010).
[46] See pp 88–91.
[47] The conclusions of the 1989 Special Commission were reiterated by that of 2003: Conclusions
and Recommendations, para 69, and again in 2009: Conclusions and Recommendations, paras 13–14.

position which should obtain when service was required on someone strongly suspected of being in a particular country but whose address within the country was unknown. The discussion centred on the extent to which the authorities of the state of destination should be placed under an obligation to trace the person concerned.[48] The United Kingdom, in its observations on the preliminary draft, expressed the hope that the Convention would not apply at all in cases in which the address of the person on whom documents were to be served was unknown. Although there was only fragmentary discussion of the matter at the Tenth Session, the United Kingdom view prevailed; an example, perhaps, of the effect of shortage of time on the content of international conventions.[49] The express exclusion of this case from the scope of the Convention leaves the Contracting States free to make whatever provision they judge appropriate,[50] for example the use of 'alternative methods', formerly known as 'substituted service' in English law.[51]

The notion of an 'unknown address' is interpreted strictly. If the person seeking service gives an address for service, having reason to believe that it is accurate, the case is not made one of an 'unknown address' merely by the fact that the person to be served has disappeared from that address and cannot be found.[52]

3. The system of Central Authorities

The main innovation in the 1965 Convention was the creation of the system of Central Authorities. Each Contracting State must designate such a Central Authority to receive requests for service from other Contracting States;[53] the expectation, borne out in practice, was that this would involve not the creation of some new agency but the designation as Central Authority for the purposes of this Convention of some existing office or ministry.[54] Most Contracting States have designated their Ministries of Justice (or some organ of the Ministry, for example the French Ministry's specialist *service civil de l'entraide judiciaire internationale*); other countries have placed the Central Authority within the courts service (for example the Irish designation of the Master of the High Court and the Netherlands' designation of the *Officier van Justitie* or public prosecutor attached to the District

---

[48] See the report of M Taborda Ferreira, *AetD(10)*, vol 3, pp 108–11.

[49] See ibid, pp 259 and 293, and Convention, art 1(2).

[50] Amtsgericht Böblingen 27 October 1987, 13 F 274/87, IPRax 1988, 114 (Asser 4/98); *Popular Entertainers LLC v Webcom Media Group Inc* 225 FRD 560 (ED Tenn, 2004); *BP Products North America Inc v Dagra* 236 FRD 270 (ED Va, 2006); *Chanel Inc v Liu Zhixian* (SD Fla, 2010). A court in The Hague adopted a similar solution in the case of a defendant whose address was known, but the address was in a part of a Contracting State, the northern area of Cyprus, over which the government of that state had no effective control; a sensible outcome, but one not covered by the text of the Convention: Arrondissementsrechtbank 's-Gravenhage, 22 December 1993, NIPR 1995 no 418 (Asser 5/356).

[51] CPR, r 6.15.

[52] *Charly Holding AG v Gomelsky* (Hoge Raad, 2 December 1988), NJ 1989, 374 (Asser 5/355).

[53] Convention, art 2(1).

[54] See *AetD(10)*, vol 3, p 174 (M Taborda Ferreira, the Rapporteur).

Court of The Hague);[55] and relatively few have retained the Foreign Ministry.[56] The United Kingdom was in this last category, the Secretary of State for Foreign and Commonwealth Affairs being the designated Central Authority until 2008 when the Senior Master in the Royal Courts of Justice took over.[57] While the US Department of Justice acts as Central Authority it has 'outsourced' the main practical functions to Process Forwarding International, a private contractor based in Seattle.

Article 18 of the Convention, introduced at the suggestion of the United Kingdom, allows a Contracting State to designate 'other authorities' in addition to the Central Authority. The purpose of this provision for what were referred to in discussion as 'subsidiary authorities' was to cater for the needs of composite states such as the United Kingdom, where different systems of law are to be found within the same state.[58] An applicant in another state may be unaware of the nature and significance of the divisions within the country of destination, so it is expressly provided that he or she always has the right to address a request directly to the Central Authority itself.[59] The system was complicated by the introduction at a late stage of a further provision enabling federal states to designate more than one Central Authority;[60] this was done on the suggestion of the German Federal Republic (which had previously resisted the British proposal as tending to multiply Central Authorities) to enable expression to be given to the sovereignty of the German *Länder* in the field of justice, and does require the applicant to identify the *Land* in question.[61] The United Kingdom and the Netherlands have designated 'other authorities' under article 18(1); in the case of the United Kingdom, the Senior Master for England and Wales, the EU and International Law Branch of the Scottish Government, and the Master (Queen's Bench and Appeals) for Northern Ireland.[62]

---

[55] Other examples are Israel (Director of Courts), Italy (registry of the Rome Court of Appeal), Luxembourg (public prosecutor, Superior Court), and Serbia (the First Instance Court of Belgrade). In most of the territories to which the Convention was extended when they were dependent territories of the United Kingdom, the Registrar of the Supreme (or High) Court is appointed. In some of the German Länder the Central Authority is the President of the Oberlandesgericht, in others the Ministry of Justice.

[56] Argentina, Greece, Japan, Mexico, and Venezuela. See also Botswana (Minister of State in the Office of the President).

[57] The designations and objections made by Contracting States are usefully collected in the *Practical Handbook* on the Convention published by the Permanent Bureau of the Hague Conference, and the current position can be ascertained via the Hague Conference's website.

[58] This device has been used by Australia and by China in respect of the Hong Kong and Macau Special Administrative Regions.

[59] Convention, art 18(2).

[60] Convention, art 18(3). Canada and Switzerland have used this power.

[61] See *AetD(10)*, vol 3, pp 172–83 and 315.

[62] The Netherlands has designated the public prosecutors of all its District Courts other than that of The Hague as 'other authorities'. Cyprus, Pakistan, and Poland have a similar system.

4. Initiation of the request

During the discussions of the draft Convention it was argued by some delegates that the Central Authority should have a double task, acting as a transmitting or forwarding agency as well as receiving requests from abroad, but their opinion did not prevail.[63] The case for using a Central Authority as a transmitting agency rests on the argument that the familiarity of its officers with the system of the Convention and with the practice of other countries would ensure that requests which it prepared or approved for transmission were in order and so would be handled expeditiously and without any need to refer a request back for clarification. The strength of this argument is increasingly recognized, as the expertise of Central Authorities has grown; some countries have chosen to use their Central Authorities as transmitting agents, although not required to do so by the Convention, and have discovered that the advantages outweigh any risk of slight delays caused by the extra agency involved within the state of origin. However, a significant number of countries remain wedded to a principle which requires all outgoing requests to emanate directly from a court; for such countries the superimposition of an administrative agency in the context of a judicial function is impossible.

In the result, the Convention provides that the request is initiated by an 'authority or judicial officer competent under the law of the state in which the documents originate'.[64] Some countries, including the United Kingdom, have chosen to provide that outgoing requests must be forwarded through the Central Authority; others allow local court officials or *huissiers* to act. Private parties may not themselves originate requests, but a party's lawyer may do so if the law of the state of origin so allows, as is the case with attorneys in several states of the USA. The Canadian and Irish governments have made declarations specifying those (including practising lawyers) who may initiate requests.

Practice appears to be fairly relaxed on this matter. The Special Commission of the Hague Conference held in 1977 to review the working of the Convention found that there was no systematic monitoring of the competence of forwarding authorities:

It appeared to the Commission that, aside from certain cases involving fantasy or malice, a request for service forwarded abroad met a precise need, and it could be presumed that such a request was in compliance with the procedural law of the forum, since this step would otherwise make no sense.[65]

The 2003 Special Commission recommended that in any question of doubt as to the competence of the forwarding authority, rather than rejecting the request, the authorities in the state requested should seek to confirm that competence by either

---

[63] *AetD(10)*, vol 3, pp 170–2.
[64] Convention, art 3(1). See *Marschhauser v Travelers Indemnity Co* 145 FRD 605 (SD Fla, 1992).
[65] *AetD(14)*, vol 4, p 386.

consulting the Hague Conference's website or by making expeditious informal enquiries of the forwarding authorities.[66]

5. Procedures for service

The Convention prescribes in some detail the documentation to be used, the extent to which translations may be required, and the actual mode of service to be employed in the state of destination; these various issues are interconnected.

An Annex to the Convention prescribes a form of 'Request for Service' which is to be used, which is in three parts. The actual request is set out in the first part, which gives the relevant addresses and which may specify a particular mode of service. The second, printed on the reverse of the first, is a Certificate either that service was effected on a stated date or that service has proved impossible for stated reasons; the Certificate will be tendered in proof of service in any proceedings in the state of origin, and the law of that state will determine whether its contents can be challenged[67] or whether the absence or incomplete nature of the Certificate is fatal.[68] The third is a Summary of the document to be served, which is served with the document itself.[69] Unless the Contracting States concerned have agreed to dispense, in dealings between their two countries, with this requirement,[70] all three parts of the Request must be completed either in the language of the state of destination or in French or English.[71]

There must be sent to the Central Authority of the state of destination two copies of the Request and of the document to be served (either the original or a copy);[72] so far as the Request is concerned this requirement for duplicates is always applicable, but pairs or groups of states may agree between themselves to dispense with the need for duplicate copies of the document to be served.[73] The practice is for the second copy of the Request to be retained in the files of the Central Authority as a record of its action in the matter, and for the second copy of the

---

[66] Conclusion and Recommendations, para 49.

[67] See *Gould Entertainment Corpn v Bodo* 107 FRD 308 (SDNY, 1985) (challenge to accuracy of Italian certificate failed on facts); *Northrup King Co v Compania Productora Semillas Algodoneras Selectas SA* 51 F 3d 1383 (8th Cir, 1995) (court unwilling to look behind certificate to examine alleged breaches of Spanish procedural law).

[68] See *Fox v Régie Nationale des Usines Renault* 103 FRD 453 (WDTenn, 1984) (absence of French certificate not fatal: 'The Hague Convention should not be construed so as to foreclose judicial discretion when such discretion needs to be exercised' (at p 455)); *Greene v Le Dorze* (NDTex, 1998) (French certificate incomplete, but accepted); *Burda Media v Viertel* 417 F 3d 292 (2nd Cir, 2005) (French police report adequate substitute for absent certificate); *Combs v Iorio* (ED Okla, 2008) (absence of Kuwaiti certificate not fatal. Cf a decision of the Italian Corte di Cassazione, 28 May 1984 (no 3257) (Asser 4/101) (no certificate; appellant could not prove service of notice of appeal by other means and appeal dismissed).

[69] See Convention, arts 3, 5(4), and 6.

[70] Convention, art 20(b).

[71] Convention, art 7(2).

[72] See *Rivers v Stihl Inc* 434 So 2d 766 (Ala, 1983) (German Central Authority refused request because document not in duplicate).

[73] Convention, arts 3(2), 20(a).

document itself to be returned with the completed Certificate of Service so as to eliminate any doubt as to which document is covered by the Certificate.

If the applicant requests a particular method of service (which in practice is seldom done)[74] that request will be complied with unless to do so would be incompatible with the law of the country of destination. The text of the Convention suggests that in all other cases the Central Authority may choose to serve the document either by the method prescribed by its internal law for the service of documents in actions brought against defendants within the jurisdiction or by 'delivery to an addressee who accepts it voluntarily', ie *remise simple*.[75] However, the Request as set out in the Annex suggests that the applicant may delete either of these possibilities, and so limit the Central Authority's options. The matter is further complicated by the rules as to translations: if the document[76] is to be served under article 5 by any method other than that of simple delivery,[77] the Central Authority may require the document to be written in, or translated into, an official language of the state of destination.[78] Unless the applicant for service has good reason to believe that service by simple delivery will be accepted, he or she should supply a translation, for there is otherwise a risk of delay while the Central Authority reports that that mode of delivery has failed and requests a translation of the document.[79] If a translation is required, the whole document must be translated including any appended material treated by the law of the state of origin as an essential part of the document.[80]

In practice, each Central Authority has a preferred method of dealing with requests for service. For example, in the United States where the Central Authority is an agency of the Federal Government, service is effected by the use of US

---

[74] At the 1989 Special Commission to review the Convention, the US Delegation reported that applicants familiar with US practice sometimes asked for a variation in it, eg that the Marshal attempt personal service at once rather than use that only after the failure of postal service.

[75] Convention, art 5; for *remise simple*, see p 3, above. It must be clear that the addressee accepts the document: see *Isabelle Lancray SA v Peters und Sickert KG* (Bundesgerichtshof, 20 September 1990 (IX ZB 1/88)), [1992] ILPr 52, NJW 1991, 641 (Asser 5/358) (service on secretary in addressee's office insufficient); *V v De Raad voor de Kinderbescherming te Rotterdam* (Hoge Raad, 20 May 1994), NJ 1994, 589 (Asser 5/368) (refusal to accept document); Oberlandesgericht Hamm, 30 September 1994 (35 U 29/94), [1996] RIW 156 (secretary sent to collect registered letter from Post Office; that did not constitute voluntary acceptance of contents).

[76] As opposed to the Request for Service, the language of which is governed by art 7: *Taylor v Uniden Corpn of America* 622 F Supp 1011 (DC Mo, 1985).

[77] Arrondissementsrechtbank Middelburg, 4 July 1984, NIPR 1984, 329 (Asser 4/101) (no translation required on *remise simple*).

[78] Convention, art 5(3). In countries with several official languages, attention may need to be paid to the prevalent language of the region in question, eg Flemish in Antwerp (Oberlandesgericht Hamm, 27 February 1985, 20 U 222/84, IPRax 1986, 104 (Asser 4/99)). It is for the central Authority to demand a translation, not the party addressed: Liège CA, 26 May 1992, Pas 1992, II 73 (Asser 5/360). Pairs or groups of contracting States may agree to waive this provision in dealings between themselves: Convention, art 20(b).

[79] Eg Arrondissementsrechtbank Amsterdam, 2 May 1979 (Asser 2/168); Porto CA, 8 November 1994 (Asser 5/370).

[80] *Teknekron Management Inc v Quante Fernmeldetechnik GmbH* 115 FRD 175 (DC Nev, 1987). There seems no merit in the point reportedly taken by a German Central Authority that the translations should be set out on separate pages from the original text: *Rivers v Stihl Inc* 434 So 2d 766 (Ala, 1983).

Marshals attached to the (Federal) District Courts. In France and Germany, on the other hand, the informal method of 'simple delivery' is preferred.[81] Practice as to translation requirements varies greatly; although the relevant information is set out in the *Practical Handbook* published by the Permanent Bureau of the Hague Conference, which is held by all Central Authorities, other applicants often fall foul of the rules. Some countries always require the document to be translated. Others have some flexibility, being prepared to serve documents in any language which the addressee is likely to understand; a short document addressed to a commercial firm in English or a language similar to that of the state of destination (eg, a document in Norwegian for service in Sweden) will be accepted, but a long document addressed to a private individual in a relatively obscure language will not.[82]

Even if there is no formal translation requirement, the provision of a translation may be advisable. There is some US authority for the proposition that service on a person who does not understand the language of the document in question is not good service on want of due process grounds. Although developed in a case to which the Hague Convention was inapplicable,[83] the point has been recognized, though held unjustified on the facts, in some Convention cases.[84] The relevance in this context of the Summary of the document to be served under the Convention system appears not to have been addressed.

The Central Authority system has many advantages, but it cannot of course ensure effective or speedy service. In the Californian case of *Quaranta v Merlini*,[85] three attempts were made to serve documents on a defendant in Italy, trying three different addresses and two different names; on each occasion the defendant could not be located or had already moved on. Even between New York and England, with no possible language problems to cause difficulty, it took in one case more than 180 days to effect service in London through the English subsidiary authority.[86] Where the Central Authority system fails to work, the courts in some countries will allow service by alternative means.[87]

---

[81] *AetD(14)*, vol 4, p 384.

[82] See also Arrondissementsrechtbank Breda, 21 April 1981 (Asser 3/136) (no translation requirements for service in Turkey).

[83] *Julen v Larsen* 25 Cal App 3d 325 (1972).

[84] *Shoei Kako Co Ltd v Superior Court for the City and County of San Fransisco* 109 Cal Rptr 402 (Cal App, 1973) (where the Japanese defendant familiar with English); Tokyo District Court, 26 March 1990 (Asser 5/362).

[85] 237 Cal Rptr 19 (Cal App, 1987).

[86] *ITEL Container International Corpn v Atlanttrafik Express Service Ltd* 686 F Supp 438 (SDNY, 1988). The 2009 Special Commission made a series of practical recommendations designed to speed the process: Conclusions and Recommendations, para 23.

[87] See the example given by the advisory committee on the US FRCP and considered in *United States Aviation Underwriters Inc v Nabtesco Corp* (WD Wash, 2007), and cases concerning the breakdown of co-operation between the US and the Russian Federation in 2003 (eg, *Nuance Communications Inc v Abbyy Software House* 626 F 3d 1222 (Fed Cir, 2010), as to which see (2009) 31 U Pa Jo Int L 593.

6. Refusal or failure to serve

If a Central Authority considers that a request for service does not fall within the Convention it may reject it.[88] Otherwise, rejection may only be on the ground of infringement of 'sovereignty or security'; neither a claim to exclusive jurisdiction by the state of destination over the subject matter with which the document deals, nor the fact that no cause of action would exist under the law of that state is a proper ground for rejection.[89] In practice rejection of requests is very rare; examples reported to the 1977 Special Commission of the Hague Conference included attempts to serve documents on the monarch of the state of destination and to bring proceedings against judges or police chiefs.[90] In a later case, the US Central Authority relied on the sovereignty basis in refusing to serve process on the captain of a US warship.[91] Article 13 has had a chequered history in the German courts, some of which have reached the questionable decision that service of an anti-suit injunction can be refused on the same ground.[92] It has twice been considered by the Constitutional Court which has stressed that although service is seen as an exercise of sovereign administrative authority, the test in article 13 is very different from one simply of public policy. Article 13 is seen as applicable when the objective pursued by the action evidently infringes the indispensable principles of a liberal state under the Rule of Law. It would, however, justify a refusal where the claim was frivolous or grossly exaggerated; the fact that punitive damages may be claimed does not in itself bring a case into that category.[93]

A more frequent cause for the return of documents unserved is the expiry of the time limit, to which attention is specifically drawn by an entry in the Summary of the Document to be Served. This may be given by reference to time elapsing after the date of issue of the document, and it is quite possible for the time limit to be passed before the document can be served or even before it is received by the Central Authority. The better practice in such cases is to attempt service even after the stated time limit: a trial or other procedural step is unlikely to follow immediately after the expiry of the time limit, so belated service may still give the defendant a useful opportunity to intervene; and under article 15[94] a six-month waiting

---

[88] Convention, art 4.

[89] Convention, art 13.

[90] *AetD(14)*, vol 4, p 383.

[91] *Edwards v Bureau Wijsmuller Scheepvart- Transport- en Zeesleepvaart Maatschappij BV* [1988] Sch en Sch 168, NIPR 1987, 469 (Amsterdam, 18 June 1987) (service not void under Dutch law; possibility of default judgment remained).

[92] *Re the Enforcement of an English Anti-suit Injunction* (Oberlandesgericht Düsseldorf, 10 January 1996 (3 VA 11/95)), [1997] ILPr 320, IPRaz 1997, 260.

[93] Bundesverfassungsgericht 91 BVerfGE 335 and 108 BVerfGE 238; Oberlandesgericht Düsseldorf, 22 September 2008 (I-3 VA 6/08), (2009) 9 Eur L F I-83, II-52; see J van Hein, 'Recent German Jurisprudence on Cooperation with the US in Civil and Commercial matters' in E Gottschalk and others (eds), *Conflict of Laws in a Globalized World: Essays in Memory of Arthur Taylor von Mehren* (CUP, 2007).

[94] See pp 47–50, below.

period is often imposed before proceedings can be taken to the stage of a default judgment.

7. Other permitted modes of service

Although the system of Central Authorities is the primary mode under the Convention, other modes of service are permitted, subject to a number of provisos. These are as follows:

(a) Service by diplomatic or consular agents directly on the addressee, without the use of any compulsion

Any Contracting State may declare its opposition in this mode of service unless the document is to be served upon a national of the state of origin.[95] Many countries, mainly those in the civil law tradition, have made this declaration;[96] accordingly an attempt to serve process via a US Vice-Consul in the German Federal Republic has been held to be ineffective,[97] and the Netherlands Ministry of External Affairs was held to have acted properly when it refused to accept a document intended for service via the diplomatic channel on a defendant in France.[98]

(b) The indirect consular channel

This mode is carried forward from the 1954 Convention, and it is expressly provided that 'if exceptional circumstances so require' diplomatic channels may be used for the same purpose.[99] Contracting States are to designate the authorities that consuls may approach.[100] Not all have done so; most have designated the Central Authority (including in the case of the United Kingdom the subsidiary authorities in each part of the UK), but others have specified the president or registrar of or public prosecutor attached to a local court within whose area the addressee is to be found.

---

[95] Convention, arts 8, 21(2)(a).

[96] Belgium, Bulgaria, China, Croatia, Czech Republic, Egypt, France, Germany, Greece, Hungary, Korea, Kuwait, Latvia, Lithuania, Luxembourg, Macedonia, Mexico, Monaco, Norway, Pakistan, Poland, Portugal, Romania, Russia, San Marino, Serbia, Seychelles, Slovakia, Sri Lanka, Switzerland, Turkey, Ukraine, and Venezuela.

[97] *Dr Ing HCF Porsche AG v Superior Court for the County of Sacramento* 177 Cal Rptr 155 (CalApp, 1981).

[98] Gerechtshof Den Bosch, 19 November 1980, NJ 1982, 416 (Asser 3/138).

[99] Convention, art 9.

[100] Convention, art 21(1)(c).

(c) The postal channel

The convention speaks of 'the freedom to send judicial documents, by postal channels, directly to persons abroad',[101] but makes it clear that this is subject to any objection by the state of destination.[102] In many countries, courier services provide an alternative to the post. Where a state objects to the use of the post, its objection will be taken to apply equally to the use of courier services.[103] Some Contracting States have indicated their objection (Argentina, Belgium, Bulgaria, China,[104] Croatia, Czech Republic, Egypt, Germany,[105] Greece, Hungary, India,[106] Korea, Kuwait, Lithuania, Macedonia, Mexico,[107] Norway, Poland, Russia, San Marino, Slovakia, Sri Lanka, Switzerland, Turkey,[108] Ukraine, and Venezuela; Luxembourg has withdrawn its original objection). It is of course difficult to 'police' this objection, and there is a certain ambivalence in the attitude of some countries; recognizing the usefulness of postal service, they welcome it as a supplementary method designed to back up the 'official' service effected in other ways, but are unhappy to see the postal channel treated as appropriate or sufficient in itself.[109]

The language of article 10(a), which authorizes the use of the postal channel, has been closely examined in US courts. It seems to have been assumed throughout the discussions leading up to the signature of the Convention that the use of the postal channel was indeed a mode of service, of notification. The text has remained substantially unchanged since the original 1896 Convention which spoke of '*la faculté d'addresser directement, par la voie de la poste, des actes aux intéressés se trouvant à l'étranger*'.[110] Such conduct would clearly be a form of 'delivery' rather than the formal service effected by the authorities of the state of destination, but there seems

---

[101] Convention, art 10(a). There is no specification of registered or certified mail; it will be for the *lex fori* to determine how service by post is to be proved: *Randolph v Hendry* 50 F Supp 2d 572 (SD WVa, 1999).

[102] Convention, arts 10, 21(2)(a).

[103] *Intercontinental Industries Corp v Qingquan Luo* (CD Cal, 2011), citing the Hague Conference's *Practical Handbook* and the view of the 2003 Special Commission.

[104] But not in the Hong Kong (see *Tracfone Wireless Inc v Bequator Corp Ltd* 717 F Supp 2d 1307 (SD Fla, 2010); *Willis v Magic Power Co Ltd* (EDPa, 2011)) or Macau Special Administrative Regions.

[105] A fact which is overlooked by practitioners with some frequency. See eg, Oberlandesgericht Frankfurt, 21 February 1991 (20 W 154/90), RIW 1991, 587 (Asser 5/358) (English writ); *Re an English Judgment* (Oberlandesgericht Hamm, 25 September 1992 (20 W 27/92)), [1993] ILPr 65; *Re Enforcement of an Israeli Judgment* (Oberlandesgericht Köln, 1 June 1994 (16 W 68/93)), [1996] ILPr 573, RIW 1994, 683), and for a French decision *Heddens v Esseydric* (Cour de Cassation, 28 March 2006), [2007] ILPr 6.

[106] See *Tuckerbrook Alternative Investments LP v Banerjee* (DC Mass, 2010).

[107] An error on the US State Department's website led some courts to conclude that Mexico did not object: *International Transactions Ltd vEmbotelladora Agral Regiomontana SA de CV* 277 F Supp 2d 654 (ND Tex, 2002); *Unite National Retirement Fund v Ariela Inc* 643 F Supp 2d 328 (SD NY 2008); the error was corrected in *OGM Inc v Televisa SA de CV* (CD Cal, 2009) and *Mitchell v Volkswagen Group of America Inc* (ND Ga, 2010).

[108] See *Shiblaq v Sadikoglu* [2004] EWHC 1890 (Comm), [2004] ILPr 51.

[109] Cf *AetD(14)*, vol 4, p 387. See also *Frankel v Kaufman* (1976) 30 PD 449 (Sup Ct of Israel) (Asser 3/137) (service by post valid in Israel); *Pycke v Office National d'Allocations Familiales pour Travailleurs Salariés* (Belgian Cour de cassation, 30 September 1986), Pas 1986, II 89 (Asser 4/102) (postal service in the Netherlands valid).

[110] 1896 Convention, art 6(1).

to be nothing in the various Hague Conventions to suggest that the postal channel was any less valid than any other permitted mode.

However, several US courts have considered cases in which service has been effected by registered mail upon defendants in Japan, a state which has objected to the other modes of service listed in article 10 but not to the use of the postal channel. Some of those courts have seized upon the use of the word 'send' in article 10(a), as opposed to 'serve'. Although this distinction could be explained by reference to civil law ideas of formal service as opposed to informal delivery, these courts including the Court of Appeals for the Eighth Circuit in *Bankston v Toyota Motor Corpn*[111] have concluded that article 10(a) does not allow effective 'service' in Japan. This reasoning has also been applied to service in Italy[112] and Spain[113] (which have objected to none of the methods listed in article 10), with the assertion that article 10(c) does not authorize a separate method of service. It is submitted that these conclusions are wholly unjustified. They were repudiated by the US State Department,[114] have been much criticized in the academic literature,[115] and are contrary to the clear understanding expressed by Special Commissions of the Hague Conference.[116] It is difficult to see what purpose would be served by the inclusion of article 10(a) in a convention on service of process were that not its subject matter. The fact, much relied on in some cases in the *Bankston* line, that service by mail is not allowed in domestic Japanese cases cannot be relevant; Japan could have objected to article 10(a) but chose not to do so.[117] The Court of Appeals for the Second Circuit has, in *Ackermann v Levine*,[118] taken the opposite view and this decision has been followed by the Ninth Circuit.[119] Decisions of District Courts in other Circuits are divided.

---

[111]   889 F 2d 172 (8th Cir, 1989).

[112]   *Hantover Inc v Omet SNC* 688 F Supp 1377 (WD Mo, 1988); cf *Knit With v Knitting Fever Inc* (ED Pa, 2010).

[113]   *Intelsat Corp v Multivision TV LLC* (SD Fla, 2010). See also the same argument in *Connuscio v Seabrand Shipping Ltd.* 908 F Supp 823 (DC Ore, 1995) (service in Greece which has objected to service by post).

[114]   Letter of the Department's Assistant Legal Advisor, A J Krecko, of March 1991; see 30 ILM 260.

[115]   P N McCausland, 'How May I Serve You?' 12 Pace L Rev 177 (1992); F B Mann, Comment, 21 Col L Rev 647 (1991). See also B A Ristau, *International Judicial Assistance* (International Law Institute, 1995), vol 1, para 4–28, supporting this line of cases but on the ground that 'send' in art 10 (a) represents 'careless drafting'.

[116]   See the Conclusions and Recommendations of the 2003 Special Commission, para 55.

[117]   This was emphasized in a formal statement made by the Japanese delegation to the 1989 Special Commission of the Hague Conference and the judgment of a court in Tokyo, 26 March 1990 (Asser 5/362), holding that Japan would recognize the *de facto* effects of service by post in Japan, but would not necessarily recognize the resulting judgment: in that case a Hawaiian judgment was refused recognition as the documents sent to the defendant were not accompanied by a translation into Japanese.

[118]   788 F 2d 830 (2nd Cir, 1986). This view was adopted in *Nuovo Pignone v Storman Asia M/V* 310 F 3d 374 (5th Cir, 2002).

[119]   *Brockmeyer v May* 383 F 3d 798 (9th Cir, 2004). See Y A Tamayo, 'Sometimes the postman doesn't ring at all: Serving Process by Mail to a Post Office Box Abroad' (2005) 13 Willamette J Int L & Disp Res 269.

Although the contrary has been argued, it is clear that there are no translation requirements when article 10(a) (or, indeed, any part of article 10) is relied upon[120]

(d) From official to official

Subject again to any objection by the state of destination, the Convention recognizes a mode of service from official to official. The text speaks of:

> the freedom of judicial officers [*officiers ministériels* in the French text], officials or other competent persons of the State of origin to effect service of judicial documents directly through the judicial officers, officials or other competent persons of the State of destination.[121]

At first sight, the inclusion of this mode is puzzling; it seems so clearly inferior to the system of Central Authorities. In practice, however, it enables those countries with the institution of *huissier* to allow direct communication from *huissier* to *huissier*.[122] It has little relevance in other countries, many of which have recorded a formal objection.[123] The United Kingdom's objection limits the scope of this mode, in effect, to direct communication from a foreign judicial officer to one of the designated central or subsidiary authorities in the United Kingdom.[124] It appears to have been used in one case for communication from a US attorney to a French *huissier*.[125]

(e) 'Any person interested in a judicial proceeding'

Subject to the same rights of objection, 'any person interested in a judicial proceeding' may effect service directly through the judicial officers, officials, or other competent persons of the state of destination.[126] Little practical use seems to be made of this mode of service in the sense in which it was drafted, which envisaged an approach by a party directly to a competent local court official, for example, in the state of destination. Many Contracting States have indicated their

---

[120] Paris CA, 6 April 1979, JT 1980, 156 (Asser 3/5); Oberlandesgericht Hamm, 16 March 1981 (2 U 182/80) (Asser 3/136); *Weight v Kawasaki Heavy Industries Ltd* 597 F Supp 1082 (ED Va, 1984); *Lemme v Wine of Japan Import* 631 F Supp 456, 464 (ED NY 1986); *Sandoval v Honda Motor Co. Ltd* 527 A 2d 564 (Pa, 1987); *Parsons v Bank Leumi Le-Israel BM* 565 So 2d 20 (Ala, 1990); *Heredia v Transport SAS* 101 F Supp 2d 158 (SD NY, 2000).

[121] Convention, art 10(b).

[122] See, eg, Ghent CA, 5 October 1978 (Asser 2/169) (Belgium and Netherlands).

[123] Botswana, Bulgaria, China (other than in the Hong Kong and Macau Special Administrative Regions), Croatia, Czech Republic, Egypt, Finland, Germany, Greece, Hungary, Iceland, Ireland, Japan, Korea, Kuwait, Latvia, Lithuania, Macedonia, Mexico, Norway, Poland, Russia, St Vincent and the Grenadines, San Marino, Seychelles, Sweden, and Turkey.

[124] Similar declarations have been made by China (in respect of the Hong Kong Special Administrative Region) and Israel. See *Koehler v Dodwell* 152 F 3d 304 (4th Cir, 1998) for some discussion of the UK declaration as applied to Bermuda.

[125] *Tamari v Bache & Co (Lebanon) SAL* 431 F Supp 1226 (ND Ill, 1977) (affd on other points, 565 F 2d 1194 (7th Cir, 1977).

[126] Convention, arts 10(c), 21(2)(a).

objection to its use.[127] As with the previous mode of service, the United Kingdom's objection limits the scope of this mode, in effect, to direct communication from a foreign judicial officer to one of the designated central or subsidiary authorities in the United Kingdom.[128] The then Central Authority of the United Kingdom confirmed in a letter to the Permanent Bureau of the Hague Conference in 1980 that its declaration did not preclude any person in another Contracting State who is interested in a judicial proceeding (including that person's lawyer) from effecting service in the United Kingdom 'directly' through a competent person other than a judicial officer or official, eg, a solicitor.[129]

(f) Alternative methods under article 19

Finally, article 19 of the Convention provides:

To the extent that the internal law of a Contracting State permits methods of transmission, other than those provided for in the preceding Articles, of documents coming from abroad, for service within its territory, the present Convention shall not affect such provisions.

It has been argued that article 19 should be narrowly construed, as referring only to alternative methods of service which are specifically authorized by the foreign country.[130] A more liberal interpretation treats article 19 as permitting service by any method that is not implicitly or explicitly prohibited by the laws of the foreign country. The original proposal of the US delegation at The Hague, from which this article was derived, spoke of 'provisions of the internal law' of the state in which service was effected as not being 'repealed, modified or otherwise affected' by the Convention, which could be read as supporting a narrower interpretation; but the wording of the eventual text was different.[131] Discussion of the proposal was brief and on the controversial point unhelpful.[132] The liberal view has, unsurprisingly, been adopted in a US decision.[133]

---

[127] Botswana, Bulgaria, China (except in the Hong Kong and Macau Special Administrative Regions), Croatia, Czech Republic, Denmark, Egypt, Estonia, Finland, Germany, Greece, Hungary, Ireland, Japan, Korea, Kuwait, Latvia, Lithuania, Macedonia, Mexico, Norway, Pakistan, Poland, Russia, St Vincent and the Grenadines, Serbia, Slovakia, Sri Lanka, Sweden, Switzerland, Turkey, and Venezuela.

[128] China (in respect of the Hong Kong Special Administrative Region), Israel, and Seychelles have made similar declarations.

[129] *Tax Lease Underwriters Inc v Blackwall Green Ltd* 106 FRD 595 (ED Mo, 1985). For a case involving service in the Isle of Man, see *IM Partners v Debt Direct Ltd* 394 F Supp 2d 503 (D Conn, 2005). The Irish declaration objecting to the mode of service under art 10(c) expressly saves service via a solicitor in Ireland.

[130] See G A Magnarini, 'Service of Process Abroad Under the Hague Convention' (1988) 71 Marq L Rev 649; G B Raley, 'A Comparative Analysis: Notice Requirements in Germany, Japan, Spain, The United Kingdom and The United States', (1993) 10 Ariz Jo Intl & Comp L 301, examining the interpretation of the article in various countries.

[131] *AetD(10)*, p 229; Working Paper 21.

[132] *AetD(10)*, pp 244–5. The proposal was seen as of little concern to countries in the civil law tradition.

[133] *Banco Latino SACA v Gomez Lopez* 53 F Supp 2d 1273 (SD Fla, 1999).

8. Bilateral arrangements

The preliminary draft of the Convention contained a provision which would enable two Contracting States to permit 'direct communication between their respective authorities'. This picked up language used in earlier Hague Conventions;[134] given the establishment of the Central Authority system, the provision seemed to have little point, as the Rapporteur himself admitted.[135] It was nonetheless retained in the final text, as article 11, and extended to include any other channel of transmission not included in the earlier articles. The Rapporteur was notably unenthusiastic about this text *'que nous n'estimons pas très heureux'*;[136] its effect appears to be that a Contracting State can enter an objection to the modes of service provided for in article 10 (which would otherwise be available in respect of all Contracting States) but allow their use in respect of particular, and perhaps especially neighbouring, states. For example, although France objects to the use of the postal channel, an exception exists in favour of documents emanating from Luxembourg,[137] but it has to be admitted that as this arrangement is the subject of a bilateral convention it is actually saved by provisions in the General Clauses of the 1965 Convention and therefore does not attract article 11.[138]

9. Safeguards

In the broadest sense, the Convention is about the passing of information, something which can be of value both to the giver and to the receiver of the information. However, it is more realistic to regard the Convention as primarily about the service of process which is in turn an essential step in the conduct of proceedings designed to secure the interests of the plaintiff. So the Convention's main provisions operate to further the interests of plaintiffs rather than those of defendants. The authors of the Convention perceived the need for some balancing provision, some safeguards for defendants, so articles 15 and 16 contain carefully constructed guarantees which have been described as the keystone of the text.[139]

Article 15 contains in effect two alternative sets of rules. The first reads as follows;

Where a writ of summons or an equivalent document[140] had to be transmitted abroad for the purpose of service, under the provisions of the present Convention,[141] and the defendant has not appeared, judgment shall not be given until it is established that—

---

[134] See 1954 Convention, art 1(4).
[135] *AetD(10)*, vol 3, p 114.
[136] Ibid, p 374.
[137] Déclaration of 14 March 1884, art 2.
[138] See Convention, arts 22–25; art 25 catches the example in the text.
[139] *AetD(10)*, vol 3, p 92 (the Rapporteur, writing of the equivalent text in the preliminary draft).
[140] Eg, notice of an appeal.
[141] For the significance of this phrase, see *Shiblaq v Sadikoglu* [2004] EWHC 1890 (Comm), [2004] ILPr 51.

(a) the document[142] was served by a method prescribed by the internal law of the State addressed for the service of documents in domestic actions upon persons who are within its territory, or

(b) the document was actually delivered to the defendant or to his residence by another method provided for by this Convention,

and that in either of these cases the service or the delivery was effected in sufficient time to enable the defendant to defend.[143]

Commenting on these provisions in a case in which, through no fault of the plaintiff, process had failed to reach a defendant in France until some two months after the hearing date, a Dutch court said that 'the Convention subordinates the interests of plaintiffs in enforcing their rights as quickly as possible against foreign defendants to the latter's interest in having an opportunity of defending themselves'.[144]

It will be noted that article 15(1)(b) is satisfied if the document is actually delivered to the defendant or to his or her residence. It is sufficient if the document is, for example, handed to a part-time domestic cleaner employed by the defendant.[145]

If the matters set out in article 15(1) are not established, the court will normally adjourn to allow either the gathering of further evidence or the making of fresh attempts to effect service.[146] In some countries, however, that is not the end of the matter. The Convention, largely as a result of the efforts of the French delegation which sought some *quid pro quo* for surrendering the system of *notification au parquet*, allows individual Contracting States to opt for rules which create, in effect, a presumption in favour of a diligent plaintiff:

Each Contracting State shall be free to declare that the judge, notwithstanding the provisions of the first paragraph of this article, may give judgment even if no certificate of service or delivery has been received, if all the following conditions are fulfilled—

(a) the document was transmitted by one of the methods provided for in this Convention,

(b) a period of time of not less than six months, considered adequate by the judge in the particular case, has elapsed since the date of the transmission of the documents,

(c) no certificate of any kind has been received, even though every reasonable effort has been made to obtain it through the competent authorities of the State addressed.[147]

---

[142] ie, in its original language, not merely a translation: Arrondissementsrechtbank Amsterdam, 11 May 1983, NIPR 1984, 131.

[143] Convention, art 15(1).

[144] Arrondissementsrechtbank Breda, 16 May 1978 (Asser 2/172).

[145] *Gould Entertainment Corpn v Bodo* 107 FRD 308 (SDNY, 1985).

[146] See the cases collected at Asser 2/171–2 and the decision of the Hoge Raad, 1 July 1982, NJ 1983, 781 (Asser 3/140).

[147] Convention, art 15(2).

This second option has been taken by a majority of Contracting States.[148] Practice under this option can be seen in a number of Netherlands decisions. In a case in which service had been attempted in Belgium, the Belgian Central Authority certified that service had proved impossible, the defendant not having been found at the address given. The *Hoge Raad*, treating this as a case within the Convention and not one in which the defendant's address was unknown,[149] ordered that the plaintiff might publish a notice in a Belgian daily paper with a view to obtaining judgment under article 15(2).[150] A later case before the *Hoge Raad* involved attempted service on a US corporation. Initially the documents were returned with an indication that the defendant was not at the address given; it might be in another state. At that stage, article 15(2)(c) was not satisfied, as 'every reasonable effort' has not been made. A further attempt to serve failed and it was reported that the defendant could not be traced. The Netherlands court was then satisfied that article 15(2) was fully satisfied.[151]

In another case,[152] repeated attempts were made to serve a defendant in Germany: the first failed as the documents were rejected as not giving the first name of the defendant; no reply was received when the documents were sent a second and third time; on the fourth occasion it was reported that the defendant had moved to another city; finally, it was said that the defendant could not be found at the new address. 'Every reasonable effort' had been made. As paragraph (a) requires service by one of the methods provided for in the Convention, the article cannot be relied on if another form of service (such as service at an 'elected domicile') valid under the *lex fori* is used.[153] In a US case in which service had been attempted through the Israeli Central Authority, which had not effected service after nine months, the court regarded article 15(2) as satisfied, but in its discretion, aware that the defendants wished to contest the suit, refused a default judgment.[154]

Whichever set of rules has been adopted, nothing in article 15 prevents a court in the state of origin from taking, in case of urgency, any provisional or protective measures.[155]

---

[148] Australia, Belgium, Botswana, Bulgaria, Canada, China, Croatia, Cyprus, Czech Republic, Denmark, Estonia, France, Germany, Greece, Hungary, Iceland, India, Ireland, Japan, Korea, Latvia, Lithuania, Luxembourg, Macedonia, Monaco, Monaco, Netherlands, Norway, Pakistan, Portugal, Russia, St Vincent and the Grenadines, San Marino, Serbia, Seychelles, Slovakia, Spain, Sri Lanka, Turkey, Ukraine, United Kingdom, the United States, and Venezuela.

[149] Excluded by Convention, art 1(2).

[150] Hoge Raad, 25 November 1977, NJ 1978, 313 (Asser 2/172).

[151] Hoge Raad, 10 May 1985, NJ 1985, 700 (Asser 4/98). Again there is some ambivalence as to whether this was an 'unknown address' case and so outside the Convention. See also Arrondissements-rechtbank Alkmaar, 3 February 1977 (Asser 2/171); Hoge Raad, 1 May 1981, RvdW 1981, 71 (Asser 3/136); Cour de cassation, 16 December 1980 (Asser 3/141) (see Droz (1981) Revcrit.d.i.p. 714) (six month delay not observed); Arrondissementsrechtbank Alkmaar, 5 August 1982, NIPR 1983, no 239 (Asser 4/106).

[152] *Holland Repair Services v Adam* (Arrondissementsrechtbank Amsterdam, 30 October 1991), NIPR 1992, no 426 (Asser 5/366).

[153] *Slok v La Chemise Lacoste SA* (Arrondissementsrechtbank 's-Gravenhage, 18 January 1990), NIPR 1991 no 459 (Asser 5/364).

[154] *Marschhauser v Travelers Indemnity Co* 145 FRD 605 (SD Fla, 1992).

[155] Convention, art 15(3).

A further protection for defendants is contained in article 16 which contains provisions safeguarding the position of a defendant against whom judgment in default has been entered:

When a writ of summons or an equivalent document had to be transmitted abroad for the purpose of service, under the provisions of the present Convention, and a judgment has been entered against a defendant who has not appeared, the judge shall have the power to relieve the defendant from the effects of the expiration of the time for appeal from the judgment if the following conditions are fulfilled—

(a) the defendant, without any fault on his part, did not have knowledge of the document in sufficient time to defend,[156] or knowledge of the judgment in sufficient time to appeal, and

(b) the defendant has disclosed a prima facie defence to the action on the merits.

An application for relief may be filed only within a reasonable time after the defendant has knowledge of the judgment.[157]

However, a Contracting State is entitled to declare that an application must be filed within a stated period from the date of entry of the judgment, a period which must not be less than one year.[158] Most Contracting States have made such a declaration, and all but three[159] of declarant states have specified a one-year time limit. Article 16 is expressly declared not to apply to judgments concerning status or capacity of persons, fields in which certainty is essential.[160]

10. Extra-judicial documents

Chapter II of the Convention, consisting solely of the brief article 17, applies the provisions of the Convention to extra-judicial documents 'emanating from authorities and judicial officers of a Contracting State'. The cited words are important. Without them the phrase 'extra-judicial documents' would appear almost unlimited in scope, while its French equivalent '*actes extra-judiciares*' has been given, at some times and in some jurisdictions, a narrow and technical meaning. The Convention text emphasizes the source of the document, and the capacity in which the person concerned is acting; a notary may be acting as a public officer

---

[156] See a judgment of an Italian court seised of an action against a Swedish firm, holding 60 days sufficient for this purpose: Monza, 9 November 1985, Revdir.int.proc. 1987, 102 (Asser 4/108).

[157] Convention, art 16(1)(2). See Bundesgerichtshof, 24 September 1986 (VIII ZR 320/85), IPRax 1988, 159 (Asser 4/107). On the question of the 'reasonable time' referred to in the final paragraph of art 16(2), the Luxembourg Court of Appeal (16 March 1987, no 9259; Asser 4/109) refused to disturb a decision that an application under art 16 made on 19 September 1985 in respect of a judgment notified to the defendant on 12 July 1985 was out of time. The defendant was a company based in Trier, not many miles from Luxembourg.

[158] Convention, art 16(3).

[159] Spain, which specifies 16 months; and Estonia and Norway, which specify three years. The Pakistan declaration refers to the limitation period set by Pakistan law.

[160] Convention, art 16(4).

or as the agent of a private party, and only in the former case will the Convention apply to documents issued by him.[161]

The discussions at the Special Commission held in 1977 to review the working of the Convention revealed that 'a great number' of extra-judicial documents were in fact sent under the Convention.[162] Examples included demands for payment, notices to quit, protests in connection with bills of exchange, and written consents to adoption or to marriage. In a civil law context these documents would have an 'official' quality, but in a common law system many would emanate from private persons. The Special Commission 'encouraged the Central Authorities to serve extrajudicial documents not emanating from an authority or from a judicial officer if these documents were of a type which normally would call for the intervention of an authority in their countries',[163] a striking example of the generous approach taken in operating this Convention.

11. Costs

The general principle as to the cost of effecting service is that the authorities of the state of destination seek no reimbursement of any costs they incur. This is expressed in article 12 of the Convention, which is an adaptation to meet the new range of modes of service of corresponding provisions in the 1954 Convention.[164] However, the applicant must pay or reimburse costs occasioned by the use of the services of a judicial officer (*officier ministériel*) or of a person competent under the law of the state of destination or by the use of a particular method of service.[165]

These provisions are rather awkwardly drafted as a result of the need to accommodate both the use of the system of Central Authorities and the other permitted modes of transmission. No attempt is made in the Convention to prescribe details of procedure for the payment or reimbursement of costs. Some countries impose a fixed fee (eg, Canada) or a payment in advance which may be adjusted later (eg, Italy, in certain cases only); others seek to recover actual charges levied by, eg, a *huissier*, and others will in practice make no charge, especially where the state of origin is known to operate a similar policy (eg the United States, which until 1978 always charged a fee). 'Simple delivery' (*remise simple*) is always free of charge.[166]

12. Relationship with other instruments

Although the 1965 Convention was designed to replace the relevant articles of the 1954 text,[167] supplementary agreements between parties to the earlier Convention

---

[161] *AetD(10)*, vol 3, p 108.
[162] *AetD(14)*, vol 4, p 388.
[163] Ibid.
[164] Convention on Civil Procedure 1954, art 7.
[165] In practice this last phrase has been treated as covering translation costs: Arnhem, 11 December 1986, NIPR 1987, 260 (Asser 4/101).
[166] See *AetD(14)*, vol 4, p 385.
[167] Convention, art 22.

are continued in respect of the new Convention unless the parties otherwise determine.[168] The Hague Convention does not derogate from other relevant Conventions to which Contracting States are, or become, parties.[169]

Many Contracting States to the Hague Convention were or became also parties to Council Regulation 44/2001 on jurisdiction and the enforcement of judgments in civil and commercial matters. The Regulation contains provisions dealing with the interrelationship of the two instruments. These provide that where a defendant domiciled in one Member State is sued in a court of another Member State the court shall stay the proceedings so long as it is not shown that the defendant has been able to receive the document instituting the proceedings or an equivalent document in sufficient time to enable him to arrange for his defence, or that all necessary steps have been taken to this end.[170] But these provisions are declared to be replaced by those of article 19 of Regulation 1348/2000[171] if the document had to be transmitted under that Regulation,[172] and by article 15 of the Hague Convention[173] if the document instituting the proceedings or notice thereof was transmitted abroad in accordance with that Convention.[174]

Under the scheme of Council Regulation 44/2001, a judgment given in one Member State is entitled, subject to certain conditions, to recognition and enforcement in the other Member States.[175] However, under article 34(2) of that Regulation:

A judgment shall not be recognized: . . .

> 2. where it was given in default of appearance, if the defendant was not served with the document which instituted the proceedings[176] or with an equivalent document in sufficient time and in such a way as to enable him to arrange for his defence . . .

This plainly parallels the text dealing with the staying of proceedings, save that there is no reference to the alternative 'taking of all necessary steps'. The European Court of Justice has held that the court in the state in which enforcement is sought must examine for itself the requirements of this provision, even if the court granting the judgment had considered similar issues in relation to article 20.[177]

---

[168] Convention, art 24.
[169] Convention, art 25.
[170] Regulation 44/2001, art 26(1)(2).
[171] Regulation 1348/2000 is now replaced by Regulation 1393/2007, but the reference has not been updated.
[172] Regulation 44/2001, art 26(3).
[173] See pp 47–49, above.
[174] Regulation 44/2001, art 26(4).
[175] See Title III (arts 32 to 56) of the Regulation.
[176] And only that document: *Société Biomécanique Intégrée v Fabrique Nationale de Herstal SA* (French Cour de cassation, 11 June 1991), [1993] ILPr 127 (decided, as are other cases cited below, under the similar but not identical language in the earlier Convention).
[177] Case 166/80 *Klomps v Michel* [1981] ECR 1593, [1982] 2 CMLR 773.

The effect of this in a Hague Convention case was examined in a later European Court case, *Pendy Plastic Products BV v Pluspunkt Handelsgesellschaft mbH*.[178] Proceedings in a Dutch court were begun by a document transmitted under the Hague Convention to a local court in Germany which certified under article 6 that it had not been possible to serve the document. The defendant had moved a few weeks before to another address in the same town, but this fact was not discovered at the time. The Dutch court, acting under article 15(2) of the Hague Convention which the Netherlands Government had declared applicable,[179] issued a default judgment. It was satisfied that every reasonable effort had been made to obtain a certificate of service. When enforcement was sought in Germany, the Oberlandesgericht Düsseldorf, holding itself required to examine the matter for itself under article 27(2) of the Brussels Convention (now article 34(2) of Regulation 44/2001), held that service had not been effected in sufficient time to allow the defendant to make a defence. After an appeal to the Bundesgerichtshof, the European Court of Justice affirmed that a fresh examination had to be made under article 27(2), and the court in the state where enforcement was sought was not bound by the determination made under article 15 of the Hague Convention.

Under article 27(2) of the Brussels Convention, the document had to be 'duly' served; the word is omitted in Regulation 44/2001. The European Court, in Convention cases, had emphasized the requirement of service in due form. Where service was attempted under the Hague Convention a failure to comply with the terms of that Convention meant that a default judgment pronounced in another Contracting State could not be recognized, even if the document was delivered in sufficient time for a defence to be arranged.[180] It is unclear how the issue would be dealt with under the new text of the Regulation.

13. Assessment of the Convention

There is little doubt that the Convention has not only produced an orderly framework within which the various forms of procedure can operate, but has also, in the Central Authority system, produced a very successful and increasingly well-used mechanism. Reviews of the operation of the Convention held in 1977, 1989, 2003, and 2009 produced no demand for its revision. The hints in the *Schlunk* opinions that 'due process' requirements are implicit in the Convention show, perhaps, a hankering for a 'model law' approach, familiar enough to those whose legal experience is of a federal system, but not yet realizable between the diverse legal systems represented at The Hague. The Convention's strength is that it copes with their diversity and provides an effective mechanism acceptable to all.

---

[178] Case 228/81, [1982] ECR 2723, [1983] 1 CMLR 665.
[179] See p 49, above.
[180] Case 305/88 *Isabelle Lancray SA v Peters und Sickert KG* [1990] 1 ECR 2725, [1991] ILPr 52. See also Oberlandesgericht Koblenz, 10 June 1991 (2 U 123/91), [1993] ILPr 289; *Re Postal Service Abroad* (Bundesgerichtshof, 18 February 1993 (IX ZB 87/90, [1995] ILPr 523 (substituted service in form not allowed in German law).

III. Regulation 1393/2007

In May 1997, the European Community drew up a Convention on the service in the Member States of judicial and extrajudicial documents in civil or commercial matters.[181] This Convention never came into force, and was overtaken by the extension of the competence of the European institutions by the Treaty of Amsterdam's establishment of an 'area of freedom, security and justice'. The draft Convention was converted, with modifications, into a Council Regulation[182] binding on Member States[183] and coming into force on 31 May 2001. After a review of the working of that Regulation[184] it was in turn replaced by Regulation 1393/2007,[185] which came into force on 13 November 2008.

The Regulation builds on the experience gained in the operation of the Hague Service Convention, but replaces that Convention in its entirety as between Member States.[186] Perhaps the most significant difference in policy is that whereas the Hague text enshrines a preference for communication between Central Authorities, the policy of the Regulation is that 'efficiency and speed in judicial procedures in civil matters means that the transmission of judicial and extrajudicial documents is to be made direct and by rapid means between local bodies designated by the Member States'.[187]

The Regulation applies in civil and commercial matters[188] where a judicial or extrajudicial document has to be transmitted from one Member State to another for service there.[189]

It was argued in *Tavoulareas v Tsavliris*[190] that where (as in Greek law) service on a person resident abroad was treated as effected when the proceedings were served on the Public Prosecutor in Greece, it was not a case in which 'a judicial . . . document has to be transmitted from one Member State to another for service

---

[181] For the text of the Convention, see OJ C 261/1, 27.8.1997; for the Explanatory Report, see ibid, p 26. Para 2 of that Report contains an account of the process by which the draft Convention was developed. See W Kennett, 'Service of Documents in Europe' (1998) 17 CJQ 284; N Betteto, 'Introduction and Practical Cases under the European Regulation on Service' (2006) 6 Eur L F I-137; R Hausmann, 'Problems of Interpretation regarding the European Regulation on Service' (2007) 7 Eur L F I-8.

[182] OJ L 160/37 30.06.2000.

[183] Denmark is not a Member State for this purpose, but an Agreement between the Community and Denmark (OJ L 300/55, 17.11.2005), in similar terms to those of Regulation 1348/2000, came into force in July 2007. See Council Decision 2006/326/EC of 27 April 2006.

[184] COM/2004/0603 final, October 2004.

[185] European Parliament and Council Regulation (EC) No 1393/2007 of 13 November 2007 on the service in the Member States of judicial and extrajudicial documents in civil and commercial matters (service of documents) and repealing Council Regulation (EC) 1348/2000, OJ L 324/79, 10.12.2007.

[186] Regulation 1393/2007, art 20(1).

[187] Regulation 1393/2007, Recital (6).

[188] For this phrase, cf pp 33–34, above. See *Re Anderson Owen Ltd (in Liquidation)* [2009] EWHC 2837 (Ch), [2010] BPIR 37 (not all 'insolvency proceedings' as defined in English law will necessarily be excluded from the category of 'civil and commercial' in the Regulation).

[189] Regulation 1393/2007, art 1(1).

[190] [2004] EWCA Civ 48, [2004] 1 Lloyd's Rep 445.

there'. The Court of Appeal rejected the argument in robust language: that the terms of the Regulation could be avoided in such a way was 'inconceivable'.

Recital (8) in the Regulation deals with a rather different issue by declaring that 'This Regulation should not apply to service of a document on the party's authorised representative in the Member State where the proceedings are taking place regardless of the place of residence of that party'. In *Department of Civil Aviation of the Kyrgyz Republic v Finrep GmbH*[191] it was held that an order for service in England upon the representative acting for a party resident abroad in an English arbitration could not be seen as 'subversive of' the Regulation.

The Regulation does not apply where the address of the person to be served with the document is not known.[192]

1. Central bodies

The Regulation requires Member States to establish two types of authority. The first is a 'central body' which, unlike the Central Authorities of the Hague system,[193] will only exceptionally be involved in the actual processes of service. The central body is responsible for (a) supplying information to the 'transmitting agencies'; (b) seeking solutions to any difficulties which may arise during transmission of documents for service; and (c) forwarding, 'in exceptional cases', at the request of a transmitting agency, a request for service to the competent 'receiving agency'.[194] The Explanatory Report to the draft Convention, commenting on the equivalent provision, gave as examples of exceptional cases one where, despite repeated requests as to the receiving agency with territorial jurisdiction to serve documents and the passage of a reasonable length of time, no response had been forthcoming, and other more dramatic cases in which a receiving agency's building had been destroyed by fire, or public services were disrupted by a general strike or a natural disaster.

2. Transmitting and receiving agencies

The operational agencies are the transmitting and receiving agencies designated under the Regulation. They are specified 'public officers, authorities or other persons' competent either to transmit or receive documents, or to carry out both functions.[195] In most Member States, the receiving agencies are the local courts (or, in some cases, the holder of a designated office within the relevant court[196]); *huissier de justices* act in Belgium, France, Luxembourg, and the Netherlands, and messen-

---

[191] [2006] EWHC 1722 (Comm).

[192] The Explanatory Report to the corresponding provision in the draft Convention stated that this provision did not mean that the agency of the Member State receiving an application for a document to be served on a person whose address is incomplete or incorrect need not try to complete or correct it.

[193] See pp 35–36.

[194] Regulation 1393/2007, art 3(1). A federal or composite state may designate more than one central body: art 3(2).

[195] Regulation 1393/2007, art 2(1)(2)(3).

[196] Registrars of the local courts in Portugal and Spain; county registrars of the circuit courts in Ireland.

gers-at-arms in Scotland; the Ministry of Justice is designated in Cyprus, Denmark, Latvia, and Sweden; the United Kingdom has designated the Senior Master to act for England and Wales and the Master (Queen's Bench and Appeals) for Northern Ireland. There will normally be only one agency in a state for each of the functions, but federal states, states in which several legal systems apply, or states with 'autonomous territorial units' may designate more than one such agency.[197] Each Member State notifies the Commission of the names and addresses of the receiving agencies, the geographical areas in which they have jurisdiction, the means of receipt of documents available to them (for example fax or e-mail), and the languages that may be used for the completion of the standard form used in the Regulation's procedures for service.[198] This information is published in a manual available on the website of the European Judicial Network.

3. Transmission and service of judicial documents

Judicial documents are to be transmitted 'directly and as soon as possible' between the designated transmitting and receiving agencies.[199] Transmission of documents, and of other communications between those agencies, may be carried out by any appropriate means, provided that the content of the document received is true and faithful to that of the document forwarded and that all information in it is easily legible.[200] A document to be transmitted must be accompanied by a request using a standard form set out in Annex I to the Regulation.[201] The form must be completed in the official language of the Member State addressed[202] or in another language which that Member State has indicated it can accept.[203] The documents need not be supplied in duplicate unless the transmitting agency wishes a copy of the document to be returned together with the certificate of service.[204]

The Regulation makes detailed provision as to the procedure to be followed by the receiving agency. Normally a receipt using the standard form set out in the Annex to the Regulation should be sent at the latest within seven days of the receipt of the documents.[205]

---

[197] Regulation 1393/2007, art 2(3). Any such designation has effect for a period of five years and may be renewed at five-year intervals.
[198] Regulation 1393/2007, art 2(4).
[199] Regulation 1393/2007, art 4(1).
[200] Regulation 1393/2007, art 4(2).
[201] Regulation 1393/2007, art 4(3).
[202] In multi-lingual states, the official language or one of the official languages of the place where service is to be effected.
[203] Regulation 1393/2007, art 4(3). Each Member State is required to indicate the official language or languages of the European Union other than its own which is or are acceptable to it for completion of the form, but this would seem not to prevent a Member State from being willing to accept forms in another language such as Norwegian. The Nordic States have agreed amongst themselves that they will use Danish, Norwegian, and Swedish without distinction.
[204] Regulation 1393/2007, art 4(4).
[205] Regulation 1393/2007, art 6(1). See arts 6(2) (incomplete information or documents), 6(3) (request outside the scope of the Regulation or formal conditions required make service impossible), and 6(4) (request sent to wrong receiving agency in receiving state).

The receiving agency must itself serve the document or have it served, either in accordance with the law of the Member State addressed or by a particular method requested by the transmitting agency, unless such a method is incompatible with the law of that Member State.[206] The duties of the receiving agency were restated in Regulation 1393/2007. Like its predecessor, the Regulation provides that the receiving agency must take all necessary steps to effect the service of the document 'as soon as possible'.[207] A Recital in the earlier Regulation suggested that this should be 'within days'.[208] The 2007 Regulation provides that service should be 'in any event within one month of receipt', but that if it has not been possible to effect service within that period, the receiving agency must immediately inform the transmitting agency using a standard-form certificate set out in Annex I to the Regulation, and also continue to take all necessary steps to effect the service of the document, unless indicated otherwise by the transmitting agency, where service seems to be possible within a reasonable period of time.[209] After service, a certificate, using another prescribed standard form, is returned to the transmitting agency.[210]

The Regulation deals fully with translation requirements. In contrast to the Hague Convention, there is no distinction for this purpose between 'formal' and 'informal' service.[211] If the applicant decides to have the documents translated, he or she bears the costs involved, without prejudice to any possible subsequent decision by the court or competent authority on liability for such costs.[212]

The addressee is entitled to refuse to accept the document to be served if it is in a language other than either (a) the official language of the Member State addressed or, if there are several official languages in that Member State, the official language or one of the official languages of the place where service is to be effected; or (b) a language which the addressee understands.[213] When a transmitting agency first receives an application, it must advise the applicant of this possibility.[214] If the addressee has exercised the right of refusal, the service of the document can be remedied through the later service on the addressee in accordance with the Regulation of the document accompanied by the required translation.[215]

---

[206] Regulation 1393/2007, art 7(1).

[207] Regulation 1393/2007, art 7(1).

[208] Regulation 1348/2000, Recital (9).

[209] Regulation 1393/2007, art 7(2).

[210] Regulation 1393/2007, art 10.

[211] See pp 3 and 39, and the discussion in W Kennett, 'Service of Documents in Europe' (1998) 17 CJQ 284, 299–304.

[212] Regulation 1393/2007, art 5(2).

[213] Regulation 1393/2007, art 8(1). There is a prescribed form by which the addressee is informed of the right to refuse acceptance. An Italian court has held that the right of refusal is inapplicable where documents are served by post under art 14: Trib di Rovereto, 18 June 2008 (no 1025/07), (2008) 8 Eur L F I-214, II-107.

[214] Regulation 1393/2007, art 5(1). For a similar rule where service is effected via the diplomatic or consular service, see art 8(5).

[215] Regulation 1393/2007, art 8(3) (a provision new in 2007, but stating the effect of Case C-443/03 *Leffler v Berlin Chemie AG* [2005] ECR I-9611, [2006] ILPr 88). The date of service of the document is that on which the document plus translation is served; but where a document has to be

The meaning of the phrase 'document to be served' was examined by the European Court in *Ingenieurburo Michael Weiss und Partner GbR v Industrie-und Handelskammer Berlin*.[216] Where a document was a document instituting proceedings, it meant the document or documents which must be served on the defendant in due time in order to enable him to assert his rights in legal proceedings in the state of transmission. Such a document had to make it possible to identify with a degree of certainty at the very least the subject matter of the claim and the cause of action. Documents which had a purely evidential function and which were not necessary for the purpose of understanding the subject matter of the claim and the cause of action did not form an integral part of the document instituting the proceedings within the meaning of the Regulation, and so the addressee cannot rely on the absence of a translation of such documents.

There was considerable discussion during the preparation of the Regulation as to the determination of the date of service, given the differences between relevant procedural rules in the Member States. The compromise solution is that it is the law of the receiving Member State that in general determines the date of service.[217] However, where a document is to be served within a particular period in the context of proceedings to be brought or pending in the Member State of origin, the date to be taken into account with respect to the applicant is that fixed by the law of that Member State.[218]

4. Costs

The service of judicial documents coming from a Member State does not give rise to any payment or reimbursement of taxes or costs for services rendered by the Member State addressed. However, the applicant must pay or reimburse the costs occasioned by (a) the employment of a judicial officer or of a person competent under the law of the Member State addressed, for which a fixed fee must be prescribed; or (b) the use of a particular method of service.[219]

5. Other permitted modes of service

Subject to various conditions, the Regulation permits the use of some other modes of service.

---

served within a particular period, the date to be taken into account is the date of the service of the initial document: art 8(3).

[216] Case C-14/07, [2008] ECR I-3367.

[217] Regulation 1393/2007, art 9(1). If service is accomplished in two different ways, eg via the transmitting and receiving agencies and by post, the date of the first successful service applies: Case C-473/04 *Plumex v Young Sports NV* [2006] ECR I-1417, [2006] ILPr 301.

[218] Regulation 1393/2007, art 9(2).

[219] Regulation 1393/2007, art 11.

(a) Service by diplomatic or consular agents

As under the Hague Convention, service may be effected by diplomatic or consular agents directly on the addressee, without the application of any compulsion. Any Member State may declare its opposition to this mode of service, unless the documents are to be served on nationals of the Member State in which the documents originate.[220]

(b) The indirect consular channel

This mode, using consular or diplomatic channels to forward judicial documents to the receiving agency of another Member State, is permitted 'in exceptional circumstances'.[221]

(c) The postal channel

This mode is permitted, but any Member State may specify 'the conditions under which' it will accept service of judicial documents by post by registered letter with acknowledgement of receipt or equivalent.[222] A Member State may not refuse to allow the use of the postal channel.

(d) Direct service

In language following that of the Hague Convention, the Regulation preserves the freedom of any person interested in a judicial proceeding to effect service of judicial documents directly through the judicial officers, officials, or other competent persons of the Member State addressed, where such direct service is permitted under the law of that Member State.[223]

6. Extrajudicial documents

Chapter III of the Regulation consists of the terse article 16 which provides that 'extrajudicial documents may be transmitted for service in another Member State in accordance with the provisions of this Regulation'.

The Explanatory Report to the earlier draft Convention observed that 'extrajudicial documents' may be taken to cover documents drawn up by a public officer, for example a notarial deed or a writ, documents drawn up by Member States' official authorities, or documents of a type or importance which require them to be transmitted and brought to the addressee's attention by official procedure. In *Roda Golf and Beach Resort SL*[224] it was held that a document could be within the term

---

[220] Regulation 1393/2007, art 13.
[221] Regulation 1393/2007, art 12.
[222] Regulation 1393/2007, art 14.
[223] Regulation 1393/2007, art 14.
[224] Case C-14/08, [2009] ECR I-5439.

'extrajudicial document' even if it was not related to any current or contemplated legal proceedings. In that case the documents were notarial acts terminating a number of contracts for the sale of immovable property, and the service of these documents which had cross-border implications was held within Regulation 1348/2000 (and by implication the later Regulation 1393/2007).

7. Safeguards

Although the Regulation supersedes, as between Member States, the provisions of the Hague Convention, it reproduces in full, with only minimal changes of terminology, the provisions of articles 15 and 16 of that Convention. Reference is made to the discussion of the Hague provisions.[225]

IV. Inter-American Arrangements

Latin American lawyers are conscious of a strong regional tradition in private international law. An early expression of this was the great *Congreso Sudamericano de Derecho Internacional Privado* held in Montevideo in 1888–89. One result of that Congress was the Convention on Civil Procedure of 11 January 1889, article 9 of which read as follows:

Letters rogatory which have as their object the service of legal notices, the taking of testimony of witnesses, or the performance of any other judicial act, shall be complied with in any Contracting State provided such Letters meet the requirements of this Convention.

Just over fifty years later a second Montevideo Congress produced a revised Convention, that on International Procedural Law of 19 March 1940.[226] To the existing text of what became article 11 were added two further sentences, one requiring that letters rogatory be translated into the language of the state of destination and the other dispensing with the requirement of legalization provided transmission was through the diplomatic (or, in their absence, consular) agents of the state of origin. Meanwhile the Bustamente Code of 1928 contained similar provisions, dealing additionally with the power of the judges issuing and receiving letters rogatory to determine questions as to the jurisdiction they were asked to exercise.[227]

It has been commented, not unfairly, that a reader from the common law tradition finds the sparse language of these texts almost unintelligible.[228] They take for granted that the service of process requires the involvement of state officials, the usual civil law approach; that international co-operation between officials of different states in matters of civil procedure is initiated by letters rogatory

---

[225] Regulation 1393/2007, art 19. See pp 47–50.
[226] See J Irizarry y Puente, 'Treaties on Private International Law', (1943) 37 Am J Int L (Supp) 95, 119.
[227] See Code, arts 388–93.
[228] H L Jones, 'International Judicial Assistance', (1953) 2 Am J Comp L 365.

transmitted by the diplomatic channel; and that in these respects the service of documents is in exactly the same category as the taking of evidence abroad. For many years, courts in the United States failed to understand the Latin American approach; the failure was so fundamental that a plaintiff in a Latin American republic had no means of serving process on a defendant in the United States.

In 1919, a US District Court held that foreign letters rogatory seeking the service of process could not be executed. The judgment in the case, *Re Letters Rogatory out of the First Civil Court of City of Mexico*,[229] is badly flawed but was followed almost without exception for half a century.[230] Judge Hand's refusal to comply with the request addressed to him in the Mexico City case rested on two grounds. The first was the narrow perception of letters rogatory as 'exclusively limited by understanding and in practice' to requests for the taking of evidence; their use in the context of service of process he described as 'novel', one requiring express statutory authority. The second was that, on theories of jurisdiction then prevailing in the United States, Mexico's claim to assert personal jurisdiction against a non-resident defendant was regarded as exorbitant; Judge Hand thought that he should not 'aid a foreign tribunal to acquire jurisdiction' in these circumstances, a phrase really quite inappropriate, since a civil law system would not regard the service of process as a basis for jurisdiction.

Practitioners gradually became aware of the extent of the problems created not only by this approach but also by the inability of any Latin American country to recognize a US judgment given after service had been effected by post on a defendant resident in such a country. The pressure grew for some international action.

Eventually, the Inter-American Council of Jurists, meeting at Rio de Janeiro in 1950, asked the Inter-American Juridical Committee to examine the matter. Its report[231] suggested some principles which might provide a basis for action. These principles[232] would accept both the formal approach of letters rogatory and the informal approach of direct (and usually postal) service, but would also note that no such service would be sufficient of itself to extend the jurisdiction of the state of origin. The Hague Convention of 1965 reflects this general approach and in later inter-American discussions the United States pressed for the acceptance of that Convention as the basis for regional co-operation, but unavailingly. The absence of any authentic Spanish or Portuguese text of the Hague Conventions militates against their acceptance in Latin America, and the Latin American attachment to the letters rogatory procedure proved too strong to allow a more broadly based solution in that region. What was there seen as more desirable was clear international agreement on the operation of the letters rogatory procedure.

---

[229] 261 F 652 (SD NY, 1919). See, to similar effect, *Matter of Romero* 107 NYS 621 (NY SupCt, 1907).

[230] For some variations in judicial practice see the (unreported) cases discussed in G Everett, 'Letters Rogatory—Service of Summons in Foreign Action', (1944) 44 Col L Rev 72.

[231] Report on Uniformity of Legislation in International Co-operation in Judicial Procedures, September 1952.

[232] Reproduced at (1953) 2 Am J Comp L 368–70.

After a good deal of further debate in the various inter-American bodies, the General Assembly of the Organization of American States (OAS) resolved in 1971 to convene an Inter-American Specialized Conference on Private International Law (CIDIP from its Spanish title, *Conferencia Especializada Inter-Americana sobre Derecho Internacional Privado*). This produced six conventions, including the Inter-American Convention on Letters Rogatory signed in Panama on 30 January 1975.[233] This convention retained something of the laconic style of drafting of its Latin American predecessors, and like them applied in principle to both the service of documents and the taking of evidence. It found little favour in the United States, where there was, however, considerable interest in securing some workable arrangement. As a result, the US delegation at the Second Inter-American Specialized Conference on Private International Law (CIDIP 2), held in Montevideo in 1979, secured the adoption of an Additional Protocol, limited to service of documents but containing a fuller treatment of that topic, drawing inspiration from some aspects of the Hague Convention. Of the total of eighteen states now party to the Convention, all but four have ratified the Protocol.[234] It is far from clear that these instruments have been successful in ensuring speedy service. Although it has been declared 'a dependable mechanism',[235] evidence given to a US court in 2011 was that 'service of process in Brazil pursuant to [the Convention] can take more than three years to complete, and only two of 100 requests for such service since 2003 have been successful'.[236] Use of the Convention and Protocol is nonetheless the preferred method of service, even though it is not the only method.[237]

1. The Inter-American Convention on Letters Rogatory of 1975

The Convention was drafted by Committee II of CIDIP on the basis of a preliminary draft prepared by the Inter-American Judicial Committee in 1973.

(a) Scope

The scope of the convention is indicated by article 2: the convention applies to:

letters rogatory, issued in conjunction with proceedings in civil and commercial matters held before a judicial or other adjudicatory authority[238] of one of the States Parties to this Convention, that have as their purpose:

---

[233] For text, see (1975) 14 ILM 339. There were 18 States Parties in 2011.

[234] Parties to the Protocol are Argentina, Brazil, Chile, Colombia, Ecuador, El Salvador, Guatemala, Mexico, Panama, Paraguay, Peru, the United States, Uruguay, and Venezuela; parties only to the Convention are Bolivia, Costa Rica, Honduras, and Spain. For an extraordinary decision, to allow the plaintiff to serve process in South Africa under the Inter-American Convention, see *Fyfee v Bumbo Ltd* (SD Tex, 2009).

[235] *Kreimerman v Casa Veerkamp SA de CV* 22 F 3d 634 (3rd Cir, 1994).

[236] *Lyman Morse Boatbuilding Co v Lee* (DC Me, 2011).

[237] *Tucker v Interarms* 186 FRD 450 (ND Ohio, 1999); *C & F Systems LLC v Limpimax SA* (WD Mich, 2010).

[238] The original version of the English text spoke merely of 'the appropriate authority'; the language cited in the text was later substituted under the OAS 'slip rule'.

a the performance of procedural acts of a merely formal nature, such as service of process, summonses or subpoenas abroad;

b the taking of evidence and the obtaining of information abroad, unless a reservation is made in this respect.

The drafting of this key article leaves some questions unresolved. The limitation to 'civil and commercial matters' accords with the approach taken at The Hague,[239] and the phrase is not formally defined. However, article 16 allows 'the States Parties' (and the use of the plural is puzzling, as the action contemplated seems to be by individual states, and will be effective in this context only insofar as the declarant state is the state of destination) to declare that the convention's provisions cover the execution of letters rogatory in criminal, labour, and 'contentious-administrative' cases. It is clear from the *travaux préparatoires*[240] that this declaration operates to 'extend' the assumed meaning of 'civil and commercial' which therefore must be taken to exclude all such cases. Only one state, Chile, has actually made a declaration under article 16.

The reference in article 2 to the judicial or other adjudicatory authority before which proceedings are held would seem, by a similar process of reasoning, not to cover all the courts and official tribunals of the state of origin. Article 16 allows extension to arbitrations and 'other matters within the jurisdiction of special courts'; it is not at all clear how this latter phrase is to be picked up in a declaration, as different states (of origin and of destination) may establish specialist courts for a variety of purposes, including adjudication on matters plainly civil or commercial in nature.

The limitation to procedural acts 'of a merely formal nature' seems to be explained, albeit indirectly, by the provision in article 3 that the Convention is not to apply to acts involving measures of compulsion.

(b) Modes of transmission

The actual transmission of letters rogatory to the authority to which they are addressed is governed by article 4 which allows six possible modes of transmission. These involve action by diplomatic or consular agents (presumably of the state of origin, though this is not made clear in the text), by the Central Authority designated for the purposes of the convention in either the state of origin or that of destination, by 'the interested parties', or 'through judicial channels'. This last

---

[239] See pp 33–34. For the approach of US courts, see *Malone v Holder* (DC Col, 2009) (Chilean letter rogatory asked for service of process in an anti-trust matter in accordance with the Convention; references to the Convention interpreted by US court 'as simply reflecting generalized understandings, as filtered through the peculiarly stilted argot of international diplomacy . . . rather than limited, specific directives intended to narrow the authority and discretion of the [US Department of Justice] in effecting service'; even if outside the 'civil and commercial' category, art 15 of the Convention allowed States Parties to engage in more favourable practices than the Convention provided).

[240] See Report of Committee II, 25 January 1975, CDIP/35, p 5.

phrase presumably means that action to transmit a letter rogatory is to be taken by the staff of the court of origin. The clarity of the phrase is not advanced by the inclusion in article 7 of the statement that 'courts in border areas of States Parties' (meaning, presumably, areas close to a common frontier between states of origin and destination) 'may directly execute the letters rogatory contemplated in this Convention'. It appears from the context that this is not intended as a limitation on the use of 'judicial channels' but rather as a preliminary observation before a specific provision that in such border cases legalization is not required. Legalization is required in other cases unless the letters rogatory are transmitted through consular or diplomatic channels or through 'the' Central Authority (semble of the state of origin);[241] a letter rogatory legalized by a competent consular or diplomatic agent is 'presumed to be duly legalized in the State of origin'.[242] The drafting of these provisions, at least as they appear in the English text, is of very poor quality.

(c) Documentation required

When transmitted, the letter must be accompanied by certain other documents, intended for delivery to the person on whom the process, summons, or subpoena is to be served, and all must be translated into the official language of the state of destination.[243] The other required documents are:

a An authenticated copy of the complaint with its supporting documents, and of other exhibits or rulings that serve as the basis for the measure requested;
b Written information identifying the authority issuing the letter, indicating the time-limits allowed the person affected to act upon the request, and warning of the consequences of failure to do so;
c Where appropriate, information on the existence and address of the court-appointed defense counsel or of competent legal aid societies in the State of origin.[244]

(d) Procedure for execution

The execution of letters rogatory is governed by the law of the state of destination, though special procedures or formalities requested by the issuing authority may be observed if to do so would not be contrary to that law.[245] An authority in the state of destination which finds that it lacks jurisdiction to execute the letter of request, for example because the defendant is not resident in its area, must forward 'the

---

[241] Convention, art 6.
[242] Convention, art 5(a). See also art 18 which obliges States Parties to inform the General Secretariat of OAS as to their legal requirements as to the legalization and translation of letters rogatory.
[243] Convention, arts 5(b), 8, 18.
[244] Convention, art 8.
[245] Convention, art 10.

documents and antecedents of the case to the authority of the State [ie, within the same state[246]] which has jurisdiction'.[247]

(e) Costs and expenses

Article 12 of the Convention specifies that costs and other expenses must be borne by the interested parties. The state of destination is given a discretion (though the convention does not specify by which organ of the state the discretion is to be exercised) to execute a letter rogatory which does not indicate the person to be held responsible for the costs and expenses; the point here is that there is a discretion to refuse to execute letters in such circumstances. In addition, the convention contains an express provision allowing a state of destination to refuse to execute a letter rogatory that is manifestly contrary to public policy (*ordre public*).[248]

(f) Protection for defendants

The Inter-American Convention contains no material comparable to that on safeguards for defendants in articles 15 and 16 of the Hague Convention. It does, however, provide expressly[249] that execution of letters rogatory does not imply ultimate recognition of the jurisdiction of the authority issuing the letter rogatory or a commitment to recognize or enforce any judgment.

(g) Relationship to other instruments

Finally, three articles of the Convention deal with other international arrangements that may be used. Article 13 allows the service of documents and the taking of evidence by consular and diplomatic agents in the state in which they are accredited, provided their acts are not contrary to the law of that state and involve no means of compulsion.[250] Article 14 allows states which belong to 'economic integration systems', by which was meant groupings such as the Latin American Free Trade Association or the Andean Common Market, to agree upon 'special methods and procedures more expeditious than those provided for' in the convention. These could presumably include methods not involving the use of letters rogatory at all,[251] though given the legal traditions of the region such radicalism seems unlikely. Article 15 preserves the liberty of States Parties to apply existing or future bilateral or multilateral agreements as to letters rogatory, including of course the earlier Latin American instruments. In line with their approach to the Hague Service Convention, US courts have interpreted this article as allowing the

---

[246] Cf Report of Committee II, CIDIP/35, p 9.
[247] Convention, art 11.
[248] Convention, art 17.
[249] Convention, art 9.
[250] See *Southwest Livestock & Trucking Co v Ramon* 169 F 3d 317 (5th Cir, 1999).
[251] Cf to the contrary, but without giving reasons, B M Carl, 'Service of Judicial Documents in Latin America' (1976) 53 Denver L J 455, 462.

continued use of procedures under US law, even though they are unilaterally imposed, not bilaterally agreed.[252]

2. The Inter-American Protocol of 1979

The Protocol was prepared by Committee I of the Second Inter-American Specialized Conference on Private International Law, almost entirely on the basis of successive proposals from the United States' delegation. Although in form supplementary to the 1975 Convention, it is in truth a substantial revision of it, creating an alternative treaty regime.

(a) Scope and modes of transmission

This is best illustrated by reference to article 1 of the Protocol. This declares that the Protocol applies only to those procedural acts set forth in article 2(a) of the Convention. This immediately excludes from the scope of the Protocol the whole area of taking evidence and obtaining information abroad; this area could be excluded by Reservation from the scope of the Convention, and is also the object of a distinct Inter-American Convention.[253] Remaining within the scope of the present instrument were only 'the performance of procedural acts of a merely formal nature, such as service of process, summonses or subpoenas abroad'.[254] These are redefined for the purposes of the Protocol as:

procedural acts (pleadings, motions, orders and subpoenas) that are served and requests for information that are made by a judicial or administrative authority of a State Party to a judicial or administrative authority of another State Party and are transmitted by a letter rogatory from the Central Authority of the State of origin to the Central Authority of the State of destination.[255]

Not only does this clarify the nature of the authorities competent to issue and execute letters rogatory, but it makes mandatory as between parties to the Protocol the use of Central Authorities both for the outward transmission and inward receipt of letters rogatory; that there is an obligation to designate a Central Authority, a matter not wholly clear in the text of the Convention, is specifically provided in article 2 of the Protocol. The duties of the receiving Central Authority are set out in detail in article 4. The understanding of the United States in drafting the Protocol was that while the United States would ratify the Convention as well as the Protocol, ratification of the latter alone not being permitted, this would create treaty obligations binding upon the United States only with other states which had ratified the Protocol and in accordance with its terms. It is submitted that this leaves

---

[252] *Pizzabiocche v Vinelli* 772 F Supp 1245 (MD Fla, 1990)*; Kreimerman v Casa Veerkamp SA de CV* 22 F 3d 634 (3rd Cir, 1994).

[253] ie, the Inter-American Convention on the Taking of Evidence Abroad examined at pp 112–113.

[254] Convention, art 2(a).

[255] Protocol, art 1.

in place the binding character of article 13 of the original Convention as to service of documents by accredited consular or diplomatic agents.[256]

(b) Documentation

There are elaborate provisions in articles 3 and 4 of the Protocol as to the appropriate documentation, and these provisions are very obviously inspired by provisions of the Hague Convention. In particular three forms are prescribed, which, to minimize translation problems, are required to be printed either in all four official languages of the Organization of American States (English, French, Portuguese, and Spanish) or at least in the languages of the states of origin and destination. The forms are of the Letter Rogatory itself, which follows the functional layout of the Hague 'Request' rather than the formal, almost supplicatory, style of a traditional letter rogatory; a statement of Essential Information for the Addressee, corresponding to the Hague 'Summary of the Document to be Served'; and a Certificate of execution or non-execution, again on the model of the corresponding Hague document. Two copies, in addition to the originals, are to be supplied; one is for service, one for retention by the state of destination; one for return with the relevant Certificate to the Central Authority of the state of origin.

The translation requirements are considerably lightened. As the Report of Committee I observed:[257] 'One of the greatest obstacles to international judicial co-operation is the necessity of translating innumerable documents into the official language of the country of destination for each international procedural act, given the high cost of translation services.' Under the Protocol the only document which need be translated is the complaint or pleading that initiated the action in which the letter rogatory was issued. Attached documents and the actual rulings ordering that a letter rogatory be issued are to be supplied, but need not be translated. The precise scope of the translation requirements is not completely clear, especially in cases in which the letter rogatory is issued at some interlocutory stage; the specific motion relevant at that stage surely should be translated, but the Protocol speaks only of the document which 'initiated the action'. The interpretation of this would appear to be within the competence of the state of origin, and it is to be hoped that an interpretation reflecting the realities of the position would always be adopted; what is important to the defendant is prompt access to the information necessary to judge how to respond to the current move by the other party.

Legalization is not required, as the Convention already provided for the exclusion of this requirement when transmission was through a Central Authority.[258]

---

[256] See p 63.
[257] CIDIP-II/64.
[258] Convention, art 6.

(c) Costs and expenses

The other area which is given detailed attention in the Protocol is that of responsibility for costs and expenses; the text comes close to adopting the principles used in the Hague Convention, but in practice is rather different.

The relevant article, article 5, begins by declaring a new principle, that 'the processing of letters rogatory by the Central Authority of the State Party of destination and its judicial or administrative authorities shall be free of charge'. However, as the *travaux préparatoires* indicate, many countries in the Americas require the costs of judicial acts to be borne by the interested parties,[259] and the Protocol reflects this by allowing a state of destination to seek payment from the party seeking execution of the letter rogatory of charges payable under its local law. The Protocol makes detailed provision to cover the practicalities: each State Party must provide the OAS General Secretariat with a schedule of costs and expenses payable under its law, together with a statement of a fixed amount which it estimates will cover the sums due in a typical case.[260] The applicant party must either pay this latter amount by cheque in advance, or indicate in the letter rogatory form the person who is responsible in the state of destination for the payment of sums due. If the actual charges exceed the sum paid in advance, the letter rogatory is still to be executed and the balance claimed after the event.

There would be obvious advantages for the parties, and probably a saving in administrative costs, were reciprocal waiver of charges between states to be adopted. This is not possible in some of the legal systems of the region, but article 7 of the Protocol encourages moves in this direction wherever possible. A state may declare that, provided there is reciprocity, it will make no charge for the services necessary for executing letters rogatory or will accept in complete satisfaction of the cost of such services either the fixed amount mentioned above or some other amount.

V. English practice

1. Service of English process abroad

Service outside the jurisdiction is governed by rule 6.40 of the Civil Procedure Rules. Where the claimant wishes to serve a claim form or any other document on a defendant out of the United Kingdom, it may be served:

(a) in accordance with by any method provided for by the Service Regulation, ie Regulation 1393/2007[261] as amended from time to time and as applied by the Agreement made on 19 October 2005 between the European Community and the Kingdom of Denmark;[262]

---

[259] Report of Committee I, CIDIP-II/64 p. 6.
[260] Protocol, art 6.
[261] See pp 54–60.
[262] CPR, rr 6.40(3)(a)(i), 6.41.

(b) through the Central Authority designated under the Hague Convention in respect of the state of destination;[263]

(c) where the state of destination is a party to a Civil Procedure Convention with the United Kingdom providing for service in that country and if the law of that country permits, through the judicial authorities of that country, or through a British Consular authority in that country (subject to any provisions of the applicable convention about the nationality of persons who may be served by such a method);[264]

(d) where there is no such Convention, if the law of that country so permits through the government of that country, where that government is willing to serve it, or through a British Consular authority in that country;[265] or

(e) by any other method permitted by the law of the country in which it is to be served.[266]

However, where the claimant wishes to serve the claim form or other document in any Commonwealth state which is not a party to the Hague Convention, the Isle of Man or the Channel Islands, or any British overseas territory, the claimant or the claimant's agent must effect service direct, except where the authorities of one of the British overseas territories require service to be through the judicial authorities of that territory.[267]

Nothing in these provisions or in any court order authorizes or requires any person to do anything which is contrary to the law of the country where the claim form or other document is to be served.[268] The effect of the predecessor provision fell to be considered in *Ferrarini SpA v Magnol Shipping Co Inc, The Sky One*.[269] The English court had given leave for the service of a writ upon the president of a Panamanian shipping operation at a stated address in Lugano or elsewhere in Switzerland. It was personally served on the president at the Lugano address by an agent of the plaintiffs. The defendants successfully applied to the English court for this service to be set aside on the grounds that personal service by the agent of a foreign litigant without the approval of the Swiss authorities was a criminal offence under the Swiss Penal Code and could not be regarded as valid service, as no English court could authorize service which was contrary to the internal law of the country in which service was to be effected. The court recognized that it did have a discretion under the Rules of the Supreme Court to allow service to stand despite the failure to comply with the Rules, for example express representation by the

---

[263] CPR, rr 6.40(3)(ii), 6.42(1)(a).

[264] CPR, rr 6.40(3)(ii), 6.42(1)(b).

[265] CPR, rr 6.40(3)(ii), 6.42(2).

[266] CPR, r 6.40(3)(c). See *Arros Invest Ltd v Nishanov* [2004] EWHC 576 (Ch), [2004] ILPr 22 (onus on claimant to show that the method of service used was adequate and in compliance with the law of the state of destination). For service in Scotland or Northern Ireland, see r 6.40(2); for service on a state, see r 6.44.

[267] See PD 6B, paras 5.1 and 5.2.

[268] CPR, r 6.40(4).

[269] [1988] 1 Lloyd's Rep 238 (CA).

defendant that the method of service adopted was lawful, before the discretion would be exercised. The court did, however, renew the validity of the writ for a period of four months, notwithstanding the expiry both of the writ and the limitation period, to allow alternative means of service to be used.

In *Phillips v Symes (No 3)*[270] it was held that in 'truly exceptional circumstances' the English court could take action to remedy a defect in service under the law of the state of destination. There a misunderstanding had caused a relevant document to be omitted from the bundle of documents served, though a translation was included. Even though the relevant limitation period had expired, the House of Lords held that service could be dispensed with.[271] This was followed in *Olafsson v Gissurarson (No 2)*[272] where the necessary documents were served and understood by the addressee, but he was not asked to sign the receipt required by Icelandic law.

In cases under the Service Regulation the claimant must file the claim form or other document, any translation, and any other documents required by the Regulation.[273] In cases under the Hague Convention, another Civil Procedure Convention, or where service is to be effected through a foreign government or a British consul, the claimant must file a request for service of the claim form or other document specifying one or more of the available methods of service, a copy of the claim form or other document, any other documents or copies of documents required by the relevant Practice Direction,[274] and usually a translation of the claim form or other document.[275] A request for service must contain an undertaking by the person making the request to be responsible for all expenses incurred by the Foreign and Commonwealth Office or foreign judicial authority and to pay those expenses to the Foreign and Commonwealth Office or foreign judicial authority on being informed of the amount.[276]

2. Service of foreign process in England

The Service Regulation, ie Regulation 1393/2007, contains rules as to the service of documents in cases governed by that Regulation. All other cases in which any document in connection with civil or commercial proceedings in a foreign court or tribunal is to be served in England and Wales are governed by Section V of Part 6 of the Civil Procedure Rules. Under those Rules, the Senior Master will serve a document upon receipt of a written request for service (i) where the foreign court or tribunal is in a State Party to the Hague Convention or other Civil Procedure Convention, from a consular or other authority of that country; or (ii) from the Secretary of State for Foreign and Commonwealth Affairs, with a recommendation

---

[270] [2008] UKHL 1, [2008] 1 WLR 180.
[271] Under what is now CPR, r 6.16.
[272] [2008] EWCA Civ 152, [2008] 1 WLR 2016.
[273] CPR, r 6.41.
[274] PD 6B, para 4.1
[275] CPR, r 6.43. For detailed requirements as to the documents to accompany the translation and the cases in which a translation is not required, see r 6.45.
[276] CPR, r 6.46.

that service should be effected; a translation of that request into English; two copies of the document to be served; and unless the foreign court or tribunal certifies that the person to be served understands the language of the document, two copies of a translation of it into English.[277] The Senior Master determines the method of service.[278]

---

[277] CPR, r 6.50.
[278] CPR, r 6.51. For subsequent action by the Senior Master and any process server, see r 6.52.

3

Taking of Evidence

Previous chapters have noted the differing approaches to the service of process taken by legal systems in the common law and civil law traditions and have given some account of the early work at The Hague. This chapter examines the modern international instruments and current practice in respect of the taking of evidence abroad.

I. The Hague Convention on the Taking of Evidence Abroad 1970

The United States, whose law on the subject had recently been overhauled,[1] played a prominent part in the process of revision of the earlier Hague conventions

---

[1] See pp 75–76.

undertaken in the late 1960s. In its Memorandum, circulated at the start of the revision process,[2] the United States Government argued that 'Letters rogatory are a useful but scarcely perfect technique for securing evidence from persons abroad' and listed a number of limitations of the technique, limitations which were especially important where the two legal systems involved differed in their practice. It suggested a number of objectives for the revision:

1. A relaxation of barriers against voluntary testimony by 'willing' parties or witnesses.
2. A willingness to permit, under court supervision, use of the techniques of examination of the foreign forum.
3. A resort to a more efficient and less expensive method of transmitting documents of international judicial assistance; and
4. An expansion of the categories of officers before whom testimony may be taken to include, for example, commissioners and consuls.

The ensuing revision successfully attained these objectives.

The Convention on the Taking of Evidence Abroad in Civil or Commercial Matters, drafted at the Eleventh Session of the Conference in 1968, was signed on 18 March 1970. It has proved to be one of the most successful of the Hague conventions, with fifty-three parties by 2011. The Convention provides for the taking of evidence or the performing of other judicial acts abroad, by means of Letters of Request or by the use of diplomats and consuls, and of and commissioners. Chapter I deals with the contents of Letters of Request, the establishment of Central Authorities, and related matters. Chapter II regulates the taking of evidence by diplomats, consuls, and commissioners. Chapter III contains general clauses and preserves existing state laws which permit evidence to be taken by other equally liberal procedures.

Special Commissions of the Hague Conference reviewed its operation in 1978, 1985 and 1989, 2003, and 2009.

1. Letters of request

(a) Scope

Chapter I of the Convention contains fresh provisions for the operation of the system of Letters of Request. Article 1 provides that a judicial authority of a Contracting State may, in civil or commercial matters, request the competent authority of another Contracting State, by means of a Letter of Request, to obtain evidence or to perform some other judicial act.

---

[2] *AetD*(11), pp 15–18.

(b) Mandatory?

The Permanent Bureau of the Hague Conference in a lengthy paper prepared for the 2009 Special Commission reported that 'a full analysis of the preparatory and subsequent material suggests that the question whether the Convention is mandatory or non-mandatory was not actively considered at the time of negotiation, nor for some time thereafter'.[3] Countries in the civil law tradition tended to assume that it was; common law countries saw it rather as a supplementary means of obtaining evidence which could be used as an alternative to the provisions in national law.

The use of the word 'may' seems to make it clear that use of the Convention is not mandatory, but the Permanent Bureau's paper noted arguments to the contrary. One was that the permissive language of the Convention should not be understood as an indication that the Convention was intended to be non-mandatory, and that the word 'may' was chosen in recognition of the fact that the Convention contains a number of methods by which evidence may be taken abroad, between which a court is permitted to choose. It had also been argued that to focus upon the permissive language of the Convention involved an overly technical interpretation that was not appropriate when interpreting instruments drafted by civil law states. The Special Commission duly considered the matter but reached the lame conclusion 'that there are still differing views among States Parties as to the mandatory or non-mandatory character of the Convention'.[4]

The whole issue has been a prominent feature of United States case law. Predictably that case law has been almost wholly in the context of pre-trial discovery (including the use of depositions for this purpose). This is in some ways a special context: pre-trial discovery is a very important part of US litigation practice, but is seen as excessive and intrusive by many other countries. Most of the parties to the Convention have exercised their right to object to the use of the Convention procedures for this purpose.[5]

(c) A note on US discovery practice

It may be helpful to set out at this point parts of Rule 26 of the United States Federal Rules of Civil Procedure:

Unless otherwise limited by court order, the scope of discovery is as follows: Parties may obtain discovery regarding any nonprivileged matter that is relevant to any party's claim or defense—including the existence, description, nature, custody, condition, and location of any documents or other tangible things and the identity and location of persons who know of any discoverable matter. For good cause, the court may order discovery of any matter relevant to the subject matter involved in the action. Relevant information need not be admissible at the trial if the discovery appears reasonably calculated to lead to the discovery

---

[3] Preliminary Document 10 of December 2008, para 42.
[4] Conclusions and Recommendations, para 53.
[5] See pp 84–88.

of admissible evidence. All discovery is subject to the limitations imposed by Rule 26(b) (2)(C).[6]

The provision just referred to states:

On motion or on its own, the court must limit the frequency or extent of discovery otherwise allowed by these rules or by local rule if it determines that:

    (i) the discovery sought is unreasonably cumulative or duplicative, or can be obtained from some other source that is more convenient, less burdensome, or less expensive;

   (ii) the party seeking discovery has had ample opportunity to obtain the information by discovery in the action; or

  (iii) the burden or expense of the proposed discovery outweighs its likely benefit, considering the needs of the case, the amount in controversy, the parties' resources, the importance of the issues at stake in the action, and the importance of the discovery in resolving the issues.

It will be noted that this permits the discovery, which may be enforced by court order, of information which is not admissible in evidence. As the advisory committee on the Rules notes:

The purpose of discovery is to allow a broad search for facts, the names of witnesses, or any other matters which may aid a party in the preparation or presentation of his case . . . In such a preliminary inquiry admissibility at trial should not be the test as to whether the information sought is within the scope of proper examination. Such a standard unnecessarily curtails the utility of discovery practice. Of course, matters entirely without bearing either as direct evidence or as leads to evidence are not within the scope of inquiry, but to the extent that the examination develops useful information, it functions successfully as an instrument of discovery, even if it produces no testimony directly admissible.

(d) Use of the forum state's procedures

The essential issue was the extent to which the procedural rules of the forum court could be used notwithstanding the Convention. Early cases, especially in state courts, tended to give some priority to the Convention. The plaintiff's bar responded vigorously, developing a series of arguments, many of which were accepted in a leading case in the Fifth Circuit, *Re Anschuetz & Co GmbH*, in 1985.[7] Finally the Supreme Court addressed the matter in *Société Nationale Industrielle Aérospatiale v US District Court for the Southern District of Iowa*[8] ('*Aérospatiale*'); while rejecting many of the arguments previously deployed, the Supreme Court gave a limited, and somewhat uncertain, place to the Convention.

---

[6] FRCP, r 26(b)(1).

[7] 754 F 2d 602 (5th Cir, 1985).

[8] 482 US 522 (1987). See generally, S F Black 'United States Transnational Discovery: the Rise and Fall of the Hague Evidence Convention' (1991) 40 ICLQ 901.

So, in the early case of *Volkswagenwerk AG v Superior Court of Sacramento County*,[9] a Californian court adopted 'a policy of avoiding international discovery methods productive of friction with the procedures of host nations'. Those procedures, resting on the civil law understanding of judicial sovereignty, required the use of letters rogatory, and 'whatever the generous provisions of the California discovery statutes, courts ordering discovery abroad must conform to the channels and procedures established by the host nation'. The policy was re-affirmed after the United States ratified the Hague Convention.[10] The majority of reported decisions over the next few years in other state courts took the Californian position, that first resort was to be had to the Convention procedures.

The first resort position was, however, rejected by many federal courts. A number of strands can be identified in the judgments.

The Convention required no change in US practice

It was certainly the case that a leading member of the United States delegation at The Hague wrote to that effect.[11] However, *some* impact on US practice was surely to be expected from the ratification of the Convention. At one stage the United States Government supported the position that the Convention dealt comprehensively, and so exclusively, with the procedures to govern the taking of evidence abroad,[12] but it later resiled from this.[13]

So long as the evidence-taking was in the US, it was immaterial that the document was disclosed or the person whose deposition was sought was in another state party to the Convention

This view was clearly articulated in *Graco Inc v Kremlin, Inc*:[14]

This court believes that discovery does not take place within [a state's] borders merely because documents to be produced somewhere else are located there. Similarly, discovery should be considered as taking place here, and not in another country, when interrogatories are served here, even if the necessary information is located in another country. The court's view is the same with respect to people residing in another country. If they are subject to the court's jurisdiction, or if the court can compel a party to produce them . . . violation of the other country's judicial sovereignty is avoided by ordering that the deposition take place outside the country.

So, compliance in the United States with discovery orders requiring 'preparatory acts' abroad was regarded as not constituting 'discovery in a foreign nation as addressed by the Hague Convention'.[15]

---

[9] 109 Cal Rptr 219 (Cal App, 1973).

[10] *Volkswagenwerk AG v Superior Court, Alameda County* 176 Cal Rptr 874 (Cal App, 1981).

[11] P W Amram, 'The Proposed Convention on the Taking of Evidence Abroad' (1969) 55 ABAJ 651. See also the Report of the US Delegation, reprinted at (1969) 8 ILM 785, 807–15.

[12] See Solicitor-General's *amicus* brief in *Volkswagenwerk AG v Falzon* 461 US 1303 (1983).

[13] See Solicitor-General's *amicus* brief in *Club Mediteranée SA v Dorin* 469 US 913 (1984).

[14] 101 FRD 503 (ND Ill., 1984), Asser 3/171. See also *Adidas (Canada) Ltd v SS Seatrain Bennington* (SD NY, 1984, unreported) (noted Asser 3/173 sub nom. *Navi Fonds KG v Les Toles Inoxydables*).

[15] *Re Anschuetz & Co GmbH* 754 F 2d 602 (5th Cir, 1985).

It scarcely needs to be observed that from the viewpoint of the defendant's country these arguments are unacceptable. Witnesses and documents located there are required to be taken out of that country for production before the authorities of the United States or before persons acting with the backing of the courts of that country; it must appear to be an attempt to give worldwide application to the procedural rules of the United States. There is, of course, no such difficulty if the evidence sought, though owned by a foreign corporation, is physically located within the territorial jurisdiction of the United States.

The truth of this matter seems to be that the authors of the Convention never really took into account the mobility of people and documents. Testimony and documentary evidence would, they envisaged, be presented either to the forum court or obtained by Letter of Request in the foreign country in which they were to be found. The Convention simply does not address the movement of persons or documents from that country to the forum state or a third state; nor, of course, the extensive nature of such movement required to comply with some American discovery orders.

The Convention did not apply where the proposed witness was a party and subject to the *in personam* jurisdiction of the United States

A number of courts distinguished between party and non-party witnesses.[16] One Circuit Court of Appeals held that the Convention did not 'supplant the application of the discovery provisions of the Federal Rules over foreign, Hague Convention State nationals, subject to *in personam* jurisdiction in a United States court'.[17] This distinction has no basis in the text of the Convention.

The Convention expressly allowed the maintenance of existing US practices

A number of courts relied on a superficial reading of article 27(c) of the Convention, which allows Contracting States to permit 'by internal law or practice, methods of taking evidence other than those provided for in this Convention'.[18] The better view, however, is that this freedom is given only to the requested country and does not refer to the country from which the discovery request originates.[19] Article 27, strangely, has also been used as the basis for an argument that use of the Convention was mandatory, but the Permanent Bureau of the Hague Conference has rejected that view: the sole purpose of article 27 was to preserve the laws of states that permit evidence to be taken within their own

---

[16] *Graco, Inc v Kremlin, Inc* 101 FRD 503 (ND Ill, 1984), Asser 3/171; *Slauenwhite v Bekum Maschinenfabriken GmbH* 104 FRD 616 (DC Mass, 1985).

[17] *Re Anschuetz & Co GmbH* 754 F 2d 602 (5th Cir, 1985).

[18] *Lasky v Continental Products Corpn* 569 F Supp 1227 (ED Pa, 1983); *Graco, Inc v Kremlin, Inc* 101 FRD 503 (ND Ill, 1984), Asser 3/171; *International Society for Krishna Consciousness, Inc v Lee* 105 FRD 435 (SD NY, 1984).

[19] See to this effect *Philadelphia Gear Corpn v American Pfauter Corpn* 100 FRD 58 (ED Pa, 1983), Asser 3/170; *Gebr Eickhoff Maschinenfabrik und Eisengieberei mbH v Starcher* 328 SE 2d 492 (WVa, 1985).

territory. It does not address the laws of states that permit evidence to be taken elsewhere, outside their own territory.[20]

Fairness to US plaintiffs

Pervading the judgments is a belief that US practice is good and is to be preserved from change. Courts have repeatedly spoken of the perceived cost and difficulty of proceeding under the Convention, and noted that the breadth of material ordinarily expected from a fully fledged American-style discovery deposition might be constricted under its rules,[21] that the Convention did not guarantee the full range of discovery available in a United States court.[22]

As the plaintiffs in *Aérospatiale* shrilly asserted:

Without just, speedy and inexpensive discovery, the courthouse is effectively barred to those who so desperately need it—United States citizens injured by defective foreign products.[23]

One District Court asserted that:

if the Convention were deemed to supplant the Federal Rules as the governing law on discovery from a litigant, in this case it would entirely deprive plaintiffs of a major tool of discovery against [the defendant]. The unfairness of such a result is compounded by the fact that, as a litigant, [the defendant] would be able to avail itself of the . . . procedures against plaintiffs.[24]

This argument is distinctly unappealing to lawyers outside the United States system. Part of the alleged unfairness is that some plaintiffs in the United States courts will be denied the extensive discovery available to plaintiffs generally; but that is to give absolutely no weight to the specifically international aspects present in particular cases. The supposed unfairness, or disparity of treatment, between plaintiff and defendant is more apparent than real; at least in the present context, discovery is a device beloved of plaintiffs as they seek relevant material on which to rest their claims. One could, not unfairly, argue that it is an inherently biased device, that its limitation actually improves the balance of abstract fairness between the parties.

Aérospatiale

In the *Aérospatiale* case,[25] the Supreme Court rejected what it characterized as the 'extreme position' that the Convention was exclusive and mandatory. That position

---

[20] Preliminary Document 10 of December 2008, para 32, citing the Explanatory Report, *AetD(11)*, vol 4, p 215.

[21] *Re Anschuetz & Co GmbH* 754 F 2d 602 (5th Cir, 1985).

[22] *Pain v United Technologies Corpn* 637 F 2d 775 (DC Circ, 1980), citing J Borel and S M Boyd, 'Opportunities for and Obstacles to Obtaining Evidence in France for Use in Litigation in the United States' (1979) 13 Int L 35; J H Carter, 'Obtaining Foreign Discovery and Evidence for Use in Litigation in the United States: Existing Rules and Procedures', (1979) 13 Int L 5.

[23] Brief for Respondents and Real Parties in Interest.

[24] *International Society for Krishna Consciousness, Inc v Lee* 105 FRD 435 (SD NY, 1984).

[25] *Societé Nationale Industrielle Aérospatiale v US District Court for the Southern District of Iowa* 482 US 522 (1987).

had been urged in *amicus* briefs filed by the French Republic and (less emphatically) by the Federal Republic of Germany, although the petitioners who had taken this position in the lower courts did not maintain it in the Supreme Court. The Court saw no mandatory language in the text of the Convention, and contrasted it with the language of the Hague Service of Process Convention.[26] The very existence of article 23 (discussed below)[27] was regarded as indicating that the Convention was not mandatory, on the rather tortuous argument that if the Convention had been intended to replace the broad discovery powers previously exercised by the United States, acceptance of article 23 (which enables other states to refuse to operate the Convention in this area) 'would have been most anomalous'. The Court also favoured the interpretation of article 27(d) which would enable requesting as well as requested states to use domestic law procedures, but even on a narrower reading saw nothing in article 27 to limit the power of a requesting state.

On the other hand, the Supreme Court rejected the argument, successful in the Court of Appeals,[28] that the Convention 'did not apply' where discovery was sought from a foreign litigant who was subject to the jurisdiction of an American court. The text of the Convention drew no distinction between evidence obtained from third parties and that obtained from litigants themselves. Nor did it support the 'geographic fiction' that evidence to be produced in the United States was not 'abroad' even though it was in fact located in a foreign country or must be gathered or otherwise prepared abroad.[29] In rejecting these arguments, the Supreme Court destroyed the authority of many of the previous decisions on the matter.

The majority's own starting point is perhaps best identified in this passage:

An interpretation of the Hague Convention as the exclusive means for obtaining evidence located abroad would effectively subject every American court hearing a case involving a national of a contracting state to the internal laws of that state. Interrogatories and document requests are staples of international commercial litigation, no less than of other suits, yet a rule of exclusivity would subordinate the court's supervision of even the most routine of these pre-trial proceedings to the actions or, equally, to the inactions of foreign judicial authorities.

The first sentence in that passage is, of course, a gross exaggeration. The second accepts as normative American practice, with which foreign judicial authorities must not be allowed to interfere.

However, the Supreme Court saw a place for comity analysis, as was urged upon it by several of the briefs, including that of the UK Government. Its position was that considerations of comity should be fully addressed before discovery should be allowed to proceed by means not fully recognized by the foreign sovereign state concerned. In practical terms this meant that a court should not lightly disregard

---

[26] A contrast which was to prove a source of embarrassment when the court later held that the Service Convention was not mandatory either, ie in the *Schlunk* case, 108 S Ct 2104 (1988), see p 31.

[27] See p 84.

[28] 782 F 2d 120 (8th Cir, 1986).

[29] See the *amicus* brief of Switzerland on these points.

foreign blocking statutes or 'defensive laws';[30] that perceived national interests should be carefully defined and weighed, so that some delay might well be accepted in the interest of promoting respect for the sovereign equality of states under international law; and that evidence of the willingness of the foreign state to assist United States courts (eg by a civil law country enacting legislation to enable cross-examination to take place)[31] should be taken into account.

The judgment of the Supreme Court does little to resolve the evident difference of opinion as to the nature and likely outcome of comity analysis. It does, however, clearly reject any approach requiring first resort to the Convention, whether based upon an interpretation of the Convention text or on comity, as a blanket rule. There had to be prior scrutiny in each case of the particular facts, sovereign interests, and the likelihood that the Convention procedures would prove effective.[32] American courts were to exercise a special vigilance to protect foreign litigants from abusive discovery, for example demands for excessive numbers of depositions or documents involving high transportation costs and capable of being used as a device to secure a settlement of the case. But the court declined to articulate specific rules to guide the 'delicate task of adjudication'.

Four of the court's nine justices joined in a separate opinion by Blackmun J. This opinion favoured a presumption of first resort to the Convention's procedures, and feared that the majority's preference for case-by-case comity analysis, unaccompanied by any guidance as to its conduct, would lead to the Convention's procedures being invoked infrequently.[33] Blackmun J proposed a tripartite analysis that would consider the foreign interests, the interests of the United States, and the mutual interests of all nations in a smoothly functioning international legal regime.

After *Aérospatiale*

The 1989 Special Commission of the Hague Conference considered the *Aérospatiale* judgments. It resolved, despite the views of the Supreme Court, that in all Contracting States, whatever their views as to its exclusive application, priority should be given to the procedures offered by the Convention when evidence located abroad is being sought.[34]

So far as the position in United States law was concerned, the Supreme Court having removed quite a few familiar landmarks without issuing much in the way of fresh navigational guidance, the courts faced some difficulties in addressing

---

[30] The *amicus* brief of the United States Solicitor General had urged that objections based on a blocking statute should be greeted with caution and scepticism in any proper comity analysis.

[31] As France had done: Nouveau Code de Procedure Civil, art 740.

[32] The Court dismissed an argument advanced both in *Re Anschuetz* and in the Court of Appeals in *Aérospatiale* itself that to resort first to the Convention but reserving the possibility of subsequent reliance on domestic rules would be a great insult to foreign states; in effect, the Court says they know the score.

[33] The separate opinion supports the majority's rejection of the 'geographic fiction' and of the supposed distinction between litigants and non-party witnesses, but rejects the majority's favoured interpretation of art 27, and its references to the 'unfairness' of depriving plaintiffs of access to domestic discovery rules.

[34] Conclusions and Recommendations, para 34(c).

the issue of the Convention's applicability.[35] Indeed one Circuit Judge[36] wrote a concurring opinion to express his concerns:

Unfortunately, I believe the language used in *Aérospatiale* has unintentionally compounded the problem inherent with the Convention: that 'relatively few judges are experienced in the area [of international law] and the procedures of foreign legal systems are often poorly understood'... Many times, rather than wade through the mire of a complex set of foreign statutes and case law, judges marginalize the Convention as an unnecessary 'option'. I believe the *Aérospatiale* decision should be re-examined to ensure that lower courts are in fact exercising 'special vigilance to protect foreign litigants' and demonstrating respect 'for any sovereign interest expressed by the foreign state'. Currently, I fear that many courts are simply discarding the treaty as an unnecessary hassle.

The Court of Appeals for the Fifth Circuit, reconsidering *Re Anschuetz* on remand from the Supreme Court in the light of *Aérospatiale*, declined to re-interpret the *Aérospatiale* decision as requiring first resort to the Convention or as sanctioning the use of Blackmun J's tripartite analysis.[37] The discretion was for the District Courts to exercise, but they were urged to be sensitive to the interests expressed in the Convention.

Courts under pressure tend to rely on devices which take attention away from the underlying issues. Appeal courts emphasize that the discretion is vested in the court of first instance and are reluctant to interfere;[38] first instance judges fall back on issues such as that of the burden of proof. The majority of courts, starting from the assumption that the Convention was or could be time-consuming and expensive, have held that the party wanting to 'impose' the use of those procedures must show good cause.[39]

This does tend to give priority to United States understandings of procedural fairness. For example in *First American Corp v Price Waterhouse LLP*,[40] where discovery was sought from a non-party in the United Kingdom, the Court of Appeals for the Second Circuit conceded that non-party status was a relevant factor in the comity analysis. Citing English decisions on the limited scope of bank confidentiality, the court held that there was no risk of an American court

---

[35] See J Chalmers, 'The Hague Evidence Convention and Discovery Inter Partes: Trial Court Decisions Post Aérospatiale', (2000) 8 Tul J Int & Comp L 189; P J Borchers, 'The Incredible Shrinking Hague Evidence Convention', (2003) 38 Tex Int L J 73 ('The United States has not been a particularly good sport when it comes to private international law conventions').

[36] Roth J in *Re Automotive Refinishing Paint Antitrust Litigation* 358 F3d 288 (3rd Cir, 2004), omitting internal citations.

[37] 838 F 2d 1362 (5th Cir, 1988).

[38] See *Sandsend Financial Consultants Ltd v Wood* 743 SW 2d 364 (Tex App, 1988) noting the overruling of the first resort approach of *Th Goldschmidt AG v Smith* 676 SW 2d 443 (Tex App, 1984), but emphasizing the importance of judicial discretion.

[39] *Benton Graphics v Uddeholm Corpn* 118 FRD 386 (DC NJ, 1987); *Haynes v Kleinwefers* 119 FRD 335 (ED NY, 1988) (where the court is sharply critical of *Hudson v Hermann Pfauter GmbH*, *supra*); *Scarminach v Goldwell GmbH* 531 NYS 2d 188 (NY Sup Ct, 1988); *Re Automotive Refinishing Paint Antitrust Litigation* 358 F 3d 288 (3rd Cir, 2004) (holding that first resort to the Hague Convention was not required even where discovery was for the purposes of establishing the yet uncertain *in personam* jurisdiction); *Re Vivendi Universal SA Securities Litigation* (SD NY, 2006).

[40] 154 F 3d 16 (2nd Cir, 1998).

misinterpreting foreign law, and that the Hague Convention did not really offer a meaningful avenue of discovery, for English case law would not allow the unspecific discovery sought by the plaintiffs. So in one breath the court relies on the similarity of English and American law as supporting its approach; in another it relies on the contrast between English and American approaches to justify applying the US rules rather than the Convention. As the court put it starkly, 'exclusive resort to the Hague Convention would unduly limit [the plaintiff's] access to potentially critical documents'.[41]

The courts pay lip-service to the requirement of the Supreme Court that American courts should take care to demonstrate due respect for any special problem confronted by the foreign litigant on account of its nationality or the location of its operations, and for any sovereign interest expressed by a foreign state. Their approach can be gauged from this extract from the judgment in *Jones v Deutsche Bank AG*:[42]

In this case, the Court is not persuaded that the burdens on Deutsche Bank, an international entity with worldwide operations, that would arise from requiring it to comply with its discovery obligations under the Federal Rules of Civil Procedure are such that Jones should be required instead to proceed under the Hague Convention. Nor has Deutsche Bank shown how the limited document production at issue here, to consist of its production of its own documents from its own offices, would seriously impair the sovereign interests of other nations. Deutsche Bank has pointed out that taken literally, the requests would appear to require it to search *all* of its offices throughout the world. Doing so would, of course, involve a greater burden and implicate the interests of additional foreign states. However, at least at this time Jones does not appear to be seeking to compel Deutsche Bank to search beyond its United Kingdom and German offices, and this order will be so limited. Additionally, this order does not require Deutsche Bank to conduct a wholesale review of all of its documents and files in those countries. Rather, Deutsche Bank shall request that its personnel in those offices search for and produce any documents or files reasonably identifiable (by virtue of document name, label, or other identifying information) as pertaining to the subject matter of the requests at issue.

Blocking statutes

A number of countries have passed 'blocking statutes' forbidding compliance with the type of discovery orders made by US courts. The best known is probably the provision in the French Penal Code[43] which provides in part that 'subject to treaties or international agreements and applicable laws and regulations, it is prohibited for any party to request, seek or disclose, in writing, orally or otherwise, economic, commercial, industrial, financial or technical documents or information leading to the constitution of evidence with a view to foreign judicial or administrative proceedings or in connection therewith'.

It was held in the *Aérospatiale* case that it was well settled that such statutes did not deprive an American court of the power to order a party subject to its

---

[41] At p 23.
[42] (ND Cal, 2006).
[43] Law 80–538.

jurisdiction to produce evidence even though the act of production may violate the foreign statute:

> It is clear that American courts are not required to adhere blindly to the directives of such a statute. Indeed, the language of the statute, if taken literally, would appear to represent an extraordinary exercise of legislative jurisdiction by the Republic of France over a United States district judge, forbidding him or her to order any discovery from a party of French nationality, even simple requests for admissions or interrogatories that the party could respond to on the basis of personal knowledge.[44]

United States courts have repeatedly refused to respect blocking statutes and have ordered compliance notwithstanding the foreign prohibition.[45] They commonly consider four factors: (1) the competing interests of the nations whose laws are in conflict; (2) the hardship of compliance on the party or witness from whom discovery is sought; (3) the importance to the litigation of the information and documents requested; and (4) the good faith of the party resisting discovery. However, the consideration does not seem to the outside observer to be even-handed. So one court noted that the United States had an obvious interest in the application of its procedural rules to discovery, but that the French blocking statute was a manifestation of French displeasure with American pre-trial discovery procedures, not intended to be enforced against French subjects but was intended rather to provide them with tactical weapons and bargaining chips in foreign courts. This, it was held, meant that France's real interests in promulgating the statute were dwarfed by American interests in complete discovery.[46] Even evidence that the French statute had been enforced did not persuade a US court to give it any determinative weight.[47]

(e) Pre-trial discovery of documents and the Convention

Article 1(2) of the Convention provides that:

> A Letter shall not be used to obtain evidence which is not intended for use in judicial proceedings, commenced or contemplated.[48]

---

[44] *Société Nationale Industrielle Aérospatiale v US District Court for the Southern District of Iowa* 482 US 522 (1987), citing *Société Internationale Pour Participations Industrielles et Commerciales SA v Rogers* 357 US 197 (1958).

[45] *Rich v KIS California Inc* 121 FRD 254 (MD NC, 1988) (French blocking statute both overly broad and vague; it need not be given the same deference as a substantive rule of law); *Re Vivendi Universal SA Securities Litigation* (SD NY, 2006) (French blocking statute); *Calixto v Watson Bowman Acme Corp* (SD Fla, 2008) (Swiss Penal Code, art 271(1)).

[46] *Re Vivendi Universal SA Securities Litigation* (SD NY, 2006), citing *United States v Gonzalez* 748 F 2d 74 (2nd Cir, 1984); *Compagnie Française d'Assurance Pour le Commerce Extérieur v Phillips Petroleum Co* 105 FRD 16 (SD NY, 1984).

[47] *MeadWestvaco Corp v Rexam plc* (ED Va, 2010), noting *Re Avocat Christopher X* (Cour de Cassation, 12 December 2007).

[48] The 2009 Special Commission noted the practice of States Parties that the expression 'contemplated' in art 1(2) included proceedings for the taking of evidence before the main proceedings have been instituted, and where there is a danger that evidence may be lost: Conclusions and Recommendations, para 47.

Article 23 further provides:

A Contracting State may at the time of signature, ratification or accession, declare that it will not execute Letters of Request issued for the purpose of obtaining pre-trial discovery of documents as known in Common Law countries.

Neither provision featured in the draft text prepared before the Eleventh Session of the Hague Conference. Both had their origin in a Working Document presented by the United Kingdom delegation[49] and designed to apply the Convention only to evidence 'for use in proceedings pending in the State of origin'. As the text emerged from the drafting committee, the English text, but not the French text, of article 1 made express reference to 'discovery': a request was not to be used for the purpose of obtaining discovery between the parties before the trial.[50] After some unhelpful discussion, which did at least confirm that the main concern of the United Kingdom delegation was that of discovery, that was dealt with in article 23, article 1 retaining some residual signs of the drafting history. What nobody seemed to notice was that the text of article 23, by referring to 'pre-trial discovery of documents as known in Common Law countries', and especially in omitting the earlier reference to discovery between the parties, covered some types of discovery known in the United States but not in other common law countries.

The limitation of article 23 of the Convention to discovery of documents leaves other forms of pre-trial discovery, such as oral depositions under United States practice, outside its scope. As Collins has convincingly argued,[51] the exclusion permitted by article 23 is in one sense very surprising, as very few of the countries present would have regarded discovery, especially when ordered against third parties, as within the concepts of evidence or other judicial acts. What must be clear is that no reservation under article 23, however worded, can operate to extend the scope of the Convention beyond that established in article 1.

So far as English law is concerned, a crucial distinction was drawn in *Radio Corporation of America v Rauland Corpn*,[52] decided under the Foreign Tribunals Evidence Act 1856. The Divisional Court in that case distinguished between the obtaining of evidence for use in a trial, 'direct' material, which constituted 'testimony' under that Act and which would be gathered in response to a Letter of Request, and the obtaining of 'indirect' material, which might lead to a line of enquiry pointing to actual evidence; the English courts would not assist a foreign court to obtain such 'indirect' material.[53] It would seem that this distinction was in the mind of the United Kingdom delegation in formulating their Working Document No 10, and that the subsequent references to 'discovery' served only to confuse the issues.

---

[49] Working Document 10, *AetD(11)*, Vol 4, p 94.
[50] Ibid, p 137.
[51] L Collins, 'The Hague Evidence Convention and Discovery: A Serious Misunderstanding?' (1986) 35 ICLQ 765.
[52] [1956] 1 QB 618 (DC).
[53] See also *American Express Warehousing Co v Doe* [1967] 1 Lloyd's Rep 222 (CA).

Very many states made the declaration, commonly called 'the Article 23 reservation' that they would not act on requests for the pre-trial discovery of documents.[54] But the United Kingdom, the proponent of article 23, made a declaration in particular terms. It declared that it understood the scope of the Letters of Request which it would not execute as including[55] Letters of Request which require a person:

(a) to state what documents relevant to the proceedings to which the Letter of Request relates are, or have been, in his possession, custody or power; or

(b) to produce any documents other than particular documents specified in the Letter of Request as being documents appearing to the requested court to be, or to be likely to be, in his possession, custody or power.

It is possible to read paragraph (b) of this declaration as implying that the United Kingdom will execute Letters of Request seeking the production of particular documents specified in the Letter and required by way of 'discovery', even if they do not (in the words of the corresponding Rule of the Supreme Court then in force)[56] 'relate to a matter in question in the cause or matter'. In the *Westinghouse* case, the House of Lords, in interpreting the Evidence (Proceedings in Other Jurisdictions) Act 1975, which gives effect to the Convention in the United Kingdom, did not share this view. Both Lord Wilberforce and Viscount Dilhorne referred to the distinction drawn in the earlier cases between 'direct' evidence and other 'indirect' material. Lord Wilberforce, noting that the United Kingdom declaration corresponded to section 2(4) of the Act, held that the distinction was preserved in section 2. If anything, the 1975 Act took 'a stricter line' on pre-trial discovery than its predecessor. Viscount Dilhorne similarly held that if the requested court was not satisfied that evidence was required, direct evidence for use at a trial as contrasted with information which might lead to the discovery of evidence, it had no power to assist. Without relying on pre-1975 cases, Lord Diplock interpreted section 2(3)(4) as excluding the obtaining, by oral deposition or the disclosure of documents, of anything other than evidence which would be admissible at the trial of the action. Lord Keith held that the distinction between evidence and discovery was recognized both in the Act and in article 23 of the Convention; it was not disputed by counsel that effect could not be given to a request merely seeking discovery.

The matter has been further discussed in two Special Commissions. In 1978, the Special Commission heard explanations from both the United States and United Kingdom experts.[57] The United States expert sought to re-assure the Commission

---

[54] As at March 2011, 26 states had an unqualified declaration under art 23: Albania, Argentina, Australia, Bulgaria, China in respect of the Macau SAR, Croatia, France, Germany, Greece, Hungary, Iceland, Italy, Liechtenstein, Lithuania, Luxembourg, Macedonia, Monaco, Poland, Portugal, Romania, Seychelles, South Africa, Spain, Sri Lanka, Turkey, and Ukraine.

[55] So the words which follow do not necessarily exhaust the category.

[56] RSC Ord 24, r 11. Disclosure and inspection of documents are now regulated by CPR Part 31.

[57] See *AetD(14)*, Vol 4, p 420.

that pre-trial discovery procedures in his country were all after the commencement of proceedings (the relevance of this being, presumably, that it picks up the requirement of article 1(2) of the Convention) and were under the control of a judge. It will be seen that this explanation does not touch the question of whether what is sought is in any sense 'evidence'. The United Kingdom expert, very surprisingly, was equally silent on this matter; he explained the purpose of article 23 as being to enable Contracting States to refuse to execute Letters of Request which lacked specificity in that they did not describe precisely enough the documents to be obtained or examined. This appears to rest on the view of the United Kingdom position which was expressly rejected in the *Westinghouse* case. The Commission responded by urging Contracting States which had made the Reservation under article 23 to withdraw it, or at least adopt the language of the United Kingdom Reservation.[58]

In 1985, the United States delegation made similar remarks to those at the earlier Special Commission, but the United Kingdom expert offered a much fuller statement of the position as it had emerged in the *Westinghouse* and *Asbestos Insurance Coverage* cases; but he still identified the article 23 Reservation in the United Kingdom version as meeting the case. The Commission again urged adoption of that language or language based on article 16 of the additional Protocol 1984 to the Inter-American Convention on the Taking of Evidence Abroad.[59] It reads as follows:

The States Parties to this Protocol shall process a letter rogatory that requests the exhibition and copying of documents if it meets the following requirements:

   (a) The proceeding has been initiated;
   (b) The documents are reasonably identified by date, contents, or other appropriate information;
   (c) The letter rogatory specifies those facts and circumstances causing the requesting party reasonably to believe that the requested documents are or were in the possession, control, or custody of, or are known to the person from whom the documents are requested.

The person from whom documents are requested may, where appropriate, deny that he has possession, control or custody of the requested documents, or may object to the exhibition and copying of the documents, in accordance with the rules of the Convention.

At the time of signing, ratifying or acceding to this Protocol a State may declare that it will process the letters rogatory to which this article applies only if they identify the relationship between the evidence or information requested and the pending proceeding.[60]

As discussion at the 1985 meeting of Experts made clear, the sensitivity of the issues surrounding article 23 is increased by the use of United States discovery processes

---

[58] The Nordic countries, Denmark, Finland, Norway, and Sweden, all amended their declarations in 1980 so as to adopt the UK formulation. That formulation is also used in the declarations by China in respect of the Hong Kong SAR (the mainland has a variant), Cyprus, India, Korea, Netherlands, Switzerland (with slightly different wording), Singapore, and the UK itself.

[59] This recommendation was repeated by the 2009 Special Commission.

[60] As at March 2011, Estonia, Mexico, and Venezuela had declarations using this formulation.

in anti-trust actions and other contexts in which the United States courts claim
to have jurisdiction more extensive than other countries are willing to approve, to
combat which a series of 'blocking statutes' have been enacted to deal with some
features of this problem. In this context, two agreed conclusions of the 1985
meeting of experts can usefully be quoted:

Statutes which prohibit the production of evidence abroad, commonly known as 'blocking
statutes', many of which have been adopted since the 1978 meeting . . . are in part a response
to what are perceived in some countries as exorbitant assertions of jurisdiction by the courts
of other countries. Such statutes however constitute a complicating factor and emphasize the
need for long-term solutions through international understanding.

The combined effect of a blocking statute and an unqualified reservation under article 23,
when both are adopted by a State, may be to discourage use by other States of the Hague
Convention.

(f) Civil and commercial

The text, and indeed the full title, of the Convention limits its field of application to
'civil or commercial matters'. The difficulties inherent in the use of this phrase, and
the view taken by a Special Commission of the Conference examining the Service
Convention, but hoping to give guidance in this context also, have already been
noted.[61]

The meaning of this troublesome phrase was a central issue in the English case of
The State of Norway's Application, which was twice considered by the Court of
Appeal and once by the House of Lords. A request under the Convention was
received in England from the Sandefjord City Court, Norway, asking that a
director and a senior employee of a London merchant bank be examined as
to the ownership and control of certain assets and of a charitable trust said
to control those assets. The context was an action in the Norwegian court to set
aside a retrospective tax assessment which had been raised by the Norwegian tax
authorities against the estate of a deceased taxpayer who, it was alleged, was the
beneficial owner of the assets which he had not declared for tax purposes.

The English courts had to consider the meaning of the phrase 'civil or commercial matter' as used in section 9(1) of the Evidence (Proceedings in Other
Jurisdictions) Act 1975, passed mainly to give effect to the Convention; the
precise question was whether the evidence sought was 'for the purposes of *civil
proceedings* . . . before the requesting court' within section 1 of the Act, the italicized
phrase being interpreted in section 9 to mean proceedings in any civil or commercial matter.

---

[61] See pp 33–34. The 1985 Special Commission on the Evidence Convention noted that many
bankruptcy cases, other than those with a penal aspect, would properly be regarded as 'civil or
commercial': Report, p 8. See Hoge Raad, 21 February 1986, NJ 1987, 149 (Asser 4/113); *Re Tucker
(a bankrupt)* [1987] 1 WLR 928 (on the Service Convention).

When the case first came before the Court of Appeal,[62] the court, finding no assistance in the text of the Convention itself, held in effect that the proceedings had to be regarded as in a 'civil or commercial matter' both under the law of the requesting country, which must necessarily be the starting point, and that of England, the courts of which had to be satisfied that the request did fall within the terms of the Act. As Glidewell LJ pointed out, the latter requirement might be wholly theoretical, given the breadth of the English concept of 'civil proceedings' as anything which is not criminal in nature.[63] Kerr LJ said that there was no generally accepted international meaning of the phrase; he recognized that in some jurisdictions, public law matters were regarded as outside the categories of civil and commercial, but that this was not universally the case; he, but not the other members of the court, felt that there was insufficient evidence as to the approach of Norwegian law, but was prepared to give the request the benefit of the doubt.

The first Letters of Request were, however, rejected as too widely drawn, under principles as to 'fishing expeditions' to be considered below.[64] The Norwegian court issued a second Letter of Request and the 'civil or commercial' point was taken again, and argued before a differently constituted Court of Appeal.[65] A majority (May and Balcombe LJJ), considering substantial additional material[66] and encouraged by academic criticism of the first decision,[67] held that 'civil or commercial matter' not only could but should be given an 'international' interpretation. May LJ recognized that the phrase had no intelligible meaning in a wholly common law context, which suggested that attention had to be given to the civil law origins of the phrase. Viewed in this light, the Norwegian proceedings would be categorized as being concerned with fiscal, and therefore public law, matters and not with matters civil or commercial. Woolf LJ reached a similar result by a different route; he could not identify an 'international' meaning of the phrase, but interpreting it by reference to English law (but not adopting 'any parochial classification of a procedural nature') he held that fiscal matters were a special category, outside that of 'civil or commercial'.

In the House of Lords, the argument went off on a rather different tack. The 1975 Act had been accepted in the Court of Appeal as having been passed mainly to give effect to the Hague Convention, but that purpose nowhere appears in the text of the Act which was also designed to replace earlier United Kingdom legislation, notably the Foreign Tribunals Evidence Act 1856 in which the phrase 'civil or commercial matter' was used in a context wholly divorced from any international convention and which formed part of the law of many Commonwealth (and common law) countries. This, and the deliberate decision of those who drafted

---

[62] *Re State of Norway's Application (No 1)* [1987] QB 433 (CA).
[63] Note that, as was pointed out by Balcombe LJ in the second Court of Appeal decision, criminal 'proceeding' may not be the same as criminal 'matter'.
[64] See pp 116–117.
[65] *Re State of Norway's Application (No 2)* [1989] 1 All ER 701 (CA).
[66] Including C Szladits' chapter on 'The Civil Law System' in 2 Ency Comp L.
[67] F A Mann, 'Any Civil or Commercial Matter' (1986) 102 LQR 505; though in some respects the Court of Appeal rejected Dr Mann's reasoning.

the Hague Convention to include no definition of the phrase in that context,[68] led Lord Goff, with whom the other members of the House agreed, to reject any 'international' meaning. Instead he applied, as had the first Court of Appeal, a combination of the laws of the requesting and requested countries. It was found that the matter was viewed as 'civil' in Norwegian law, and it was held that (contrary to the view of Woolf LJ) there was nothing to take fiscal matters outside the civil category in English law, which embraced everything which was not a criminal matter. The House rejected, it is submitted quite correctly, an argument that the refusal of the English courts to enforce foreign penal or revenue law[69] precluded the English court from giving the assistance requested; to provide evidence which is to be used in foreign proceedings, even enforcement proceedings, is not to 'enforce' the foreign law in England.

In the end result, therefore, the *State of Norway* litigation provides no real guidance as to the meaning of the phrase in the Hague context. As Dr Mann has argued,[70] it does allow the English courts to provide assistance, in practice under the Hague Convention, in certain fiscal and administrative contexts which would be judged by some other countries to fall outside its scope; Dr Mann's unease at this needs to be balanced against the enormous and considered growth, recounted elsewhere in this book, in international co-operation in such fields.[71]

One closely related question has also been the subject of much recent discussion. If a request is made to obtain evidence abroad for use in what are clearly civil proceedings, is it a sufficient ground for rejecting the request that there is a possibility that the evidence might subsequently be used in the requesting country in a criminal matter?

The general opinion amongst Central Authorities is that a request should not be rejected on this ground;[72] and this appears to accord with the views expressed in the House of Lords in the *Westinghouse* case.[73] As Lord Wilberforce pointed out,[74] once evidence is brought out in court it is in the public domain; unless the terms of relevant legislation or international agreements provide otherwise, there is nothing to prevent other interested persons or authorities acting upon the information thus made available. However, it is quite proper to reject a request if the evidence is really being sought with a view to its use in criminal proceedings. This was emphasized in the *Westinghouse* case by Viscount Dilhorne who said:

---

[68] See *AetD(11)*, Vol 4, pp 56–7 (explanatory report of Mr Amram on the preliminary draft of the Convention).

[69] See Dicey Morris and Collins, *The Conflict of Laws* (14th edn, 2006), para 5R-019.

[70] (1989) 105 LQR 341.

[71] See also *Securities and Exchange Commission v Certain Unknown Purchasers of the Common Stock of and Call Options for the Common Stock of Santa Fe International Corpn* (QBD, 23 February 1984, unreported) where SEC proceedings were treated as a civil matter. In *S v E* [1967] 1 QB 367 affiliation proceedings were held to be civil proceedings within the Foreign Tribunals Evidence Act 1856.

[72] See the conclusions of the 1978 Special Commission, at *AetD(14)*, Vol 4, pp 419–20.

[73] *Rio Tinto Zinc Corporation v Westinghouse Electric Corporation* [1978] AC 547 (HL).

[74] Ibid, at p 610.

I hope that the courts of this country will always be vigilant to prevent a misuse of the convention and will not make an order requiring evidence to be given . . . unless it is clearly established that, even if required for civil proceedings, it is not also sought for criminal proceedings.[75]

A converse situation arose in *BOC Ltd v Barlow*.[76] The Court of Appeal held that information obtained under the Criminal Justice (International Co-operation) Act 1990 could be used in subsequent civil proceedings.

Although the primary purpose of the Convention is to obtain evidence in connection with a pending action, an Israeli court has held that *exequatur* proceedings for the enforcement of an existing judgment can be a civil matter, and a Letter of Request can properly seek evidence needed for those proceedings.[77]

(g) Judicial authorities

The request must emanate from a 'judicial authority', but there is no definition of this expression. The Commission responsible for preparing the Convention decided not to include courts of arbitration,[78] but there is no clarity on the position of administrative tribunals, many of which closely resemble ordinary courts, whilst others do not. Each case must be examined on its own facts, examining the function rather than just the formal categorization of the requesting authority.[79] An illustration, from a not dissimilar field, of this approach in practice is *Re Letters Rogatory Issued by the Director of Inspection of Government of India*,[80] where a US Court of Appeals decided, after an analysis of the powers and duties of a tax assessment agency in India, that it was not a 'tribunal' entitled to the execution in New York of a Letter of Request seeking action under 28 USC 1782.[81]

(h) 'Evidence'

No definition of this term is given, but some guide to the meaning of 'obtain evidence' is given in article 3(e), (f), and (g) which refer to witnesses, questions to be asked, and documents or property to be inspected. The preliminary draft of article 1 did in fact contain, in the English text only, an explanatory gloss to the word 'evidence' as 'including the taking of statements of witnesses, parties or experts and the production or examination of documents or other objects or property'; its eventual omission was for reasons of style rather than of substance.

---

[75] Ibid, at p 631.
[76] *The Times*, 10 July 2001 (CA).
[77] Tel Aviv, 5 August 1992 (Asser 5/374).
[78] *AetD(11)*, Vol 4, pp 97–9.
[79] See the Report of the 1985 Special Commission, p 8. In some countries, the Minister of Justice may qualify: see *Ste IPCL v Elf Aquitaine* (Cour de Cass, 22 May 2007), (2008) Rev Crit de d i priv 278 (Nigeria and Congo).
[80] 385 F 2d 1017 (2nd Cir, 1967).
[81] For this provision, see pp 134–135. See also *Fonseca v Blumenthal* 620 F 2d 322 (2nd Circ, 1980) (similar decision re the Superintendent of Exchange Control of the Republic of Colombia).

A French court has held that the inspection of a building by a technical expert in the context of a dispute as to the fitness of materials used in the construction of the building did not involve the taking of evidence, as it required no action by a judicial authority of the country in which the building was situated.[82]

Article 1(2), excluding attempts to obtain evidence which is not intended for use in judicial proceedings, commenced, or contemplated, has already been considered in the context of pre-trial discovery.[83]

(i) 'Other judicial act'

This is a phrase retained from the earlier Hague Conventions. In order to minimize doubts as to its scope, article 1(3) makes it clear that certain matters which are either dealt with in other conventions, or which might involve the exercise of the court's discretion, such as the service of process, the enforcement of judgments and orders, and orders for provisional or protective measures, are excluded.[84] The act must be 'judicial'; if it is not within the functions of the judiciary in the state of execution, eg conducting conciliation in matrimonial proceedings or valuing property, the Request may be refused (even if it is a judicial act in the requesting state).[85]

In practice, many states seem willing to adopt a generous view of the scope of the Convention, responding to requests to obtain the results of blood-grouping tests (at least where the subject is willing) and to provide copies of public documents or of entries in registers of civil status.[86] In England, obtaining extracts of public records would not be seen as a judicial act, and the phrase 'other judicial acts' seems to remain a source of puzzlement.[87]

(j) Central Authorities

Each Contracting State must establish a Central Authority to receive Letters of Request,[88] and there is freedom to designate additional 'other authorities' or, in the case of federal states, more than one Central Authority.[89] It is customary for the same body to be designated as the Central Authority for other Hague Conventions dealing with civil procedure, notably that on Service of Process.[90]

---

[82] *Sté Luxguard v Sté SN Sitraco* (Versailles CA, 9 April 1993), [1996] ILPr 5.

[83] See pp 84–85.

[84] eg, many types of injunctions, forced sales, and receiverships: see the Explanatory Report of Mr Amram, *AetD(11)*, Vol 4, p 203.

[85] Convention, art 12(a).

[86] See the 1978 Special Commission report, *AetD(14)*, Vol 4, p 420.

[87] See ibid, p 411, where the United Kingdom's response to the Hague Conference questionnaire assumes that 'other judicial acts' form a middle category between 'judicial' and 'non-judicial' acts, which was never the intention.

[88] Convention, art 2. Letters purporting to be sent under the Convention but sent by a party directly to the foreign court, and not via the Central Authority may be ignored: *Panamerican Resource and Development Inc v Huancayo SAF* Buenos Aires, 8 July 1988 (Asser 5/372).

[89] Convention, art 24.

[90] See what is said in the context of that Convention, pp 35–36.

In the United Kingdom, the Senior Master is the Central Authority. In Commonwealth jurisdictions, the designated Central Authority is frequently the Registrar of the Supreme Court or its equivalent (as in Barbados, Singapore, Hong Kong) but sometimes the Ministry of Justice (as in Cyprus) or the Governor (as in the Cayman Islands).

To ensure the simplicity of the system, it is expressly provided in article 2 that no intervening agency in the requested state is to deal with the Letter of Request on its way to the Central Authority. However, article 27(a) permits a state to declare that it will accept transmission of Letters of Request to its judicial authorities by other channels (no state has done so); article 28(a) enables two or more Contracting States to make other arrangements *inter se*; and article 32 protects existing bilateral Conventions.

The Convention does not prescribe how a Letter of Request should be despatched from within the requesting state. In the United States the courts transmit Letters directly to the Central Authority abroad. In the United Kingdom and France Letters are transmitted through their own Central Authorities, a procedure which has the advantage of making it more likely that the formal requirements of the Convention will be fully complied with.

(k) Contents of Letters of Request

The detailed information which the Letter of Request must contain is set out in article 3. It includes the name of the requesting authority, and the name of the requested authority if known; otherwise the Letter could simply refer to 'the appropriate authority'. Details of the parties, the proceedings, the evidence to be obtained, or other judicial act to be performed and questions to be put must be included. The precise details required will depend on the circumstances: although the names and addresses of the proposed witnesses are to be included 'where appropriate',[91] such information will normally be required whenever witnesses are required, and a court may decline to issue Letters of Request containing a mere list of names with no additional data.[92] If, under the law of the requesting authority, the evidence is to be given on oath or any special form is to be used, this should be included, along with any special procedure to be followed under article 9.[93] No legalization of the Letter or other like formality may be required.

The Special Commissions of 1978 and 1985 considered that there was a need for a model or standard form of Letter of Request to overcome the problem of inadequate information, eg as to the precise nature of the evidence to be obtained, or the authority to whom the Letter should be returned, as well as difficulties

---

[91] Convention, art 3(2).

[92] Arnhem, 8 April 1993, NIPR 1993, 474 (Asser 5/377).

[93] See p 96. The Letter may also contain information about the privileges and duties of witnesses required under art 11. If necessary, a Letter of Request may be supplemented or amended by a further Letter: Amsterdam, 21 September 1989, NJ 1990, 617 (Asser 5/376).

of interpretation over legal terminology used in different systems. Accordingly a model form was devised, and revised in 1985. It is designed to operate as a checklist of all information which is considered to be desirable or necessary for the successful execution of the Request and its prompt return to the requesting authority. The model form is not obligatory but is recommended in the interest of both requesting and requested states. What is most needed is a clear explanation of the particular point on which evidence is sought; the model form includes requests for summaries of the parties' positions and suggests that relevant documentation (court orders, pleadings) might be attached; but these should be restricted to matters illuminating the particular request for evidence and should not seek to rehearse the whole case.

(l) Language of the Request

Letters of Request must be in the language of the authority requested to execute it (or be accompanied by a translation into that language); or in English or French, unless a party has made a reservation under article 33 excluding the use of English or French; or in another language which a Contracting State has declared its readiness to accept.[94] A state with more than one official language may, if necessary under internal law, declare the language of Letters to be used in specified parts of its territory. Failure to comply with this declaration, 'without justifiable excuse', renders the state of origin liable to pay the cost of translation.[95]

The Convention does not prescribe the language to be used in responding to the Letter; the normal expectation is that the language to be used will be that in which the Letter was sent, but documents and evidence taken orally will be sent in the original language, whatever that may be.

(m) Rejection of Letter of Request

The Convention creates an obligation to execute Letters of Request falling within its terms; and the Letter is to be executed 'expeditiously'.[96] The exceptional circumstances in which execution may be refused are very narrowly defined.

A Central Authority may object to a Letter on the ground that it does not comply with the Convention, for example because the contents are insufficiently full, whereupon it must promptly inform the sending authority.[97] If the Letter of Request complies with the Convention, its execution may be refused only on the grounds set out in article 12, and only to the extent that it is objectionable on those grounds. They are that in the state of execution the execution of the Letter does not fall within the province of the judiciary; and that the state addressed considers that its sovereignty or security would be prejudiced thereby.

---

[94] Convention, art 4.   [95] Ibid.   [96] Convention, art 9.   [97] Convention, art 5.

The *Westinghouse* case[98] illustrates the reference to prejudice to the sovereignty of a state, the Attorney-General appearing to represent that HM Government regarded as an unacceptable invasion of its own sovereignty the use of proceedings in the United States courts as a means by which the United States Government sought to investigate activities outside the United States of British companies and individuals which might infringe American anti-trust laws.[99] As has already been noted, a request for extracts from a public record is an example of a Request falling outside the judicial function in some states.

The Special Commission of 1978 discussed a difficult question, raised by the United States, as to whether or not a Central Authority was obliged to prosecute or to defend an appeal against a decision of the judicial authority granting or refusing execution of a Letter. In the United States, the Central Authority has, on several occasions, responded to appeals made to higher courts by one of the parties. The discussion was not conclusive but views were expressed that, while there was no such obligation on the Central Authority, if it felt that good grounds existed for an appeal, it could properly act.[100]

(n) Execution of Letters of Request

Letters of Request are to be executed by an 'authority competent to execute them',[101] later referred to as a 'judicial authority'.[102] If a Request is sent to an authority which is not competent to execute it, it must be sent forthwith to the correct authority,[103] either by the former authority direct, or by the Central Authority.

A question was raised in the 1978 Special Commission as to whether a 'judicial authority' meant a judge. The practice of states was more liberal: the United States, for example, is prepared to appoint as commissioners any persons who are entitled to administer oaths. In England, the competent authorities are the Masters, who make orders appointing examiners, almost always barristers, to take the testimony. In other countries, such as Austria, Sweden, Norway, and Denmark, the authority is the local court where the witness resides. In France, the authorities include not only the judiciary but also other persons designated as commissioners by the French Government. The Commission felt that, to save time and expense, authorities able to execute requests should include not only courts, but commissioners, notaries public, lawyers and others, insofar as they could be given 'certain attributes of a judicial authority'.[104]

---

[98] *Rio Tinto Zinc Corp v Westinghouse Electric Corp* [1978] AC 547. See further pp 115–118.
[99] See also *Time Inc v Attorney-General* (1984) 38 PD 385, 561, Asser 4/131 (Israeli High Ct) (refusal to accept request that a government minister give evidence as to the reputation of a colleague in respect of his official duties).
[100] *AetD(14)*, Vol 4, p 423.
[101] Convention, art 2.
[102] Convention, art 9.
[103] Convention, art 6.
[104] *AetD(14)*, Vol 4, p 422.

(o) Attendance at the execution of the Letter of Request

Notice of the time and place of the proceedings must, on request, be sent to the requesting authority or direct to the parties, to enable them and their representatives to be present.[105] The notice can be given either by the Central Authority or, to save time, directly by the competent authority.[106] The Convention makes no provision for a case in which no notice is given, despite a request having been made. In a case under the 1954 Convention, in which a Belgian court had failed to notify the other party as asked in the Dutch letter of request, the Hoge Raad held that the evidence taken in Belgium could not be relied upon.[107] If no request for information as to the date and time of the hearing is made, it seems the evidence will be admissible despite the absence of the element of confrontation normally required in many legal systems.[108]

Contracting States may declare that 'judicial personnel of the requesting authority' may be present at the execution of the letter.[109] The declaration may also require prior authorization by the competent authority to be obtained in each particular case. Although the text was carefully drafted to limit the rights of the visiting judge, in that he or she could be present at, but play no active part in, the proceedings, more active participation is in practice allowed in some countries.[110] In some, eg the United Kingdom and France, judges are permitted to attend (pursuant either to a declaration under the Convention or other procedures) but it has been rare for them to do so and they could normally ask questions only with the leave of the court. The United States adopts a liberal approach, and some foreign judges have actually been sworn in as commissioners by American courts, eg German and Italian judges have been allowed to execute the Letters themselves in the United States by examining witnesses in their own language and according to their own procedures. United States judges also have gone abroad on rare occasions, eg to England in the *Westinghouse* case, but it is understood that the United States now discourages this practice.

(p) Special procedures and methods

The judicial authority executing the request applies its own laws and procedures, save where a request is made to follow a special method or procedure, which is not incompatible with the law of the state of execution or impossible of performance by reason of its internal practice and procedure or by reason of other practical difficulties.[111]

---

[105] Convention, art 7.
[106] In England, the information is sent to the requesting authority by the Queen's Bench Masters' Secretary on behalf of the Senior Master.
[107] Hoge Raad, 25 October 1991, NJ 1992, 6 (Asser 5/332).
[108] Trieste CA, 26 February 1992, Riv d i p proc 1993, 751 (Asser 5/375).
[109] Convention, art 8.
[110] See *AetD(14)*, Vol 4, p 422.
[111] Convention, art 9.

Some requesting states may only accept evidence taken in a particular way and the Convention tries to ensure that a request for a special procedure (for example, for verbatim transcripts or, on the other hand, for a summary of the evidence in deposition form; or for videotaped evidence)[112] will not be refused merely because it is inconvenient to the requested state. 'Incompatible' with internal law does not mean simply 'different' from such law, but that there must be some constitutional or statutory prohibition. It is, of course, for the requested state to determine whether the special method is impractical or impossible of performance.[113]

In appropriate cases a commissioner from the requesting state might be appointed to carry out the special method or procedure requested, eg to overcome the difficulty which a civil law state may have in satisfying a Request from a common law state to take evidence under cross-examination, because no judge or local lawyer in the requested state had any experience in that field. There are indications, however, that the operation of the Convention leads to a greater willingness on the part of requested countries to adapt their procedures so that the needs of countries with different traditions are more readily met. The German courts, for example, have developed a procedure for taking depositions in response to requests from foreign countries, with provision for cross-examination, which appears entirely to meet the needs of common law countries; the French Code of Civil Procedure now allows verbatim recording and a limited form of cross-examination to meet the needs of parties using the Convention.[114]

Letters of Request are to be executed expeditiously.[115] At the 1985 Special Commission, various estimates were given as to the length of time taken to comply with a Letter of Request. A fair number of countries indicated that a response could be given within three months. Those with a slower response time indicated that special treatment would be given to Requests which indicated genuine urgency. The recommended model form of Letter of Request as revised in 1985 includes questions as to the date by which a response is needed, and the reasons for the choice of that date.

(q) Measures of compulsion against a witness

The requested authority is required by article 10 to apply the same measures of compulsion against an unwilling witness as it would do under its internal law in

---

[112] The Special Commission of 2009 made a series of recommendations showing how video technology could assist the working of the Convention: Conclusions and Recommendations, paras 55–7. Cf M Davies, 'By-Passing the Hague Evidence Convention' (2007) 55 Am J Comp L 205.

[113] For example, the Dutch courts have held that they are unable to require a witness named in a Letter of Request to produce specified documents as opposed to giving oral testimony about them: Hoge Raad, 11 March 1994, NJ 1995, 3 (Asser 5/377); Amsterdam, 23 February 1995, NIPR 1995, 415 (Asser 5/379). See also the discussion in the (seemingly non-Convention) case of *Wigley v Dick* (Royal Ct, Jersey, 24 November 1989) (Asser 5/381).

[114] See arts 739–740 of the Code. For Germany, see D R Shemanski, 'Obtaining Evidence in the Federal Republic of Germany: The Impact of the Hague Evidence Convention on German-American Judicial Co-operation' (1983) 17 Int L 465.

[115] Convention, art 9(3).

local proceedings. Although no serious problems have arisen under this article, there is a divergence of practice in applying compulsion for blood tests in paternity cases, where the Convention is often used. Some countries, including England but not Scotland, will use compulsory powers, but this is not the case in many countries, including France, the Netherlands, Portugal, Scotland, and the United States, where it may be unconstitutional to force a person to give body samples.

(r) Privileges and duties of witnesses

A witness may refuse to give evidence if he or she has a privilege or duty to do so either under the law of the state where the Letter of Request is to be executed or under the law of the requesting state.[116] So in the *Westinghouse* case, one group of witnesses successfully claimed a privilege existing in English law, while another group of witnesses successfully relied upon a privilege existing in the law of the United States, the requesting state. Where the privilege arises under the law of the requesting state and the privilege has not been stated in the Letter, the requested authority may ask the requesting authority to confirm whether such privilege or duty exists,[117] in order to safeguard the witness's interests. It is obviously more convenient if the requesting authority anticipates any possible claim of privilege under its own law, preferably by supplying a copy of the relevant legal provisions with the Letter of Request.

Several English cases have examined the relevance of the French 'blocking statute'[118] which provides that:

without prejudice to international treaties or agreements or of the statutory or regulatory laws in force, it is forbidden for any person to request, seek or produce in writing, orally or by any other means, economic, commercial, industrial, financial or technical documents or information with a view to it being used as evidence in foreign judicial or administrative proceedings or in the context of such proceedings.

The opening words would seem to safeguard the position under the Convention, but in non-Convention contexts the English courts have regarded the French statute as virtually a dead letter and have asserted that they have a discretion to order the provision of evidence abroad even if the witness might be in technical breach of the law, even the criminal law, of his or her country.[119]

---

[116] Convention, art 11. See Hoge Raad, 11 March 1994, NJ 1995, 3 (Asser 5/377) (position of notaries under Dutch law).

[117] See Convention, art 11(1)(b).

[118] Art 1 *bis* of Loi 80–583 of 16 July 1980. For US case law, see p 84.

[119] *Morris v Banque Arabe et Internationale d'Investissement SA* [2001] ILPr 37 (Comm Ct) citing two cases decided under earlier rules of court (*Partenreederei M/s Heidberg v Grosvenor Grain and Feed Co Ltd (The Heidberg)* [1993] 2 Lloyd's Rep. 324 (Asser 5/380) and *Canada Trust Ltd v Stolzenberg* [1998] ILPr 290) and the related issues examined in *Brannigan v Davison* [1997] AC 238 (PC). Related issues arise in connection with the European Union's Data Protection Directive (Directive 95/46/EC of the European Parliament and of the Council of 24 October 1995 on the protection of individuals with regard to the processing of personal data and on the free movement of such data, OJ L 281, 23.11.1995) which may in effect prohibit compliance with a discovery order from the United

In the negotiation of the Hague Convention, the question of privileges under the law of third states proved difficult.[120] There was seen to be a need to protect such witnesses as a Swiss banker who is prevented by Swiss law from disclosing bank details, or a French physician whose duty of professional secrecy is enforced under severe professional sanctions. In place of a draft provision which gave protection in all cases where criminal or disciplinary proceedings were possible in a third state, the final Convention text allows states to declare that they will respect privileges and duties under the law of third states to the extent specified in the declaration.[121] The United Kingdom has made no such declaration.

(s) Return of executed Letter of Request

The documents establishing the execution of the Letter are to be sent by the requested authority to the requesting authority by the same channel as was used for transmission of the Request. If the Letter is not executed in whole or in part, the requesting authority must be informed immediately.[122] In practice, some states (including the United Kingdom and the United States) always return the documents through their Central Authorities because it enables them to monitor the implementation of the Convention. Other states, in the interests of speed, leave it to the competent authority to return the documents, or to inform the requesting authority that the Letter of Request has not been executed.

(t) Taxes and costs

A state may not claim reimbursement of taxes and costs of any nature for executing a Letter, but it may recover from the requesting state any fees paid to experts and interpreters, as well as the cost of any special procedure requested under article 9.[123] Furthermore, a requested authority, whose law obliges the parties themselves to secure the evidence, and which is not able itself to execute the Letter, may, with the consent of the requesting authority, appoint a suitable person to do so and recover the appropriate costs.[124] The requesting state and not the state seeking the evidence is liable for these costs, and it is of interest that this provision enables a judge of the requesting state to impose an international fiscal obligation on his or her government.

Under article 26 a state may, if required to do so because of constitutional limitations (and on the basis of reciprocity), request reimbursement by the requesting state of fees and costs for the service of process on an unwilling witness and for

---

States. See C L Reyes, 'The US Discovery—EU Data Privacy Directive Conflict' (2009) 19 Duke J Comp & Int L 357.

[120] See *AetD(11)*, Vol 4, pp 60–1, 116–18, 136 and 166–7.
[121] Convention, art 11(2).
[122] Convention, art 13.
[123] Convention, art 14(1)(2).
[124] Convention, art 14(3). This provision enables a common law jurisdiction such as England to recover the fees of private examiners appointed by the court.

the attendance of a witness, and for transcripts or evidence. This provision does not appear to have been formally invoked, but it may prove of particular assistance in some federal systems where there can be constitutional problems in appropriating funds for these expenses.

Certain requested states in fact claim reimbursement of high fees and daily allowances and travel costs of witnesses who have to travel long distances, although these costs should normally be borne by the requested state unless article 26 can be invoked.

2. Taking of evidence by diplomatic officers, consular agents, and commissioners

The drafting of the Convention brought out interesting differences between the common law and civil law countries as to the degree of acceptability of consuls and commissioners. In a common law country, the preparation of a case for trial is the private responsibility of the parties, and so the taking of evidence, without compulsion, by a consul or a commissioner does not necessarily offend such a country's concept of judicial sovereignty; but the position may be very different where, as in many civil law countries, the obtaining of evidence is part of the judicial function, and official permission is be required before the evidence can be taken privately. The Convention, partly drawing on United Kingdom bilateral conventions, sought to harmonize these different concepts by providing a procedural device acceptable to all systems. In so doing, it achieved a successful bridge between the two traditions.

It is convenient to reproduce the summary of the English legal position concerning the taking of evidence by consuls and similar officers, a summary prepared as part of the preliminary work leading up to the Convention:

There is no legal objection to the taking of evidence in England for use outside the jurisdiction without the intervention of the English court. Evidence can be freely taken by agents acting on behalf of foreign litigants; but no compulsory processes may be used, nor may the evidence be taken on oath. A foreign court is at liberty to appoint a consul in England of its own country, or any other person it desires as an examiner to take evidence. So long as the witnesses are willing to attend to give evidence the examination may be completed and the result returned to the foreign court without the intervention of the court in England. The administration of an oath in England without lawful authority is an offence, but a person appointed by order of a foreign court or other judicial authority has the necessary authority by virtue of section 1 of the Oaths and Evidence (Overseas Authorities and Countries) Act 1963, for use in civil proceedings carried on under the law of that country, and a consul may administer an oath under certain other statutory provisions.[125]

Civil law countries take a much stricter line on the permissibility of such actions in their jurisdiction by the agents of foreign courts. For this reason the whole of Chapter II of the Hague Convention, while providing much fuller and clearer

---

[125] *AetD(11)*, Vol 4, pp 41–2. For the 'other statutory provisions', see now the Consular Relations Act 1968, s10.

guidance than the earlier 1954 text, is subject to optional clauses and rights of reservation. Indeed the whole Chapter may be excluded by a reservation under article 33 and several countries have taken this course.[126]

In Chapter II, the reference is only to the taking of 'evidence', which is a well-recognized function of consuls, as reflected, eg in United Kingdom bilateral conventions and in the 1954 Convention, and not the performance of 'other judicial acts' (regarded as exclusively judicial functions). Moreover, the proceedings for which the evidence is required must be actually 'commenced', and not merely 'contemplated'.

(a) Taking of evidence by diplomats and consuls

From nationals of the state the consul represents
The Convention provides first that a diplomatic officer and consular agent may take evidence without compulsion in civil or commercial matters from nationals of the accrediting state in aid of proceedings commenced in the courts of the state represented.[127] However, even the exercise of this right may, by the declaration of the Contracting State in which the evidence is to be taken, be made subject to the permission of the appropriate authority designated by that state.[128] Although several countries have made the declaration requiring permission, many encourage the use of consuls as saving the expense of employing personnel of the receiving state.

From nationals of the host state and of third states
In contrast, article 16 provides that a diplomatic officer or consular agent may only take evidence, without compulsion, of nationals of the state in which he exercises his or her functions, or of third states, if a competent authority in the requested state has given its permission, either generally or in the particular case, and subject to any conditions imposed. A state may, however, by declaration dispense with the need for such permission.[129] Many states have made such declarations, subject, however, to a variety of conditions, mainly requiring the requested state to be informed about, or to be present at, the taking of the evidence. The United Kingdom does not require prior permission, if reciprocity is accorded. The United States does not require advance permission. France has indicated the terms upon which permission will be given, and these include an insistence that the evidence be taken exclusively within the premises of the foreign Embassy or Consulate.

---

[126] They include Argentina, Germany, Singapore, Sri Lanka, and Turkey. Other states (Bulgaria, China, Poland, and Ukraine) have excluded almost the whole of Chapter II except for art 15).
[127] Convention, art 15(1).
[128] Convention, art 15(2).
[129] Convention, art 16(2).

(b) Taking of evidence by commissioners

Commissioners may, without compulsion, take evidence in one state in aid of court proceedings commenced in another state, on the same conditions as apply under article 16.[130] Declarations similar to those referred to in the last paragraph have also been made in this context.

Commissioners may be appointed by a judicial authority of either the requesting or the requested state, and the Convention enables courts to appoint foreign judges as 'commissioners' to examine witnesses directly in their own language and under their own procedures and without the intervention of the local courts.

Some indication of practice under these provisions can be gleaned from the discussions in the Special Commissions on the Convention. So, commissioners have mainly been used by the United States in its relations with France and the United Kingdom. The American authorities appoint as commissioners persons from the United States itself, or American consuls, or judicial authorities or other persons residing in the requested state. This procedure can minimize costs, eg where the alternative would be to transport witnesses to the United States, but, as the French authorities have pointed out, where the request is a straightforward one, it is sometimes cheaper to use a Letter of Request, rather than appoint a commissioner.

(c) Measures of compulsion

A state may declare that a diplomatic officer, consular agent or commissioner may apply to the designated competent authority for 'appropriate' assistance to obtain evidence by compulsion.[131] The declaration may impose conditions. The measures of compulsion will be those prescribed by law for use in internal proceedings.[132] Belarus, Cyprus, the Czech Republic, Greece, Hungary, India, Italy,[133] Serbia, Slovakia, Ukraine, the United Kingdom, and the United States have made the declaration under this article.

States vary in their practice. The United Kingdom and United States can be expected to employ their ordinary procedures for issuing subpoenas or other measures. In contrast, France, which has made no declaration under article 18, will only make compulsion available to a commissioner if he or she is a French judicial authority, appointed as commissioner.

(d) Conditions on grant of permission

In giving permission for diplomats, consuls, or commissioners to take evidence under articles 15–17, or in granting measures of compulsion, the competent

---

[130] Convention, art 17.
[131] Convention, art 18.
[132] Convention, art 18(2).
[133] See Brescia CA, 28 November 1991, 1992 Rev dir i p proc 397 (Asser 5/383).

authority of the state in which the evidence is to be taken may prescribe such conditions as it deems fit, including the time and place of the taking of evidence and the giving of reasonable advance notice of hearing.[134] So, a representative of the authority is entitled to be present at the taking of the evidence; for example, the authority may wish to ensure that there is no infringement of its state's sovereignty or security, or to uphold privileges of the witness. Examples of other conditions might be to limit the scope and subject matter of the examination, to specify the persons who may be present at the taking of the evidence other than the parties and the witnesses, and to limit the right to enter and inspect real property. These conditions may not affect the following provisions as to legal representation and certain other matters.

(e) Legal representation

Persons concerned in the taking of evidence under Chapter II of the Convention may be legally represented.[135] They would, no doubt, include the parties and witnesses, but whether others such as the employer of a witness, or an insurance company, would be so entitled, is not clear.

(f) Administrative rules

The diplomatic officer or consular agent or commissioner may take all kinds of evidence which are not incompatible with local law or contrary to any permission granted and, within such limits, they may administer oaths. (The power to administer oaths may thus be limited, where local law provides that only judges and notaries may administer oaths.) A request to a person to appear or to give evidence must be in the language of the place where the evidence is to be taken, unless the witness is a national of the requesting state. The person must be told that he or she may be legally represented. If the requested state has not filed a declaration under article 18, and measures of compulsion are not available by other means under internal law, the request must state that the person concerned is not compelled to appear or to give evidence. The evidence may be taken in the manner provided by the law of the requesting state if this is not forbidden in the requested state. The privileges and duties to refuse to give evidence contained in article 11[136] are also available under Chapter II.[137] As any privilege to refuse to give evidence can be invoked by witnesses, the 'commission' or other document appointing the diplomatic officer or consular agent or commissioner should contain the necessary details about such privilege.

---

[134] Convention, art 19.   [135] Convention, art 20.
[136] See pp 98–99.   [137] Convention, art 21.

II. Council Regulation No 1206/2001

In 2001 the European Union adopted a Council Regulation on co-operation between the courts of the Member States in the taking of evidence in civil or commercial matters.[138] This was one of the many actions which followed from the decisions of the European Council held in Tampere in October 1999. The Regulation came fully into effect on 1 January 2004.[139] A *Practice Guide*, produced in consultation with the European Judicial Network, was published in 2005.

As the account which follows will make clear, the Regulation builds on the Hague Convention of 1970, the Recitals noting as part of the justification for the making of the Regulation that only eleven of the existing Member States were parties to the Hague instrument.[140] A major difference is that the Regulation provides for the direct transmission of requests from court to court, dispensing with the Central Authorities which are such an important feature of the Hague Convention, though preserving a limited role for what are termed 'central bodies'. It was felt that direct communication from court to court would be the most effective method; as the Recitals note: 'The efficiency of judicial procedures in civil or commercial matters requires that the transmission and execution of requests for the performance of taking of evidence is to be made directly and by the most rapid means possible between Member States' courts.'[141]

The Regulation prevails over other provisions contained in bilateral or multilateral agreements or arrangements concluded by the Member States and in particular the Hague Convention.[142] It does not preclude Member States from maintaining or concluding agreements or arrangements between two or more of them to further facilitate the taking of evidence, provided that they are compatible with the Regulation.[143]

1. Scope

The Regulation applies in civil or commercial matters (a phrase not further defined, but on which the jurisprudence of the European Court in the context of jurisdictional rules will be relevant)[144] where the court of a Member State (except Denmark),[145] in accordance with the provisions of the law of that state, requests (a) the competent court of another Member State to take evidence; or (b) to take evidence directly in another Member State.[146] As in the Hague Convention, it is provided

---

[138] Council Regulation (EC) No 1206/2001 of 28 May 2001, OJ L174, 27.6.2001.
[139] Regulation, art 24(2).
[140] Recital (6). The relevant provisions of the Hague Convention may be relied on in order to interpret the Regulation: Case C-283/09 *Weryński v Mediatel 4B spółka z o o* (ECJ, 17 February 2011).
[141] Recital (8).
[142] Regulation, art 21(1). It prevails also over the Hague Convention on Civil Procedure of 1954.
[143] Regulation, art 21(2).
[144] Cf pp 33–34, above.
[145] See Recital (12) and art 1(3).   [146] Regulation, art 1(1).

that a request shall not be made to obtain evidence which is not intended for use in judicial proceedings, commenced or contemplated.[147] As the *Practice Guide* observes, the concept of 'evidence' is not defined, but it includes hearings of witnesses of fact, of the parties, of experts, the production of documents, verifications, and the establishment of facts.[148] The Commission noted in 2007 significantly diverging interpretations of what is considered as 'evidence', in particular with respect to taking DNA and blood samples.[149] It was held in *Dendron GmbH v Regents of the University of California*[150] that the Regulation had a limited purpose: it could not be used for the purpose of obtaining evidence for use in non-judicial proceedings, not to obtain evidence and documents for use in criminal proceedings, or in any proceedings in a state outside the European Union or in Denmark. The limited purpose of the Regulation was matched by a limitation on the power to use material produced under it, so that any collateral use outside that limited purpose is prohibited save with the permission of the requesting court or the person or parties from whom the evidence is being sought.

The Regulation contains no special provision as to 'pre-trial discovery';[151] the problems caused by the extensive discovery practices in the United States and some other countries do not arise between Member States, and it was judged sufficient to rely on the general language of the Regulation.

The possibly mandatory or exclusive nature of the Regulation was examined by the Court of Appeal in *Masri v Consolidated Contractors International (UK) Ltd and others (No 4)*.[152] In that case, a judgment creditor obtained an order under CPR r 71.2 for an officer of the company, domiciled in Greece, to be examined in England in respect of the company's foreign assets. On appeal against the order, arguments were advanced reminiscent of those deployed in the United States cases.[153] It was argued for the appellant that Regulation 1206/2001 exhaustively covered the possible ways in which evidence could be sought by a court of one Member State in the territory of another Member State; it was a complete code for the taking of evidence between Regulation states. It was argued that an application against a non-party for an order that he should travel from another Member State and bring documents from another Member State amounted to obtaining evidence from, and indeed in, the territory of another Member State, and thus fell within the scope of, or is a matter that should be dealt with under, the Regulation. Article 1 was to be broadly interpreted as including an order for evidence to be obtained from but not in another Member State. Moreover, the Regulation contained important

---

[147] Regulation, art 1(2).

[148] *Practice Guide*, para 8.

[149] Report from the Commission to the Council, the European Parliament and the European Economic and Social Committee on the application of the Council Regulation (EC) 1206/2001 of 28 May 2001 on co-operation between the courts of the Member States in the taking of evidence in civil or commercial matters, COM(2007) 769 final, para 2.9.

[150] [2004] EWHC 589 (Ch), [2004] ILPr 35.

[151] Cf the Hague position: pp 84–88, above.

[152] [2008] EWCA Civ 876, [2010] 1 AC 90, HL. See A Nuyts, 'Le règlement communautaire sur l'obtention des preuves: un instrument exclusif?' (2007) Rev crit de d i p 53.

[153] See pp 77–79.

protections for addressees and the sovereignty of the receiving state[154] which are not to be circumvented by taking evidence outside its provisions.

In support of the order appealed from, it was argued that Regulation 1206/2001 only applied where the English court wished to take evidence in another Member State and not where the English court, acting under a provision of national law, required the provision of evidence or information in England from a party over whom it had jurisdiction to grant such an order. The Court of Appeal accepted this argument.[155] The safeguards in the Regulation were simply irrelevant: the Regulation admittedly did not apply where evidence was sought from a person already a party to litigation, as for example by an order for *inter partes* disclosure, and the instant context was seen as analogous.

In the House of Lords, it was held that an order under CPR r 71.2 was not available on the facts, and points concerning the Regulation were not reached.

A rather different point concerns the relationship between Regulation 1206/2001 and the power to take provisional or protective measures under what is now article 31 of Regulation 44/2001, the Brussels I Regulation. This reads:

Application may be made to the courts of a Member State for such provisional, including protective, measures as may be available under the law of that state, even if, under this Regulation, the courts of another Member State have jurisdiction as to the substance of the matter.

In *St Paul Dairy Industries NV v Unibel Exser BVBA*[156] there was an application in the Netherlands to take a deposition there with a view to its use in the substantive proceedings in Belgium. The European Court of Justice held that a request for a deposition was not a claim for provisional or protective measures. This can be contrasted with the facts in *Tedesco v Tomasoni Fittings SrL*:[157] here a request was made under the Brussels I Regulation for the description of an allegedly patent-infringing product. The case was withdrawn before the European Court was able to give judgment, but Advocate General Kokott published an opinion that this was a matter within Regulation 1206/2001, one of evidence. Steps to secure the substance of a claim were provisional or protective measures under Brussels I; procedural measures to secure or preserve evidence were for Regulation 1206/2001.[158]

2. Transmission of requests

Requests are to be transmitted by the court before which the proceedings are commenced or contemplated, 'the requesting court', directly to the competent

---

[154] Regulation, arts 5, 10(2), 10(4), 17(2), 17(4).

[155] Following a decision to the same effect in earlier proceedings before Gloster J: *Masri v Consolidated Contractors International (UK) Ltd (No 2)* [2007] EWHC 3010 (Comm), [2008] 1 All ER (Comm) 305 (not in issue in the appeal against that decision).

[156] Case C-104/83, [2005] ECR I-3481.

[157] Case C-175/06, (2008) 8 Eur L F I-42.

[158] See J van Hein, 'Drawing the Line between Brussels I and the Evidence Regulation', (2008) 8 Eur L F I-34; A Rushworth, 'Demarcating the Boundary between the Brussels I Regulation and the Evidence Regulation', [2009] LMCLQ 196.

court of another Member State, 'the requested court', for the performance of the taking of evidence.[159] For this procedure to be effective, information must be available as to the competent courts in each Member State: which court, for example, has jurisdiction in respect of commercial matters in, say, Barcelona? To make this possible, each Member State must draw up a list of the courts competent for the performance of taking of evidence under the Regulation, indicating the territorial and, where appropriate, the special jurisdiction of those courts.[160]

Requests are not normally routed via any central agency in the requested state, but each Member State must designate a 'central body' (or in federal and composite states more than one such body)[161] responsible for (a) supplying information to the courts; (b) seeking solutions to any difficulties which may arise in respect of a request; and (c) forwarding, 'in exceptional cases', at the request of a requesting court, a request to the competent court.[162] One type of request may be routed through a central body: this is a request for the direct taking of evidence by the requesting court under article 17, considered further below.

3. Contents of requests

The Regulation contains an Annex of Forms which specify the detailed information to be provided. Form A is the standard form for requesting the taking of evidence by the requested court; Form I is for use when the requesting court seeks to take evidence directly in the territory of the requested state. In each case the request contains the identity of the relevant courts; the names and addresses of the parties to the proceedings and their representatives, if any; the nature and subject matter of the case and a brief statement of the facts; a description of the taking of evidence to be performed; where the request is for the examination of a person, that person's name and address, the questions to be put or a statement of the facts about which the person is to be examined; where appropriate, a reference to a right to refuse to testify under the law of the requesting state;[163] any requirement that the examination is to be carried out under oath or affirmation in lieu thereof, and any special form to be used; and any other information that the requesting court deems necessary.[164]

Requests and other communications sent under the Regulation must be in the official language of the requested state or, if there are several official languages in that state, in the official language or one of the official languages of the place where the requested taking of evidence is to be performed, or in another language which

---

[159] Regulation, art 2(1).

[160] Regulation, art 2(2). The information is available on the website of the European Judicial Network; see arts 19, 22.

[161] Regulation, art 3(2).

[162] Regulation, art 3(1).

[163] The Regulation uses in this and other contexts the cumbersome phrase 'the law of the Member State of the requesting (or requested) court', presumably to deal with federal and other composite states in which the location of the court within the state will determine the applicable law. There is no 'federal clause', the alternative device for dealing with such cases.

[164] See Regulation, art 4(1).

the requested state has indicated it can accept.[165] Any documents which the requesting court deems it necessary to enclose for the execution of the request must be accompanied by a translation into the language in which the request was written.[166]

Requests and other communications are to be transmitted by the swiftest possible means that the requested state has indicated it can accept: in many cases this will include electronic means. The only essential is that the document received accurately reflects the content of the document forwarded and that all information in it is legible.[167]

If the request is complete and otherwise in order, the requested court is to send within seven days an acknowledgement of receipt to the requesting court using a prescribed form, Form B in the Annex.[168] There are detailed procedural rules as to what is to be done if the requested court lacks competence in the matter, or the request is incomplete or not accompanied by the deposit or advance required in certain cases.[169]

4. Execution of requests

In the more usual case involving taking of evidence by the requested court, that court is to execute the request without delay and, at the latest, within ninety days of receipt of the request.[170] The Commission reported in 2007 that most requests for the taking of evidence were executed within this ninety-day limit, but that there was also a significant number of cases in which that limit was exceeded, some cases taking even more than six months.[171] If the requested court is not in a position to execute the request within ninety days of receipt, it must inform the requesting court, using a form prescribed in the Annex, explaining the reasons and giving an estimated time for the execution of the request.[172] The request is to be executed in accordance with the law of the requested state; if, however the request is for the use of a special procedure provided for by the law of the requesting state or the use of communications technology for a videoconference or teleconference, this procedure will be used unless it is incompatible with the law of the requested state or by reason of 'major practical difficulties'.[173] Special forms are provided for use in these cases.

---

[165] Regulation, art 5.

[166] Regulation, art 4(3).

[167] Regulation, art 6.

[168] Regulation, art 7.

[169] Regulation, arts 8 and 9. For the deposit or advance, see art 18(3), considered below.

[170] Regulation, art 10(1).

[171] Report from the Commission to the Council, the European Parliament and the European Economic and Social Committee on the application of the Council Regulation (EC) 1206/2001 of 28 May 2001 on cooperation between the courts of the Member States in the taking of evidence in civil or commercial matters, COM(2007) 769 final, para 2.1.

[172] Regulation, art 15.

[173] Regulation, art 10(2)(3)(4). The Commission's 2007 report noted that technology of this sort was actually used to a very limited extent: para 2.4.

5. Attendance and participation of parties and representatives

As in the Hague Convention, the Regulation contains provisions allowing the presence of the parties and their representatives if any, and of representatives of the requesting court (defined to include the judicial personnel or other persons such as experts in each case as designated by the requesting court).[174] Such presence will be allowed if it is provided for in (or in the case of representatives of the requesting court, is compatible with) the law of the requested state: it is for the requested court to settle the conditions under which the persons attending may participate in the proceedings.[175]

6. Coercive measures

Where necessary, in executing a request the requested court is to apply the appropriate coercive measures in the instances and to the extent as are provided for by the law of the requested state for the execution of a request made for the same purpose by its national authorities or one of the parties concerned.[176]

7. Privileges of witnesses

Where the request involves testimony by a witness,[177] it is not to be executed when the person concerned claims the right to refuse to give evidence or to be prohibited from giving evidence (a) under the law of the requested state; or (b) under the law of the requesting state, where that right has been specified in the request, or, if need be, at the instance of the requested court, has been confirmed by the requesting court.[178] There is no provision, such as exists in the Hague Convention,[179] relating to privileges or prohibitions under the law of third states.

8. Other grounds for refusing to execute a request

The only other grounds on which the execution of a request may be refused are that (a) the request does not fall within the scope of the Regulation; or (b) the execution of the request under the law of the requested state does not fall within the functions of the judiciary; or (c) the requesting court fails to repair the omissions in an incomplete request within thirty days of being asked to do so; or (d) a deposit or advance is not made within sixty days after the requested court asked for one.[180]

---

[174] Regulation, arts 11 and 12.
[175] Regulation, art 10(3), 11(4).
[176] Regulation, art 13.
[177] The Regulation uses the quaint language 'implies that a person shall be heard'.
[178] Regulation, art 14(1).
[179] See p 99.
[180] Regulation, art 14(2).

Execution may not be refused by the requested court solely on the ground that under the law of the requested state a court of that state has exclusive jurisdiction over the subject matter of the action or that the law of that state would not admit the right of action on it.[181]

9. Costs

The general principle is that the execution of a request is not to give rise to a claim for any reimbursement of taxes or costs.[182] The terms 'taxes' and 'costs' are given an autonomous meaning: 'taxes' means sums received by the court for carrying out its functions, and 'costs' are the sums paid by the court to third parties in the course of proceedings, in particular to experts or witnesses.[183] Nevertheless, if the requested court so requires, the requesting court must ensure the reimbursement, without delay, of the fees paid to experts and interpreters, and the costs occasioned by the use at the request of the requesting court of a special procedure or of communications technology.[184] Where the opinion of an expert is required (and only in such cases), the requested court may, before executing the request, ask the requesting court for an adequate deposit or advance towards the requested costs.[185] Whether the parties must bear these fees or costs or make the deposit or advance is a matter for the law of the requesting state.[186]

In the *Weryński* case,[187] a Polish court requested an Irish court to take evidence from a witness. Under Irish law, witnesses can only be required to give evidence if they are paid their expenses in advance. The issues taken to the European Court were whether the Irish court could require the Polish court to pay these sums, either in advance or by way of reimbursement. The court held that to impose a requirement of an advance payment would amount to a rejection of the request and none of the grounds allowing such refusal applied. So far as reimbursement was concerned, the text of the regulation dealt only with experts and not other witnesses; drawing on article 14 of the Hague Convention, the court held that witness expenses could not be claimed from the Polish court.

10. Procedure after execution of request

The requested court is to send without delay to the requesting court the documents establishing the execution of the request and, where appropriate, return the documents received from the requesting court. The documents are to be accompanied by a confirmation of execution using a form prescribed in the Annex.

---

[181] Regulation, art 14(4).
[182] Regulation, art 18(1).
[183] Case C-283/09 *Weryński v Mediatel 4B spółka z o o* [2011] 3 WLR 1316 (ECJ).
[184] Regulation, art 18(2).
[185] Regulation, art 18(3).
[186] Regulation, art 18(2)(3).
[187] Case C-283/09 *Weryński v Mediatel 4B spółka z o o* [2011] 3 WLR 1316 (ECJ).

11. Direct taking of evidence by the requesting court

The Regulation makes an advance on the Hague text by including developed provisions as to the taking by the requesting court of evidence on the territory of another Member State.[188] In this type of case, the request is submitted to the designated central body of the requested state. The direct taking of evidence may only take place if it can be performed on a voluntary basis without the need for coercive measures.[189] Where the direct taking of evidence means that a witness is required to testify, the requesting court must inform the person concerned that this can only be on a voluntary basis. The evidence is taken by a member of the judicial personnel of the requesting court or by any other person such as an expert, designated in accordance with the law of requesting state.

When a request is received by a central body it must, within thirty days, inform the requesting court if the request is accepted and, if necessary, under what conditions according to the law of its state such performance is to be carried out. The central body may assign a court to take part in the taking of evidence in order to ensure the proper application of the Regulation and the conditions that have been set out. The central body is directed by the Regulation to encourage the use of communications technology, such as videoconferences and teleconferences.[190] The central body may refuse direct taking of evidence only if (a) the request does not fall within the scope of the Regulation; (b) the request does not contain all of the necessary information; or (c) the direct taking of evidence requested is contrary to fundamental principles of law in the requested state.[191] Subject to the conditions laid down, the requesting court executes the request in accordance with the law of that state.[192]

III. Inter-American Instruments

The Organization of American States through its Specialized Conference on Private International Law has produced the Inter-American Convention on the taking of Evidence Abroad of 1975[193] and the Additional Protocol to that Convention, agreed in 1984.[194]

---

[188] Little used in practice: see the Commission's 2007 report, para 2.7.
[189] Regulation, art 17(2).
[190] Regulation, art 17(4).
[191] Regulation, art 17(5).
[192] Regulation, art 17(6).
[193] As at March 2011 this had 15 States Parties: Argentina, Chile, Colombia, Costa Rica, Dominican Republic, Ecuador, El Salvador, Guatemala, Honduras, Mexico, Panama, Paraguay, Peru, Uruguay, and Venezuela.
[194] Only five states have become parties to the Additional Protocol: Argentina, Ecuador, Mexico, Uruguay, and Venezuela.

1. The Inter-American Convention

The Convention deals with letters rogatory issued in conjunction with proceedings in civil or commercial matters for the purpose of taking evidence or obtaining information abroad and addressed by a judicial authority of one of the States Parties to the convention to the competent authority of another.[195] Such letters rogatory are to be executed in accordance with the terms of the convention, provided that the procedure requested is not contrary to legal provisions in the state of destination that expressly prohibit it, and provided also that the interested party places at the disposal of the authority of the state of destination the financial and other means necessary to secure compliance with the request.[196]

The authority of the state of destination is given jurisdiction over disputes arising in connection with the execution of the measure requested, and may apply the measures of compulsion provided for in its law.[197] More generally, letters rogatory concerning the taking of evidence are to be executed in accordance with the laws and procedural rules of the state of destination.[198] At the request of the authority issuing the letter rogatory, the authority of the state of destination may accept the observance of additional formalities or special procedures in performing the act requested, unless the observance of those procedures or of those formalities is contrary to the laws of the state of destination or impossible of performance.[199]

Letters rogatory may be transmitted to the authority to which they are addressed through judicial channels, diplomatic or consular agents, or the Central Authority of the state of origin or of the state of destination, as the case may be.[200] A letter rogatory must be legalized, unless it is transmitted or returned through consular or diplomatic channels or through the Central Authority;[201] and the letter itself and the appended documentation must be translated into the official language of the state of destination.[202]

Article 9 of the Convention follows article 23 of the Hague Convention in declaring that the authority of the state of destination may refuse execution of a letter rogatory whose purpose is the taking of evidence prior to judicial proceedings or 'pretrial discovery of documents' as the procedure is known in Common Law

---

[195] Convention, art 2; see art 1 for an explanation of the terms used in the different language versions of the convention, which are in Spanish, English, French, and Portuguese; and art 4 for the prescribed contents of the letter.

[196] Convention, art 2.

[197] Convention, art 3.

[198] Convention, art 5.

[199] Convention, art 6.

[200] Convention, art 11.

[201] Convention, arts 10(1), 13. Not every State Party seems to have designated a Central Authority. Central Authorities are in El Salvador and Guatemala the Supreme Court of Justice; in Chile, Ecuador, Mexico, and Panama within the Foreign Ministry; and in Uruguay in the Ministry of Education and Culture.

[202] Convention, art 10(2).

countries. The state of destination may also refuse to execute a letter rogatory that is manifestly contrary to its public policy ('*ordre public*').[203]

The costs and other expenses involved in the processing and execution of letters rogatory are to be borne by the interested parties, but the state of destination is given a discretion to execute a letter rogatory that does not indicate the person to be held responsible for costs and other expenses.[204]

A person called to give evidence in the state of destination pursuant to a letter rogatory may refuse to do so when he or she invokes impediment, exception, or duty to refuse to testify under the law of the state of destination; or under the law of the state of origin, if the invoked impediment, exception, or duty to refuse has been specified in the letter rogatory or has been confirmed by the requesting authority at the instance of the court of destination.[205]

The Convention declares that execution of letters rogatory is not to imply ultimate recognition of the jurisdiction of the authority issuing the letter rogatory or a commitment to recognize the validity of the judgment it may render or to execute it.[206]

2. The Additional Protocol of 1984

Only five states have become parties to the Additional Protocol, and most did so with reservations.[207] The Additional Protocol made it mandatory for States Parties to designate a Central Authority;[208] the matter was unclear in the Convention itself. It also introduced prescribed forms for a letter rogatory and for a certificate by which the Central Authority of the state of designation attests to the execution or non-execution of the letter.

The Additional Protocol sets out, in much greater detail than the Convention, the procedure for the sending and processing of a letter rogatory seeking the taking of evidence.[209] In particular it provides that the judicial or other adjudicatory authority of the state of origin may request notice of the date, time, and place of the execution of a letter rogatory. The judicial or other adjudicatory authority of the state of destination that will execute the letter must then provide that information to the judicial or other adjudicatory authority of the state of origin, as requested. The legal representatives of the parties or their lawyers may attend the execution of the letter, their intervention being subject to the law of the state of destination.[210]

The rules as to costs and expenses are revised. The processing of letters rogatory by the Central Authority of the state of destination and by its judicial or other adjudicatory authorities is to be free of charge. However, this state may seek payment by the party requesting the evidence or information for those services

---

[203] Convention, art 16.   [204] Convention, art 7.   [205] Convention, art 12.
[206] Convention, art 8. When it signed the Convention, Mexico made a declaration that it understood art 8 to refer to the international validity of foreign judgments.
[207] Argentina, Ecuador, Mexico, Uruguay, and Venezuela; the reservations are noted in the following footnotes.
[208] Additional Protocol, art 1.
[209] Additional Protocol, arts 3–5.   [210] Additional Protocol, art 5.

which, in accordance with its local law, are required to be paid for directly by that party.[211] Each State Party has to provide a schedule of services, itemizing the pertinent costs and expenses that, in accordance with its local law, must be paid for directly by the party requesting the evidence or information.[212]

The Additional Protocol also regulates the taking of evidence by diplomatic or consular agents, which may be limited to taking evidence from persons of the nationality of the state accrediting the agent. The agent himself may not use measures of compulsion but may ask the appropriate judicial authority of the state of destination to use the measures of compulsion available under the law of that state.[213]

Article 16 of the Additional Protocol deals, without using the term, with discovery of documents:

The States Parties to this Protocol shall process a letter rogatory that requests the exhibition and copying of documents if it meets the following requirements:

The proceeding has been initiated;

The documents are reasonably identified by date, contents, or other appropriate information; and

The letter rogatory specifies those facts and circumstances causing the requesting party reasonably to believe that the requested documents are or were in the possession, control, or custody of, or are known to the person from whom the documents are requested.

The person from whom documents are requested may, where appropriate, deny that he has possession, control, or custody of the requested documents, or may object to the exhibition and copying of the documents, in accordance with the rules of the Convention.

At the time of signing, ratifying or acceding to this Protocol a State may declare that it will process the letters rogatory to which this article applies only if they identify the relationship between the evidence or information requested and the pending proceeding.[214]

IV. English practice

1. Evidence in England for use in foreign proceedings

(a) Requests from Regulation states

Where a request is received in England from another EU Member State under Regulation 1206/2001,[215] it is dealt with in accordance with that Regulation and rule 34.24 of the Civil Procedure Rules. The court may order an examination to be

---

[211] Additional Protocol, art 6.

[212] Additional Protocol, arts 7, 8. Mexico and Venezuela declared, however, that the parties must defray experts' fees, the costs of personnel and any apparatuses required, expenditures caused to third parties, and payment of legal fees for the issuance of copies and other documents.

[213] Additional Protocol, arts 9–13. Argentina and Brazil entered reservations against all these articles; Chile against arts 11–13. Mexico made a detailed declaration qualifying the effect of this part of the Additional Protocol.

[214] Brazil entered a reservation against art 16. Mexico and Venezuela made the declaration referred to in the final paragraph.

[215] See pp 104–111.

taken before (a) any fit and proper person nominated by the person applying for the order; (b) an examiner of the court; or (c) any other person whom the court considers suitable.[216]

(b) Other cases

Jurisdiction to deal with requests from other states is governed exclusively by the Evidence (Proceedings in Other Jurisdictions) Act 1975. Although its text nowhere mentions the Hague Convention, this was enacted to enable the United Kingdom to ratify the Convention. The Act is drafted so as to apply to any foreign state.

The Act gives certain powers to the High Court where an application is made for an order for evidence to be obtained in England, and the court is satisfied that the application is made in pursuance of a request[217] issued by or on behalf of a court or tribunal[218] exercising jurisdiction in another part of the United Kingdom or some other country,[219] and that the evidence sought is to be obtained for the purposes of civil proceedings[220] which have either been instituted before the requesting court or whose institution is contemplated.[221] The English courts afford foreign courts all the assistance they can: 'It is the duty and the pleasure of the English courts to do all it can to assist the foreign court, just as it would expect the foreign court to help it in like circumstances.'[222] The English court will not investigate the likely relevance of the evidence sought to issues raised in the foreign proceedings, regarding that as a matter for the foreign court (which will not have made its request without due consideration).[223]

The court, in practice a Master, can make an appropriate order to give effect to the request underlying the application.[224] Such orders may make provision for the examination of witnesses, either orally or in writing; for the production of documents; for the inspection, photographing, preservation, custody, or detention of any property; for the taking of samples of any property and the carrying out of any experiments on or with any property; for the medical examination of any person; and for the taking and testing of samples of blood from any person.[225]

---

[216] CPR, r 34.18, applied by r 34.24.

[217] Including any commission, order, or other process (Evidence (Proceedings in Other Jurisdictions) Act 1975, s 9(1)) as well as a Letter of Request.

[218] Cf the Convention term 'judicial authority': p 91.

[219] Or by the Court of Justice of the European Communities: Evidence (European Court) Order 1976, SI 1976 No 428.

[220] Defined to mean proceedings in any civil or commercial matter: Evidence (Proceedings in Other Jurisdictions) Act 1975, s 9(1) and see pp 88–91.

[221] Evidence (Proceedings in Other Jurisdictions) Act 1975, s 1. Cf *Re International Power Industries Inc, The Times*, 25 July 1984.

[222] *Genira Trade & Finance Inc v Refco Capital Markets Ltd* [2001] EWCA Civ 1733, citing Lord Denning MR in *Rio Tinto Zinc Corporation v Westinghouse Electric Corporation* [1978] AC 547 (HL) at 560.

[223] *Rio Tinto Zinc Corporation v Westinghouse Electric Corporation* [1978] AC 547 (HL); *Re Asbestos Insurance Coverage Cases* [1985] 1 WLR 331 (HL).

[224] Evidence (Proceedings in Other Jurisdictions) Act 1975, s 2(1).

[225] Ibid, s 2(2).

Under the Convention, a requested state is to apply the same measures of compulsion as would be available in purely domestic cases;[226] this is reflected in the provision in section 2(3) of the Act that an order under that section may not require any particular steps to be taken unless they are steps which can be required to be taken by way of obtaining evidence for the purposes of civil proceedings in the court making the order, ie, the High Court.[227] To this there is one exception, to comply with article 9 of the Convention:[228] an order may be made that a person should give evidence otherwise than on oath where this is asked for by the requesting court.[229]

Section 2(3) was not referred to in the judgment in *J Barber & Sons v Lloyd's Underwriters*,[230] where despite the opposition of the defendants it was ordered that the taking of depositions before an examiner of the court should, as had been requested by the foreign court, be videotaped. Evans J held that a request by the foreign court for a particular mode of examination to be followed should be complied with, in the exercise of discretion, unless what was asked for was so contrary to English established procedures that it should not be permitted. However much in the spirit of the Convention, this ruling is not altogether easy to reconcile with the language of the Act. A more straightforward illustration of the effect of section 2(3) is provided by the Scottish case of *Re Lord Advocate, Petitioner*.[231] The plaintiffs in proceedings in Texas hoped to establish that an aircraft accident had been caused by the flight crew misinterpreting warning lights on the aircraft's instrument panel. They sought to have evidence taken from a representative of the aircraft manufacturers as to their experience of misinterpretations of such lights on their aircraft. The Court of Session regarded this as an attempt to obtain, by means of pre-trial discovery, material which might lead to a line of enquiry which in turn might reveal relevant documents or other evidence. Such an order could not be made in Scottish litigation, and section 2(3) therefore prevented the Letter of Request being complied with.

An order may not be made under section 2 requiring a person to state what documents relevant to the proceedings to which the application relates are, or have been, in his or her possession, custody, or power; or to produce any documents other than particular documents specified in the order as being documents appearing to the High Court to be, or to be likely to be, in his or her possession, custody, or power.[232] This provision reflects the language of the reservation made by the United Kingdom under article 23 of the Convention, the origins and effect of which have already been discussed.[233] So far as the production of documents is

---

[226] See pp 97–98.
[227] For the implications of this for requests that corporations should give evidence see *Penn-Texas Corpn v Murat Anstalt* [1964] 1 QB 40 (CA) and *Penn-Texas Corpn v Murat Anstalt (No 2)* [1964] 2 QB 647 (CA), both decided under the Foreign Tribunals Evidence Act 1856.
[228] See p 96.
[229] Evidence (Proceedings in Other Jurisdictions) Act 1975, s 2(3).
[230] [1987] QB 103.
[231] 1998 SC 87.
[232] Evidence (Proceedings in Other Jurisdictions) Act 1975, s 2(4).
[233] See pp 84–88.

concerned much attention has focused on the words 'particular documents specified in the order'. This phrase is to be given a strict construction;[234] to avoid
countenancing 'fishing expeditions', the documents must be either individual
documents separately described or documents falling within a compendious description which nonetheless indicates the exact documents required.[235] Requests
for classes or categories of documents, as distinct from particular documents, are
excluded; it has been suggested that 'the moment it becomes necessary to include in
the request the words "if any" or similar, then it is almost bound to be fatal'.[236]
A request too widely drawn can sometimes be acted upon in part, the court striking
out the parts which are unacceptable; but the court will not undertake the task of
redrafting the request.[237]

The notion of 'fishing expedition' is not readily applicable where oral evidence is
to be taken.[238] In relation to oral evidence, a request can be accepted where the
intention was to obtain evidence for use at trial and there was reason to believe that
the person had knowledge of matters relevant to issues at trial.[239] In the typical case
oral examination relates almost exclusively to the requested documents, so, if
the documents are not properly sought, oral examination falls away,[240] but in
some cases the oral evidence can be regarded as free-standing and can proceed even
if the request in relation to documents is refused on the grounds of 'fishing'. The
court may, however, impose conditions, eg that 'the examination of witnesses shall
be for the purpose only of eliciting and recording testimony appropriate to be given
at trial' and that 'no question may be asked of the witness that in the opinion of the
examiner is not a question of the nature that could properly be asked by counsel
examining a witness-in-chief at a trial before the High Court of England and
Wales'.[241]

An order under section 2 may also not be made if it is shown that the request
infringes the jurisdiction of the United Kingdom or is otherwise prejudicial to the
United Kingdom; on these matters a certificate of the Secretary of State is conclusive.[242] This last provision, part of the United Kingdom's 'blocking statute', builds
upon the opinions in the House of Lords in the *Westinghouse* case,[243] where the

---

[234] *Rio Tinto Zinc Corporation v Westinghouse Electric Corporation* [1978] AC 547 (HL) per Lord
Wilberforce at 609 and Lord Diplock at 635; *Re Asbestos Insurance Coverage Cases* [1985] 1 WLR 331
(HL) per Lord Fraser at 337–8.
[235] eg, 'monthly bank statements for the year 1984 relating to [a specified] account'; but not 'all X's
bank statements for 1984': *Re Asbestos Insurance Coverage Cases* [1985] 1 WLR 331 (HL) per Lord
Fraser at 337–8.
[236] Per Evans LJ in *Conopco Inc v Ernst and Young*, unreported, 1 September 1993 (CA).
[237] See *Boeing Co v PPG Industries Inc* [1988] 3 All ER 839 (CA); *Genira Trade & Finance Inc v
Refco Capital Markets Ltd* [2001] EWCA Civ 1733.
[238] *Re State of Norway's Application (No 2)* [1990] 1 AC 723, at 781 per Woolf LJ.
[239] *First American Corporation v Zayed* [1999] 1 WLR 1154; *Windh v Land Rover North America
Inc* [2005] EWHC 432 (QB); *Charman v Charman* [2005] EWCA Civ 1606, [2006] 1 WLR 1053.
[240] *Netbank v Commercial Money Center* [2004] Bda LR 46 (Sup Ct Bermuda), cited with approval
in *Charman v Charman* [2005] EWCA Civ 1606, [2006] 1 WLR 1053.
[241] *Golden Eagle Refinery Co Inc v Associated International Insurance Co* (CA, unreported,
19 February 1998).
[242] Protection of Trading Interests Act 1980, s 4.
[243] *Rio Tinto Zinc Corporation v Westinghouse Electric Corporation* [1978] AC 547 (HL).

Attorney-General intervened to express the policy of the Government against the recognition of investigatory orders made in the United States against UK companies. If an order is made, a person is not to be compelled to give evidence where this would be prejudicial to the security of the United Kingdom; here again, a certificate of the Secretary of State is conclusive.[244]

Provision is made as to claims of privilege in section 3 of the Act. Where the claim arises under the law of the requesting state, and is neither supported by material in the request nor conceded by the applicant for the order, the court may order that the evidence be taken, but the evidence is not transmitted to the requesting court if that court, on the matter being referred to it, upholds the claim.[245]

Section 9 of the Act precludes the English court from making an order for the taking of evidence addressed to 'any person in his capacity as an officer or servant of the Crown'. A broad interpretation was given to this provision in *Re Pan American World Airways Inc's Application*.[246] In litigation arising out of the Lockerbie air disaster, the applicants sought an order under the 1975 Act for the examination of a forensic scientist who had examined the explosive device which caused the crash as part of his duties in the Ministry of Defence. The particular point that arose was that the scientist was now retired, and so no longer a Crown servant. The Court of Appeal held that the relevant time for the purposes of section 9(4) was the time the information was obtained by the proposed witness (and so when he examined the device) and not the time at which he was asked to give evidence. There was therefore no power to order him to give evidence.

2. Evidence from abroad for use in England

Quite apart from the courts' power to order the taking of evidence out of the jurisdiction, which is considered below,[247] there are various procedures available during the pre-trial phase which lead to the exposure of information or material relevant to the matter in hand. Where the information concerns, or the material consists of, property outside the jurisdiction, the effect of the procedures is akin to the taking of evidence abroad.

There has been no profound analysis of the precise basis for the English court making orders which have, in this sense, an extra-territorial effect. It has, however, long been recognized that the court can exercise jurisdiction *in personam* against an individual present in England or capable of being made a party to English proceedings in cases in which Equity so requires, even where the subject matter is foreign immovable property.[248] A court must be able to exercise

---

[244] Evidence (Proceedings in Other Jurisdictions) Act 1975, s 3(3).

[245] Ibid, s 3(2). See on the procedure to be followed where other objections are raised in the course of the examination, *R v Rathbone, ex p Dikko* [1985] QB 630.

[246] [1992] 1 QB 854 (CA).   [247] See pp 124–132.

[248] See *Penn v Lord Baltimore* (1750) 1 Ves Sen 444; Dicey Morris and Collins, *The Conflict of Laws* (14th edn, 2006), rule 122. This principle is now subject to significant exceptions in respect of land in other European countries as a result of EU legislation and the Lugano Convention.

some measure of control over the cases which are brought before it, to prevent injustice to either party and to ensure that the various issues can be fully and effectively dealt with. These objectives could not be attained were the court's powers to be strictly limited to its territorial jurisdiction. In recent years, the English courts have been making greater and more assertive use of their powers; they retain, however, a proper sensitivity to the position of foreign countries, and exercise their discretion with that in mind. The result is a much more restrained use of orders with extra-territorial effects than is the practice in the United States.[249]

(a) Discovery or disclosure

Nature of English practice

In England, the process traditionally referred to in common law jurisdictions (though with diverse understandings) as 'discovery' is now dealt with under Part 31 of the Civil Procedure Rules as 'disclosure and inspection of documents'.[250] What is referred to in the Rules as 'standard disclosure' will be ordered as part of the case management process unless it has already happened by agreement between the parties. Standard disclosure requires a party to disclose only (a) the documents on which he relies; and (b) the documents which adversely affect his or her own case, adversely affect another party's case, or support another party's case; and (c) the documents which required to be disclosed by a relevant practice direction.[251] When giving standard disclosure, a party is required to make a reasonable search for documents falling within categories (b) and (c). The factors relevant in deciding the reasonableness of a search include (a) the number of documents involved; (b) the nature and complexity of the proceedings; (c) the ease and expense of retrieval of any particular document; and (d) the significance of any document which is likely to be located during the search.[252]

Disclosure is limited to documents which are or have been in a party's control.[253] Several features of this system of discovery are noteworthy because of the contrast between discovery in England and the very much broader concept, known by the same name, in United States practice.[254] In the English system generally, disclosure follows the identification of the issues, normally by the delivery of the written defence. There is no procedure to assist the claimant who is still deciding how to formulate a claim, or whom to sue; that would be to countenance 'fishing

---

[249] See pp 134–135.

[250] In this context 'document' is defined to mean anything in which information of any description is recorded: CPR, r 31.4. Part 31 is a complete code: *SmithKline Beecham plc v Generics (UK) Ltd* [2003] EWCA Civ 1109, [2004] 1 WLR 1476.

[251] CPR, r 31.6. For the procedure for disclosure, see r 3.10.

[252] CPR, r 31.7.

[253] CPR, r 31.8.

[254] See pp 75–76; *South Carolina Insurance Co v Assurantie Maatschappij 'De Zeven Provincien' NV* [1987] AC 24, 35–6; and L A Collins, 'The Hague Evidence Convention and Discovery: A Serious Misunderstanding?' (1986) 35 ICLQ 765, 768–70.

expeditions'. Also, generally, the obligation to make disclosure is limited to those who are parties to the action.

There are exceptions to both these general statements though the courts apply them with notable caution. Under section 33(2) of the Supreme Court [now renamed the Senior Courts] Act 1981 and rule 3.16 of the Civil Procedure Rules, the High Court has power to order a person who appears to the court to be likely to be a party to the proceedings[255] and to be likely to have or to have had in his possession, custody, or power any documents which are relevant to an issue arising or likely to arise out of that claim to disclose the existence of and produce documents which are in his possession, custody, or power.[256] In *Black v Sumitomo Corp*[257] the element of discretion was emphasized. Without it an order for pre-action disclosure would be made in almost every dispute of any seriousness, irrespective of its context and detail, whereas by and large the concept of disclosure being ordered at other than the normal time was unusual, at any rate where the parties at the pre-action stage have been acting reasonably. The discretion was not confined and its exercise depends on all the facts of the case, including the nature of the injury or loss complained of; the clarity and identification of the issues raised by the complaint; the nature of the documents requested; the relevance of any protocol or pre-action enquiries; and the opportunity which the complainant has to make his or her case without pre-action disclosure.

So far as third parties are concerned, under section 34(2) of the Supreme Court [now renamed the Senior Courts] Act 1981 and rule 3.17 of the Civil Procedure Rules, the High Court has power to order a person who is not a party to the proceedings and to be likely to have in his possession, custody, or power any documents which are relevant to an issue arising or likely to arise out of that claim to disclose the existence of and produce documents which are in his possession, custody or power. It has been emphasized that disclosure against third parties should be regarded as the exception rather than the rule and not simply ordered by way of routine.[258] The exercise of the court's power is again a matter of discretion.[259] Applications under rule 3.18 are still sometimes referred to as '*Norwich Pharmacal* applications' from a case in which a narrower power was identified. In that case,[260] Lord Reid said:

If through no fault of his own a person gets mixed up in the tortious acts of others so as to facilitate their wrongdoing he may incur no personal liability but he comes under a duty to assist the person who has been wronged by giving him full information and disclosing the identity of the wrongdoers. I do not think that it matters whether he became so mixed up by voluntary action on his part or because it was his duty to do what he did. It may be that if this causes him expense the person seeking the information ought to reimburse him. But

---

[255] On this phrase see *Black v Sumitomo Corp* [2001] EWCA Civ 1819, [2002] 1 WLR 1562.

[256] An order cannot be made under s 33(2) if compliance with it would be likely to be injurious to the public interest: s 33(5).

[257] [2001] EWCA Civ 1819, [2002] 1 WLR 1562, at [85]–[88].

[258] *Frankson v Home Office* [2003] 1 WLR 1952.

[259] See eg *Gary Flood v Times Newspapers Ltd* [2009] EWHC 411 (QB).

[260] *Norwich Pharmacal Co v Customs and Excise Commissioners* [1974] AC 133.

justice requires that he should co-operate in righting the wrong if he unwittingly facilitated its perpetration.

There has been only a small number of *Norwich Pharmacal* orders made in aid of foreign legal proceedings.[261]

Territorial reach

Is it in any way relevant that the person required to make disclosure, or a document, is outside the jurisdiction? It seems that such facts are wholly irrelevant, at least in the normal case of disclosure by a party to the action. It has long been established that a defendant may be required to discover documents under his control but situated abroad; in the early cases, the fact that relevant documents were in Calcutta[262] or in Tobago[263] led merely to an extension in the time allowed for their production. In 1985, Hoffman J, in dealing with a case concerning an order under the Bankers' Books Evidence Act 1879 and a *subpoena duces tecum*, distinguished cases of discovery by 'ordinary parties to English litigation who happen to be foreigners'.[264] As he put it:

If you join the game you must play according to the local rules. This applies not only to plaintiffs but also to defendants who give notice of intention to defend . . . Of course, a party may be excused from having to produce a document on the grounds that this would violate the law of the place where the document is kept.[265] But in principle, there is no reason why he should not have to produce all discoverable documents wherever they are.[266]

It would seem that different considerations apply in the exceptional cases in which discovery may be obtained from a third party. Hoffman J expressed the view that discovery under the principle in *Norwich Pharmacal*[267] was more akin to the subpoena directed to a witness than the discovery required of an ordinary defendant.[268] It followed that the proper jurisdictional limits were the same as those applying to subpoenas, which cannot be addressed to persons outside the United Kingdom.[269]

(b) Detention, custody, and preservation of property

Under the English Civil Procedure Rules (and comparable rules of court in other Commonwealth jurisdictions), the court may make an order for the 'detention, custody or preservation' of any relevant property, and may order the inspection of

---

[261] *United Company Rusal plc v HSBC Bank plc* [2011] EWHC 404 (QB) at [9].
[262] See *Freeman v Fairlie* (1812) 3 Mer 29, 44–5 (Lord Eldon LC).
[263] See *Farquharson v Balfour* (1823) Turn & R184, 190–1 (Lord Eldon LC).
[264] *MacKinnon v Donaldson, Lufkin and Jenrette Securities Corpn* [1986] Ch 482.
[265] Hoffman J cites *Société Internationale pour Participations Industrielles et Commerciales SA v Rogers* 357 US 197 (1958).
[266] [1986] Ch 482, 494–5.
[267] [1974] AC 133. See p 120, above.
[268] *MacKinnon v Donaldson, Lufkin and Jenrette Corpn* [1986] Ch 482, 498–9.
[269] See p 124.

such property in the possession of a party.[270] Related powers deal with orders for the taking of samples of the property, and the carrying out of experiments upon it.[271] All these orders are made after an application with notice to the other party, though applications may be made without notice if good reason is shown.[272]

The court seems to give a broad interpretation to these powers. The power to make orders for the 'preservation' of property has been used in the context of the transfer of the mortgage of land by a mentally disordered person, even though the land was in Monte Carlo.[273] References in the text of the rules to 'custody' and 'observation' (the latter word being absent from the most recent text of the Rules) support a decision that the court could properly order the sending of an item of property out of the jurisdiction, in the instant case to South Africa, so that it could be identified by a witness whose evidence was being taken on commission there.[274]

(c) Freezing (or Mareva) injunctions

A freezing or *Mareva* injunction is one granted, either after judgment to the successful claimant or before trial to a claimant who has a good arguable case on the merits, restraining a defendant 'from dealing with any assets whether located within the jurisdiction or not'.[275] Its purpose is to prevent the enforcement of a judgment being rendered impossible, and so justice defeated, by the dissipation of assets which would be available to satisfy the judgment. It takes its name from one of the first cases in which such an injunction was granted, *Mareva Compania Naviera SA v International Bulkcarriers SA*.[276] Closely associated with freezing injunctions, and of direct relevance to the subject matter of the present work, are orders requiring a defendant to disclose the location of relevant assets.[277]

Territorial reach

Injunctions can be issued in aid of foreign proceedings, wherever they are commenced. It was thought at one time that a freezing injunction was a remedy only available against foreign defendants, but section 37(3) of the Supreme Court [now renamed Senior Courts] Act 1981 provides:

The power of the High Court under [section 37(1)] to grant an interlocutory injunction restraining a party to any proceedings from removing from the jurisdiction of the High Court, or otherwise dealing with, assets located within that jurisdiction shall be exercisable

---

[270] CPR, r 25.1(c)(i), (ii).
[271] CPR, r 25.1(c)(iii), (iv).
[272] CPR, r 25.3(1).
[273] *Chaplin v Burnett* (1912) 28 TLR 256 (CA).
[274] *Chaplin v Puttick* [1898] 2 QB 160.
[275] CPR, r 25.1(f).
[276] [1975] 2 Lloyd's Rep. 509 (CA). Authority to issue freezing injunction has a statutory basis in Supreme Court Act 1981, s 37(3).
[277] CPR, r 25.1(g).

in cases where that party is, as well as in cases where he is not, domiciled, resident or present within that jurisdiction.

It will be noted that section 37(3) refers to 'assets located within that jurisdiction', a reference which reflects, but does not directly confirm, the understanding of the position which prevailed in 1981, that an injunction could only attach to assets within England and Wales. This supposed principle was decisively rejected in a remarkable series of Court of Appeal decisions in June and July 1989.[278]

A worldwide *Mareva* injunction now always contains provisions designed to afford some protection for third parties from what would otherwise be 'an altogether exorbitant, extra-territorial jurisdiction'.[279] These are contained in the model order set out in the Rules[280] and provide:

19(1) Except as provided in paragraph (2) below, the terms of this order do not affect or concern anyone outside the jurisdiction of this court.
  (2) The terms of this order will affect the following persons in a country or state outside the jurisdiction of this court—
    (a) the Respondent or his officer or agent appointed by power of attorney;
    (b) any person who—
      (i) is subject to the jurisdiction of this court;
      (ii) has been given written notice of this order at his residence or place of business within the jurisdiction of this court; and
      (iii) is able to prevent acts or omissions outside the jurisdiction of this court which constitute or assist in a breach of the terms of this order; and
    (c) any other person, only to the extent that this order is declared enforceable by or is enforced by a court in that country or state.

20. Nothing in this order shall, in respect of assets located outside England and Wales, prevent any third party from complying with—

  (1) what it reasonably believes to be its obligations, contractual or otherwise, under the laws and obligations of the country or state in which those assets are situated or under the proper law of any contract between itself and the Respondent; and
  (2) any orders of the courts of that country or state, provided that reasonable notice of any application for such an order is given to the Applicant's solicitors.

Disclosure orders

In the present context, the importance of the freezing injunction lies in the associated order directing a party to provide information about the location of relevant property or assets or to provide information about relevant property or assets which are or may be the subject of an application for a freezing injunction.[281] Disclosure orders may be made in respect of assets outside the jurisdiction, for

---

[278] *Babanaft International Co SA v Bassatne* [1990] Ch 13 (CA); *Republic of Haiti v Duvalier* [1990] QB 202 (CA); *Derby & Co Ltd v Weldon (No 1)* [1990] Ch 48 (CA).
[279] See *Babanaft International Co SA v Bassatne* [1990] Ch 13, per Nicholls LJ. See also *Dadourian Group International Inc v Simms* [2006] EWCA Civ 399, [2006] 1 WLR 2499.
[280] PD 25A, Annex.
[281] CPR, r 25.1(g).

example documents relating to a Swiss bank account.[282] In some circumstances, the information thus gained may itself be relevant to issues in pending proceedings, in which case the order is a means of obtaining evidence abroad. In many more cases, once a claimant discovers that there are assets in a foreign state he will wish (and sometimes be enabled by the very presence of the assets) to commence proceedings in the courts of that state; there is what might be described as a 'jurisdiction-fishing expedition'.

Some protection is afforded by the practice of requiring the claimant to give an express undertaking not to use the information obtained without first seeking the leave of the court,[283] and it was held in *Tate Access Floors Inc v Boswell*[284] that even in the absence of an express undertaking the implied undertaking against using information for an improper or collateral purpose could be relied upon to the same effect.

(d) Orders for the taking of evidence abroad

The characteristic mode of proof in common law jurisdictions is reflected in the general rule stated in the Civil Procedure Rules[285] that any fact which needs to be proved by the evidence of witnesses is to be proved (a) at trial, by their oral evidence given in public;[286] and (b) at any other hearing, by their evidence in writing. The court may, however, allow the use of video links or other means.[287]

The attendance of a witness is secured by the issue of a witness summons; disobedience will be contempt of court. A witness summons may not be issued where the proposed witness is out of the United Kingdom. Even in the case of a willing witness, considerations of cost and convenience may make it very desirable to avoid the requirement of attendance. In some cases this can be achieved by obtaining an order that the witness be examined before the hearing and the evidence presented in the form of a deposition.[288] Such an order will not be made where the evidence is strongly contested or in cases where the trial judge will need to form an impression of the demeanour of the witness in order to assess his or her credibility. In some circumstances, the course of the trial will be such that a witness whose affidavit has been received will after all be required to attend for cross-examination;[289] this applies no less to witnesses abroad as to those within the jurisdiction.[290]

---

[282] *Bank of Crete SA v Koskotas* [1991] 2 Lloyds's Rep 587 (CA).

[283] See *Babanaft International Co SA v Bassatne* [1990] Ch 13 (CA); *Bank of Crete SA v Koskotas (No 2)* [1993] 1 All ER 748 (permission given for plaintiff to use material obtained via disclosure order in context of criminal investigation it was bound to conduct under Greek law).

[284] [1991] Ch 512.

[285] CPR, r 32.2(1).

[286] But note that a witness's prepared witness statement, duly served on the other party, stands as his evidence in chief: CPR, r 32.5(2).

[287] CPR, r 32.2.   [288] CPR, r 34.8.   [289] CPR, r 34.11(4).

[290] *Strauss v Goldschmidt* (1892) 8 TLR 239 (DC) (though on the facts foreign witness not required to attend).

If the deposition is to be taken in England (and there may be cases in which a foreign witness can be available in England but not at the date of the trial), the examination will be before a judge, an examiner of the court (the most usual procedure), or another person designated by the court.[291] If the deposition is to be taken abroad, alternative ways of proceeding are available. The distinction between them is of considerable importance.

Perhaps the neatest way of expressing the distinction is to contrast unilateral and co-operative procedures. The former is an exercise of the authority of the forum state; in the language of an old Chancery writ, *dedimus potestatem* (we have given power). The latter invokes international judicial assistance in that it requires the active involvement of the judicial authorities of the state in which the evidence is to be taken.

Unilateral procedures

In current English practice, the High Court can appoint a 'special examiner' to take evidence at any place, including a place outside the jurisdiction. The order for the appointment of such an examiner is the modern equivalent of the long-obsolete practice of issuing a commission for the taking of evidence out of the jurisdiction.[292] Because of the need to respect the sensitivities of foreign states, careful limits are set to the power to make orders:

(a) the general power to appoint a special examiner may be exercised only 'if the government of [the relevant] country allows a person appointed by the High Court to examine a person in that country';[293]

(b) a special examiner may be the British Consul or the Consul-General or his deputy in the country where the evidence is to be taken if there is a Civil Procedure Convention with the relevant country providing for the taking of evidence in that country for the assistance of proceedings in the courts of the United Kingdom; or with the consent of the Secretary of State[294] (who would presumably have regard to the known attitude of the foreign government and the terms of any relevant Convention as to consular relations).

These procedures are not available where the evidence is to be taken in a state to which Regulation 1206/2001[295] applies.

Co-operative procedures

The alternative mode of procedure is for the court to seek the assistance of the authorities of the country in which the proposed deponent is, asking that they take the evidence of that person or arrange for it to be taken. If that country is a state to which Regulation 1206/2001 applies, its procedures will be used. In other cases the

---

[291] CPR, r 34.8(3); for the appointment of examiners, see r 34.15.
[292] See Evidence by Commission Act 1859 for the operation of the old procedure between different parts of HM's dominions; it was repealed by the Evidence (Proceedings in Other Jurisdictions) Act 1975.
[293] CPR, r 34.13(4).
[294] PD 34A Depositions and Court Attendance of Witnesses, para 5.8.
[295] See pp 104–111.

court may make an order under CPR rule 34.13 for the issue of a letter of request. The draft letter of request annexed to the relevant Practice Direction describes the nature of the proceedings, with a summary of the facts, and asserts the necessity for the purposes of justice of the examination of the witnesses whose names and addresses are given. As to the mode of their examination, the letter contains this paragraph:

> The witnesses should be examined on oath or if that is not possible within your laws or is impossible of performance by reason of the internal practice and procedure of your court or by reason of practical difficulties, they should be examined in accordance with whatever procedure your laws provide for in these matters.

It is then asked that the witnesses be examined either in accordance with a given list of questions, which will have been drafted by the applicant party, or regarding certain matters summarized in the letter of request itself; an example might be 'a road traffic accident believed to have taken place in the sight of the witness at such-and-such a place and time'. The former might appear a more powerful technique from the point of view of the applicant; but, comparing it with a 'live' examination, in which the questioner can frame follow-up questions in terms of the way in which the facts evolve from earlier answers, a US court has described the framing of questions in advance as 'a supreme test of the questioning lawyer's powers of prescience'.[296] The foreign court is asked to notify the English court or any appointed agents of the parties of the date and place of the examination, and to reduce the evidence into writing.

What is notable about all this is that certain things are not included in the letter of request. Nothing is said about cross-examination, not even a request for the facility to be afforded if it would be compatible with foreign procedures; no detail is given as to the manner in which the evidence is to be 'reduced into writing', so that, for example, no preference is expressed for a verbatim transcript rather than a summary minute prepared by the foreign judge.

The practice of the courts

Rules of court in many Commonwealth jurisdictions follow the relevant English text, so there is quite a voluminous body of case law in which the practice of taking evidence out of the jurisdiction is examined.

The former Rules of the Supreme Court expressly stated what is undoubtedly current practice, that an order for such examination will be made 'where it appears necessary for the purposes of justice'.[297] The courts have repeatedly stressed that the making of an order is discretionary; it is not a matter of right, something to which a litigant is entitled *ex debito justitiae*.[298] 'The purposes of justice' does not

---

[296] *Androux v Geldermann, Inc* (ND Ill, 1990).
[297] RSC Ord 38, r 1.
[298] *Merry v R* (1884) 10 VLR.(E.) 135; *Coristine Ltd v Haddad* (1915) 21 DLR 350 (Sask.); *New Zealand Towel Supply and Laundry Ltd v NZ Tri-cleaning Co Ltd* [1935] NZLR 204 (CA).

mean 'in the interest of either party to the litigation'; the interests of all parties need to be considered.[299]

Courts in various jurisdictions have developed lists of factors which should regularly be taken into account in exercising the discretion. For example, Canadian courts have approved a statement in the Canadian *Annual Practice*[300] listing as criteria:

(1) that the application is made bona fide; (2) that the issue in respect of which the evidence is required is one that the Court ought to try; (3) that the witnesses to be examined may give evidence material to the issue; (4) that there is good reason why they cannot be examined here; and (5) that the examination abroad will be effectual.

A longer list of criteria was developed by Canadian courts in a criminal context:[301]

(1) whether the requested jurisdiction will or is likely to respond favourably to a request for judicial assistance;

(2) whether the manner of response, if favourable, is compatible with the manner in which evidence is taken in Canada;

(3) whether the circumstances of the witness's residence out of Canada render return to Canada for trial likely or unlikely, thereby affecting the necessity for the taking of evidence on commission;

(4) whether the witness has relevant and material evidence to give receivable in accordance with the rules of evidence applicable in the Canadian proceedings;

(5) whether the witness is willing to attend to give evidence on commission and, if not, the means whereby his or her evidence may be compelled or otherwise ensured;

(6) whether there will be unfair prejudice to the party opposite by the order of a commission;

(7) whether there will be any serious disruption of the trial proceedings by the taking of such evidence;

(8) whether the trier of fact will be disadvantaged to the prejudice of the parties or either of them, by being unable to observe the demeanour of the witnesses.

(9) whether the applicant for the taking of commission evidence has made meaningful efforts to procure the witness' attendance to testify in Canada;

(10) whether the application is made in good faith in contradistinction to those cases where the application constitutes little more than a manipulative gimmick to avoid a timely trial on the merits.

A slightly less elaborate statement is much cited in Australia: the applicant must satisfy the court 'that the witness is out of the jurisdiction of the court, that

---

[299] *Berdan v Greenwood* (1880) 20 ChD 764n (CA), per Bagallay LJ at p 765n. In some circumstances, greater weight will be given to the convenience of the defendant: *Emanuel v Soltykoff* (1892) 8 TLR 331 (CA) (see further below on this point).
[300] See *Haynes v Haynes* (1962) 35 DLR (2d) 602 (BC).
[301] *R v Neeb (No 2)* [1989] OJ No 447; *R v Hanson* [1998] OJ No 429.

his evidence is material and that his attendance within the jurisdiction cannot be procured';[302] it seems to have been derived from a similar observation of Lindley LJ in an early English case.[303] These tests provide reliable guidance in straightforward cases, but often there are additional factors varying with the circumstances which must be considered before the court will authorize a departure from the normal method of trial.[304] It is possible to identify rather more closely some of the relevant considerations:

Non-availability of the witness at the trial

The witness must be outside the jurisdiction[305] and there must be some good reason why he or she cannot attend for examination in the usual way. The serious ill-health of the witness is a strong reason,[306] but it needs to be clearly proved; the courts have shown themselves suspicious of mere assertions of unfitness to travel.[307] The cost of travel to the place of trial will also be relevant; in an extreme case, the expense of the claimant's own journey to the only available forum might exceed the value of the claim,[308] though in other cases legal aid may be available to cover those costs.[309] Given the non-availability of subpoenas, a mere refusal by a potential witness to attend in England may be sufficient, as may evidence that the person's employer would not grant the necessary leave of absence.[310]

Where the witness is also a party to the proceedings, the courts will be less eager to dispense with attendance. The fact that bigamy charges were pending against the defendant in the forum Province was accepted as a valid reason in one case;[311] not surprisingly, a Saskatchewan judge was markedly unimpressed by a defendant's assertion that he could not travel from Oregon because the trial would occur at 'a very busy period in the building industry'.[312]

---

[302] Per Gibbs J in *Hardie Rubber Co Pty Ltd v General Tire and Rubber Co* (1973) 129 CLR 521 at 528. See also *Willis v Trequair* (1906) 3 CLR 912.

[303] *Armour v Walker* (1883) 25 ChD 673 at 677.

[304] See *Lucas Industries Ltd v Chloride Batteries Australia Ltd* (1978) 45 FLR 160 (Fed Ct).

[305] The witness's presence within the jurisdiction at some earlier date (with the possibility of taking evidence in some form then) does not preclude the making of an order: *Mason v Delargy* (1884) 1 WN (NSW) 68.

[306] *Haynes v Haynes* (1962) 35 DLR (2d) 602 (evidence by elderly plaintiff, resident in England, with serious heart complaint); *Weingarden v Noss* (1953) 9 WWR (NS) 335 (Man) (advanced age and serious ill-health of plaintiff).

[307] *Berndan v Greenwood* (1880) 20 ChD 764 (CA) (heart condition said to make crossing of English Channel dangerous to life); *Park v Schneider* (1912) 6 DLR 451.

[308] eg, *Wong Doo v Kana Bhana* [1973] NZLR 1455 (CA) (travel from China).

[309] *Ammar v Ammar* [1954] P 468.

[310] *Hardie Rubber Co Pty Ltd v General Tire and Rubber Co* (1973) 129 CLR 521; *Lucas Industries Ltd v Chloride Batteries Australia Ltd* (1978) 45 FLR 160 (Fed Ct) (Swedish employer would allow witness to travel to London but not to Australia). Cf *Romano v Maggiora* [1936] 2 DLR 329 (BC CA) where very precise evidence of unwillingness and expense demanded.

[311] *Mills v Mills* (1888) 12 PR (Ont) 473.

[312] *Murray v Plummer* (1913) 11 DLR 764.

Materiality of the evidence

Taking evidence abroad can involve both delay and added expense. The courts will not make an order with these consequences unless they are satisfied that the evidence proposed to be taken is genuinely material to the issues in the case. While the court will avoid going into the merits of the case at the interlocutory stage, the applicant for an order must establish materiality on the balance of probabilities.[313] In marginal cases, courts have sometimes allowed the applicant an opportunity to provide more details pointing to materiality[314] or agreed to an order subject to the applicant giving security for costs.[315] An order will not be made to secure evidence which merely serves to 'bolster up' other evidence.[316]

Some Canadian courts fell into the practice of declaring that 'controversial' evidence should not be taken by an examiner out of the jurisdiction; it was better that such evidence be fully tested in the trial court. It is now recognized that this approach, seldom if ever actually applied in practice, is based on a confusion of thought. Questions of witnesses' credibility may be relevant, and will be considered below; that their evidence is controversial, taken alone, merely establishes that it is material to the issues in the case; it is a reason for making an order, not for refusing to do so.[317]

Even if the evidence sought is material, a court will not order the taking of evidence abroad if equally satisfactory evidence on the same point can be obtained from another source within the jurisdiction.[318]

Credibility; and issues of identity

By making an order, the trial court denies itself the chance to observe the demeanour of the witness and especially his or her reaction to cross-examination. Although the examiner appointed by the court may in some circumstances submit a report which accompanies the deposition,[319] this is merely intended to give the opportunity of recording facts, including incidents during the examination (for example, that the witnesses fainted, or rose up and tried to assault cross-examining counsel); the examiner cannot indicate an opinion as to the credibility of the witness or his or her own impressions of the witness's demeanour.[320] In some cases, and especially where the witness has no interest in the outcome of the case, the lost opportunity to assess demeanour is of no great significance; in others it is too great a price to pay.

A leading illustration is *Berdan v Greenwood*.[321] The Russian Government had purchased firearms, and the claimant claimed that this was a result of influence he had exerted; if this were true, he would be entitled to commission on the sale value.

---

[313] *Hardie Rubber Co Pty Ltd v General Tire and Rubber Co* (1973) 129 CLR 521; *Lucas Industries Ltd v Chloride Batteries Australia Ltd* (1978) 45 FLR 160 (Fed Ct); *New Zealand Towel Supply and Laundry Ltd v NZ Tri-cleaning Co Ltd* [1935] NZLR 204 (CA).

[314] *Langen v Tate* (1883) 24 ChD 522 (CA).

[315] *Hawes, Gibson and Co v Hawes* (1912) 3 DLR 396 (Ont); *Re Corr* (1912) 5 DLR 367 (Ont).

[316] *Ehrmann v Ehrmann* (1896) 2 ChD 611 (CA); *Maynard v Maynard* [1947] OWN 493.

[317] See *Niewiadomski v Langdon* (1956) 6 DLR (2d) 361 (Ont).

[318] See, eg, *Park v Scheider* (1912) 6 DLR 451 (Alta).

[319] See PD 32A Depositions and Court Attendance of Witnesses, para 4.8.

[320] *Re Wipperman* [1955] P 59 (where Pearce J gives the examples used in the text).

[321] (1880) 20 ChD 764n (CA).

The defendants contested the claim, and the relevant Russian officials were to give evidence on their behalf. The claimant's case rested solely on his own evidence, and he asked that it be taken on commission in Bucharest, pleading ill-health. Reversing the courts below, the Court of Appeal refused his application; his credibility was the key issue, and in such a case it was of 'extreme importance' that his evidence be tested by cross-examination in open court. There is an even stronger case for such cross-examination where the evidence the claimant wishes to give (eg, as to the state of his knowledge at a particular date) is very difficult to challenge by calling other witnesses; if he is believed, his point is established.[322]

A similar result is likely where the witness is suspected of complicity in a fraudulent scheme, especially where he can be regarded as the 'real' claimant.[323] An element in a number of such cases is a tendency to apply the tests more strictly when the application is made by the claimant, after he had selected the forum, especially where the application concerns the claimant's own evidence.[324] However, the 'credibility' factor can be relevant where the evidence is that of the defendant (for example, in a contested divorce case[325]) or of some other key witness.[326]

Questions of the witness's identity are an especially strong illustration of the principle. In *Nadin v Bassett*,[327] the claimant, who had lived in New Zealand for over twenty years, claimed to be the heir-at-law of an intestate who had died some ten years before the claim. The issue was whether he was the person he claimed to be, and the Court of Appeal held that this must be tested by his appearance in court where cross-examination could be fully informed by the recollections of several people in England who knew the missing heir before his emigration. The court allowed a deposition to be taken in New Zealand, which might convince the other parties of the genuineness of the claim, but it was only to be admitted in evidence with their consent.[328]

Likely outcome and adequacy of foreign procedure

No court will make an order, especially one likely to cause delay, unless it is clear that doing so will serve some useful purpose. In the absence of powers of compulsion, the evident determination of the proposed witness not to co-operate in any way may well dissuade the court from making an order.[329] Even if the witness is

---

[322] See *Park v Schneider* (1912) 6 DLR 451 (Alta), distinguished on this point in *Kaye v Burnsland Addition Ltd* (1915) 24 DLR 232 (Alta).

[323] eg, *Fidelity Trust Co v Schneider* (1913) 14 DLR 224 (Alta); *Lawson v Vacuum Brake Co* (1884) 27 ChD 137 (CA) (suspected accomplice; application of a 'shadowy, frivolous and vexatious' character); *Murray v Plummer* (1913) 11 DLR 764 (Sask) (witness a co-defendant, allegedly implicated in fraud).

[324] *Coch v Allcock & Co* (1888) 21 QBD 178 (CA); *Emanuel v Soltykoff* (1892) 8 TLR 331 (CA); *Ross v Woodford* [1894] 1 Ch 38; *Richard Beliveau Co v Tyerman* (1911) 16 WLR 492 (Sask).

[325] *Ammar v Ammar* [1954] P 468.

[326] eg, *Re Boyse* (1882) 20 ChD 760 (where witness had interest in outcome, and his behaviour judged suspicious).

[327] (1883) 25 ChD 21 (CA).

[328] See *Bangkok Bank Ltd v Swatow Lace Co Ltd* [1963] NSWR 488; *La Baloise Compagnie d'Assurances contre l'Incendie v Western Australian Insurance Co Ltd* [1939] VLR 363.

[329] *Re Tucker (A Bankrupt)* [1990] Ch 148 (CA).

willing, the law of the place in which he is to be examined may be such as to render the examination inadequate. There might, for example, be some legal reason why the examiner could not administer the oath. Where a Letter of Request is addressed to a foreign court, that court may be unaccustomed to the process of cross-examination. A century ago, an English judge could say:

the habits and practice of the French courts are different from our own, and . . . when the cross-examination of [the] witness is most material, and will alone enable me to judge of the effect of his examination-in-chief, I decline to delegate my discretion to any other tribunal.[330]

In modern conditions, courts are increasingly willing to operate modes of procedure, including cross-examination, with which they are unfamiliar.[331] There are inevitable difficulties in giving instructions as to cross-examination when those instructions must be settled before the examination-in-chief, and before other witnesses have been heard.[332] The courts recognize these limitations, which are inherent in any system of taking evidence abroad ahead of the trial, but cannot regard them as a sufficient objection to the making of the order.[333] In some circumstances, a locally resident examiner may have special expertise, as where evidence as to a marriage in China was ordered to be taken in Hong Kong.[334]

The video alternative

The development of video facilities may be thought to reduce the need for evidence to be taken abroad, but some of the factors already listed may tell against the use of video technology. A New South Wales judgment[335] helpfully reviewed the practice to be followed. As the court noted, apart from dealing with obvious practical matters such as comparative costs and the difficulty created by differences in time zones, the previous cases touched upon some recurring themes: the appropriateness of audiovisual facilities for centrally important evidence; the assessment of credit where evidence is given by audiovisual link; difficulties raised by the use of documents for cross-examination in audiovisual evidence; technological difficulties due to lapse of time between transmission and receipt of questions and answers; and difficulties posed by the use of audiovisual facilities where the cross-examination is lengthy.

The court held that the fact that the witness's evidence would be centrally important should not of itself persuade the court against using audiovisual facilities.

---

[330] *Re Boyse* (1882) 20 ChD 760 at 772 per Fry J.

[331] For practice under the Hague Evidence Convention, see pp 96–97.

[332] Cf *Stewart v Sovereign Bank of Canada* (1912) 2 DLR 913, where it was made a condition of the order that the evidence should be taken only after certain other evidence had been received, and *The Adolf Leonhardt* [1973] 2 Lloyd's Rep 318 where Brandon J appointed himself a special examiner and sat to hear evidence in Rotterdam for two days in the middle of the trial.

[333] See *Hardie Rubber Co Pty Ltd v General Tire and Rubber Co* (1973) 129 CLR 521 (difficulties of cross-examination in Japan surmountable); *Credit Suisse v Lim Soon Fang Bryan* [2007] SGHC 52 (letter of request from Singapore to Taiwan despite absence of cross-examination in Taiwan).

[334] *Wong Doo v Kana Bhana* [1933] NZLR 1455 (CA).

[335] *Asic v Rich* [2004] NSWSC 467, with a full review of (mainly Australian) case law.

But if the court could anticipate that the cross-examination of the witness would be lengthy and complex, and that the credit of the witness would be challenged, and the issue of credit depending upon the witness's responses to questions based on documents shown to him by the cross-examiner, that combination of factors is likely to persuade the court against audiovisual evidence unless there is a good reason for choosing it (such as, for example, a large difference in costs or the illness of the overseas witness). The management of documents could be a source of frustration and delay where audiovisual evidence was taken, but the problem could be reduced to manageable proportions if the cross-examiner made sure that copies of the documents were available to the witness overseas and there was someone with the witness who could assist the witness to identify and locate the documents. The extent of the problem will vary from case to case.

Overall, the court should strongly encourage the use of current-generation electronic aids to its work, provided they were cost-effective and their reliability had been adequately established, recognizing that a technological innovation which saves time and money may be acceptable even if it delivers a product not quite as good as the traditional alternative. But there would be exceptional cases where, presented with a choice between taking evidence by electronic means or using the tried and true viva voce method, the court will decide that there are good grounds for proceeding by *viva voce* evidence.

Other considerations

As with any other interlocutory application, the applicant must act promptly[336] and with frankness.[337] The courts will not allow the taking of evidence abroad to develop into a 'roving enquiry', but in many jurisdictions it is not essential to name in advance all the witnesses to be examined.[338]

Production of documents

Most of the cases concern the giving of oral testimony by the witness, and there was some uncertainty as to whether a Letter of Request could be issued seeking the assistance of a foreign court in obtaining the production of documents. Nicholls V-C held in *Panayiotou v Sony Music Entertainment (UK) Ltd*[339] that such action could be taken, under the court's inherent jurisdiction, provided the specificity of the documents satisfied the same test as would be applied by an English court in responding to a foreign request.[340]

---

[336] *New Zealand Towel Supply and Laundry Ltd v NZ Tri-cleaning Co Ltd* [1935] NZLR 204 (CA) (lack of promptness a factor in decision to refuse order).

[337] *Hardie Rubber Co Pty Ltd v General Tire and Rubber Co* (1973) 129 CLR 521.

[338] *Hardie Rubber Co Pty Ltd v General Tire and Rubber Co* (1973) 129 CLR 521, where relevant officers or employees of two named companies were to be examined. The court cited *Nadin v Bassett* (1883) 25 ChD 21 (CA) and *Armour v Walker* (1883) 25 ChD 673 (CA) as showing a similarly liberal practice in England.

[339] [1993] Ch 142.

[340] As to which see pp 116–118.

(e) Use of pre-trial procedures of other jurisdictions

By comparison with some other jurisdictions, and especially those in the United States, the scope of discovery and related procedures available in England is quite limited. Is there any reason why a party to litigation in England, either as claimant or defendant, should not take advantage of any procedures which might be open to him or her to obtain discovery or other access to relevant material in some such foreign jurisdiction?

This point arose for decision in *South Carolina Insurance Co v Assurantie Maatschappij 'de Zeven Provincien' NV*.[341] The defendants in an English action wished to inspect documents of admitted relevance to the subject matter of the case (which involved a series of reinsurance contracts) in the possession of a company not itself a party to the litigation and having no place of business in England; the documents were situated in the State of Washington. As the company was not a party, discovery as understood in England was not available; as it was not within the United Kingdom no *subpoena duces tecum* could be issued (and that would only secure the production of documents at the trial, not for pre-trial inspection). The defendants sought an order under a US statutory provision[342] dealing specifically with assistance to litigants in foreign courts. Under it, 'any interested person' could seek an order of a US District Court that any person within its district should produce documents for use in the foreign proceedings.

Before Hobhouse J and in the Court of Appeal, the claimants were successful in arguing that the defendants should be restrained by injunction from seeking or enforcing such a District Court order. The defendants had not contested the jurisdiction of the English court and must be taken to have accepted that the dispute would be settled in accordance with English procedure; the English court must be in full control of its own procedures and not allow procedural battles to develop in other countries which would add to the expense and dislocate the timetable of English litigation.

The House of Lords unanimously allowed the defendants' appeal. Given the freedom which the parties enjoy in a common law system in the matter of gathering evidence, their resort to foreign procedures could not be said to interfere with English procedures or the control over those procedures which the English court would exercise. The defendants' conduct was not unconscionable, nor an interference with any legal or equitable right of the claimants. Any possibility of excessive delay could be met by the English court fixing a date for trial; and it could control the allocation of costs.

As a result, therefore, there may be foreign pre-trial procedures available to the parties which will enable them to overcome the limitations on the territorial scope of the procedures normally available in England. Of particular practical importance are two important federal statutory provisions in the United States.

---

[341] [1987] AC 24.   [342] 28 USC 1782. See further below.

The first provision, the one used in the *South Carolina* case, gives a means whereby a United States court may provide material for use in foreign proceedings.[343] This provides, in relevant part:

The district court of the district in which a person resides or is found may order him to give his testimony or statement or to produce a document or other thing for use in a proceeding in a foreign or international tribunal. The order may be made pursuant to a letter rogatory issued, or request made, by a foreign or international tribunal or upon the application of any interested person and may direct that the testimony or statement be given, or the document or other thing be produced, before a person appointed by the court.

The power of United States federal courts to take evidence in aid of foreign proceedings was first introduced in 1855, but as a result of a series of what are now seen as misunderstandings[344] fell into disuse. It was revived in 1948 and the present law emerged in 1964 after a report from a Congressional Commission and the Advisory Committee on International Rules of Judicial Procedure.

The United States Supreme Court considered the scope of section 1728 in *Intel Corp v Advanced Micro Devices Inc.*[345] A dispute between two Californian companies led to one complaining to the European Commission's Directorate-General for Competition that the other had violated European competition law. The complaint was being investigated when the complainant sought an order under section 1728 for the production of certain documents. The Supreme Court held that an order could be made. Given the nature of the proceedings which could lead to a final administrative decision both responsive to the complaint and reviewable in court, a complainant qualified as an 'interested person' and the European Commission was a 'tribunal' when it acted as a first-instance decision-maker. A 'proceeding' for which discovery was sought had to be in reasonable contemplation, but did not need to be pending or imminent. An order could be made even where the material sought was not discoverable under the law of the relevant foreign state. However, a District Court had discretion in deciding whether to make an order. In exercising that discretion, a court should note that where discovery was sought from a third party, such discovery might not be available in the foreign state and the assistance of the US courts would be needed. A court should also consider the nature of the foreign tribunal, the character of proceedings underway abroad, and the receptivity of the foreign government, court, or agency to US judicial assistance. A court could also consider whether the request concealed an attempt to circumvent foreign proof-gathering limits or other policies of a foreign country or the United States. Unduly intrusive or burdensome requests may be rejected or trimmed.

---

[343] 28 USC 1782.

[344] See W B Stahr, 'Discovery under 28 USC 1782 for Foreign and International Proceedings' (1990) 30 Va Jo Int L 597 at 600–5. For another study see 'Much Ado about 1782: A Look at Recent Problems with Discovery in the United States for Use in Foreign Litigation under 28 USC 1782' (1989) 20 Inter-Am L Rev 429.

[345] 542 US 241 (2004). See C D Wallace, (2003) 37 Int L 1055 (2003) (principally a comment on the lower court decision, but with useful history).

It seems, however, that section 1728 cannot be used to compel the production of documents located outside the United States.[346] It was formerly thought not to be available in support of arbitral proceedings, but some courts have taken the view that *Intel Corp v Advanced Micro Devices Inc*[347] justifies its use in this context.[348]

In addition, the US courts have a wide subpoena power applying to persons in foreign countries:

A court of the United States may order the issuance of a subpoena requiring the appearance as a witness before it, or before a person or body designated by it, of a national or resident of the United States who is in a foreign country, or requiring the production of a specified document or other thing by him, if the court finds that particular testimony or the production of the document or other thing by him is necessary in the interests of justice, and, in other than a criminal action or proceeding,[349] if the court finds, in addition, that it is not possible to obtain his testimony in admissible form without his personal appearance or to obtain the production of the document or other thing in any other manner.[350]

---

[346] *Re Godfrey* (SD NY, 2007) not following *Re Gemeinschaftspraxis* (SD NY, 2006), and citing *Re Sarrio SA* 119 F 3d 143 (2nd Cir, 1997), *Norex Petroleum Ltd v Chubb Insurance Company of Canada* 384 F Supp 2d 45 (DDC, 2005). See H Smit, 'American Assistance to Litigation in Foreign and International Tribunals: Section 1728 of Title 28 of the USC Revisited', (1998) 25 Syracuse J Int L & Com 1.

[347] 542 US 241 (2004). See C D Wallace, (2003) 37 Int L 1055 (2003) (principally a comment on the lower court decision, but with useful history).

[348] For the earlier view, see *National Broadcasting Co v Bear Sterns & Co* 165 F 3d 184 (2nd Cir, 1999). See now O L Knöfel, 'Judicial Assistance in the Taking of Evidence Abroad in Aid of Arbitration: a German Perspective' (2009) J Priv Int L 281 at 291–5.

[349] For the international implications of this subpoena power in the criminal context, see pp 204–208.

[350] 28 USC 1783.

4

Other Forms of Co-operation in Civil Matters

The issues of service of process and taking of evidence abroad, examined in the last two chapters, do not exhaust the field. The Hague Conventions of 1905 and 1954 dealing with civil procedure dealt not only with those matters but also with a range of other issues: security for costs, legal aid, the free issue of documents of civil status and physical detention. These matters have been the subject of several more recent international instruments; they are examined in this chapter together with the developing area of mediation in cross-border disputes. The European Union has adopted a number of further Regulations aimed at removing obstacles in the way of those with civil claims. These are related to, but outside, the scope of this book, as they are measures of harmonization or deal with the enforcement of judgments: the European Enforcement Order,[1] the European order for payment procedure,[2] and the European small claims procedure.[3]

---

[1] European Parliament and Council Regulation No 805/2004 of 21 April 2004 creating a European Enforcement Order for uncontested claims, OJ L 14315, 30.4.2004, amended by Commission Regulation No 1869/2005, OJ L 300/6, 17.11.2005.
[2] European Parliament and Council Regulation No 1896/2006 of 12 December 2006 creating a European order for payment procedure, OJ L 399/1, 30.12.2006.
[3] European Parliament and Council Regulation No 861/2007 of 11 July 2007 establishing a European Small Claims Procedure, OJ L 199/1, 31.7.2007.

I. Abolition of legalization

Some states have traditionally insisted that anyone seeking to rely in that state on a public document produced in another state should have that document 'legalized'. This is a cumbersome process, sometimes known as 'chain certification'. As that latter term suggests, the process is one in which the authenticity of the document is certified by an appropriate officer, his or her certification itself requiring authentication by a further process which may require the attention of diplomatic or consular personnel.[4]

1. The Hague Convention of 1961

In 1961 the Hague Conference adopted a Convention Abolishing the Requirement of Legalisation for Foreign Public Documents.[5] The convention applies to public documents which have been executed in the territory of one Contracting State and which have to be produced in the territory of another Contracting State. 'Public documents' includes (a) documents emanating from an authority or an official connected with the courts or tribunals of the state, including those emanating from a public prosecutor, a clerk of a court, or a process server (*huissier de justice*); (b) administrative documents; (c) notarial acts; and (d) official certificates which are placed on documents signed by persons in their private capacity, such as official certificates recording the registration of a document or the fact that it was in existence on a certain date, and official and notarial authentications of signatures. However, the Convention does not apply to documents executed by diplomatic or consular agents or to administrative documents dealing directly with commercial or customs operations.[6] There is, however, a Council of Europe convention excluding legalization of the former group of documents.[7]

Under the Hague Convention, Contracting States are required to exempt from legalization documents to which the convention applies.[8] The only formality that may be required in order to certify the authenticity of the signature, the capacity in which the person signing the document has acted, and, where appropriate, the identity of the seal or stamp which it bears, is the addition of an 'apostille', a certificate issued by the competent authority of the state from which the document emanates.[9] The apostille is in a form annexed to the convention, and may be placed

---

[4] See Georges A L Droz, *La légalisation des actes officiels étrangers* (Hague Conference Preliminary Document No 1 of March 1959).

[5] The Convention was signed on 5 October 1961.

[6] Convention, art 1.

[7] European Convention on the Abolition of Legalisation of Documents executed by Diplomatic Agents or Consular Officers, CETS No 063; it has 21 parties.

[8] Convention, art 2. They must take the necessary steps to prevent the performance of legalization by its diplomatic or consular agents in cases where the convention applies: art 9.

[9] Convention, art 3. Even this formality is unnecessary if legalization has been abolished in respect of particular types of document under applicable law or by international agreement: ibid.

on the document itself or on an *allonge*, that is on a separate paper attached to the primary document.[10]

The security of the system is guaranteed by the authority designated in each Contracting State as competent to issue apostilles keeping 'a register or card index' in which it records each apostille issued with identifying details. At the request of any interested person, the authority which has issued the certificate verifies whether the particulars in the certificate correspond with those in the register or card index.[11]

The operation of the convention was reviewed by a Special Commission held in 2009. The Special Commission noted that the definition of 'public document' in article 1 of the convention was not exhaustive. It was for the law of the state of origin to determine the public nature of a document, and the Commission suggested that states should give a broad interpretation to the category of public documents. In practice, some states issue apostilles for documents such as import or export licences, health certificates, and certificates of origin or conformity.[12] At present the convention cannot be applied to documents issued by intergovernmental organizations, including Regional Economic Integration Organisations such as the European Union.[13]

One matter of concern to the Special Commission was the fraudulent misrepresentation of the convention as guaranteeing the *truth* as opposed to the authenticity of a document. It is the signature on the document and not the content of the document that is authenticated. There was evidence that 'diploma mills' (bogus universities awarding degrees in return for payment) sought an apostille to give the degree certificate the semblance of official recognition by the state.[14]

The convention uses what now seems the charmingly dated term 'card index' as if it were an advanced information storage method. Electronic developments have not been overlooked, and an Electronic Apostille Pilot Program, 'e-APP', has been initiated by the Hague Conference and the National Notary Association of the United States of America, and it has received funding from the European Commission. Several states are already making practical use of the e-APP aspect of this project.

2. Copies of entries and decisions

The Hague Convention on International Access to Justice of 1980[15] provides that nationals of any Contracting State and persons habitually resident in any Contracting State are entitled to obtain in any other Contracting State, on the same terms and conditions as its nationals, copies of or extracts from entries in public

---

[10] Convention, art 4.
[11] Convention, arts 6–7.
[12] Conclusions and Recommendations, paras 72 and 77.
[13] Ibid, para 76.
[14] Ibid, para 84 and see 'The application of the Apostille Convention to diplomas including those issued by diploma mills', Preliminary Document No 5 of December 2008.
[15] See further, p 141.

registers and decisions relating to civil or commercial matters and may have such documents legalized, where necessary.[16]

3. Possible EU action

In December 2010 the European Commission published a Green Paper examining related issues.[17] It spoke of the obstacles EU citizens experienced on moving to another Member State, notably the need to present public records from their previous state of residence to the authorities of that Member State in order to provide the proof needed to benefit from a right or to comply with an obligation. This was especially true of 'civil status records', such as records of births, marriages, or paternal recognition of a child born out of wedlock. The Commission indicated that in 2013 it would make proposals concerning the free movement of documents by eliminating legalization formalities between Member States and providing for the recognition of the effects of certain civil status records, so that legal status granted in one Member State could be recognized and have the same legal consequences in another.

The Green Paper noted that all Member Sates were party to the Hague Convention of 1961, but reported that even the apostille procedure under that convention required administrative steps and involved some loss of time and a cost which varied from one Member State to another[18]. In the Commission's view, it was time to consider abolishing the apostille as well as legalization for all public documents in order to ensure that they could circulate freely throughout the EU.

II. Legal aid

A useful survey of legal aid issues was contained in a European Commission Green Paper, 'Legal aid in civil matters: the problems confronting the cross-border litigant', published in 2000.[19] It offered a definition of legal aid as including provision of free or low-cost legal advice or court representation by a lawyer; partial or total exemption from other costs, such as court fees, which would normally be levied; and direct financial assistance to defray any of the costs associated with litigation, such as lawyers' costs, court fees, witness expenses, liability of a losing party to support winners' costs, etc. It noted that a person threatened with proceedings, or wishing to bring proceedings, abroad might need legal aid at three stages: pre-litigation advice; the assistance of an advocate at a trial and exemption from court fees; and assistance at the stage of having a foreign judgment declared enforceable or being enforced.

---

[16] Convention, art 18.
[17] 'Less bureaucracy for citizens: promoting free movement of public documents and recognition of the effects of civil status records', COM(2010) 747 final, 14.12.2010.
[18] In some Member States an apostille is provided free of charge; others charge up to €50.
[19] COM/2000/0051 final.

Even within the EU, there were fundamental differences in the philosophy and organization and management of the legal aid systems. The broad objective in some Member States was to be to make legal services and access to justice generally available, whereas in others the legal aid system could be seen as an adjunct of welfare law, available only to the very poorest. In some countries there was a well-developed system whereby the state or a state agency directly provided realistic reimbursement to the lawyers involved, whereas in others the scheme consisted of lawyers themselves offering (whether voluntarily or compulsorily) pro-bono services or services which were not realistically remunerated. Legal aid systems were, however, crafted with litigation in the enacting states between residents of that state in mind; a litigant from another state, or a person seeking to litigate in another state, may be ineligible.

1. The Hague Convention on International Access to Justice

After the Hague Conference had adopted its conventions on service of process and taking evidence abroad, it addressed the revision of the earlier texts dealing with other matters, including especially legal aid. The result was a Convention on International Access to Justice agreed on 25 October 1980.[20] It has (as at January 2012) twenty-five parties, almost all from the civil law tradition.

The Convention provides that nationals of any Contracting State and persons habitually resident in any Contracting State are to be entitled to legal aid for court proceedings in civil and commercial matters[21] in each Contracting State on the same conditions as if they themselves were nationals of and habitually resident in that state.[22] The same applies to persons who formerly had their habitual residence in a Contracting State in which court proceedings are to be or have been commenced, if the cause of action arose out of their former habitual residence in that State.[23] These provisions apply to legal advice provided the person seeking advice is present in the state where advice is sought.[24]

The Convention makes the familiar provision for a Central Authority in each Contracting State to receive, and take action on, applications for legal aid submitted under the Convention; and for transmitting authorities for the purpose of forwarding applications for legal aid to the appropriate Central Authority in the requested state.[25] However, the Convention does not prevent applications being made via the diplomatic channel or directly to the competent authorities of the requested

---

[20] See the full Explanatory Report by Gustaf Möller, *AetD (14)*, vol 4, p 260.

[21] And in proceedings in administrative, social, or fiscal matters in states where legal aid is provided in that context: Convention, art 1(3), the provisions of this article shall apply to cases brought before the courts or tribunals competent in such matters.

[22] Convention, art 1(1). The Special Commission of 2009 expressed the opinion that the wording of article 1 does not accommodate the inclusion of legal persons within its scope of application: Conclusions and Recommendations, para 61.

[23] Convention, art 1(2). For the power to enter a reservation excluding cases based on current or former habitual residence where there is no reciprocity, see art 28.

[24] Convention, art 2.

[25] Convention, arts 3, 4, 6, and 8.

state.[26] A prescribed form of application is set out in the Annex to the Convention, and there are detailed requirements as to the translation of the application, supporting documents, and any communications in response to requests for further information.[27]

2. European Agreement on the Transmission of Applications for Legal Aid

A European Agreement on the Transmission of Applications for Legal Aid was concluded under the auspices of the Council of Europe, being signed on 27 January 1977.[28] A relatively simple instrument, it provides that every person who has his or her habitual residence in the territory of one of the Contracting Parties and who wishes to apply for legal aid in civil, commercial, or administrative matters in the territory of another Contracting Party may submit an application in the state where he or she is habitually resident. That state is to transmit the application to the other state.[29] Transmitting and receiving authorities are designated for this purpose.[30] In January 2012 it had thirty-seven parties, including the United Kingdom. An Additional Protocol was signed in 2001.[31] This aimed to improve the efficiency of the operation of the Agreement and to supplement it in certain aspects, in particular as regards questions relating to mutual assistance between central authorities and to the communications between lawyers and applicants for legal aid. In January 2012 it had nine parties.

3. Directive 2003/8

The European Commission's Green Paper, already referred to, expressed serious doubts as to the legitimacy under European law of conditions on eligibility to receive legal aid such as residence, nationality, or even presence in the forum state.[32] Whether or not discrimination of this sort was prohibited, it was judged desirable that all Union citizens, domiciled or habitually resident in the territory of any Member State, should be eligible for legal aid in cross-border disputes, and that this should also apply to third-country nationals who habitually and lawfully resided in a Member State.[33] The outcome was Council Directive

---

[26] Convention, arts 4(3) and 5. An applicant for legal aid who does not reside in a Contracting State may submit an application through consular channels: art 9.

[27] Convention, art 7.

[28] ETS 92.

[29] Agreement, art 1.

[30] Agreement, art 2.

[31] CETS 179.

[32] The Commission drew on the implications of a number of cases, none directly concerned with legal aid: Case 137/84, *Mutsch*, [1985] ECR 2681; Case C-85/96 *Sala v Freistaat Bayern* [1998] ECR I-2694; Case 186/87 *Cowan v Trésor public* [1989] ECR 195; Case C-43/95 *Data Delecta Aktiebolag v MSL Dynamics Ltd* [1996] ECR I-4661; Case C-274/96 *Bickel & Franz* [1998] ECR I-7637.

[33] See Directive 2003/8, Recital (13).

2003/8,[34] which as between Member States[35] takes precedence over both the Hague Convention provisions on legal aid and the European Agreement.

The Directive establishes minimum common rules relating to legal aid in cross-border disputes. It applies, in such disputes, to civil and commercial matters whatever the nature of the court or tribunal. It does not extend, in particular, to revenue, customs, or administrative matters.[36] In this context, a cross-border dispute is one where the party applying for legal aid is domiciled[37] or habitually resident, at the time when the application is submitted, in a Member State other than the Member State where the court is sitting or where the decision is to be enforced.[38]

Natural persons[39] involved in a dispute covered by the Directive are entitled to receive appropriate legal aid in order to ensure their effective access to justice in accordance with the conditions laid down in the Directive. Legal aid is considered to be appropriate when it guarantees pre-litigation advice with a view to reaching a settlement prior to bringing legal proceedings; or legal assistance and representation in court, and exemption from, or assistance with, the cost of proceedings.[40] In some Member States a losing party is liable for the costs of the opposing party. If in such a state the recipient loses the case, the legal aid is to cover the costs incurred by the opposing party, if the same would have been true had the recipient been domiciled or habitually resident in the Member State in which the court is sitting.[41] There is a general non-discrimination principle that Member States must grant legal aid without discrimination to Union citizens and third-country nationals residing lawfully in a Member State.[42]

The Directive is in fact more nuanced than these general statements suggest. It contains conditions relating to financial resources, a means test: legal aid is to be granted to qualified persons who are partly or totally unable to meet the relevant costs of proceedings as a result of their economic situation. A person's economic situation is to be assessed by the competent authority of the Member State in which the court is sitting, in the light of various objective factors such as income, capital, or family situation, including an assessment of the resources of persons who are financially dependent on the applicant. Member States may define thresholds above which legal aid applicants are deemed partly or totally able to bear the costs of

---

[34] Council Directive 2003/8/EC of 27 January 2003 to improve access to justice in cross-border disputes by establishing minimum common rules relating to legal aid for such disputes. Member States were to transpose the Directive into national law by 30 November 2004.

[35] Except Denmark: see Directive, art 1(3).

[36] Directive, art 1.

[37] For the meaning of 'domicile' see Directive, art 2(2) applying Council Regulation (EC) No 44/2001 of 22 December 2000 on jurisdiction and the recognition and enforcement of judgments in civil and commercial matters, art 59.

[38] Directive, art 2.

[39] On the position of legal persons needing legal aid, see Case C-279/09 *DEB Deutsche Energie-handels- und Beratungsgesellschaft mbH v Bundesrepublik Deutschland* [2011] 2 CMLR 21.

[40] Directive, art 3; fees to persons mandated by the court to perform acts during the proceedings are covered.

[41] Directive, art 3(2).

[42] Directive, art 4.

proceedings, but this may not prevent legal aid applicants who are above the thresholds from being granted legal aid if they prove that they are unable to pay the cost of the proceedings as a result of differences in the cost of living between the Member States of domicile or habitual residence and of the forum.[43] Member States may request that legal aid recipients pay reasonable contributions towards the costs of proceedings, taking into account their economic situation; and Member States may provide that the competent authority may decide that recipients of legal aid must refund it in whole or in part if their financial situation has substantially improved or if the decision to grant legal aid had been taken on the basis of inaccurate information given by the recipient.[44]

Member States need not provide legal assistance or representation in the courts or tribunals in proceedings especially designed to enable litigants to make their case in person, except when the courts or any other competent authority otherwise decide in order to ensure equality of parties or in view of the complexity of the case.[45] Further, legal aid does not need to be granted to applicants in so far as they enjoy, in the instant case, effective access to other mechanisms that cover the cost of proceedings.[46]

There are also conditions relating to the substance of disputes, a merits test. Member States may provide that legal aid applications for actions which appear to be manifestly unfounded may be rejected by the competent authorities. If pre-litigation advice is offered, the benefit of further legal aid may be refused or cancelled on grounds related to the merits of the case in so far as access to justice is guaranteed. When taking a decision on the merits of an application, Member States must consider the importance of the individual case to the applicant, but may also take into account the nature of the case when the applicant is claiming damage to his or her reputation but has suffered no material or financial loss, or when the application concerns a claim arising directly out of the applicant's trade or self-employed profession.[47]

The Directive also identifies costs to be borne by the forum state and by the state of domicile or habitual residence. Legal aid granted in the Member State in which the court is sitting must cover the following costs directly related to the cross-border nature of the dispute: interpretation; translation of the documents required by the court or by the competent authority and presented by the recipient which are necessary for the resolution of the case; and travel costs to be borne by the applicant where the physical presence of the persons concerned with the presentation of the applicant's case is required in court by the law or by the court of that Member State and the court decides that the persons concerned cannot be heard to the satisfaction of the court by any other means.[48] However, the Member State in which the legal aid applicant is domiciled or habitually resident must provide legal aid necessary to cover costs relating to the assistance of a local lawyer or any other person entitled by

---

43 Directive, art 5.   44 Directive, art 4(3)(4).   45 Directive, art 3(3).
46 Directive, art 5(5).   47 Directive, art 6.   48 Directive, art 7.

the law to give legal advice, incurred in that Member State until the application for legal aid has been received, in accordance with the Directive, in the Member State where the court is sitting; and the translation of the application and of the necessary supporting documents when the application is submitted to the authorities in that Member State.[49]

Legal aid must continue to be granted totally or partially to recipients to cover expenses incurred in having a judgment enforced in the Member State where the court is sitting. A recipient who in that Member State has received legal aid must receive legal aid provided for by the law of the Member State where recognition or enforcement is sought. Legal aid continues to be available if an appeal is brought either against or by the recipient.[50]

Legal aid applications may be submitted to either the competent authority of the Member State in which the applicant is domiciled or habitually resident, acting as transmitting authority; or to the competent authority of the Member State in which the court is sitting or where the decision is to be enforced, acting as receiving authority.[51]

The Directive required the establishment of a standard form for legal aid applications and for the transmission of such applications, and the Commission published two Decisions accordingly.[52]

III. Security for costs

The Hague Convention on International Access to Justice prohibits Contracting States from requiring a security, bond, deposit of any kind, or any payment as security for court fees from persons (including legal persons) habitually resident in a Contracting State who are plaintiffs or parties intervening in proceedings before the courts or tribunals of another Contracting State where the requirement is imposed by reason only of their foreign nationality or of their not being domiciled or resident in the State in which proceedings are commenced.[53] This provision is balanced by one making it easy to enforce an order for payment of costs and expenses of proceedings, made in one of the Contracting States against any person exempt from such requirements by virtue of the Convention or of the law of the state where the proceedings have been commenced. Such an order must, on the

---

[49] Directive, art 8.

[50] Directive, art 9.

[51] Directive, art 13. For language requirements, see art 14.

[52] Commission Decision 2004/844/EC of 9 November 2004 establishing a form for legal aid applications under Council Directive 2003/8/EC to improve access to justice in cross-border disputes by establishing minimum common rules relating to legal aid for such disputes, and Commission Decision 2005/630/EC of 26 August 2005 establishing a form for the transmission of legal aid applications under Council Directive 2003/8/EC.

[53] Convention, art 14. The 2009 Special Commission considered that nationals of a Contracting State who are habitually resident in the forum state fell within the scope of art 14: Conclusions and Recommendations, para 63.

application of the person entitled to the benefit of the order, be rendered enforceable without charge in any other Contracting State.[54]

IV. Physical detention and safe-conduct

Further provisions of the Hague Convention on International Access to Justice 1980 deal with these issues. Arrest and detention, whether as a means of enforcement or simply as a precautionary measure, must not, in civil or commercial matters, be employed against nationals of a Contracting State or persons habitually resident in a Contracting State in circumstances where they cannot be employed against nationals of the arresting and detaining state.[55] Witnesses and experts who are nationals of or habitually resident in another Contracting State are given safe-conduct and are not liable to prosecution or detention, or subjected to any other restriction on their personal liberty in the forum state for a period commencing seven days before the date fixed for the hearing of the witness or expert and ceasing when the witness or expert having had, for a period of seven consecutive days from the date when he was informed by the judicial authorities that his presence is no longer required, an opportunity of leaving, has nevertheless remained in the territory, or having left it, has returned voluntarily.[56]

V. Mediation

In many states, much attention has been paid in recent years to alternative dispute resolution, including mediation. The European Commission published a Green Paper on alternative dispute resolution in civil and commercial law in 2002,[57] and there is a European Association of Judges for Mediation (GEMME), which is active in developing transnational mediation.

The first piece of legislation dealing with this was European Parliament and Council Directive 2008/52/EC of 21 May 2008 on certain aspects of mediation in civil and commercial matters.[58] The declared objective is to facilitate access to alternative dispute resolution and to promote the amicable settlement of disputes by encouraging the use of mediation and by ensuring a balanced relationship between mediation and judicial proceedings.[59] The Directive applies, in cross-border disputes, to civil and commercial matters except as regards rights and obligations that are not at the parties' disposal under the relevant applicable law. It does not extend, in particular, to revenue, customs, or administrative matters, or

---

[54] Convention, art 15. For the role of transmitting and Central Authorities and the required documentation, see arts 16 and 17.

[55] Convention, art 19.

[56] Convention, art 20.

[57] COM(2002) 196 final, 19.04.2002.

[58] OJ L 136/3, 24.5.2008. Member States are to implement the Directive by 21 May 2011.

[59] Directive, art 1(1).

to the liability of the state for acts and omissions in the exercise of state authority (*acta iure imperii*).[60]

A cross-border dispute is defined as one in which at least one of the parties is domiciled[61] or habitually resident in a Member State [62] other than that of any other party on the date on which (a) the parties agree to use mediation after the dispute has arisen; (b) mediation is ordered by a court; (c) an obligation to use mediation arises under national law; or (d) an invitation is made to the parties under article 5 of the Directive.[63] That provides that a court before which an action is brought may, when appropriate and having regard to all the circumstances of the case, invite the parties to use mediation in order to settle the dispute. The court may also invite the parties to attend an information session on the use of mediation if such sessions are held and are easily available.

'Mediation' is defined to mean 'a structured process, however named or referred to, whereby two or more parties to a dispute attempt by themselves, on a voluntary basis, to reach an agreement on the settlement of their dispute with the assistance of a mediator.' The process may be initiated by the parties or suggested or ordered by a court or prescribed by the law of a Member State. It includes mediation conducted by a judge who is not responsible for any judicial proceedings concerning the dispute in question, but it excludes attempts made by the court or the judge seised to settle a dispute in the course of judicial proceedings concerning the dispute in question.[64]

The Directive imposes a number of obligations on Member States in seeking to ensure the quality of mediation, including by the training of mediators;[65] to ensure that it is possible for the parties, or for one of them with the explicit consent of the others, to request that the content of a written agreement resulting from mediation be made enforceable;[66] and to ensure the confidentiality of mediation;[67] and to ensure that parties who choose mediation in an attempt to settle a dispute are not subsequently prevented from initiating judicial proceedings or arbitration in relation to that dispute by the expiry of limitation or prescription periods during the mediation process.[68]

1. UK implementation

The Directive has been implemented in the United Kingdom. The Cross-Border Mediation (EU Directive) Regulations 2011[69] implement articles 7 and 8 of the Directive, dealing with the confidentiality of mediation and the effect of cross-border mediation on limitation periods. The confidentiality of cross-border

---

[60] Directive, art 1(2).
[61] Domicile is determined in accordance with arts 59 and 60 of Regulation 44/2001.
[62] Denmark is not a Member State for the purposes of the Directive: art 1(3).
[63] Directive, art 2(1).   [64] Directive, art 3(a).
[65] Directive, art 4.   [66] Directive, art 6.
[67] Directive, art 7. For the purposes of arts 7 and 8, 'mediation' has a slightly wider meaning: art 2(2).
[68] Directive, art 8.
[69] SI 2011/1133, applying where a mediation in relation to a relevant dispute starts on or after 20 May 2011. There are corresponding regulations applying in Scotland and Northern Ireland.

mediation is protected by a general provision that a mediator or a mediation administrator has the right to withhold mediation evidence in civil and commercial judicial proceedings and arbitration.[70] This is, however, subject to the power of the court to order that a mediator or a mediation administrator must give or disclose mediation evidence where all parties to the mediation agree to the giving or disclosure of the mediation evidence; or where the giving or disclosure of the mediation evidence is necessary for overriding considerations of public policy;[71] or where the mediation evidence relates to the mediation settlement, and the giving or disclosure of the mediation settlement is necessary to implement or enforce the mediation settlement agreement.[72] The enforcement of mediation settlements is governed by provisions in the Civil Procedure Rules,[73] and further provisions implementing the Directive are in Part 35 of the Family Procedure Rules.

[70] Regulations, reg 9.
[72] Regulations, reg 10.
[71] See art 7(1)(a) of the Directive.
[73] CPR, r 78.24 and 78.25.

5

Criminal Matters: Old Hesitations and Modern Activity

The practice of international judicial assistance in civil and commercial matters is well established and relatively well known. But, at least in countries of the common law tradition, similar co-operation in criminal matters has been, until recent times, strangely neglected. Why is this so?

As a topic, mutual assistance in criminal matters has no obvious place in the legal categories familiar to common lawyers. It lies rather forlornly in a no man's land between private international law on the one hand and criminal procedure on the other. For understandable, but on examination insufficient, reasons it is shunned by specialists in both those areas.

I. Grounds for hesitation

1. Conflict of laws principles: foreign penal laws

Private international lawyers ('conflicts' specialists) feel that their subject has little or nothing to do with criminal matters of any sort. This attitude is largely derived from the principle expressed in Rule 3 of the leading English treatise: 'English courts have no jurisdiction to entertain an action...for the enforcement, either directly or indirectly, of a penal...law of a foreign State'.[1] The Rule expresses

---

[1] Dicey Morris and Collins, *The Conflict of Laws* (14th edn, 2006), para. 5R-019. The English courts will apply their own characterization of the foreign law; that it is regarded as civil and not penal by the foreign state is immaterial: *Iran (Government of) v Barakat Galleries Ltd* [2007] EWCA Civ

a principle found in judicial pronouncements and the writings of commentators in many jurisdictions:

- 'Penal laws of foreign countries are strictly local, and affect nothing more than they can reach, and can be seized by virtue of their authority';[2]
- 'The courts of no country execute the penal laws of another';[3]
- 'No society takes concern in any crime, but what is hurtful to itself'.[4]

These statements of principle, most clearly the last-cited, were made in a time in which virtually all criminal activity was local in its effects. Even the most serious crimes would be 'hurtful' only to one society, and other states could afford to stand aloof. The position is now very different. As Lord Griffiths observed in the Privy Council case of *Liangsiriprasert v United States Government*,[5] 'international crime has to be fought by international co-operation between law enforcement agencies... Unfortunately in this century crime has ceased to be largely local in origin and effect. Crime is now established on an international scale and the criminal law must face this new reality'.

There is a growing realization that organized crime, with its profits from drug-trafficking and major commercial fraud, and corruption, with political leaders able with impunity to steal enormous sums from their national Treasury, can threaten the economic stability and security of whole nation states. States are still proudly sovereign, so that, for example, some refuse to consider the extradition of their nationals whatever the alleged offence, but there is now a willingness to share resources in the fight against international crime.

In these changed circumstances, the hallowed principle that one state will not take cognizance of the penal law of another state requires re-examination. It is now recognized, so far as English law is concerned in the House of Lords' decision in *Re State of Norway's Application*,[6] that the provision of assistance to the prosecution authorities of another state may not amount to even 'indirect' enforcement of the penal law of that state. In that case, the Letters of Request sought evidence for use in proceedings in a Norwegian court concerning allegedly unpaid tax, and it was argued that this contravened the principle (which applies to revenue law no less than to penal law), but it was held that the execution of the Letters of Request, even though the result might assist in the enforcement of the foreign law in the foreign proceedings, did not constitute enforcement, direct or indirect, of that law in England. It is believed that this judgment is of general application, and that it removes any doubts as to the legitimacy at common law of the provision of assistance in criminal matters.

1374, [2009] QB 22; *Pocket Kings Ltd v Safenames Ltd* [2009] EWHC 2529 (Ch), [2010] 2 WLR 1110.

   [2] *Folliott v Ogden* (1789) 1 Hy Bl 123, per Lord Loughborough at 135.

   [3] *The Antelope* (1825) 10 Wheat 123 (US Sup Ct), per Marshall CJ.

   [4] Lord Kames, *Equity*, Book 3, chap 8, s 1 (cited by Story as representing the Scottish position: *Conflict of Laws*, s 622).

   [5] [1991] 1 AC 225 at 242 and 251.

   [6] [1900] 1 AC 723.

2. Criminal procedure: confrontation

From the point of view of criminal procedure, an important principle of the common law tradition had the effect of appearing to render mutual assistance in criminal matters of limited value. This applied to the taking of evidence abroad, which seems to conflict with the principle that, in the words of the Confrontation Clause in the Sixth Amendment to the US Constitution, 'in all criminal prosecutions, the accused shall enjoy the right . . . to be confronted with the witnesses against him'. As the Supreme Court observed, this necessarily implies that the evidence against a defendant 'shall come from a witness stand in a public courtroom where there is full judicial protection of the defendant's right of confrontation, of cross-examination, and of counsel'.[7]

(a) US practice

On its face, that seems to exclude the possibility of using against a defendant evidence taken in his absence, and especially evidence taken abroad. In fact, rule 15 of the US Federal Rules of Criminal Procedure enables a court to allow a prospective witness to be deposed in order to preserve testimony for trial, 'because of exceptional circumstances and in the interest of justice'. The importance of that rule has grown with advances in technology and with the growing impact of international crime and of terrorism. At first telephone links and video recordings were used.[8] Newer technology, video-conferencing in particular, enables courts, in the words of one US judge 'to replicate the face-to-face, eyeball-to-eyeball circumstances of a courtroom.'[9]

In the controversial case of *US v Abu Ali*,[10] the defendant was accused of belonging to an al-Qaeda terrorist cell in Saudi Arabia and making plans to carry out a number of terrorist acts in the United States. The Court of Appeals asserted that the US criminal justice system 'is not without those attributes of adaptation that will permit it to function in the post-9/11 world'. Evidence was required from officials in Saudi Arabia as to the conditions under which the defendant made confessions, which he claimed were made under torture. The officials were not willing to give evidence except in Riyadh; it was judged impossible to take the defendant to Riyadh. A procedure was devised, and what follows is based on its description by the Court of Appeals.

The trial court directed that two defence attorneys should attend the taking of the officials' depositions in Saudi Arabia, while a third attorney was to sit with Abu Ali in Virginia. Two attorneys for the prosecution and a translator were also present

---

[7] *Turner v State of Louisiana* 379 US 466, 472–3 (1964); *Pointer v Texas* 380 US 400 (1965) (applicability to state courts).
[8] See, eg, *US v Salim* 855 F 2d 944 (2nd Circ, 1988) (prosecution evidence taken in France) and *US v Des Marteau* 162 FRD 364 (MD Fla, 1995) (defence evidence taken in Canada).
[9] *US v Zubair Ahmed* 587 F Supp 2d 853 (ND Ohio, 2008).
[10] 528 F 3d 210 (4th Cir, 2008).

in the room in Saudi Arabia while the officers were being deposed. A live, two-way video link was used to transmit the proceedings to a courtroom in Virginia, so that Abu Ali and one of his attorneys could see and hear the testimony contemporaneously; it also allowed the officials to see and hear Abu Ali as he testified. Both the witnesses and Abu Ali were videotaped during the depositions, so that the jury could see their reactions. The trial court presided over the depositions from the courtroom in Virginia, ruling on objections as they arose. Abu Ali was able to communicate via mobile phone with his defence counsel in Saudi Arabia during the frequent breaks in the proceedings. In addition, the court was willing to stop the depositions if Abu Ali's counsel in Saudi Arabia wanted to consult with their client. Deposition testimony was taken under these conditions for seven days. Abu Ali's counsel actively participated throughout these depositions, objecting frequently during the Government's direct examination and cross-examining each of the witnesses at length. In particular, Abu Ali's counsel were able to question the interrogating officers about Abu Ali's claims that he was tortured and beaten; deprived of sleep, food, and water; and denied use of a bathroom and mattress.

The Court of Appeals based its approval of this procedure, which it saw as not violating the Confrontation Clause, partly on public policy grounds:

Insistence on face-to-face confrontation may in some circumstances limit the ability of the United States to further its fundamental interest in preventing terrorist attacks. It is unquestionable that the struggle against terrorism is one of global dimension and that the United States depends upon its allies for logistical support and intelligence in this endeavor. This cooperation can result in foreign officials possessing information vital to prosecutions occurring in American courts. If the government is flatly prohibited from deposing foreign officials anywhere but in the United States, this would jeopardize the government's ability to prosecute terrorists using the domestic criminal justice system.

(b) English practice

In England, the principle behind the Confrontation Clause proved equally influential. It was plainly recognized in the Merchant Shipping Act 1995, section 286 of which (derived from the Merchant Shipping Act 1894) is of much wider application than the Short Title of the Act suggests. In relevant part, the section provides that whenever the testimony of any witness is required in any legal proceedings in the United Kingdom and the witness cannot be found in the Kingdom, any deposition made on oath by such witness before a British consular officer should be admissible in evidence, subject to certain conditions. One of these was that the deposition must 'if the proceedings are criminal proceedings, have been taken in the presence of the accused.'

Where foreign evidence was required not for the prosecution but for the defence, the difficulties of principle were very much reduced. The practice of admitting such evidence seems to have been established at a relatively early date. In the eighteenth century, a woman accused of obtaining a pension by the false pretense that she was the widow of a deceased officer, to whom it was alleged she had never been married, wished to produce evidence of a marriage in Scotland. As the witnesses were in

Scotland and could not be compelled to appear at the trial in England, the court adjourned the proceedings pending the taking of evidence before a judge of the Court of Session in Scotland.[11] Nor did the common law principles stand in the way of the provision of assistance to a foreign court, including the taking of evidence in England for use in foreign proceedings where such evidence would be admissible.[12]

In the changed circumstances of international crime, legislation allows evidence to be taken abroad, and taken in England for use abroad, by live television link.[13]

II. Movement to the modern position

1. Early efforts to secure international co-operation

The spread of multilateral and bilateral agreements for international judicial assistance in civil and commercial matters was not accompanied by similar developments in the criminal context; progress in mutual assistance in criminal matters can fairly be said to be half a century behind.

Some work was done on the subject by the League of Nations Committee of Experts for the Progressive Codification of International Law. A Draft Convention was prepared by a sub-committee, whose rapporteur was Professor Schücking, in 1928.[14] This provided for requests to be sent, in the normal case, through diplomatic channels.[15] The Draft Convention covered 'measures of enquiry', the summoning of witnesses and experts to attend in the requesting state (with immunity from prosecution in respect of earlier conduct), the transfer of persons in custody to appear as witnesses (available only on the basis of reciprocity), and the surrender of exhibits.[16] The striking omission from the text is any reference to the actual taking of evidence in the requested state; presumably it was thought that this was, or could be, covered by international practice as to letters of request.

It was some years after the Second World War before the first modern multilateral mutual assistance treaty was signed. This was the European Convention on Mutual Assistance in Criminal Matters of 1959,[17] which antedated by a decade or more the recent wave of activity in the field.

2. The current scene

If mutual assistance in criminal matters developed relatively slowly, the last decade or so of the twentieth century saw almost frenetic activity, which continues

---

[11] See Lord Mansfield's account of the case in *Mostyn v Fobrigas* (1774) 1 Cwp 161, 174.

[12] See, eg, Extradition Act 1870, s 24 (testimony of any witness may be obtained in relation to any criminal matter pending in any court or tribunal in a foreign state).

[13] Crime (International Co-operation) Act 2003, s 30 ff; see p 231.

[14] League of Nations Doc A.15.1928.V.

[15] Draft Convention, art 5.

[16] Draft Convention, arts 1–3.

[17] See pp 170–177.

unabated. Concern about the drugs trade, international terrorism, and commercial crime generally have led to the creation of a considerable number of *ad hoc* international groups supplementing the work of longer-established organizations. In Europe, the gradual extension of the competence of the European Union has fuelled this process. Generally, it seems that the impetus has come in recent years from bodies which are essentially political in nature rather than, as one might expect, primarily from the specialist bodies in the law enforcement community. The material which follows is intended to sketch the nature of some of this activity, which has either produced or forms an important background to the particular legal measures which constitute international judicial assistance. The conventions, regulations, and other instruments are examined in the appropriate context in the chapter which follow.

(a) Interpol

The best known of all the specialist organizations is the International Criminal Police Organization or Interpol.[18] First established in 1923, it was revived in 1946 after World War II and has grown to an organization with, by 2012, 188 member countries. It has an annual General Assembly and headquarters in France, with regional offices in Argentina, Cameroon, Côte d'Ivoire, El Salvador, Kenya, Thailand, and Zimbabwe. It works through a network of National Central Bureaux (NCBs) staffed by police officers in each member country. Interpol spokespersons tend to be defensive about its work, anxious to dispel the popular perception of the organization as an international investigative agency, but equally concerned that it should not be seen as a mere communications centre.[19]

Its communications role is nonetheless a very important one. It operates a system of international notices, for example red notices for wanted persons (of which more than 5,000 were issued in 2009) and green notices about professional offenders believed to be operating in several countries, and circulates modus operandi reports and organized crime bulletins. Interpol maintains very large databases, not only on international offenders, including fingerprints and DNA profiles, but also on stolen motor vehicles, stolen works of art, traffic in explosives and firearms, and stolen or lost travel documents.

The ethos of Interpol, with its strong emphasis on practical police work, reflected in the fact that police officers make up a high proportion of its international staff, has prevented it taking major initiatives in the strictly legal field. It has tended to follow rather than lead the development of legal provision for international judicial assistance.

---

[18] See M Anderson, *Policing the World: INTERPOL and the Politics of International Police Co-operation* (OUP, 1989); M Deflem, *Policing Worlds Society* (OUP, 2002); N Gerspacher, 'The Roles of International Police Co-operation Organizations' (2005) 13 Eur J Crime Crim L & Crim Just 413.

[19] See also the professional criticisms of Interpol's work, at least in previous years, recorded in the report of the House of Commons Home Affairs Committee on Practical Police Co-operation in the European Community (HC363, Session 1989–1990).

(b) World Customs Organization

Although it uses as its working name the title World Customs Organization (WCO), this body is formally constituted as the Customs Co-operation Council. Originally a wholly European grouping dating from 1953, it now has a worldwide membership.[20] It serves as the international body for co-operation between customs administrations, work made more complex by the different allocation of functions in member states as between customs, police forces, border militia or coastguards, and revenue authorities. The WCO headquarters are in Brussels; its Council's Enforcement Committee is important in the present context.

A central legal instrument in its work is the International Convention on Mutual Administrative Assistance for the Prevention, Investigation and Repression of Customs Offences adopted in Nairobi in June 1977; an amending Protocol of 1985, enabling administrations which were not members of the Council to be parties to the Nairobi Convention, came into force in July 1989. The Convention has a number of Annexes and its structure allows Contracting Parties[21] to accept each Annex separately. For example, Annex IV deals with assistance, on request, in surveillance operations; Annex V with the appearance of customs officials before a court or tribunal abroad; and Annex X with assistance in the drugs field. The Convention is supplemented by Recommendations of the Council dealing with technical aspects of customs operations. It was supplemented in 2003 by the Johannesburg Convention, the International Convention on Mutual Administrative Assistance in Customs Matters, but by 2012 this had only three ratifications and had not come into force.

(c) United Nations

The United Nations has an Office on Drugs and Crime (UNODC) based in Vienna, which facilitates international co-operation and sponsors research. It is responsible for a range of programmes, such as the Global Programme against Money-Laundering, Proceeds of Crime and the Financing of Terrorism, established in 1997. Every five years the United Nations organizes a Congress on the Prevention of Crime and the Treatment of Offenders, the most recent being the Twelfth Congress, held in Brazil in 2010. The nature of these gatherings has varied over the years, that held in Habana in 1990 being unusually well-prepared and productive, with an elaborate series of Regional and Interregional Preparatory Meetings. In particular, it adopted Model Treaties on a number of matters, including Mutual Assistance in Criminal Matters, the Transfer of Proceedings in Criminal Matters, and Extradition. The United Nations has also been very active in the drugs field, notably in sponsoring the negotiation which led to the 1988 Vienna Convention against Illicit Traffic in Narcotic Drugs and Psychotropic Substances.

---

[20] 177 national customs bodies in 2012.   [21] There were 51 parties as at June 2010.

In 2000, it opened for signature a UN Convention on Transnational Organized Crime, and a UN Convention against Corruption followed in 2003.

(d) G8

The Group of Eight (originally Seven) leading industrial nations has taken an interest in this field, having established in 1989 an influential Financial Action Task Force. This concentrated on money laundering, and its work is considered more fully in that context. In 1990, the G7 Summit established a Chemical Action Task Force to deal with issues relating to the diversion of precursor and essential chemicals into illicit drug production. It did much work over the next few years, but its role was then transferred to the United Nations.[22]

(e) The Commonwealth Secretariat

The Commonwealth Secretariat, based in London, provides a range of services to Commonwealth governments; it is answerable ultimately to the Commonwealth Heads of Government Meetings. It has long been active in international efforts to combat crime,[23] early evidence of which was the production of the London Scheme for the Rendition of Fugitive Offenders; what now seems a rather quaint title conceals a modern instrument for extradition as between Commonwealth member countries. Its Legal and Administrative Affairs Division has responded to requests by Law Ministers by developing a series of schemes for mutual assistance in the administration of justice, including the Harare Scheme of 1986 for Mutual Assistance in Criminal Matters.

(f) The Council of Europe

The Council of Europe, a regional organization established in 1949, pre-dates and has a wider membership than the European Union; non-European states can and do take part in many of its activities. It has always taken a keen interest in criminal matters, and was early in the international assistance field with the European Convention on Mutual Assistance in Criminal Matters being signed in 1959, with an Additional Protocol signed in 1978, and a Second Additional Protocol in 2001.

It has produced a large number of conventions relevant to this work: the European Convention on the International Validity of Criminal Judgments 1970; the European Convention on the Transfer of Proceedings in Criminal Matters 1972; the European Convention on the Suppression of Terrorism 1977;

---

[22] See W C Gilmore, 'The G7 and Transnational Drug Trafficking: The Task Force Experience' in P J Cullen and W C Gilmore (eds), *Crime sans Frontières: International and European Approaches* (Edinburgh University Press, 1998), pp 30–8.

[23] See D Stafford, 'Combating Transnational Crime: The Role of the Commonwealth' in ibid, pp 44–9.

the Convention on the Transfer of Sentenced Persons 1983; the Convention on Laundering, Search, Seizure and Confiscation of the Proceeds from Crime 1990; the Convention on Cybercrime 2001 with an Additional Protocol in 2003; the Council of Europe Convention on the Prevention of Terrorism 2005; the Council of Europe Convention on Action against Trafficking in Human Beings 2005; and the Council of Europe Convention on Preventing and Combating Violence Against Women and Domestic Violence 2011.

Within its structures, where acronyms flourish, are a Committee of Experts on Terrorism (CODEXTER), a Committee of Experts on the Evaluation of Anti-Money Laundering Measures and the Financing of Terrorism (MONEYVAL), a Committee for the Prevention of Torture and Inhuman or Degrading Treatment or Punishment (CPT), a Group of States against Corruption (GRECO), a Group of Experts on Action against Trafficking in Human Beings (GRETA); there is an Economic Crime Division within its Directorate of Co-operation.

(g) The European Union

The development of the European Community's or Union's involvement in criminal matters is a rather complicated story, and reflects the changes in the structure and governance of the Union itself.

Before Maastricht

In the first phase, until the Treaty of Maastricht in 1982, there was no Community competence: co-operation between Member States in relevant fields took place outside the formal Community framework. So, in 1976 the United Kingdom suggested a new European inter-governmental forum for co-operation at a practical and operational level in combating terrorism, drugs trafficking, and serious crime and public order generally. Its name, TREVI, was a reference to the fountain in Rome, where the initial meeting was held, and to M Fontaine a leading participant; such whimsical humour is a rare commodity in international organizations.[24] TREVI had a number of Working Groups, dealing with terrorism, a range of public order (including football crowd control) and equipment issues; and drugs and organized crime, ultimately guided by a Programme of Action agreed in 1990.

The Schengen agreements

The first Schengen Agreement, the Agreement between the Governments of the States of the Benelux Union, the Federal Republic of Germany, and the French Republic on the gradual abolition of controls at frontiers, was signed in June 1985. The context was the desire of the European Commission and many Member States to abolish border controls as part of the Single European Market. The necessity and desirability of such a development were alike controversial, and there are important

---

[24] Indeed, it was so out of line with the prevailing earnestness of European institutions that TREVI was declared to be an acronym for Terrorisme, Radicalisme, Extremisme et Violence Internationale.

implications for law enforcement.[25] The removal of internal barriers to the free movement of criminals places more weight on security at the external border of the Union, and creates new requirements for co-operation between law enforcement agencies within each Member State.

Schengen I drew on the experience of the Benelux countries in removing border controls, and was followed by a much more sensitive document, known as Schengen II and more formally as the Convention implementing the earlier Agreement, in June 1990.[26] This contemplates 'hot pursuit' by national police forces across frontiers, contains mutual assistance provisions in Chapter 2 (articles 48 to 53), and established an Executive Committee with considerable powers. The Convention provided for a computerized database, the Schengen Information System (SIS), capable of serving a maximum of eighteen states; the second generation SIS was to prove a decade-long project, conceived in 2001, established in 2006, and incomplete in 2010. By Protocol No 19 to the Treaty on the Functioning of the European Union, the Schengen *acquis* is integrated into the structures of the Union, the Council replacing the Executive Committee.

All the then Member States acceded to the Convention except for the United Kingdom and Ireland, which remained aloof. In 1999, however, the United Kingdom announced its wish to participate in many aspects of the Schengen system, including the mutual assistance arrangements and the SIS, and later the European Agency for the operational management of large-scale IT systems in the area of freedom, security, and justice, but not the 'hot pursuit' provisions.[27]

Maastricht and the 'Third Pillar'

The position of criminal matters within the EU changed with the implementation in 1993 of the Maastricht Treaty, Title VI of which created the so-called 'Third Pillar' dealing with co-operation in the fields of Justice and Home Affairs (JHA). A new body, the 'K4 Committee',[28] drew together the work of the previously separate groups such as TREVI. The Community acquired competence to negotiate agreements for mutual assistance in customs matters with foreign countries.[29]

A number of significant actions followed. Europol and the European Judicial Network were created; they are considered further below. In 1996, the Council adopted a Joint Action concerning the approximation of the laws and practices of the Member States of the European Union to combat drug addiction and to prevent and combat illegal drug trafficking.[30] In the following year, it adopted an

---

[25] See a report of the House of Lords Select Committee on the European Communities, *Border Control of People* (HL 90, Session 1988–89).

[26] Signed originally between the five parties to the 1985 Agreement.

[27] Council Decision of 29 May 2000 (2000/365/EC), OJ L 131, 1.6.2000 and Council Decision of 14 December 2010 (2010/779/EU, OJ L 333/58, 17.12.2010.

[28] The name is derived from the relevant article of the Treaty.

[29] See the Agreement with the United States, agreed at The Hague in May 1997, OJ L 222, 12.8.1997.

[30] Joint Action 96/750/JHA, OJ L 342, 31.12.1996.

Action Plan to Combat Organized Crime[31] containing fifteen 'political guidelines' and thirty detailed action points; a Multidisciplinary Group on Organized Crime was established to take the Action Plan forward.

As part of the implementation of that Action Plan, in June 1998 the Council adopted a Joint Action on good practice in mutual legal assistance in criminal matters,[32] and later in 1998 further Joint Actions on money laundering[33] and on the criminalization of participation in organized crime.[34]

Amsterdam: the area of freedom, security, and justice

The Treaty of Amsterdam 1997 made significant changes in the institutional geography, with new Community competence in an 'area of freedom, security and justice' which covers such matters related to the free movement of persons as immigration and asylum, and a slimmed-down version of the Third Pillar covering police and customs co-operation and judicial co-operation in criminal matters. Within that Third Pillar, the range of available forms of action by the European institutions was expanded to include 'framework decisions' as to the approximation of national laws. A special European Council held at Tampere, Finland, in October 1999, set the political agenda for the new 'area of freedom, security and justice'. Its conclusions included references to extradition, the mutual recognition of criminal judgments and orders, the establishment of joint investigative teams, a European Police College, the revision of the Directive on money laundering, the extension of Europol's competence in money laundering to cover predicate offences of all types, and the establishment of Eurojust.

The European Crime Prevention Network was established by a Council Decision in May 2001,[35] and re-established by a fresh Decision in 2009.[36] It consists of designated contact points (competent national authorities or academic specialists), and is directed to pay particular attention to the fields of juvenile, urban, and drug-related crime.

Probably the most significant actions were the establishment in May 2000 of a Convention on Mutual Assistance in Criminal Matters and the creation of the European Arrest Warrant (EAW). Work was also done on money laundering, on victims of crime, on combating terrorism, on freezing orders, and on combating human trafficking; and, in terms of operational co-operation, on joint investigation teams and liaison officers.

---

[31] OJ C 251, 15.8.97. See also the Council Resolution of 21 December 1998 on the prevention of organized crime with reference to the establishment of a comprehensive strategy for combating it (OJ C 408, 29.12.1998); this adds little, and may be a sign of the need of each Presidency to be seen to be 'doing something' about crime.

[32] Joint Action 98/427/JHA, OJ L 191, 7.7.98.

[33] Joint Action 98/699/JHA, OJ L 333, 9.12.1998.

[34] Joint Action 98/733/JHA, OJ, L 351 29.12.1998.

[35] Decision of 28 May 2001 setting up a European crime prevention network (2001/427/JHA), OJ L 153, 8.6.2001.

[36] Council Decision 2009/902/JHA of 30 November 2009 setting up a European Crime Prevention Network (EUCPN) and repealing Decision 2001/427/JHA, OJ L 321/44, 8.12.2009.

The Hague Programme

The 'Hague Programme' for the years 2004 to 2009 emphasized fighting against terrorism; developing a strategy to tackle organized crime at EU level, for example through Europol and Eurojust; and promoting effective access to civil and criminal justice. During this period there was a series of Council Framework Decisions applying the principle of mutual recognition to various types of penalty and dealing with the taking into account of convictions in other Member States, and further instruments were adopted dealing with the proceeds of crime, the victims of crime, and trafficking in human beings. A number of Decisions addressed the continuing threats posed by terrorism and organized crime, and a new network was established on corruption. A significant Framework Decision created the European Evidence Warrant (EEW).

The Stockholm Programme

The 'Stockholm Programme' for 2010 to 2014[37] included devising a strategy to ensure that an integrated and co-ordinated approach is provided to victims of crime, if necessary by creating one comprehensive legal instrument on the protection of victims; implementing a 'road map' for strengthening procedural rights of suspected and accused persons in criminal proceedings; and exploring the results of the evaluation of the EAW.[38] The last two items are examined further, below.

Treaty of Lisbon

After the adoption of the Treaty of Lisbon, which came into effect in 2009, judicial co-operation in criminal matters forms Chapter 4 (articles 82 to 86) of Title V in Part Three of the Treaty on the Functioning of the European Union. Under Protocol No 21, the United Kingdom (and Ireland) are not bound by decisions taken under these provisions of the Treaty but may 'opt-in' on a case-by-case basis.

The European Arrest Warrant

This book does not seek to deal with the complex topic of extradition, which is the subject of many international treaties, previous EU instruments[39] and a Commonwealth Scheme. The operation of the EAW, leading to the surrender of a person to the authorities of another Member State, could well be seen as a form of extradition. The same is true of the system of 'backing of warrants' which operates between England or Wales and the Isle of Man and the Channel Islands, and formerly between other parts of the United Kingdom, and between the UK and Ireland.

The Framework Decision which introduced the EAW[40] presents it in a different light. It takes as its starting point the decisions of the European Council at Tampere

---

[37] OJ C 115/1, 4.5.2010.

[38] See the report of the House of Commons Justice Committee, *Justice Issues in Europe* (Seventh Report of Session 2009–10; HC 162).

[39] See M Mackarel and S Nash, 'Extradition and the European Union' (1997) 46 ICLQ 954.

[40] Council Framework Decision 2002/584 of 13 June 2002 on the EAW and the surrender procedures between Member States, OJ L 190/1, 18.7.2002. See R Blekxtoon and W van Ballegooij, *Handbook on the European Arrest Warrant* (T M C Asser Press, 2005), M Jimeno-Bulnes, 'The

in October 1999, the identification of the principle of mutual recognition as the cornerstone of future co-operation, and the specific identification of mutual enforcement of arrest warrants in the Tampere Conclusions. So 'the objective set for the Union to become an area of freedom, security and justice leads to abolishing extradition between Member States and replacing it by a system of surrender between judicial authorities'.[41] It is a very significant instrument in the development of international co-operation in Europe and some account must be given of it.

Under the Framework Decision, Member States must execute an EAW, defined as a judicial decision issued by a Member State with a view to the arrest and surrender by another Member State of a requested person, for the purposes of conducting a criminal prosecution or executing a custodial sentence or detention order.[42] There is no mandatory system of central authorities, but a Member State may appoint one or more central authorities to assist its competent judicial authorities.[43] An EAW may be issued for acts punishable by the law of the issuing Member State by a custodial sentence or a detention order for a maximum period of at least twelve months or, where a sentence has been passed or a detention order has been made, for sentences of at least four months.[44] Expenses incurred in the territory of the executing Member State for the execution of a EAW are to be borne by that Member State; all other expenses by the issuing Member State.[45]

In some cases, execution of an EAW may be subject to double criminality.[46] This is not necessary in cases involving one or more of the offences listed in article 2 (2) which are punishable in the issuing state by a custodial sentence or a detention order for a maximum period of at least three years.[47] If the EAW is not related to any of those offences and its execution would require a search or seizure,

---

Enforcement of the European Arrest Warrant: A Comparison Between Spain and the UK' (2007) 15 Eur J Crime Crim L & Crim J 263, and for an account of the development of the Decision and the issues which gave rise to concern in the preparatory stages, see M Plachta, 'European Arrest Warrant: Revolution in Extradition?' (2003) 11 Eur J Crime Crim L & Crim J 178.

[41] Framework Decision, Recital (5).

[42] Framework Decision, art 1. For the form and content of an EAW, see art 8 and the Annex to the Framework Decision. In certain cases, an alert in the Schengen Information System (SIS) is deemed equivalent to a EAW: art 9(3). An EAW may be transmitted directly to the relevant executing judicial authority, or via the SIS, the secure telecommunications system of the European Judicial Network or Interpol: arts 9 and 10; the Interpol channel is used in some 60 per cent of all cases: see the Commission's 2007 report on the implementation of the Framework Decision, COM/2007/407 final.

[43] Framework Decision, arts 6 and 7.

[44] Framework Decision, art 2(1). See *Pilecki v Circuit Court of Legnica, Poland* [2008] UKHL 7, [2008] 1 WLR 325.

[45] Framework Decision, art 30. See *Dabas v High Court of Justice in Madrid, Spain* [2007] UKHL 6, [2007] 2 AC 31 per Lord Hope of Craighead at [42]: 'It must be borne in mind too that, for obvious practical reasons, a large number of European arrest warrants are not directed at only one member state . . . The person who issues a European arrest warrant is not required to address it to any particular member state. Once issued, it is available to be used wherever the requested person happens to be when it is executed.'

[46] Framework Decision, art 2(3).

[47] The list is the same as in other Framework Decisions: see p 333, n 112. See *Office of the King's Prosecutor, Brussels v Cando Armas* [2005] UKHL 67, [2006] 2 AC 1.

recognition or execution of the EAW may be subject to the condition of double criminality.[48]

There are a number of grounds for a refusal to execute an EAW, some mandatory and others optional. Execution must be refused:

(a) if the offence on which the warrant is based is covered by amnesty in the executing Member State, where that state had jurisdiction to prosecute the offence under its own criminal law;

(b) if the executing judicial authority is informed that the requested person has been finally judged by a Member State in respect of the same acts provided that, where there has been sentence, the sentence has been served or is currently being served or may no longer be executed under the law of the sentencing Member State;

(c) if the person who is the subject of the EAW may not, owing to his age, be held criminally responsible for the acts on which the warrant is based under the law of the executing state.[49]

The optional grounds, where execution may be refused, are more numerous. They are:

(a) where double criminality is required and is not established;

(b) where the person who is the subject of the EAW is being prosecuted in the executing Member State for the same act as that on which the EAW is based;

(c) where the judicial authorities of the executing Member State have decided either not to prosecute for the offence on which the EAW is based or to halt proceedings, or where a final judgment has been passed upon the requested person in a Member State, in respect of the same acts, which prevents further proceedings;

(d) where the criminal prosecution or punishment of the requested person is statute-barred according to the law of the executing Member State and the acts fall within the jurisdiction of that Member State under its own criminal law;

(e) if the executing judicial authority is informed that the requested person has been finally judged by a third state in respect of the same acts provided that, where there has been sentence, the sentence has been served or is currently being served or may no longer be executed under the law of the sentencing country;

(f) if the EAW has been issued for the purposes of execution of a custodial sentence or detention order, where the requested person is staying in, or is a national or a resident of the executing Member State and that state undertakes to execute the sentence or detention order in accordance with its domestic law;

---

[48] Framework Decision 2008, art 14.   [49] Framework Decision, art 3.

(g) where the EAW relates to offences which are regarded by the law of the executing Member State as having been committed in whole or in part in the territory of the executing Member State or in a place treated as such; or have been committed outside the territory of the issuing Member State and the law of the executing Member State does not allow prosecution for the same offences when committed outside its territory.[50]

In certain cases, the law of the executing Member State may impose conditions on the execution of the EAW. These are certain cases of decisions rendered in absentia, and certain cases of life sentences.[51] Similarly, where a person who is the subject of a EAW for the purposes of prosecution is a national or resident of the executing Member State, surrender may be subject to the condition that the person, after being heard, is returned to the executing Member State in order to serve there the custodial sentence or detention order passed against him in the issuing Member State.[52]

The Framework Decision contains detailed provisions as to the requested person's rights to counsel and an interpreter, and the possibility of provisional release on bail.[53] The requested person may consent to his or her surrender to the requesting Member State,[54] but in any other case he or she is entitled to be heard by the executing judicial authority, in accordance with the law of the executing Member State, and the executing judicial authority is to decide whether the person is to be surrendered.[55]

Once a decision has been taken to surrender the requested person, the surrender must take place within ten days.[56] It may exceptionally be temporarily postponed for serious humanitarian reasons, for example if there are substantial grounds for believing that it would manifestly endanger the requested person's life or health.[57] Surrender may also be postponed so that the requested person may be prosecuted in the executing Member State or, if he or she has already been sentenced, so that he or she may serve, in its territory, a sentence passed for an act other than that referred to in the EAW.[58]

After surrender, the issuing Member State must deduct all periods of detention arising from the execution of a EAW from the total period of detention to be served in the issuing Member State as a result of a custodial sentence or detention order being passed.[59] Article 27 addresses the 'specialty rule' familiar in extradition cases, under which a surrendered person may not be prosecuted for offences other than

---

[50] Framework Decision, art 4.
[51] Framework Decision, art 5(1),(2).
[52] Framework Decision, art 5(3).
[53] Framework Decision, arts 11 and 12.
[54] Framework Decision, art 13.
[55] Framework Decision, arts 14 and 15. For time limits (60 days from arrest to final decision) see art 17. For conflicting requests or conflicts with other international obligations, see arts 16 and 21.
[56] Framework Decision, art 23(2). For the handing over of property required as evidence or which has been acquired by the requested person, see art 29.
[57] Framework Decision, art 23(4).
[58] Framework Decision, art 24.
[59] Framework Decision, art 26.

those which are the subject of the extradition request. This rule applies in EAW cases, but may be the subject of general waiver by individual Member States in their relations with other Member States that have given the same waiver; but the effect of the waiver may be disapplied in any particular case. The requested person may waive the specialty rule, which is also inapplicable in certain other prescribed cases.[60]

The implementation of the Framework Decision was not uneventful.[61] It escaped a challenge before the European Court of Justice, which alleged conflict with the Treaty provisions,[62] but the provisions allowing the surrender of nationals, for some Member States a major innovation, ran into serious difficulties. It was held unconstitutional, or in conflict with other provisions of national law, in Cyprus, Germany, and Poland, but in each case amendments were made to national law, though in the case of Germany only after a hiatus of thirteen months.[63] Nonetheless, the EAW is an undoubted success at least in securing prompt surrender.

An unusually frank assessment is to be found in the 2011 report by the Commission on the implmentation of the EAW Framework Decision:[64]

The Commission has received representations from European and national parliamentarians, defence lawyers, citizens and civil society groups highlighting a number of problems with the operation of the EAW: no entitlement to legal representation in the issuing state during the surrender proceedings in the executing state; detention conditions in some Member States combined with sometimes lengthy pre-trial detention for surrendered persons and the non-uniform application of a proportionality check by issuing states, resulting in requests for surrender for relatively minor offences that, in the absence of a proportionality check in the executing state, must be executed.

From the issues raised in relation to the operation of the EAW it would seem that, despite the fact that the law and criminal procedures of all Member States are subject to the standards of the European Court of Human Rights, there are often some doubts about standards being similar across the EU.[65] While an individual can have recourse to the European Court of Human Rights to assert rights arising from the European Convention on Human Rights, this can only be done after an alleged breach has occurred and all domestic legal avenues have been exhausted. This has not proved to be an effective means of ensuring that signatories comply with the Convention's standards.

---

[60] Framework Decision, art 27(3).

[61] See M Mackarel, 'The European Arrest Warrant—the Early Years: Implementing and Using the Warrant' (2007) 15 Eur J Crime Crim L & Crim J 37, which examines, inter alia, the Commission's criticisms of UK legislative implementation.

[62] Case C-303/05 *Advocaten voor de Wereld VZW v Leden van de Ministerraad* [2007] ECR I-3633. See P O'Reilly, 'The Exit of the Elephant from the European Arrest Warrant Parlour' (2007) 2 J Eur Crim Law 23; D Sarmiento 'The European Arrest Warrant and the Quest for Constitutional Coherence' (2008) 6 Int J of Const L 171.

[63] See the Commission's 2007 report on the implementation of the Framework Decision, COM/2007/407 final and Z Deen-Racsmány, 'The European Arrest Warrant and the Surrender of Nationals Revisited: The Lessons of Constitutional Challenges' (2006) 14 Eur J Crime Crim L & Crim J 271.

[64] COM(2011) 175 final,11.4.2011, section 4.

[65] See *Minister for Justice Equality and Law Reform v Rettinger* [2010] IESC 45.

With hindsight, many feel that the 'roadmap' for strengthening the procedural rights of suspected or accused persons in criminal proceedings should have been pursued before the introduction of the EAW.

The 'roadmap' for strengthening procedural rights of suspected and accused persons in criminal proceedings,[66] indentified six priority measures: the right to interpretation and translation;[67] the right to information about rights (Letter of Rights);[68] pre-trial legal advice and at-trial legal aid; a detained person's right to communicate with family members, employers, and consular authorities; protection for vulnerable suspects;[69] and a Green Paper on pre-trial detention.[70]

A second 'roadmap' was adopted in June 2011, addressing the need to strengthen the rights and protection of victims of crime, especially in criminal proceedings.[71] This will lead to the review and development of existing EU instruments in this area.[72]

(h) Eurojust

The creation of Eurojust, bringing together prosecutors, judges, and police officers to reinforce the fight against serious organized crime, was clearly seen as a desirable political gesture, but there was for some time considerable uncertainty as to what Eurojust was actually meant to do: as the European Commission put it with some delicacy, 'notions and concepts on what tasks and powers Eurojust should have varied rather widely'.[73] At the end of 2000, the Council decided to establish a Provisional Judicial Co-operation Unit, later referred to as Pro-Eurojust, the main task of which was 'to improve co-operation between the competent national authorities with regard to investigations and prosecutions in relation to serious crime, particularly when it is organised, involving two or more Member States'.

Eurojust itself was established by a Council Decision of 28 February 2002.[74] It was to comprise one national member seconded by each Member State, who could

---

[66] Resolution of the Council of 30 November 2009, OJ C 295/1, 4.12.2009.

[67] Already acted upon in Directive 2010/64/EU of the European Parliament and of the Council of 20 October 2010 on the right to interpretation and translation in criminal proceedings, OJ L 280/1, 26.10.2010.

[68] See the Proposal for a Directive of the European Parliament and of the Council on the right to information in criminal proceedings, COM(2010)392 final.

[69] See the Proposal for a Directive of the European Parliament and of the Council on the right of access to a lawyer in criminal proceedings and on the right to communicate upon arrest, COM(2011) 326 final.

[70] See 'Strengthening mutual trust in the European judicial area: A Green Paper on the application of EU criminal justice legislation in the field of detention, COM(2011)327 final.

[71] Resolution of the Council of 10 June 2011, OJ C 187/1, 28.6.2011.

[72] Council Framework Decision 2001/220/JHA of 15 March 2001 on the standing of victims in criminal proceedings and Council Directive 2004/80/EC of 29 April 2004 relating to crime victims, OJ L 261/15, 6.8.2004. See the Proposal for a Directive of the European Parliament and Council establishing minimum standards on the rights, support and protection of victims of crime, COM/ 2011/0275 final.

[73] Communication to the Council, COM(2000) 746 final, 21.11.2000.

[74] Council Decision of 28 February 2002 setting up Eurojust with a view to reinforcing the fight against serious crime (2002/187/JHA), OJ L 63/1, 6.3.2002.

be a prosecutor, a judge, or a police officer of equivalent competence, and whose term of office has to be at least four years. Each member was to have one deputy and one assistant. It was only in 2009 that it was required that the members be based in the Eurojust headquarters in The Hague.[75] There are elaborate rules as to personal data and a Joint Supervisory Body to monitor their observance. The national members could act individually or as a College.

In 2009 an 'On-Call Coordination' facility was established, available throughout the year on a 24-hour basis.[76] A further development in 2009 was a new requirement that each Member State should have one or more national correspondents for Eurojust and a Eurojust national co-ordination system to ensure co-ordination of the work carried out by the national correspondents for Eurojust, the national correspondent for Eurojust for terrorism matters, the national correspondent for the European Judicial Network and up to three other contact points of the European Judicial Network, and the national members or contact points of the Network for Joint Investigation Teams and of the networks of contact points in respect of persons responsible for genocide, crimes against humanity and war crimes and corruption.

The scale of Eurojust's activities was initially, and in operational terms remains, modest. Its contribution was declared to have been 'positive' in a rather defensive report by the Commission in 2007, which noted the increase in operational cases from 588 in 2005 to 771 in 2006.[77] There were 1,372 cases in 2009, when its expenditure was €28,177,688.

Under what is now article 85 of the Treaty on the Functioning of the European Union, Eurojust's mission is to support and strengthen co-ordination and co-operation between national investigating and prosecuting authorities in relation to serious crime affecting two or more Member States or requiring a prosecution on common bases, on the basis of operations conducted and information supplied by the Member States' authorities and by Europol. Regulations of the European Parliament and the Council may determine Eurojust's structure, operation, field of action, and tasks[78].

(i) Europol

The establishment of a European Police Office or Europol, originally proposed by Germany, was envisaged at the time of the Maastricht Treaty in 1992; it was seven years before Europol became operational, in July 1999. The first proposal was for a European Criminal Investigation Office, modelled on the United States' FBI, but this proved unacceptable. By 1993 there was agreement to establish a European Drugs Unit (EDU) based in The Hague, but there was continuing disagreement

---

[75] Council Decision, arts 2, as amended by Council Decision 2009/426/JHA of 16 December 2008, OJ L 138, 14 4.6.2009, and 9.

[76] Council Decision, art 5a, inserted by Council Decision 2009/426/JHA.

[77] Communication on the role of Eurojust and the European Judicial Network in the fight against organised crime and terrorism in the European Union, COM(2007) 644 final, 23.10.2007.

[78] Under art 86 TFEU, a European Public Prosecutor's Office may be established from Eurojust in order to combat crimes affecting the financial interests of the Union.

about many aspects of the future Europol. The Europol Convention was eventually signed in 1995, amended on a number of occasions, and eventually replaced in 2009 by a Council Decision.[79] Europol is governed by a Management Board and has, like Eurojust, a joint supervisory body concerned with data protection issues.

Europol is based in The Hague and relates to designated national units, corresponding to the Interpol's NCBs, and each unit designates one or more liaison officers. It can be involved in the work of joint investigation teams and maintains the Europol Information System, searched 150,000 times a year, and a Secure Information Exchange Network Application (SIENA) under which 300,000 messages are exchanged each year. It operates in connection with organized crime, terrorism, and other forms of serious crime as listed in the Annex to the Decision and affecting two or more Member States in such a way as to require a common approach by the Member States owing to the scale, significance, and consequences of the offences.[80]

(j) European Judicial Network in Criminal Matters

The European Judicial Network was originally set up in 1998.[81] The creation of Eurojust and the gradual implementation of the principle of mutual recognition of decisions prompted a reconsideration of the Network and it now operates under a new Council Decision taken in December 2008.[82]

The European Judicial Network is made up of the central authorities responsible for international judicial co-operation and the judicial or other competent authorities with specific responsibilities within the context of international co-operation. In each Member State there are to be found one or more contact points, care being taken to ensure effective coverage of the whole of its territory; a national correspondent for the European Judicial Network, chosen from among the contact points; and another with, in English, the very odd title 'tool correspondent for the European Judicial Network'. Liaison magistrates, where appointed, may also be linked to the Network.[83]

The Network operates by facilitating the establishment of appropriate contacts between the contact points in the various Member States; through periodic meetings of the Member States' representatives; and by providing up-to-date

---

[79] Council Decision of 6 April 2009 establishing the European Police Office (Europol), OJ L 121/37, 15.5.2009.

[80] Council Decision, art 4. See M Sabatier, *La Co-opération Européenne Policière* (Paris 2001); N Gerspacher, 'The Roles of International Police Co-operation Organizations' (2005) 13 Eur J Crime Crim L & Crim Just 413.

[81] Joint Action of 29 June 1998 adopted by the Council on the basis of Article K.3 of the Treaty on European Union, on the creation of a European Judicial Network, OJ L 191/4, 7.7.1998.

[82] Council Decision 2008/976/JHA of 16 December 2008 on the European Judicial Network OJ L 348/130, 24.12.2008.

[83] Council Decision, art 2.

background information, in particular by means of a website and a secure telecommunications network.[84]

The contact points are to be active intermediaries with the task of facilitating judicial co-operation between Member States, particularly in actions to combat forms of serious crime. They must be available to enable local judicial authorities and other competent authorities in their own Member State, contact points in the other Member States, and local judicial and other competent authorities in the other Member States to establish the most appropriate direct contacts. They are to provide the local judicial authorities in their own Member State, the contact points in the other Member States, and the local judicial authorities in the other Member States with the legal and practical information necessary to enable them to prepare an effective request for judicial co-operation or to improve judicial co-operation in general.[85]

The national correspondent is responsible, in his or her Member State, for issues related to the internal functioning of the Network, including the co-ordination of requests for information and replies issued by the competent national authorities; is the main person responsible for the contacts with the Network's Secretariat; and may advise on the appointment of new contact points.[86] The tool correspondent is responsible for the accuracy and currency of prescribed information disseminated via the Secretariat.[87]

The Network and Eurojust are to 'maintain privileged relations with each other, based on consultation and complementarity, especially between the contact points of a Member State, the Eurojust national member of the same Member State and the national correspondents for the European Judicial Network and Eurojust'.[88]

(k) Mutual assistance in specialized fields

In a number of other contexts, international instruments provide, usually in the most general terms, for states to afford one another measures of assistance in connection with criminal proceedings. Examples are to be found in the various conventions seeking to protect civil aviation from terrorism and hijacking.[89]

---

[84] Council Decision, art 3. For plenary meetings, see arts 5 and 6; for the information provisions see arts 7–9.

[85] Council Decision, art 4(1)–(3).

[86] Council Decision, art 4(4).

[87] Council Decision, arts 4(5), 7, and 8.

[88] Council Decision, art 10.

[89] See pp 258–260.

6

General Mutual Assistance Instruments

A number of international instruments, taking various forms as convention, scheme, or model treaty, provide for the giving of mutual assistance in criminal matters. This chapter reviews the general provisions in the major multilateral instruments, later chapters examining how specific types of assistance, and particular types of crime, are dealt with. There has been a clear developmental process, each new instrument building on what had been achieved in earlier texts, so this chapter has a chronological arrangement in looking at the work of the Council of Europe, the Commonwealth, the United Nations, the Organization of American States, and the European Union.

I. European Convention on Mutual Assistance in Criminal Matters

It was inevitable that the traditional reluctance of states to co-operate in criminal law matters would ultimately break down. The greatest shift in attitudes dates from the 1970s and 1980s, and that makes all the more remarkable the pioneering work of the Council of Europe which led to the European Convention on Mutual Assistance in Criminal Matters 1959.[1] The influence of that Convention has been profound, notably in its influence on other instruments, such as the Commonwealth Scheme.

In 1953 a Committee of Governmental Experts was convened under the auspices of the Council of Europe to discuss the possibility of a European Convention in relation to extradition. In the report of the Committee the question of mutual assistance in criminal matters was raised as being of great importance. It was felt that extradition was only one aspect of this co-operation and, in view of the development of international relations in general and European relations in particular, it was becoming essential to apply common standards to other matters. It was noted that although some states already had rules in this area, these tended to regulate on the municipal rather than the international level. The Committee of Ministers therefore agreed to the widening of the experts' terms of reference to allow preparation of a draft convention in this area, and after deliberation this was opened for signature on 20 April 1959.[2] As at January 2012, it had forty-eight States Parties.

As part of the process of monitoring the working of the European Convention and of encouraging more ratifications, a meeting was held in June 1970 of the persons responsible at national level for its implementation, and certain proposals were made aimed at facilitating its practical application. These led to an Additional Protocol to the Convention signed in 1978.[3] It deals with fiscal matters, the enforcement of penalties, and information on criminal records. As at 2012, it has forty parties. A Second Additional Protocol[4] was opened for signature in November 2001; as at 2012 there were twenty-two parties, including the United Kingdom.

---

[1] ETS No 30.

[2] *Explanatory Report* on the European Convention on Mutual Assistance in Criminal Matters, at p 5. Further information is contained in *Problems Arising from the Practical Application of the European Convention on Mutual Assistance in Criminal Matters*, Council of Europe 1971. This document is cited hereafter as *PPA*.

[3] Additional Protocol to the European Convention on Mutual Assistance in Criminal Matters, 17 March 1978, European Treaty Series No 99.

[4] ETS No 182.

It made a number of improvements in the Convention text, noted at appropriate points in this chapter, and incorporated, often with very little change, material derived from the European Union Convention considered below,[5] or in some cases the Schengen Convention. This material covers hearing by video or telephone conference, provisions on restitution, the temporary transfer of detained persons to the requested party, new rules as to the languages of documents, the use of service by post, cross-border observations, controlled delivery, covert investigations, joint investigative teams, criminal and civil liability regarding officials, and data protection issues. The point of this wholesale 'borrowing' is that the relevant Council of Europe texts can be ratified by a wider geographical group than that comprising the European Union.

As the 1959 Convention was the first multilateral agreement in this area, it was decided that the main objective was to produce a convention which was sufficiently flexible to allow it to be adapted to the diversity of legal systems in Europe, with recognition of a general obligation to render assistance in criminal matters and minimum rules laying down the limits on the provision of that assistance. It was felt to be easier to draw up rules in relation to mutual assistance, as in this field, unlike that of extradition, there was no question of affecting the liberty of the individual. Therefore, if assistance were granted independently of extradition there was no necessity for a requirement of dual criminality, and more minor offences could also be included.[6] It was, however, still felt to be advisable to exclude military offences, and to allow discretion in relation to the more contentious areas of political and fiscal offences.[7] It was also felt that the convention need not deal with detailed matters of police co-operation, as this was better handled through the work of the International Criminal Police Organization (ICPO)—Interpol.

The resulting convention has achieved these aims in that it is sufficiently simple to allow it to be applied without the need for elaborate implementing legislation,[8] but it is not a uniform and comprehensive text on criminal procedure, as it often leaves execution of the request to be governed by the law of the requested state. The convention entered into force on 12 July 1962. In 1990 the United Kingdom belatedly became a party to what was undoubtedly one of the Council of Europe's most successful agreements to date.

1. Scope of the convention

The convention is divided into eight chapters, each of which deals with a different area of the provision of mutual assistance; the first of these chapters lays down the foundation on which the rest of the convention rests. Article 1(1) provides that the parties are[9] to afford each other the 'widest measure of mutual assistance in

---

[5] See pp 190–195.
[6] *Explanatory Report*, at p 7; *Bundesamt für Polizeiwesen v S* (Fed Ct, 27 February 1991) [1991] I BGE 53.
[7] The convention was later extended in relation to fiscal offences and administrative criminal law.
[8] For example, the convention was brought into force for France by a law which simply gave effect to the actual text: Decret No 67–636, 23 July 1967.
[9] The Second Additional Protocol of 2001 inserted the adverb 'promptly'.

proceedings in respect of offences, the punishment of which, at the time of the request for assistance, falls within the jurisdiction of the judicial authorities of the requesting Party'. It appears to be immaterial on what date the offence was committed, and the Swiss courts have held the convention applicable in respect of crimes committed before it came into force.[10] Article 1(1) is intended to be interpreted in a broad sense as extending not only to the sorts of mutual assistance specifically covered by the convention, but also every other kind of mutual legal assistance which might be sought.[11] The Second Additional Protocol of 2001 made it clear that offences by legal persons (eg, companies) are within the scope of the convention.

It is clearly necessary that 'proceedings' have been commenced, though this will cover formal investigatory proceedings. The provision is so drafted as to apply to proceedings which 'at the time of the request' are within the jurisdiction of the judicial authorities; this is to enable the convention to extend to certain offences in Germany which are initially dealt with by an administrative body but which may be transferred to a judicial authority.[12] The Second Additional Protocol of 2001 clarified the scope of the convention so as to clearly cover 'administrative criminal law', defined as covering proceedings by administrative authorities for infringements of rules of law where the decision might give rise to proceedings in the criminal courts.[13]

It has been held by the Swiss courts that the discontinuance of penal proceedings for reasons of expediency does not prevent the provision of mutual assistance, as no decision on the culpability of the accused has been made, and the maxim *ne bis in idem* is not in jeopardy.[14] States Parties are entitled to make a declaration in which they define what they deem to be judicial authorities.[15] Mutual assistance is not to be provided in respect of arrests or the enforcement of verdicts or offences under military law which are not offences under ordinary criminal law.[16]

2. Refusal of assistance

The cases in which there is a discretion to refuse to provide assistance are set out in article 2. Firstly, assistance may be refused if the request concerns an offence which the requested party considers to be a political offence, an offence connected with a political offence, or a fiscal offence.[17] Even the Swiss, with their reputation for

---

[10] *S v Camera dei Ricorsi Penali del Tribunale di Appello del Cantone Ticino* [1987] I BGE (112/6) 576.

[11] *Explanatory Report*, at p 11.

[12] *PPA*, at p 14.

[13] See the *Explanatory Report* on the Second Additional Protocol, paras 21–29.

[14] *Mercedes Zunder v Chambre d'Accusation du Canton de Genève* [1986] I BGE (110/1) 385.

[15] Convention, art 24.

[16] Convention, art 1(2).

[17] Convention, art 2(a). Although the Additional Protocol of 1978 amends this exception in relation to fiscal offences, the adoption of the Protocol is not obligatory and therefore for those states which have not become party to it the original form of art 2(a) is still valid.

protecting all information in matters fiscal, have decided that the information provided by Swiss authorities may be used by a foreign state in the investigation of political and associated offences and tax offences unless a condition expressly prohibiting this has been made by the relevant Swiss authority.[18] The discretionary nature of article 2 is important as co-operation in these areas is not automatically precluded. However, the categorization of the crime within the requesting state is irrelevant as refusal depends on the subjective opinion of the authorities of the requested state.

That last point was made clear in *R v Secretary of State for the Home Department, ex p Fininvest SpA*[19] where the relevant request concerned illicit payments to politicians. The Home Secretary considered article 2(a) and took the view that the payments referred to were offences of bribery and corruption, false accounting, and use of monies for criminal purposes; they were not political offences or offences connected with political offences. In effect upholding that decision, the Divisional Court held that the question whether or not an offence is political is to be determined by the law of the requested state on the meaning of 'political offence' for this purpose, and citing a number of dicta, including that of Lord Radcliffe in an extradition context in *Schtraks v Government of Israel*[20] that:

the idea that lies behind the phrase 'offence of a political character' is that the fugitive is at odds with the state that applies for his extradition on some issue connected with the political control or government of the country ... It does indicate, I think, that the requesting state is after him for reasons other than the enforcement of the criminal law in its ordinary, what I may call its common or international, aspect.

The court held that the Italian magistracy's desire to expose and punish corruption in public and political life, and the conflict that had created between the judges and the politicians there, did not operate to transform the offences into political ones. The magistracy was standing apart as the relevant arm of central government and the politicians (or some of them) as the offenders against whom 'the criminal law in its ordinary ... aspect' was being enforced.

Secondly, assistance may be refused if the requested party considers that execution is 'likely to prejudice the sovereignty, security, *ordre public* or other essential interests of its country'.[21] The essential interests referred to are those of the state and not any individual,[22] and extend to the protection of economic interests.[23]

The authors of the convention admitted only these grounds for refusing assistance. It was considered that accepting obligations in relation to mutual assistance implies some surrender of sovereignty to the extent which the requested state considers compatible with its fundamental concepts and its essential political or economic interests.[24] The adoption of a provision precluding assistance where the requested state felt that it might facilitate persecution on the grounds of race,

---

[18] Schweizerisches Bundesgericht [1982] I BGE 261.   [19] [1997] 1 WLR 743 (DC).
[20] [1964] AC 556 at 591–2.   [21] Convention, art 2(b).
[22] *Explanatory Report*, at p 13.   [23] Ibid.
[24] *PPA*, at p 15. See, however, art 5, considered at p 202, below.

religion, nationality, or political opinions was not felt to be necessary, because of both the narrow territorial application of the convention and the width of article 2 (b).[25] A provision preventing assistance when either the case in question was pending or had already been decided within the requested state was also felt to be undesirable, as it would have unduly restricted the scope of the convention.[26]

The limitations implied by article 1(1) are of great importance. The convention is about assistance 'in proceedings ... within the jurisdiction of the judicial authorities' and as a general rule requests are to originate from 'judicial authorities'.[27] While this pattern is a reflection of civil law practice, under which even the investigatory stage of a criminal matter may fall within the competence of a *juge d'instruction* or similar judicial officer, it is also a mark of the early date of the convention. Later international agreements have dealt more fully with assistance to prosecution and investigatory agencies at times before any proceedings have been commenced, and even in some cases before any crime has been committed. In the original text of the European Convention, the stage in the criminal matter at which assistance may first be requested was addressed obliquely; article 15(3), in the context of the procedure for sending requests, referred to 'requests for investigation preliminary to prosecution', but this language disappeared in the new text of article 15 substituted by the Second Additional Protocol of 2001.

3. Postponed execution of requests

Article 7 of the Second Additional Protocol of 2001 allows the requested party to postpone action on a request if such action would prejudice investigations, prosecutions, or related proceedings by its authorities.[28] Before refusing or postponing assistance, the requested party must, after having consulted with the requesting party where appropriate, consider whether the request may be granted partially or subject to such conditions as it deems necessary.[29] If the request is postponed, reasons must be given for the postponement. The requested party must also inform the requesting party of any reasons that render impossible the execution of the request or are likely to delay it significantly.[30]

4. Modes of transmission, translations, and costs

The requirements for contents of requests are briefly set out in article 14, but, more importantly, the manner in which these requests are to be transmitted is dealt with in article 15, the text of which was revised in the Second Additional Protocol of

---

[25] *Explanatory Report*, at p 13.
[26] Ibid.
[27] See Convention, art 15, as substituted by the Second Additional Protocol of 2001. For the designation of judicial authorities, see art 24, a new text of which was also substituted in 2001.
[28] Second Additional Protocol, art 7(1).
[29] Second Additional Protocol, art 7(2).
[30] Second Additional Protocol, art 7(3).

2001. The normal channel for Letters Rogatory and for applications for transfers of persons in custody under article 11 is to be from Ministry of Justice to Ministry of Justice.[31] This cuts through some of the delays and complexities associated with the diplomatic channel, which was the normal route prior to the Convention, but still permits for a measure of governmental supervision. Contracting Parties are, however, entitled to make a reservation under article 15(6)[32] that some or all requests are to go through channels other than those provided for in this article; some have done so, but none have used this power to insist on the diplomatic channel being used.

The Convention also makes it possible to use even more direct communication than that between Ministries of Justice. In cases of 'urgency' the original text allows direct communication between the judicial authorities of each state,[33] although the states are entitled to demand, through a reservation under article 15(6), that a copy of a request sent in this way be forwarded to the Ministry of Justice. The information provided in response to an urgent request must still be returned through the normal channel established by article 15(1). The reference to urgency vanished in the new text agreed in 2001.

Even in the original text, the direct route between judicial authorities may always be used where the request is not in the form of Letters Rogatory under articles 3 to 5 nor a request for the transfer of a person in custody under article 11. It should also be noted that the Convention does not take precedence over any bilateral agreements or arrangements between the Contracting Parties which provide for direct transmission of requests.[34]

The remaining significant procedural provision is article 16, which deals with translation of requests. Unless a reservation is made under article 16(2), translations of requests and annexed documents are not to be required; where the reservation is made the other Contracting Parties are entitled to apply reciprocity.[35] This is without prejudice to the provisions on this topic in any agreement or arrangement in force or to be made between two or more Contracting Parties.[36] In keeping with the notion that the process should be kept as simple as possible, evidence or documents transmitted under the Convention are not to require any form of authentication.[37] Where an authority receives a request which it has no jurisdiction to comply with, it is to pass that request on to the competent authority of its own country and notify the requesting party of this through the direct channels, if that was how the request was made.[38] Reasons are to be given for any refusal of assistance.[39]

The question of the expense of complying with requests for assistance is dealt with by article 20, which provides that the expenses incurred in executing requests are not to be refunded unless caused by the attendance of experts within the requested State or by the transfer of a person in custody under article 11. The

---

[31] Convention, art 15(1).   [32] Convention, art 15(9) in the 2001 text.
[33] Convention, art 15(2).   [34] Convention, art 15(7); in the 2001 text, art 15(10).
[35] Convention, art 16(2).   [36] Convention, art 16(3).
[37] Convention, art 17.   [38] Convention, art 18.   [39] Convention, art 19.

costs of video or telephone links and interpreting costs were added in the 2001 text. This has led to complaints, as in some cases the execution of Letters Rogatory may prove to be very costly.[40] This was also the subject of much debate when drafting the Commonwealth Scheme for Mutual Assistance in Criminal Matters,[41] as when authorities are required to operate on a small budget, expensive assistance to other States may significantly curtail their own activities. The compromise reached in relation to the Commonwealth Scheme was that expenses would be refunded when of an extraordinary nature, and the 2001 text of the European Convention also allows refunds of 'costs of a substantial or extraordinary nature'.[42]

5. Spontaneous information

The Second Additional Protocol provides[43] that the competent authorities of a party may, without prior request (and without prejudice to their own investigations or proceedings), forward to the competent authorities of another party information obtained within the framework of their own investigations, when they consider that the disclosure of such information might assist the receiving party in initiating or carrying out investigations or proceedings, or might lead to a request by that party under the Convention or its Protocols. The providing party may, pursuant to its national law, impose conditions on the use of such information by the receiving party, and the receiving party is[44] bound by those conditions.

6. Reservations

Reservations may be made in respect of any provision or provisions of the Convention, although where a reservation has been made a Contracting Party may not claim application of that provision except in so far as it has itself accepted it.[45] This provision is unfortunately very wide, as is often the case with agreements produced within the Council of Europe, as the large number of Member States can prevent full agreement being reached. It does, however, provide the benefit of achieving a full scheme to which exceptions are allowed, rather than a minimal approach, which would allow no scope for improvement. As will be seen, the Commonwealth Scheme is based on a similar philosophy, although expressed in a different form.

The United Kingdom enacted legislation, the Criminal Justice (International Co-operation) Act 1990, enabling it to ratify the Convention.[46] It was, however, found necessary for the United Kingdom to make a number of Reservations and Declarations in respect of the Convention.

---

[40] *PPA*, at p 53.   [41] See pp 183–184.
[42] Convention, art. 20(1)(c) as substituted by Second Additional Protocol of 2001; see the *Explanatory Report* to that Protocol, paras 48–50.
[43] Second Additional Protocol, art 11.
[44] Subject to a possible reservation requiring advance notice: art 11(4).   [45] Art 23.
[46] Now replaced by more comprehensive legislation.

The Reservations are:

(a) a reservation of the right to refuse assistance if the person concerned has been convicted or acquitted of an offence based on the relevant conduct in the United Kingdom or in a third State;

(b) in respect of article 3, a reservation of a right not to take evidence or gather other material in the face of a privilege, absence of compellability, or other applicable exemption;

(c) in respect of search and seizure, a reservation of a right to make action dependent on double criminality and consistency of the execution of the letters rogatory with the law of the United Kingdom;

(d) a refusal of requests under article 11(2) for the transit across its territory of persons in custody;

(e) a statement that the United Kingdom will consider the grant of immunity under article 12 only where it is specifically requested, and will refuse to grant it if it would be against the public interest;

(f) a reservation of the right not to apply article 21, dealing with information in respect of proceedings.

Amongst the Declarations, which mainly deal with the offices and courts to be designated under the Convention, is one reserving the right to stipulate that requests and annexed documents be accompanied by translations into English.

II. The Commonwealth Scheme

The Commonwealth Scheme for Mutual Assistance in Criminal Matters was a product of the triennial meetings of Commonwealth Law Ministers. The possibility of co-operation in this field was referred to in general terms in the Communiqués of the meetings held in 1975 and 1977, and various reports were prepared for the consideration of Ministers. Eventually, in 1983, the Law Ministers asked the Commonwealth Secretariat to prepare proposals. They expressed the hope that consultation might lead to the formulation of a scheme in which their countries would unite in the determination to respond effectively to the challenge presented by increasing levels of criminal activity. This might in the first instance take the form of a Commonwealth Scheme for Mutual Assistance in Criminal Matters which would respect the characteristics of shared Commonwealth criminal procedures.[47]

A possible Scheme was prepared by this author, drawing on the experience of earlier regional conventions, and an outline of its provisions was circulated for Government observations in June 1984.[48] A Draft Scheme was published in October 1985; it took into account the observations submitted by fourteen

---

[47] Communiqué of the Law Ministers' Meeting, Colombo, 1983, para 18.
[48] Commonwealth Secretariat Circular letter 50/84. The text of the proposed Scheme was not published at that stage, but appeared in the Working Papers for the Senior Officials' Meeting, January 1986.

Commonwealth Governments and by Interpol,[49] and was influenced by Canada's draft treaty with the United States and by the current version of a model negotiating text being prepared within the Australian Attorney-General's Department.

The negotiation of bilateral mutual assistance treaties is commonly a protracted business; it is something of an art form in its own right, with its own critical literature.[50] By contrast, the Commonwealth Scheme was settled with almost disconcerting speed. A meeting of Senior Officials from twenty-nine countries held in London in January 1986 devoted some four days of plenary sessions to the negotiations on this topic, with the equivalent of one extra day's work by a small drafting committee. This process settled a text which, after further consideration by governments, was endorsed at the Law Ministers' meeting at Harare the following July with only one small drafting amendment[51] and the incorporation of additional material on the seizure of the proceeds of crime which had been prepared in the interim.[52]

1. Nature of a Commonwealth Scheme

The negotiating process was made much easier by the initial decision to use the device of a 'Commonwealth Scheme'. It is Commonwealth practice, previously exemplified by the London Scheme for the Rendition of Fugitive Offenders (ie, the Commonwealth Extradition Scheme), to embody certain types of multilateral agreement in the form of Schemes rather than in treaties or conventions. A Scheme does not create binding international obligations, and is not registered under article 102 of the UN Charter: it represents more an agreed set of recommendations for legislative implementation by each Government. The Scheme device is not without its critics, and its use in this context was consistently opposed by the representatives of Jamaica. It is significant that the fullest critique of the Scheme device in the literature was written by the Director of the Division of International Law of the Jamaican Attorney-General's Department, albeit in a personal capacity.[53] His primary concern is the absence of any guaranteed reciprocity. If the pace, the precise mode, and even the extent of legislative implementation is left to individual Commonwealth governments,[54] one country may accept obligations, for example to provide a certain type of assistance at the request of a prosecution authority in any other Commonwealth member country, which are not accepted elsewhere. In the extradition context, in which this criticism was first made, the point has obvious force:

[49] The draft and the full text of the Government observations formed Criminal Working Paper 2 for the January 1986 meeting.

[50] See E Nadelmann, 'Negotiations in Criminal Law Assistance Treaties' (1985) 33 Am Jo Comp L 465.

[51] The use of the term 'country' for the more cumbrous 'part of the Commonwealth' used in the earlier drafts following the model of the Commonwealth Scheme for the Rendition of Fugitive Offenders.

[52] See further, pp 295–296.

[53] P L Robinson, 'The Commonwealth Scheme relating to the Rendition of Fugitive Offenders: A Critical Appraisal of some Essential Elements' (1984) 33 ICLQ 614, especially at 617–24.

[54] The Scheme states that 'Countries are encouraged to such adopt legislative or other measures as may be necessary to implement the provisions of this Scheme': Scheme, para 1(4).

[I]t may be ... that two Commonwealth countries would never, because of radical differences in foreign policy, enter into an extradition arrangement. But, if they cannot agree on a treaty regime for extradition, an expectation that they would nonetheless extradite to each other pursuant to a non-binding, non-reciprocal, non-conventional Scheme, by reason merely of a similarity in legal background, is idle, unwarranted, quaint and naive.[55]

It was on these grounds that the Jamaican representatives argued for the elaboration of a multilateral treaty; and the Jamaican Government ultimately entered a Reservation to the Scheme,[56] reserving 'the right not to grant requests from countries which would not be competent under their laws to accede to similar requests from Jamaica'.

The great majority of governments did, however, support the continued use of the Scheme technique. The features identified by the critics as weaknesses were seen by the majority as affording real advantages. It was recognized that there would have to be considerable flexibility in handling what was for most countries a wholly new area. Some countries might have real difficulties in implementing the whole Scheme, for constitutional reasons (for example, the complexity facing a federal state in legislating for immunity from prosecution for certain types of witness), or because of paucity of resources. There is nonetheless real value in all Commonwealth countries being able to take some part in determining the shape of the whole Scheme, and in using a device which permits of relatively easy amendment and development of the procedures in the light of experience. It was agreed that the Scheme would be reviewed periodically by Senior Officials meeting in the interval between the triennial meetings of Law Ministers. Amendments were made to the Scheme in 1990, 2002, and 2005, and a considerably revised Scheme was adopted in July 2011; such continuing development would have been virtually impossible had the treaty procedure been followed. References in the following material are to the revised Scheme as adopted in 2011. In that text many provisions are redrafted, references are made to assistance of various types in aid of investigations, and there is new material on the interception of telecommunications and of postal items, covert electronic surveillance, and asset recovery.

2. Scope of the Scheme

A striking feature of the Scheme, when compared with earlier multilateral conventions, is the wide range of types of assistance that it covers. Paragraph 1(5) provides:

Mutual legal assistance in criminal matters under this Scheme includes, but is not limited to, assistance in

(a) identifying and locating persons;
(b) taking evidence or statements from persons;
(c) effecting service of documents;
(d) executing searches and seizures;

---

[55] At 619.
[56] Given that the Scheme is non-binding, the precise status of such a Reservation is a matter of considerable obscurity.

(e) providing and producing relevant documents, records, items and other materials;

(f) facilitating the voluntary attendance of persons in the requesting country;

(g) effecting a temporary transfer of persons in custody to assist in an investigation or appear as a witness;

(h) the identification, tracing, freezing, restraining, forfeiture and confiscating the proceeds and instrumentalities of crime;

(i) the return and disposal of property;

(j) preserving and obtaining computer data;

(k) interception of postal items;

(l) interception of telecommunications;

(m) covert electronic surveillance.[57]

In 1983 Law Ministers considered a paper on the principles of mutual assistance,[58] which examined at length the question of jurisdiction in criminal matters, exploring a number of alternative principles upon which a claim to exercise jurisdiction could be based. However, the view taken in preparing the Scheme was that in intra-Commonwealth relations it should be sufficient that a Commonwealth country requesting assistance was in fact able to take jurisdiction under its own legal principles. That is, there should be no provision seeking to identify the 'proper' jurisdiction for trial, nor any provision that a requested country should in any way test or examine the claim to jurisdiction. Similarly, no provision was included to the effect that the provision of assistance should not imply recognition of the ultimate judgment.

In order to obtain assistance, an agency or authority in the requesting country[59] initiates a 'request for assistance' which is transmitted, and received in the requested country, by a designated 'Central Authority'[60] following the practice adopted first in the Hague Service and Evidence Conventions[61] and later in bilateral mutual assistance treaties. Communication must take place directly between Central Authorities unless the countries have agreed otherwise.[62]

The authors of the Scheme rejected a suggestion that there should be a prescribed form of Request, along the lines of the forms prescribed or recommended for use with the Hague Service and Evidence Conventions, believing that requests under the Scheme were likely to be so diverse in character that a prescribed form would be of limited value. Instead, the Scheme contains provisions specifying the information to be included.[63]

---

[57] At one stage it was proposed to include other forms of surveillance, but they were excluded as essentially matters of police-to-police co-operation rather than the more formal steps covered by the Scheme.

[58] By Dr D Chaikin (paper LMM(83)29).

[59] See Scheme, para 4(1)(a); the Scheme no longer contains any fuller definition, but earlier versions referred to a law enforcement agency or public prosecution or judicial authority competent under the law of the requesting country.

[60] Scheme, para 3.

[61] See pp 35–36.

[62] Scheme, para 3(3).

[63] Scheme, para 13.

As with other arrangements for mutual assistance, the effective limits of the Scheme are largely set by the two key decisions which had to be taken by its authors: when may a request for assistance be made; and on what grounds can assistance be refused?

3. When may assistance be sought?

The Scheme requires the giving of assistance in response to a request made in respect of a criminal matter 'arising in' the requesting country.[64] A criminal matter arises in a country if the Central Authority of that country certifies that criminal or forfeiture proceedings have been instituted in a court exercising jurisdiction in that country or that there is reasonable cause to believe that an offence has been committed in respect of which such proceedings could be instituted.[65] 'Criminal matter' is itself defined[66] to mean 'criminal proceedings as well as investigations or proceedings relating to: (a) the restraint or freezing of property that may be confiscated or forfeited by a court, or that may be needed to satisfy a pecuniary penalty imposed in respect of an offence; (b) the confiscation or forfeiture of property by a court in respect of an offence; and (c) the imposition or recovery of a pecuniary penalty in respect of an offence'. Although the word 'investigations' might seem to be governed by the items listed at (a) to (c), the text of the Scheme provides for assistance in respect of investigations more generally.

The exact stage which has been reached will be specified in the request; where criminal proceedings have not been instituted, the request must state the offence which the requesting country has reasonable cause to believe has been, is being, or will be committed, with a summary of known facts.[67] In every case, a request must establish a link between the criminal matter and the assistance sought.[68]

It must be kept in mind that the Scheme 'does not affect any existing forms of co-operation, either formal or informal, nor does it preclude the development of any future forms of co-operation'[69]. Much co-operation at the investigative stage already takes place between police forces and other law enforcement agencies, either through Interpol or by direct bilateral contacts; the fact that the Scheme can be relied upon from a particular time does not preclude earlier co-operation.

4. Refusal of assistance

Paragraph 8 of the Scheme, which sets out the grounds upon which the requested country may refuse to grant assistance as asked, was the result of much discussion when the Scheme was first adopted and has undergone some development in the 2011 revision. It will be convenient to set it out paragraph 8(1) in full:

(1) The requested country may refuse to comply in whole or in part with a request for assistance under this Scheme where the Central Authority of that country considers that:

---

[64] Scheme, para 1(2). [65] Scheme, para 2(2). [66] Scheme, para 2(3).
[67] Scheme, para 4(1)(h). [68] Scheme, para 4(1)(d). [69] Scheme, para 1(3).

a. the request relates to an offence or proceedings of a political character;[70]
b. the conduct which is the subject of the request is an offence only under military law or a law relating to military obligations of the requesting country;
c. the request relates to an offence, the prosecution of which in the requesting country would be incompatible with the requested country's law on double jeopardy;
d. compliance with the request would be contrary to the constitutions or domestic laws of that country, or would prejudice the sovereignty, national security, international relations, national interests, public order or other essential public interest of that country;
e. there are substantial grounds to believe that compliance with the request would facilitate the prosecution or punishment of any person on account of race, ethnic origin, sex, religion, nationality or political opinions or would cause prejudice for any of these reasons to any person affected by the request;
f. the steps required to be taken in order to comply with the request cannot under the law of that country be taken; and
g. by reason of the trivial nature of the alleged offending or the low value of the likely penalty or any property likely to be forfeited or confiscated, the requested country would not have made a similar request to another country in connection with a like criminal matter arising in the requested country.

Paragraph 8(1)(d) is drawn in broad terms, the phrase 'other essential public interests' (based on a similar phrase in the US–Canada Treaty) being susceptible to a generous interpretation. By way of example, the Australian Mutual Assistance in Criminal Matters Act 1987, which generally reflects the provisions of the Scheme, is very much fuller at this point. It provides for the refusal of a request if, in the opinion of the Attorney-General, the request relates to the assertion of extra-territorial jurisdiction in circumstances in which Australia would not make a corresponding claim to jurisdiction; in certain cases where the death penalty might be imposed in the foreign country; if the request relates to the prosecution of a person entitled to plead a statute of limitations or some similar bar to prosecution under Australian law; and if the provision of assistance could prejudice an investigation or proceeding in relation to a criminal matter in Australia, or the safety of any person, or impose an excessive burden on the resources of Australia or one of its States or Territories.[71]

Paragraph 8(1)(f) is of considerable significance. The general philosophy of the Scheme is that procedures and facilities available in support of criminal investigations and prosecutions initiated in one country should also be made available to assist similar endeavours undertaken in another Commonwealth country. However all requests are to be dealt with according to the law of the requested country,[72] and a requested country is not required to do more than it would do in a purely domestic case. For example, if the taking of body samples is not provided for under the law of the requested country it will refuse a request for assistance in obtaining such samples; the availability of such procedures under the law of the requesting country is immaterial.

---

[70] For offences which are *not* political offences, see Scheme, para 8(2).
[71] Mutual Assistance in Criminal Matters Act 1987, s 8 as amended.
[72] Scheme, para 6.

Paragraph 8(1)(g) was added in 2011 to signal that trivial matters should not be made the subject of a request.

When the Scheme was first drafted 'double criminality' was a major issue. The requirement (that the facts must constitute an offence under the law of the requested as well as the requesting country) features in extradition practice, but there the liberty of an individual present in the requested country is at stake. Most bilateral mutual assistance treaties contain no such requirement. However, strong support emerged in the discussions for a discretionary double criminality rule, which was ultimately included. The 2011 text of the Scheme omits this provision and includes as paragraph 10 an exhortatory provision: 'Each country is encouraged to render assistance in the absence of dual criminality.'

Three further provisions may be noted. Assistance may not be refused solely on the grounds of bank or other financial institution secrecy rules.[73] The requested country may make the provision of assistance of any sort subject to the requesting country complying with specified conditions. If the requesting country refuses to comply with the conditions, the requested country may refuse to grant the assistance sought in whole or in part.[74] Finally, each country is 'encouraged to render assistance in the absence of reciprocal arrangement'.[75]

5. Expenses of compliance

It was recognized by the authors of the Scheme that, no matter how much goodwill might exist in the Commonwealth for the success of the proposals for enhanced co-operation, the goodwill would be tested by the expenses of providing assistance. The proposal in the preliminary draft that expenses should fall to be carried by the requested country in each case, its contribution in one case being rewarded by free assistance when it acted as the requesting country in another case, proved unacceptable.

The discussions were much influenced by the course of Canada's treaty negotiations with the United States, in which considerable time was spent in deciding how this topic could be best handled. Neither country wanted to be burdened with administrative accounting tasks, but it was recognized that a requested state could incur significant costs in providing some forms of assistance. For example, a requested state might be asked to conduct surveillance of suspected criminals, which could involve assigning extra police officers to this task at great expense, eg, overtime pay, and commercial fraud cases might involve extensive examination of records. A competent authority in the requested state might not be able to afford this extraordinary expense, with the result that the request would not be proceeded with or would be carried out in an unsatisfactory manner. Article VIII(3) of the Canada–US Treaty enables the requested state to notify the requesting state of unusual expenses; if the assistance was important to the requesting state, it would bear those costs.

---

[73] Scheme, para 8(3).   [74] Scheme, para 9.   [75] Scheme, para 11.

In the end, the Scheme adopted a similar approach. The matter was further discussed by Commonwealth Law Ministers in 1999 in response to continuing expressions of concern from small jurisdictions over the impact on national resources caused by complying with requests for assistance. A set of Guidelines was adopted to deal with particular aspects of the issue, but a survey conducted in 2001 as to the working of these Guidelines found no evidence that they were expressly relied on in practice. The matter was again reviewed in the process of preparing the revised text adopted in 2011, which made only limited changes.

Paragraph 7 of the Scheme now provides that the costs of executing a request are to be borne by the requested country, unless otherwise agreed by the countries; but where expenses of 'a substantial or extraordinary nature' are or will be required to execute the request, the countries are to consult in advance to determine the manner in which the costs shall be borne.[76] A non-exclusive list is given of what will amount to 'substantial or extraordinary expenses': (a) fees and reasonable expenses of expert witnesses; (b) the costs incurred in facilitating the personal appearance of a person for the purposes of an investigation or to appear as a witness in the requesting country;[77] (c) the costs of establishing and operating live video links or other audiovisual means, and the interpretation and transcription of such proceedings; (d) the costs of temporarily transferring persons in custody;[78] (e) the costs incurred for the interception of telecommunication; and (f) the costs incurred for conducting surveillance.[79]

6. Implementation of the Scheme

A Model Bill to assist countries in preparing legislation implementing the Scheme as originally drafted was developed, and a further Model Bill was commissioned in 2011. The larger Commonwealth member countries, possessing both more highly developed mutual assistance policies and larger numbers of legislative drafters, have tended to produce their own models. Australia is one example. The Mutual Assistance in Criminal Matters Act 1987 bears many resemblances to the Commonwealth model, not surprisingly in view of the large contribution made by Australian officials in the negotiation of the Scheme and its subsequent discussion. There are some notable differences, one of which is that in section 8 of the Act refusal of assistance is mandatory on certain grounds, which under the Scheme give only a discretionary power of refusal. In treaty negotiations, Australia has found that many foreign states prefer discretionary language; in the words of a senior negotiator, 'Australia has agreed to this on the clear understanding that in respect of [those grounds] Australia could only exercise that discretion one way—namely by refusing assistance'.[80]

Canada's approach was very different. As a matter of policy, and also because of federal constitutional issues, Canada decided to insist on a treaty-based approach. Its Mutual Legal Assistance in Criminal Matters Act, originally enacted in 1988,

---

[76] Scheme, para 7(1),(2).   [77] Under para 15.   [78] Under para 16.
[79] Scheme, para 7(3).   [80] See Materials on the Scheme, Vol 4, at p 105.

limits the powers of the responsible Minister to cases in which 'the agreement provides for mutual legal assistance with respect to the subject-matter of the request'.[81] However, the Act contains other provisions which mean that the actual position in practice is less restrictive than that might suggest. Section 6(1) of the Act[82] provides that:

If there is no agreement between Canada and a state or entity, or the state's or entity's name does not appear in the schedule, the Minister of Foreign Affairs may, with the agreement of the Minister [of Justice], enter into an administrative arrangement with the state or entity providing for legal assistance with respect to an investigation specified in the arrangement relating to an act that, if committed in Canada, would be an indictable offence.

Such an administrative arrangement can be implemented as if it were a treaty.[83]

By 2011, Canada had negotiated thirty-six bilateral treaties dealing with mutual assistance in criminal matters, that with the UK being specifically on drug trafficking, the others all general in scope. For other countries within the Commonwealth Scheme, a request under the Scheme will be translated for the purposes of Canadian law into an administrative arrangement and assistance given on that basis.

III. UN Model Treaty on Mutual Assistance in Criminal Matters

In order to encourage the further development of mutual assistance in criminal matters, the United Nations agreed on the recommendation of its Eighth Congress on the Prevention of Crime and the Treatment of Offenders[84] to adopt the text of a model treaty to be used as a basis in future negotiations between its Member States. As a model treaty the text is simple, providing a mere framework and containing none of the more complex procedural provisions found in existing agreements. The Model Treaty contains little innovative material, many of its provisions bearing a close resemblance to earlier texts.

1. Scope of the Model Treaty

The general practice in the negotiation of a Mutual Legal Assistance Treaty (MLAT) is for the parties to agree to provide each other with mutual assistance with particular reference to certain types of assistance, such as the taking of evidence from witnesses, the execution of searches and seizures, the service of documents, and the provision of copies of documents and records.[85] The Model Treaty contains no surprises in this area, with the statement of the scope of the Treaty

---

[81] Mutual Legal Assistance in Criminal Matters Act s 8(1) (as substituted by the Extradition Act 1999, s 101).
[82] As substituted by Extradition Act 1999, s 100.
[83] Ibid, s 6(3).
[84] Havana, 27 August–7 September 1990.
[85] See, for example, UN Model Treaty, art 1; Commonwealth Scheme, para 1.

being taken directly from the Council of Europe Convention as a tried and tested definition.[86]

One unusual feature is that while the Treaty adopts the common practice of permitting the provision of originals or certified copies of relevant documents and records, it also specifically permits provision of copies of bank, financial, corporate, or business records;[87] the secrecy of banks and similar financial institutions is not to be used as a sole ground for refusing assistance.[88]

The making and processing of requests has now also become a matter of convention, with the accepted procedure being to require each party to such a treaty to establish a central authority through which all assistance is sought. The UN Model Treaty follows this practice.[89] Unlike some other texts, there is no provision for oral requests to be dealt with by the central authority in cases of urgency.[90]

Certain requests for assistance will always be refused as falling outside the scope of the Treaty:[91] the Model Treaty does not apply to extradition, enforcement of criminal judgments,[92] the transfer of persons in custody to serve sentences, or to the transfer of proceedings in criminal matters, which is dealt with in a separate Model Treaty.[93] The number of exclusions reflects in part difficulties in reaching agreement. While the number of exclusions from the Model Treaty is larger than, for example, that in the European Convention,[94] there is no exclusion applying to fiscal cases; this presumably reflects the attitude taken to the related issue of bank secrecy.

When a request falls within the scope of the Treaty there are a number of discretionary grounds on which assistance may be refused. What is not apparent from the text is exactly who may exercise this discretion: under the Commonwealth Scheme it is clearly stated that the requested country may refuse to comply with a request when it appears to the Central Authority that certain conditions are satisfied.[95] The text of the Model Treaty permits the refusal of assistance where the 'Requested State is of the opinion' that certain conditions are fulfilled,[96] or 'there are substantial grounds for believing' that the request has been made for a certain purpose.[97] This raises a question over whether the discretion should be exercised by the central authority, or whether government in the form of a Secretary of State or Minister for Justice should make the decision. Different practices could conceivably produce different types of decision as to the grant and level of

---

[86] UN Model Treaty, art 1(1); Council of Europe Convention, art 1(1).
[87] UN Model Treaty, art 1(2)(g).
[88] UN Model Treaty, art 4(2).
[89] UN Model Treaty, art 3 (using the expression 'competent authority').
[90] UN Model Treaty, art 5. Cf the Council of Europe Convention, art 15(2).
[91] UN Model Treaty, art 1(3).
[92] Except those within the scope of the Optional Protocol.
[93] See pp 347–349.
[94] Council of Europe Convention, arts 1(2) and 2.
[95] Commonwealth Scheme, para 8.
[96] UN Model Treaty, art 4(1)(a).
[97] UN Model Treaty, art 4(1)(c).

assistance. The grounds for the refusal of a request are not extensive, but the notes to the Treaty state that the list is merely illustrative and is therefore liable to be expanded by individual states. In particular, it should be noted that dual criminality is not included as one of the grounds for refusal.

Once the relevant body has taken the decision as to whether or not assistance should be granted, execution is to be carried out in the manner requested to the extent permitted by the law of the requested state.[98] As had become common in such treaties, the use of the information or evidence provided to the requesting state in pursuance of the request is limited to the purposes stated in the request, unless the requested state gives its consent, and the material must be returned to the requested state as soon as possible unless the right to claim its return is waived.[99] The confidentiality of the request and the information provided is also guaranteed.[100]

There was a provision in the Commonwealth Scheme as originally adopted that allowed the requested country to use measures of compulsion in connection with a request to the extent that those measures are available under its domestic law.[101] There is no equivalent provision in the United Nations Model Treaty.

The Treaty then moves on to give particular instructions for those heads of assistance that are specifically provided for; in keeping with the status of the text as a model for future agreements, these provisions are not detailed. For example, the service of documents is permitted under the Treaty,[102] but there is no guidance as to the method of service that should be used or as to how proof of service might be provided.

Similarly, requested states are to obtain evidence on request by taking testimony or requiring production of items from the witnesses;[103] the text merely provides that this is to be done in conformity with its own law, with no special instructions about cases where compliance with the law of the requesting state might be necessary to ensure that the evidence obtained is admissible in proceedings there. Provision is made for witnesses to decline to give evidence in reliance on a privilege to decline to so that exists under the law of either the requested state or that of the requesting state.[104] This is no less favourable than comparable provisions in other texts.[105]

Among the categories of assistance commonly found in MLATs is provision for the invitation of witnesses to attend for questioning in the requesting state and for the transfer of persons in custody to be examined. The Model Treaty follows this practice, and provision is made for inviting both persons at liberty and those in

[98] UN Model Treaty, art 6.
[99] UN Model Treaty, arts 7 and 8.
[100] UN Model Treaty, art 9.
[101] Commonwealth Scheme (1986 text), para 8; para 6 of the 2011 text provides more generally that the request is to be dealt with according to the law of the requested country.
[102] UN Model Treaty, art 10.
[103] UN Model Treaty, art 11.
[104] UN Model Treaty, art 12.
[105] eg, Commonwealth Scheme, para 18.

custody to appear in the requesting state. The transfer of persons in custody may only be made where permitted by the law of the requested state and agreement is given for that particular prisoner to be handed over. The prisoner himself must also consent to the transfer.[106] As it is intended purely as an outline, the text does not deal with such problems as whether the time spent in the other country is to count towards the sentence imposed in the requested state, or whether special considerations apply where the person who is requested to attend is a national of the requesting state. The Model Treaty differs from the Commonwealth Scheme and the European Convention in this area, as they each contain special grounds for refusing a request of this type, but there are no such special grounds here.[107]

As a necessary corollary to the attendance of witnesses in the requesting state, MLATs normally seek to afford some kind of immunity from prosecution. The protection given by the Model Treaty is that which is normally provided—the witness is not to be subjected to restriction of his personal liberty in respect of any acts or omissions, or convictions, that preceded his departure from the requested state; he may not be required to give evidence other than as specified in the request; and the summons may not impose any compulsion to appear or penalty for failing to comply with it, whether it purports to do so or not.[108] The immunity also ceases as is normal: where the person does not leave the requesting state within fifteen days of being told that he is no longer required for the investigations, or where he leaves the country within that period but returns to it of his own free will.

The Model Treaty also follows the common practice of permitting the provision of copies of documents and records available to the public and of such other documents and records as would be made available to domestic law enforcement agencies in similar circumstances.[109] The text dealing with search and seizure contains no more than the absolute minimum: 'the Requested State shall, in so far as its law permits, carry out requests for search and seizure and delivery of any material to the Requesting State for evidentiary purposes, provided that the rights of bona fide third parties are protected.'[110]

A noteworthy feature of the Model Treaty is that under article 18 it is expressly provided that a request for assistance and its supporting documents, and any documents or other material supplied in response to that request, are not to require certification or authentication; this is also the case under article 17 of the European Convention, which states that authentication is not necessary. Under the Commonwealth Scheme authentication may be required both of materials submitted to the requested country as part of a request, and of material transmitted by the requested country in response to a request.[111]

On the sensitive matter of costs, sensitive because small states in particular are aware that the expense of complying with a request for assistance can prove to be

---

[106] UN Model Treaty, art 13.
[107] Commonwealth Scheme, para 16; Council of Europe Convention, art 11.
[108] UN Model Treaty, art 15(1).
[109] UN Model Treaty, art 16. Cf. Commonwealth Scheme, para 13(2).
[110] UN Model Treaty, art 17.
[111] Commonwealth Scheme, para 30.

prohibitive, the United Nations text again follows standard international practice, with the ordinary costs of complying with a request to be borne by the requested state, unless otherwise agreed, but with provision for consultation in cases where expenses of an extraordinary nature are likely to be incurred.[112] The requesting state is responsible for the travel and incidental expenses of witnesses travelling to the requesting country, and for any cash advances made to a witness prior to arrival in the requesting state.[113]

IV. Inter-American Convention on Mutual Assistance in Criminal Matters

One of the Inter-American conventions prepared under the auspices of Organization of American States is that on Mutual Assistance in Criminal Matters, adopted in Nassau, Bahamas, in 1992. It has (in 2012) twenty-five States Parties.

Under its terms, States Parties are to render to one another mutual assistance in 'investigations, prosecutions, and proceedings that pertain to crimes over which the requesting state has jurisdiction at the time the assistance is requested'.[114] Its scope is further indicated by a non-exclusive list of relevant procedures: notification of rulings and judgments; taking of testimony or statements from persons; summoning of witnesses and expert witnesses to provide testimony; immobilization and sequestration of property, freezing of assets, and assistance in procedures related to seizures; searches or seizures; examination of objects and places; service of judicial documents; transmittal of documents, reports, information, and evidence; transfer of detained persons for the purpose of this convention; and any other procedure, provided there is an agreement between the requesting state and the requested state.[115] The parties also agree to assist each other, to the extent permitted by their respective laws, in precautionary measures and measures for securing the proceeds, fruits, and instrumentalities of the crime.[116]

The act that gives rise to the request must be punishable by one year or more of imprisonment in the requesting state.[117] Requests for assistance must originate from the authorities responsible for criminal investigation or prosecution in the requesting state,[118] and are transmitted and received by central authorities.[119]

---

[112] UN Model Treaty, art 19.
[113] UN Model Treaty, art 14. These are the same provisions as are made in the Commonwealth Scheme (para 15(2)) and the Council of Europe Convention (arts 9 and 20).
[114] Inter-American Convention, art 2.
[115] Inter-American Convention, art 7.
[116] Inter-American Convention, art 15.
[117] Inter-American Convention, art 6.
[118] Inter-American Convention, art 4.
[119] Inter-American Convention, art 3.

The requested state may refuse assistance when it determines that:

a. The request for assistance is being used in order to prosecute a person on a charge with respect to which that person has already been sentenced or acquitted in a trial in the requesting or requested state;

b. The investigation has been initiated for the purpose of prosecuting, punishing, or discriminating in any way against an individual or group of persons for reason of sex, race, social status, nationality, religion, or ideology;

c. The request refers to a crime that is political or related to a political crime, or to a common crime prosecuted for political reasons;

d. The request has been issued at the request of a special or *ad hoc* tribunal;

e. Public policy (*ordre public*), sovereignty, security, or basic public interests are prejudiced; and

f. The request pertains to a tax crime. Nevertheless, the assistance is to be granted if the offence is committed by way of an intentionally incorrect statement, whether oral or written, or by way of an intentional failure to declare income derived from any other offence covered by this convention for the purpose of concealing such income.[120]

The Convention does not apply to military crimes.[121] Double criminality is not generally required except where the assistance sought is the immobilization and sequestration of property, or searches and seizures, including house searches.[122]

V. EU Convention on Mutual Assistance in Criminal Matters between Member States

This Convention was finally adopted in May 2000 after a protracted period of gestation,[123] and was supplemented by a Protocol adopted in November 2001.[124] Although the European Union is sometimes accused of 'stealing the clothes' of other international bodies, by adopting as its own texts derived substantially from the work of other bodies, this Convention declares its aim to be 'to supplement the provisions and facilitate the application between the States of the European Union, of [inter alia] the European Convention on Mutual Assistance in Criminal Matters of 20 April 1959',[125] that is the Council of Europe's convention.[126] When the idea of a European Union instrument was first mooted, many felt that it would

---

[120] Inter-American Convention, art 9. The provision as to tax crimes was effectively deleted by an Optional Protocol of November 1993, which only seven states have ratified.

[121] Inter-American Convention, art 8.

[122] Inter-American Convention, art 5.

[123] For text see OJ C 197, 12.7.2000. The official *Explanatory Report* appears at OJ C 379, 29.12.2000.

[124] OJ 2001 C326, 21.11.2001.

[125] Convention, art 1(1).

[126] See pp 170–177, above.

be better to work within the Council of Europe where work on the revision of the 1959 Convention had already begun, but the argument prevailed that there was a need for 'something to be done more urgently within the EU'.[127] In the event some five years were spent on detailed negotiations before the text was settled, and within months thereafter new proposals were advanced.[128]

The starting-point for the negotiations was a recognition that mutual assistance between the States already lay on solid foundations, with the 1959 Convention and its Additional Protocol, the Schengen documents, and regional arrangements such as those between the Benelux countries. The aim of the EU Convention was to develop and modernize the existing provisions, taking into account in particular, advances in technology.

The text of the Convention identifies its 'parent Conventions': the 1959 Convention and its Additional Protocol; the provisions on mutual assistance in criminal matters in the Schengen Implementation Convention of 1990; and Chapter 2 of the Benelux Treaty of 1962, as amended by a 1974 Protocol.[129] Those provisions continue in effect as the legal basis for mutual assistance:[130] the EU Convention does not itself provide a basis which can be relied upon on its own in making a request for mutual assistance. Similarly, the new Convention does not preclude more favourable provision being made between states, for example by bilateral agreements.[131]

1. Scope of mutual assistance

One purpose of the EU Convention was to extend the range of circumstances in which mutual assistance would be afforded. Building on provisions in the Schengen Convention, the EU Convention provides that mutual assistance shall be afforded in proceedings brought by the administrative authorities in respect of acts which are punishable under the national law of the requesting or the requested state, or both, by virtue of being infringements of the rules of law,[132] and where the decision may give rise to proceedings before a court having jurisdiction in particular[133] in criminal matters.[134] It is also provided that mutual assistance must be afforded in connection with this type of proceedings and criminal proceedings which relate to offences or infringements for which a legal person may be held liable in the

---

[127] 14th Report of the House of Lords' Select Committee on the European Communities (Session 1997–1998), *Mutual Assistance in Criminal Matters* (HL Paper 72), para 51.

[128] Initiative of the French Republic with a view to adopting a Convention on improving mutual assistance in criminal matters, in particular in the area of combating organised crime, laundering of the proceeds from crime and financial crime, OJ C 243, 24.08.2000.

[129] Convention, art 1(1).

[130] However, articles 49(a), 52, 53, and 73 of the Schengen Implementation Convention are repealed (by the Mutual Assistance Convention, art 2(2)) as they are effectively replaced by provisions in the new Convention.

[131] Convention, art 1(2).

[132] eg, the *Ordnungswidrigkeit* of German law: an offence which is not classified as criminal but is punishable by fines imposed by administrative authorities.

[133] The *Explanatory Report* indicates that the phrase 'in particular', which reads awkwardly in English, means that a court with both criminal and some other form of jurisdiction suffices.

[134] Convention, art 3(1).

requesting state,[135] even if there is no such liability so far as legal persons are concerned in the law of the requested state.

2. Form and transmission of requests

Under the 1959 Council of Europe Convention most requests for mutual assistance pass from one Ministry of Justice to another.[136] The EU Convention adopts as the norm direct contact between the judicial authorities in each state.[137] A request is to be made in writing, or 'by any means capable of producing a written record under conditions allowing the receiving state to establish authenticity',[138] a phrase which will cover e-mail and similar modes of communication.

Other modes of procedure are permitted. These may include communication between central authorities in each state;[139] between a judicial authority of one state and a central authority of another state;[140] and, in case of urgency, via Interpol (or in future, Europol).[141] There are special provisions allowing communication with police or customs authorities[142] or administrative authorities.[143]

3. Procedures for carrying out requests

The principle adopted in article 3 of the 1959 Convention is that in the normal case requests are carried out in the manner provided for by the law of the requested state. The EU Convention adjusts the balance between requesting and requested states in this respect. The requested state is to comply with the formalities and procedures expressly indicated by the requesting state.[144] The expectation is that only those procedures of real importance to the requesting state will be specified: an example might be the presence of a legal representative of the defendant. There are exceptions to the principle that the procedures of the requesting state will apply: where the Convention provides to the contrary in a particular context,[145] and where the

---

[135] Convention, art 3(2).

[136] See 1959 Convention, art 11 and p 175, above.

[137] EU Convention, art 6(1). This applies equally to the spontaneous provision of information, provided for in art 7.

[138] Ibid.

[139] Certain matters must pass through central authorities: requests for temporary transfer or transit of persons held in custody, and certain notices of information from judicial records: EU Convention, art 6(8). In the United Kingdom and in Ireland, judicial authorities may not themselves have authority to execute requests. Accordingly, those states are allowed to require the use of their central authorities at least until they accept the mutual legal assistance provisions of the Schengen Implementation Convention: EU Convention, art 6(3).

[140] EU Convention, art 6(2).

[141] EU Convention, art 6(4).

[142] EU Convention, art 6(5) in respect of matters under art 12 (controlled deliveries), art 13 (joint investigation teams) and art 6 (covert investigations). But see the possible reservations re art 6(5) and (6): art 6(7).

[143] EU Convention, art 6(6) in respect of proceedings under art 3(1).

[144] EU Convention, art 4(1).

[145] For example, controlled deliveries are undertaken 'with due regard to' the law of the requested state (art 12(2)).

formalities and procedures are contrary to the fundamental principles of law in the requested state.[146] If the requirements of the requesting state cannot be met, the authorities of the two states are to confer on the procedure to be followed.[147] Corresponding provisions are made as to deadlines: the requesting state may state a deadline for compliance, with reasons (such as the expected date of a trial); the requested state must meet the deadline if it can, and must notify the requesting state if that proves impossible and confer with its authorities as to what should be done.[148]

4. Further aspects of co-operation

Article 5 of the 2001 Protocol[149] deals with the situation in which the requested state comes across further possibilities unrecognized in the request. If the competent authority of the requested Member State in the course of the execution of a request for mutual assistance considers that it may be appropriate to undertake investigations not initially foreseen, or which could not be specified when the request was made, it must immediately inform the requesting authority accordingly in order to enable it to take further action.

Similarly, article 6 spells out the possibilities of making additional or supplementary requests, including one made in the course of joint work in the requested state directly to the competent authority of that state.

5. Controlled deliveries

The controlled delivery technique is a well-established law enforcement method in combating drug trafficking. The EU Convention extends the same principle to all goods where there is an investigation into a serious, ie, an extraditable, offence.[150] The goods might be pornographic materials, stolen works of art, or even nuclear waste. A controlled delivery is to take place in accordance with the procedures of the requested state, and the right to act and to direct and control operations lies with the competent authorities of that state.[151]

6. Joint investigation teams

Joint investigations by members of the law enforcement agencies of two or more countries are of obvious value in dealing with cross-border crime. The EU

---

[146] EU Convention, art 4(1).

[147] EU Convention, art 4(3).

[148] EU Convention, art 4(2)(4). See, for 'urgent' requests, para 2 of the Joint Action (98/427/JHA) of 29 June 1998 on good practice in mutual legal assistance in criminal matters, OJ L 191, 7.7.1998.

[149] OJ C 326, 21.11.2001.

[150] EU Convention, art 12(1). This is understood, by reference to the EU Extradition Convention of 1996, art 2, to mean an offence punishable under the law of the requesting state by deprivation of liberty or a detention order for a maximum period of at least 12 months and under the law of the requested state by deprivation of liberty or a detention order for a maximum period of at least six months.

[151] EU Convention, art 12(3).

Convention provides a more secure legal framework for the operation of joint investigation teams. The general conditions for the operation of such a team include the appointment as leader of the team of a person representing the criminal investigation authority of the state in which the team operates.[152] Members of the team seconded from the other states involved have prescribed powers:

(a) they may be present when investigative measures are taken in the state of operation, unless the team leader, for particular reasons in accordance with the law of the state where the team operates, decides otherwise;[153] and

(b) they may, in accordance with the law of the state where the team operates, be entrusted by the team leader with the task of taking certain investigative measures where this has been approved by the competent authorities of the state of operation and the seconding state.

A seconded member may request his or her own national authorities to take measures which are required by the team, without any further request under the Convention.[154]

So far as information is concerned, a member of the joint investigation team may, in accordance with his or her national law and within the limits of his or her competence, provide the team with information available in the state which has seconded him or her for the purpose of the criminal investigations conducted by the team. Information lawfully obtained by a member or seconded member while part of a joint investigation team which is not otherwise available to the competent authorities of the states concerned may be used for the purposes for which the team has been set up; and, subject to the prior consent[155] of the state where the information became available, for detecting, investigating, and prosecuting other criminal offences; for preventing an immediate and serious threat to public security; and for other purposes to the extent that this is agreed between the states setting up the team.[156]

To the extent that the laws of the states concerned or the provisions of any legal instrument applicable between them permit, arrangements may be agreed for persons other than representatives of the competent authorities of the states setting up the joint investigation team to take part in the activities of the team;[157] this provision has Europol primarily in mind.[158] As the *Explanatory Report* makes clear, persons authorized to participate in an investigation team under this paragraph will act primarily in a supportive or advisory role, and are not permitted to exercise the functions conferred on members or seconded members of a team unless this is

---

[152] EU Convention, art 13(3). See the Council Resolution of 26 February 2010 on a Model Agreement for setting up a Joint Investigation Team, OJ C 70/1, 19.3.2010.

[153] EU Convention, art 13(5).

[154] EU Convention, art 13(7).

[155] To be withheld only in cases where such use would endanger criminal investigations in the state concerned or in respect of which that state could refuse mutual assistance.

[156] EU Convention, art 13(9)(10).

[157] EU Convention, art 13(12).

[158] See also Council Recommendation of 30 November 2000 to Member States in respect of Europol's assistance to joint investigative teams set up by the Member States, OJ C 357, 13.12.2000.

permitted under the relevant agreement between the Member States concerned. The United Kingdom has maintained its opposition to Europol personnel having operational powers.

7. Covert investigations

Another investigative technique involves undercover agents, or, in the language of the Convention 'officers acting under covert or false identity'. The Convention contains an article,[159] which states may opt out of, which merely provides that states may agree to assist one another in covert investigations. Such investigations are to take place in accordance with the national law and procedures of the states on the territory of which the covert investigation takes place. The states involved co-operate to ensure that the covert investigation is prepared and supervised, and to make arrangements for the security of the officers acting under covert or false identity.

8. Liability regarding officials

A matter which was of some concern during the negotiation of the Convention was the need for clarity as to the potential criminal and civil liabilities of officials engaged in controlled delivery or covert operations or working as members of joint investigation teams. So far as criminal liability is concerned, article 15 places such officials in the same position as the officials of the state where the offences are committed. Civil liability rests primarily upon the state whose officials are concerned, but is governed by the law of the state in whose territory those officials were operating.[160] However, the latter state has the duty of making good any damage under the conditions applicable to damage caused by its own officials, seeking reimbursement from the other state.[161]

The following chapter examines provisions for international co-operation in criminal matters in the service of documents and the taking of evidence. It is followed by an account of texts dealing with particular types of crime.

---

[159] EU Convention, art 14.
[160] EU Convention, art 16(1).
[161] EU Convention, art 16(2)(3).

7

Service of Documents and Obtaining Evidence

In the context of international co-operation in civil matters, the service of process and the taking of evidence abroad are dealt with as distinct topics. That is not appropriate in the context of criminal matters, as the documents that require service abroad are commonly subpoenas or similar witness summonses, seeking to obtain evidence for a criminal prosecution.

I. General service and evidence provisions

1. The 1959 Council of Europe Convention

(a) Letters Rogatory

Chapter II of the European Convention of 1959 (articles 3–6) deals essentially with the taking of evidence for use in criminal proceedings. It specifies that the request shall in this context take the form of Letters Rogatory defined in the official Explanatory Report as 'a mandate by a judicial authority of one country to a foreign judicial authority to perform in its place one or more specified actions'.[1] On the basis of this understanding, it has been held by a Swiss court that where a foreign court has made an application to question a witness through a Swiss court, the foreign court has legal standing to appeal against questioning which it feels has not been properly carried out, as the requested judge acts in place of the requesting judge in discharging his investigatory duty.[2]

This type of procedure was familiar to states from its use in international civil procedure, especially as a means for taking evidence. It had not previously been much used in the criminal context, and in subsequent international agreements, where the emphasis on co-operation between specifically *judicial* authorities has been less marked, a more neutral term (such as 'request' simpliciter) has commonly been substituted.

Article 3(1) provides that 'the requested Party shall execute in the manner provided for by its law[3] any Letters Rogatory relating to a criminal matter and addressed to it by the judicial authorities of the requesting Party for the purpose of procuring evidence or transmitting articles to be produced in evidence, records or documents'. 'Evidence' is to be construed as referring, inter alia, to hearing witnesses, experts, and accused persons, and providing for transport and search and seizure.[4] It has been suggested that it should be construed in its widest sense as meaning anything which may be evidence for the prosecution or the defence and liable to lead to the establishing of the true facts,[5] and also that the requested authority must judge whether the objects in question are connected with the alleged offence and truly required as evidence rather than as, for example, security for civil claims.[6] The Swiss courts have decided that the proceeds of crime can be handed over under the Swiss legislation giving effect to the convention (which does

---

[1] At p 14.

[2] Justizkommission Zug, 4 April 1985, [1986] SJZ 301.

[3] The Second Additional Protocol of 2001 adds a new provision (art 8 of the Protocol) that 'notwithstanding the provisions of Article 3 of the Convention, where requests specify formalities or procedures which are necessary under the law of the requesting Party, even if unfamiliar to the requested Party, the latter shall comply with such requests to the extent that the action sought is not contrary to fundamental principles of its law, unless otherwise provided for in this Protocol'.

[4] *Explanatory Report* at p 14.

[5] *PPA*, at p 42.

[6] Ibid.

not specifically refer to proceeds at any point); but they have also indicated that this will not normally be the case where the proceeds of tax fraud are concerned.[7]

The examination of witnesses and experts is to be carried out in accordance with the law of the requested state. The requesting state may, however, ask that the witnesses and experts be examined on oath, and this is to be complied with if not prohibited by the law of the requested state.[8] No provision is made to enable the record of the evidence to be taken in a particular form, or for procedures such as cross-examination to be allowed; the law of the court executing the request governs, but in practice some procedural codes will be flexible enough to accommodate the needs of requesting states. The convention does provide that where sight of documents and records is requested, certified copies or certified photostat copies are to be sufficient unless originals are expressly requested, in which case every effort is to be made to comply.[9] The Swiss authorities have indicated that, although it is accepted that information about the relatives of criminals may also be sought, this may not be used in evidence against them without the consent of the Swiss authorities.[10]

It is also to be noted that while the Letters Rogatory must be addressed to the requested party by the judicial authorities of the other state, the convention does not prohibit third parties making requests to those authorities for transmission. Officials and interested persons may also expressly request permission to attend the execution of the Letters Rogatory, but this is subject to the consent of the requested state;[11] additional language was inserted[12] by the Second Additional Protocol of 2001 to the effect that consent should not be refused where the presence of the visiting official 'is likely to render the execution of the request for assistance more responsive to the needs of the requesting Party'. The consent may only be given where not prohibited by the law of the requested state, as it was considered to be unacceptable that the authorities of the requesting state and the parties in criminal proceedings have better rights than equivalent parties in domestic proceedings in the requested state.[13]

(b) Appearance of witnesses, experts, and prosecuted persons in the requesting state

The sub-heading appears in the Convention as part of the title to Chapter III. This makes clear what might otherwise be obscure to an English reader of the text, that the 'service of writs' includes the service of witness summonses. 'Prosecuted persons' is a term which is not used in the text of the articles of the Convention;

---

[7] *S v Camera dei Ricorsi Penali del Tribunale di Appelo del Cantone Ticino* [1987] I BGE (112/6) 576.

[8] Council of Europe Convention, art 3(2).

[9] Council of Europe Convention, art 3(3).

[10] *S v Camera dei Ricorsi Penali del Tribunale di Appello del Cantone Ticino*, n 7 above.

[11] Council of Europe Convention, art 4(1).

[12] As art 4(2).

[13] *PPA*, at p 16.

it means persons in custody (for whatever reason) whose appearance as a witness in the requesting state is required. It is also clear, though only implied in the text, that articles 8 to 12 are concerned with the appearance of persons to give evidence in the requesting state; appearance in the requested state is covered by the Letters Rogatory provisions of Chapter II.

Article 8 prevents a witness or expert summoned to appear in the requesting state from being punished for failing to answer a summons unless they subsequently enter the territory of the requesting party and are again summoned.[14] This is to be the case even where the summons contains a notice of penalty,[15] and 'penalty' is to be construed as including all forms of restraint on personal liberty, including fines.[16] From the point of view of the prosecution, there are some cases in which progress cannot be made unless the witness attends in the requesting state; this is more likely to be the case if the officials of that state are not permitted to be present at the examination of a witness, perhaps after the use of compulsory powers, in the requested state in response to a Letter Rogatory. However, these considerations are outweighed by considerations of individual liberty and the unacceptability of the extra-territorial effect of subpoenas.[17]

The payment of an allowance and travelling expenses is guaranteed for witnesses and experts by article 9, which provides that they are to be paid by the requesting party at rates at least equal to those applicable in the country where the hearing is to take place. Where the appearance of a witness is especially necessary this is to be expressly mentioned in the request and the requested party is required to invite that person to appear.[18] Where this is the case the summons should indicate the approximate allowances and expenses refundable, and, when requested by the witness or expert, an advance should be made to him by the requested party which will then be refunded by the requesting party. These advances are considered necessary to encourage attendance,[19] but it has been suggested that they should be available to all witnesses and experts, as every person whose presence is requested must be considered to be especially necessary for mutual assistance to have been invoked.

Where the person summoned is being held in custody in the requested state the provisions of article 11 apply. The Convention permits temporary transfer for the purposes of personal appearance for evidentiary purposes other than standing trial,[20] with return to be within a period stipulated by the requesting party provided that certain conditions are met. Transfer may be refused if the person in custody does not consent; if his presence is necessary at criminal proceedings pending in the requested state; if transfer would be liable to prolong his detention; or if there are

---

[14] *Explanatory Report*, at p 18.
[15] Council of Europe Convention, art 8.
[16] *Explanatory Report*, at p 18.
[17] See *PPA*, at p 18, and pp 204–205 for a fuller account of the issue as it arose in the context of the Commonwealth Scheme for Mutual Assistance in Criminal Matters.
[18] Council of Europe Convention, art 10(1).
[19] *PPA*, at p 18.
[20] The reference to 'evidentiary purposes other than standing trial' is a clarification introduced in the redraft of art 11 substituted by the Second Additional Protocol of 2001.

'other overriding grounds' for refusing transfer. If a transfer takes place, the person transferred is not to be required to do anything other than give evidence or take part in a confrontation.[21]

Where the transfer involves transit through a third state which is also a party to the Convention an application requesting permission should be made to the Ministry of Justice of that state, the only ground for refusing such permission being that a Contracting Party may refuse to permit transit of its own nationals.[22] The person is to remain in custody during transit and while within the territory of the requesting state unless the requested party applies for his release.[23] There is no mention within the Convention itself of whether the time spent in custody in the requesting state should count towards the person's sentence, but the general view of the group of experts which reviewed the practical application of the Convention was that this should be the case.[24]

An important provision is article 12, which grants witnesses, experts, and persons in custody a certain immunity from prosecution when responding to a summons; a distinction necessarily being made between witnesses and experts on the one hand and persons being summoned to answer charges on the other.

Witnesses and experts are granted immunity from prosecution, detention, or other restraints on their personal liberty in respect of acts or convictions dating from before their departure from the requested state.[25] In the case of persons being summoned to face criminal proceedings it is obviously impracticable to provide such a blanket immunity from prosecution; persons summoned to answer for acts forming the subject of proceedings against them are entitled to be free from prosecution, detention, or other restraints on personal liberty in respect of acts or convictions dating from before their departure from the requested state and which are not specified in the summons.[26]

It was decided that it was equitable for the immunity to cease when the person had had an opportunity of leaving the territory of the requested state for a period of fifteen consecutive days from the date when his presence was no longer required by the judicial authorities but has nevertheless remained in the requesting state or was returned to it (eg, under normal extradition procedures).[27]

(c) Hearing by video or telephone conference

The Second Additional Protocol of 2001 makes provision for the use of video and telephone conference facilities, adopting almost unchanged the texts of articles 10 and 11 of the European Union Convention, considered below.[28]

---

[21] *PPA*, at p 48.
[22] Council of Europe Convention, art 11(2).
[23] Council of Europe Convention, art 11(3).
[24] *PPA*, at p 95.
[25] Council of Europe Convention, art 12(1).
[26] Council of Europe Convention, art 12(2).
[27] Council of Europe Convention, art 12(3).
[28] Second Additional Protocol, arts 9 and 10; for the EU text, see pp 210–211.

(d) Search and seizure

Letters Rogatory may request the search for and seizure of property, but limitations on compliance with such requests are to be found in articles 5 and 6. Firstly, the Contracting Parties may reserve the right to make execution of Letters Rogatory for the search and seizure of property dependent on one or more of the following conditions:[29]

(a) that the offence concerned is punishable under both the law of the requesting and requested states;

(b) that the offence is an extraditable offence in the requested country;

(c) that the execution of Letters Rogatory is consistent with the law of the requested state.

Where such a reservation is made, reciprocity may be applied against that state by any other Contracting State.[30]

Where property is to be handed over pursuant to a request, compliance may be delayed if the property, records, or documents are required in connection with pending criminal proceedings in the requested state; any property handed over in execution of a request is to be returned as soon as possible unless the requested state waives the right to demand its return.[31] It has been held in *X v Appellationsgericht des Kantons Baselstadt* that no breach of the convention takes place until the requested state, which had not waived the right to reclaim the property, has made a request for its return and that request has been ignored.[32] In this case the Italian authorities had requested the transfer of valuable gravestones from Switzerland for use in criminal proceedings in Italy. Italy subsequently refused to hand back the stones, claiming that they were historic treasures under public international law, but it was held that the claim could not succeed as the refusal to return the stones or to execute the Swiss court order for their seizure amounted to a breach of good faith. It was agreed by the Committee of Experts when drafting the convention that the requesting state would not be permitted to dispose of the property even when it was obliged to determine the question of ownership under its own domestic law,[33] but this has been criticized as doing nothing to protect third party rights and as failing to meet the many and varied legal problems which can arise.[34]

(e) Service of writs and records of judicial verdicts

Article 7 provides that the requested party shall effect service of writs and records of judicial verdicts transmitted to it for that purpose. This will include the service

---

[29] Council of Europe Convention, art 5(1).
[30] Council of Europe Convention, art 5(2).
[31] Council of Europe Convention, art 6.
[32] *X v Appellationsgericht des Kantons Baselstadt* [1985] I BGE (111) 52.
[33] *Explanatory Report*, at p 16.
[34] *PPA*, at p 44.

of summonses addressed to defendants; this facilitates the issuing of default judgments (ie, in the absence of any appearance by the defendant), which are common in civil law jurisdictions.

Service may either be by simple transmission or, where expressly requested, in the manner provided for the service of analogous documents under the domestic law of the requested state or in a special manner consistent with that law. This is intended to allow the requested party to make use of whichever mode of service is easiest for it to provide,[35] and although no definition of 'writs and records of judicial verdicts' is provided, it is intended to extend to notification of all matters relating solely to criminal proceedings.[36] Where service is requested in a particular form, or where provisions as to modes of service are contained in a supplementary bilateral agreement between the two states, service in some other form will be at risk of being declared invalid for the purpose of the proceedings in the requesting state.[37]

As proof of service may be required in certain jurisdictions to show that due notice has been given of the proceedings, article 7(2) provides that the requested party must provide either a receipt bearing the date and the signature of the person on whom the documents were served, or a declaration made by the requested party stating that service was effected, giving details of the form and date of service. Criticisms have been made, however, that it is a serious flaw in the Convention that there is no attempt to deal with the effects of service or whether service may be refused. Finally, because of strict requirements in the law of some Scandinavian countries that no accused can be convicted without being given specified periods of notice of the charge against him, article 7(3) allows any Contracting Party to enter a reservation that service of a summons on an accused person within its territory must be transmitted to its authorities by a certain time before the date set for appearance.

2. The Commonwealth Scheme

(a) Location of individuals; service of process

The Commonwealth Scheme applies to requests for assistance in 'identifying and locating persons',[38] but, as such assistance can be provided in most countries administratively, the text of the Scheme contains no further detail.

In many countries, especially those in the common law tradition, service of documents may similarly be an administrative matter requiring no legislative action. In fact the United Kingdom Crime (International Co-operation) Act 2003[39] makes express provision for the service of foreign process.

---

[35] *Explanatory Report*, at p 16.
[36] *PPA*, at p 45.
[37] *Officier van Justitie in het Arrondissement Middelburg v S* [1988] NJ 2458 (Hoge Raad, 15 December 1987).
[38] Scheme, para 1(5)(a).
[39] Crime (International Co-operation) Act 2003, ss 1, 2. See pp 225–234.

Provisions in the Commonwealth Scheme as to service of process[40] were drafted with an eye on the Hague Service Convention of 1965, but contain two additional safeguards. Both apply where the documents relate to attendance in the requesting country (typically a witness summons). The requesting country's Central Authority must provide information as to outstanding warrants or other judicial orders in criminal matters against the person to be served.[41] This is to ensure that if the person served decides to attend in the requesting country, his decision is a fully informed one.

The second safeguard was added to the text of the Scheme in 1990, after extensive discussion which began at a Commonwealth Regional Workshop held in Bermuda in December 1988. That Workshop had before it the text of the Treaty between the United States of America and the Commonwealth of the Bahamas on Mutual Assistance in Criminal Matters. Article 17(1) of that Treaty reads:

> The Requested State shall effect service of any document relating to or forming part of any request for assistance properly made under the provisions of this Treaty transmitted to it for this purpose by the Requesting State; *provided that the Requested State shall not be obliged to serve any subpoena or other process requiring the attendance of any person before any authority or tribunal in the Requesting State.* (emphasis added)

The proviso (emphasized above) was added in the course of negotiating the Treaty;[42] it was the absence of any corresponding provision in the Commonwealth Scheme which attracted comment in Bermuda.[43] The basic question concerns the attitude which should be taken to a request from a foreign government for assistance in serving a document in the nature of a summons or subpoena in any of four circumstances (of which the first two are the more important in the present context). These are where:

(a) the foreign government wishes measures of compulsion to be available in and under the law of the requested country; or

(b) failure to obey the summons will expose the person on whom it is served to penalties under the law of the requesting country; or

(c) to obey the summons will expose that person to prosecution for a crime in connection with which the summons was issued; or

(d) to obey the summons will expose that person to prosecution for other crimes or to other penalties or legal proceedings.[44]

---

[40] Scheme, para 12.

[41] Scheme, para 12(2).

[42] An identical text appears as art 13(1) of the United Kingdom–US Treaty concerning mutual assistance between the United States and the Cayman Islands.

[43] The issue is of considerable importance to those countries close to the United States (which applies sanctions readily) and especially those, like Bermuda, whose air routes are almost wholly via the US mainland.

[44] Immunity of witnesses from prosecution is fully dealt with in para 17 of the Commonwealth Scheme. Some countries are prepared to give more extensive immunities, eg s 19 of the Mutual Assistance in Criminal Matters Act 1987 of Australia protects the person concerned from civil actions and from having to give evidence in any proceedings other than the proceeding to which the request related.

The first issue identified here is generally referred to as the question of the 'international subpoena'. The introduction of any provision in the Scheme along the lines of the international subpoena was decisively rejected in 1986. This was despite arguments that in a number of cases evidence crucial to the success of a prosecution might be inadmissible if taken abroad on commission, perhaps because of the absence of an opportunity for cross-examination by the defendant; that reliance could not be placed on the willing co-operation of the witness; and that service of an enforceable subpoena might be an advantage to willing witnesses, who could more easily obtain leave of absence from an employer and might be released from some obligations of confidentiality which would otherwise apply.

Although useful regional arrangements for 'backing' witness summonses do exist, giving them the status of international subpoenas,[45] human rights and constitutional considerations ensure that international treaty practice reveals little support for the 'international subpoena' notion. There is, exceptionally, provision in the United States–Italian Mutual Assistance Treaty for the compulsory appearance of a witness in the requesting state;[46] persons compelled to appear are given immunity from prosecution based on truthful testimony given pursuant to a request under the Treaty.[47] In general, however, international practice is that 'witnesses and experts are completely free not to go to the requesting country'.[48] It is significant that even in the UN Convention against Illicit Traffic in Narcotic Drugs and Psychotropic Substances 1988, the obligation to provide assistance in this context is merely to 'facilitate or encourage, to the extent consistent with . . . domestic law and practice, the presence' of witnesses 'who consent to assist in investigations or participate in proceedings'.[49]

Where failure to obey the summons will expose the person on whom it is served to penalties under the law of the requesting country, international treaty practice seeks to exclude (or at least severely limit) the possibility of such penalties being applied. Amongst treaties which exclude that possibility entirely is the European Convention on Mutual Assistance, article 8 of which reads:

A witness or expert who has failed to answer a summons to appear, service of which has been requested [under the Convention] shall not, even if the summons contains a notice of penalty, be subjected to any punishment or measure of restraint, unless subsequently he voluntarily enters the territory of the requesting Party and is there again duly summoned.

Similarly, treaties entered into by Australia contain a provision on the following lines:

---

[45] eg, Australia has such arrangements with New Zealand and Fiji; Malaysia with Singapore and Brunei.
[46] Applying both to witnesses in custody for other reasons in the requested state (Treaty, art 16(1)) and those at liberty there (art 15(1)).
[47] Treaty, art 17(1).
[48] *Explanatory Report* to the European Convention on Mutual Assistance, art 8.
[49] Vienna Convention, art 7(4).

A person who does not answer a summons to appear [in the Requesting State] as a witness or expert shall not by reason thereof be liable to any penalty or be subjected to any coercive measures notwithstanding any contrary statement in the summons.[50]

Some treaties apply a similar rule only where the person served is not a national of the requesting country.[51]

The position taken by the Bahamas in its treaty negotiations with the United States goes further. It involves the reservation of a right to refuse to serve any subpoena or other process requiring the attendance of a person before a court in the requesting state. Presumably 'subpoena' is used in its literal sense, of a document to which penalties or sanctions are attached; the reservation of the right to refuse to serve 'other process', including witness summonses carrying no (overt) sanctions, takes the position still further.

In the event, Law Ministers at their meeting in 1990 accepted a recommendation to add what is now paragraph 12(5) of the Scheme, which addresses the possibility of penalties in either of the relevant countries, providing:

A person served in compliance with a request with a summons to appear as a witness in the requesting country and who fails to comply with the summons shall not by reason thereof be liable to any penalty or measure of compulsion in either the requesting or the requested country notwithstanding any contrary statement in the summons.

The Crime (International Co-operation) Act 2003 of the United Kingdom provides that service of process requiring a person to attend as a party or as a witness imposes no obligation under the law of any part of the United Kingdom to comply; and the service of such process must be accompanied by a notice to that effect.[52]

(b) Obtaining evidence in the requested country

Paragraph 14 of the Scheme deals with the examination of witnesses in the requested country, its provisions again influenced by the work of the Hague Conference, in its Evidence Convention of 1970. The earlier text was extended in 2011 to cover the taking of statements, ie, at the investigatory stage. The Scheme covers both the examination of a witness (as opposed to a person merely making a statement) by a person, typically appointed by a court, in the requested country, and also the giving of evidence through a live video link or other audiovisual means.

Following the Hague model, a witness may claim any privilege available in criminal proceedings in either the requested or the requesting country.[53] This was not uncontroversial: an alternative view was that the law of the requesting country alone should govern, so that, for example, an Australian request for the evidence of a witness who could otherwise plead the privilege against self-

---

[50] Australia–Austria Treaty, art 10(4). See to the same effect the Treaties with Italy, art 14(5); Luxembourg, art 13(5); Netherlands, art 14(4).

[51] eg, the United States–Switzerland Treaty, art 24(1).

[52] Crime (International Co-operation) Act 2003, s 2(1)(2).

[53] Scheme, para 18.

incrimination in the requested country could be acted upon if he were compellable under Australian law having been given an indemnity against prosecution by the Director of Public Prosecutions. Practice under bilateral treaties varies greatly. To deal with practical issues concerning the operation of the 'double privilege' rule adopted in the Scheme, the request for assistance must contain an indication of any provisions of the law of the requesting country as to privilege or exemption from giving evidence which appear especially relevant to the request.[54] This last provision might appear a little odd in that it invites a prosecution agency to indicate reasons why it should be denied the evidence it seeks, but it accords with the general approach of fair and open dealing between the Central Authorities, whose trust and goodwill are essential if the Scheme is to operate effectively.

Paragraph 19 deals with search and seizure of evidence, where the Central Authority of the requested country acts, in effect, as an agent for that of the requesting country in applying for any necessary warrant, and with other procedures such as inspecting or photographing evidence, or taking and analysing samples. Further provisions govern the disclosure of any document, record, item, or other material relevant to the criminal matter, meaning those held by the authorities as opposed to a private individual; requested countries are 'encouraged to provide copies of any document, record, item or other material not publicly available, to the same extent and under the same conditions as apply to the provision of such material to its own law enforcement agencies or prosecution or judicial authorities'.[55]

(c) Interception of postal items

Notably restricted provisions relating to the interception of postal items were added to the Scheme in 2011.[56] A request may seek assistance for the interception of a postal item during the course of its carriage by a postal service and the subsequent transmission to the requesting country of the postal item or, where appropriate, a copy or record thereof. Such a request may only be made where it appears to the requesting country that there are grounds to suspect that the information obtained pursuant to the interception would be relevant to the commission of a criminal offence in the requesting country; and it appears to the requested country that there are grounds to suspect that the information would be relevant to the commission of a criminal offence in the requested country; and the criminal matter arising in the requesting country is, in the view of the requesting country, of a serious character.[57] It will be seen that these conditions mean that criminal offences in both countries must be suspected, which gives a new meaning to the term 'double criminality'. The general provisions of the Scheme ensure that requests are dealt with under the law of the requested county; this is re-stated in the provisions dealing with the interception of postal items, and in addition the duration of and the detailed

---

[54] Scheme, para 14(2)(c).
[55] Scheme, para 13. See para 30 as to the actual transmission, return and authentication of material.
[56] Scheme, para 20.   [57] Scheme, para 20(2).

conditions of such activities must be agreed between the requesting and requested countries.[58] Furthermore, the requested country has an unqualified right to refuse to give such assistance, and need not give reasons for any refusal.[59]

(d) Appearance of witnesses in the requesting country

The Scheme contains quite elaborate provisions[60] designed to enable statements to be taken in the requesting country, or evidence to be taken in the courts of that country, either by facilitating the travel of a witness from the requested country or by arranging for the temporary transfer of a person in custody[61] in that country but who is willing to give evidence in the requesting country. The provisions were based on those in the European Convention on Mutual Assistance in Criminal Matters[62] and in bilateral treaties negotiated by the United States. These provisions apply only where the potential witness is willing to appear; there is no question of measures of compulsion, or of any penalty for failure to appear,[63] and the provisions grant a carefully limited immunity from prosecution while the witness is in the requesting country.

So far as the transfer of persons in custody is concerned, the United Kingdom insisted on the inclusion of what is now paragraph 16(4):

Notwithstanding the consent of the person in custody, the requested country may refuse to comply with a request for that person's transfer and shall be under no obligation to inform the requesting country of the reasons for such refusal.

It is not entirely clear why the United Kingdom's representatives were so insistent on this point. They prayed in aid practice in respect of the repatriation of prisoners, which is of course a much more long-term measure, and argued that the reasons for refusing a request might be so sensitive that it would be undesirable for them to be discussed with the requesting country or with the person concerned.

In contrast, Australia was anxious to include in the Scheme provision for 'trial transfer', that is the transfer of someone already detained in State A to stand trial in State B (while evidence was available and fresh) on the understanding that he would be returned to State A to complete his sentence there. It was felt, however, that this was a form of (temporary) extradition, with which the present Scheme did not deal, and the Law Ministers eventually agreed (despite some hesitations on the part of a few countries) to deal with the matter by way of an amendment to the Commonwealth Scheme on the Rendition of Fugitive Offenders.

---

[58] Scheme, para 20(3).   [59] Scheme, para 20(4).   [60] Scheme, paras 15–17.
[61] This term will include both convicted and remand prisoners.
[62] Council of Europe Convention, arts 10–12.
[63] See Scheme, paras 15(4) and 16(5), provisions both added in 1990 for the reasons discussed above in the context of the service of witness summonses.

3. The EU Convention

It has already been noted that the EU Convention on Mutual Assistance in Criminal Matters between Member States supplements the 1959 Council of Europe Convention and does not replace its central provisions. Specifically EU action dealing with the taking of evidence was much delayed.

(a) Service of procedural documents and summonses

The Council of Europe Convention deals quite fully with the service of documents including witness summonses, and the position of those who do or do not respond to such a summons.[64] The EU Convention contains the simple provision that each state is to send procedural documents intended for persons who are in the territory[65] of another Member State to them directly by post.[66] A less direct route, via the competent authorities of the requested state, may be used only if the address of the person for whom the document is intended is unknown or uncertain; or the law of the requesting state requires proof of service in a form which cannot be obtained by the use of postal service; or it has not been possible to serve the document by post; or the requesting state has 'justified reasons' for considering that dispatch by post will be ineffective or is inappropriate.[67]

There are some unusual and well-crafted provisions concerning information for the recipient. Where there is reason to believe that the addressee does not understand the language in which the document is drawn up, the document, or at least the important passages thereof, must be translated either into a language of the state in which the addressee is staying or another language which it is known the addressee understands.[68] The addressee must also be sent a notice, translated if necessary, stating that he or she may obtain information from the authority by which the document was issued or from other authorities in that state regarding his or her rights and obligations concerning the document.[69] Examples given in the *Explanatory Report* include information as to the consequences of a failure to comply with the document and the circumstances in which the person concerned may be assisted by a lawyer; in the case of a witness summons, there should be information as to the possibility of an advance to cover travel expenses and subsistence costs.

---

[64] See pp. 199–201, above and the 1959 Convention, arts 8, 9, and 12. The effect of those latter provisions is expressly preserved by the EU Convention, art 5(5).

[65] The *Explanatory Report* notes that this phrase should be interpreted in a broad sense and does not necessarily mean that the person is resident in the requested state.

[66] EU Convention, art 5(1).

[67] EU Convention, art 5(2).

[68] EU Convention, art 5(3).

[69] EU Convention, art 5(4).

(b) Temporary transfer of persons held in custody for purpose of investigation

The Council of Europe Convention provides for the transfer of a person in custody in a requested state to the requesting state to appear as a witness or for the purposes of confrontation; and provides some safeguards for the person concerned.[70] The EU Convention extends these provisions to cover transfers in respect of an investigation for which the presence of the person held in custody is required.[71] The transfer is the subject of an agreement between the competent authorities in each state, and a state may make a declaration that it will always require the consent of the person in custody. This has always been the United Kingdom practice.[72]

(c) Hearings by video conference or telephone conference

There are circumstances in which it is not possible or convenient for a witness, including an expert witness, to attend in person at a trial or other hearing in another state. Modern technology makes it relatively simple to arrange adequate substitutes for personal appearance, via video conferencing or a telephone conference. Both are provided for in the EU Convention.

Where a witness is in the requested state's territory and has to be heard as a witness or expert by the judicial authorities of another state, the requested state must agree to the hearing by video conference provided that the use of the video conference is not contrary to fundamental principles of its law and on condition that it has the technical means to carry out the hearing.[73] The Convention lays down rules as to how the video conference is to be conducted:

(a) a judicial authority of the requested Member State shall be present during the hearing, where necessary assisted by an interpreter, and shall also be responsible for ensuring both the identification of the person to be heard and respect for the fundamental principles of the law of the requested Member State. If the judicial authority of the requested Member State is of the view that during the hearing the fundamental principles of the law of the requested Member State are being infringed, it shall immediately take the necessary measures to ensure that the hearing continues in accordance with the said principles;

(b) measures for the protection of the person to be heard shall be agreed, where necessary, between the competent authorities of the requesting and the requested Member States;

(c) the hearing shall be conducted directly by, or under the direction of, the judicial authority of the requesting Member State in accordance with its own laws;

---

[70] Council of Europe Convention, art 11; and see pp 201–202, above.

[71] EU Convention, art 9.

[72] See 14th Report of the House of Lords' Select Committee on the European Communities (Session 1997–1998), *Mutual Assistance in Criminal Matters* (HL Paper 72), para 64.

[73] EU Convention, art 10(1)(2).

(d) at the request of the requesting Member State or the person to be heard the requested Member State shall ensure that the person to be heard is assisted by an interpreter, if necessary;

(e) the person to be heard may claim the right not to testify which would accrue to him or her under the law of either the requested or the requesting Member State.[74]

A carefully qualified provision allows, but does not compel, Member States to apply the video conferencing practice to hearings involving accused persons. A Member State may make a declaration that it will not do so (and the United Kingdom has done so) and must specifically agree to any such hearing. To safeguard the accused, the Convention makes specific reference to the European Convention on Human Rights and requires the accused person's consent to any hearing.[75]

Provisions for telephone conferences are much simpler. The witness or expert must agree, but the state in which he or she is located can only refuse its agreement if such a conference would be contrary to fundamental principles of its law.[76]

4. The 2003 Framework Decision on freezing orders

In 2003, the Council of the European Community adopted a Framework Decision[77] on the execution in the European Union of orders freezing property or evidence. Although not evident from the title, this Framework Decision was limited to orders made in criminal proceedings: its declared objective was to establish the rules under which a Member State was to recognize and execute in its territory a freezing order issued by a judicial authority of another Member State in the framework of criminal proceedings.[78] There were further limitations: the Framework Decision applied only to freezing orders issued for the purpose of securing evidence, or the subsequent confiscation of property.[79] The scope in terms of the offence alleged was defined in a fairly complex fashion: many offences, listed in article 3(2), defined by the law of the issuing state and in that issuing state by a custodial sentence of a maximum period of at least three years, were within the scope of the Decision without more; for other offences regard had also to be had to the law of the executing state.[80]

The Framework Decision provided for the transmission of a freezing order by the judicial authority which issued it directly to the competent judicial authority for execution by any means capable of producing a written record under conditions allowing the executing state to establish authenticity.[81] It was to be accompanied by

---

[74] EU Convention, art 10(5). For minutes of the proceedings, costs, and the application of perjury and related law, see art 10(6), (7), (8).
[75] EU Convention, art 10(9).
[76] EU Convention, art 11.
[77] Framework Decision 2003/577/JHA of 22 July 2003, OJ L 196/45, 2.8.2003.
[78] Framework Decision 2003, art 1.
[79] Framework Decision 2003, art 3(1).
[80] Framework Decision 2003, arts 2(e) (definition of 'evidence'), 3.
[81] Framework Decision 2003, art 4(1).

a prescribed certificate, translated into an official language of the executing state.[82] The UK and Ireland were allowed to insist that the freezing order together with the certificate must be sent via a central authority.[83]

The competent judicial authorities of the executing state were required to recognize a freezing order without any further formality being required and to take forthwith the necessary measures for its immediate execution in the same way as for a freezing order made by an authority of the executing state.[84] This was subject to a number of grounds for non-recognition or non-execution,[85] and for postponement of execution, which included cases in which execution might damage an ongoing criminal investigation.[86] Reports on the action taken in the executing state were to be made forthwith to the competent authority in the issuing state by any means capable of producing a written record.

In 2008, the Commission reported[87] that implementation by the Member States was not satisfactory, with implementing national legislation revealing numerous omissions and misinterpretations. The Framework Decision also had one obvious limitation: it is solely concerned with the freezing of material; any question of its transfer to the requesting state, for any purpose, required recourse to other mutual legal assistance instruments.

5. The 2008 Framework Decision on a European Evidence Warrant

Meanwhile, the Commission had made a Proposal[88] for what eventually became a Council Framework Decision[89] creating a European Evidence Warrant (EEW). The lengthy gestation period produced a disappointingly complex instrument. The ambitious aims of the Commission were expressed in its Proposal as follows:

38. Notwithstanding the advantages of the proposed European Evidence Warrant, it remains the case that practitioners need to rely on a variety of co-operation instruments in order to obtain evidence from other Member States. Indeed, the proposed European Evidence Warrant risks introducing the inconvenience for the practitioner of having to use different types of instruments for different aspects of the same case (for example, a European Evidence Warrant for objects and documents, but a mutual assistance request for taking witness statements).

39. It is therefore necessary to make clear that the European Evidence Warrant is, in the Commission's view, the first step towards a single mutual recognition instrument that

---

[82] Framework Decision 2003, art 9.
[83] Framework Decision 2003, art 4(2).
[84] Framework Decision 2003, art 5.
[85] Set out in Framework Decision 2003, art 7.
[86] Framework Decision 2003, art 8.
[87] Report of the Commission based on Article 14 of Council Framework Decision 2003/577/JHA of 22 July 2003 on the execution in the European Union of orders freezing property or evidence, COM/2008/0885 final.
[88] COM/2003/0688 final.
[89] Framework Decision 2008/978/JHA of 18 December 2008 on the European evidence warrant for the purpose of obtaining objects, documents and data for use in proceedings in criminal matters, OJ L 350/72.

would in due course replace all of the existing mutual assistance regime. The steps towards a single instrument could be as follows.

- The first step would be the proposed European Evidence Warrant, which provides for the obtaining of evidence that already exists and that is directly available.
- The next stage would be to provide for the mutual recognition of orders for the obtaining of other types of evidence. These can be divided into two categories.
- First, there is evidence that does not already exist but which is directly available. This includes the taking of evidence in the form of interviews of suspects, witnesses or experts, and the taking of evidence through the monitoring of telephone calls or banking transactions.
- Secondly, there is evidence which, although already existing, is not directly available without further investigation or analysis. This includes the taking of evidence from the body of a person (such DNA samples). This category also includes situations where further inquiries need to be made, in particular by compiling or analysing existing objects, documents or data. An example is the commissioning of an expert's report.
- In a final stage these separate instruments could be brought together into a single consolidated instrument which would include a general part containing provisions applicable to all co-operation.

40. Such a single consolidated instrument would within the EU replace mutual legal assistance in the same way that the European arrest warrant will replace extradition. The existing mosaic of international and EU conventions governing the cross-border gathering of evidence within the EU would thus be replaced by a single EU body of law. Achieving that end objective straightaway by means of a single instrument would, however, be unduly complex. This proposal is therefore limited to a first step.

(a) Nature of an EEW

An EEW is defined as a judicial decision issued by a competent authority of a Member State with a view to obtaining objects, documents, and data from another Member State for use in defined types of proceedings.[90] These are:

(a) criminal proceedings brought by, or to be brought before, a judicial authority in respect of a criminal offence under the national law of the issuing state;

(b) proceedings brought by administrative authorities in respect of acts which are punishable under the national law of the issuing state by virtue of being infringements of the rules of law, and where the decision may give rise to proceedings before a court having jurisdiction in particular in criminal matters;

(c) proceedings brought by judicial authorities in respect of acts which are punishable under the national law of the issuing state by virtue of being infringements of the rules of law, and where the decision may give rise to further proceedings before a court having jurisdiction in particular in criminal matters; and

---

[90] Framework Decision 2008, art 1(1).

(d) any of the above proceedings which relate to offences or infringements for which a legal person may be held liable or punished in the issuing state.[91]

An EEW may be issued by a judge, a court, an investigating magistrate, a public prosecutor, or any other judicial authority as defined by the issuing state and, in the specific case, acting in its capacity as an investigating authority in criminal proceedings with competence to order the obtaining of evidence in cross-border cases in accordance with national law.[92] The EEW is in a form specified in the Annex to the Framework Decision.[93]

An EEW may be issued with a view to obtaining in the executing state objects, documents, or data needed in the issuing state for the purpose of such proceedings. However, an EEW may not be issued for the purpose of requiring the executing authority to (a) conduct interviews, take statements, or initiate other types of hearings involving suspects, witnesses, experts, or any other party; (b) carry out bodily examinations or obtain bodily material or biometric data directly from the body of any person, including DNA samples or fingerprints; (c) obtain information in real time such as through the interception of communications, covert surveillance, or monitoring of bank accounts; (d) conduct analysis of existing objects, documents, or data; or (e) obtain communications data retained by providers of a publicly available electronic communications service or a public communications network.[94]

Before an EEW is issued the issuing authority must be satisfied that obtaining the objects, documents, or data sought is necessary and proportionate for the purpose of the proceedings in question; and that the objects, documents, or data could be obtained under the law of the issuing state in a comparable case if they were available on the territory of the issuing state, even though different procedural measures might be used.[95]

(b) Transmission of EEWs

A number of methods for transmitting EEWs are provided. The default method is direct transmission to the competent authority of a Member State in which the competent authority of the issuing state has reasonable grounds to believe that relevant objects, documents, or data are located or, in the case of electronic data, directly accessible under the law of the executing state. It is to be transmitted without delay by any means capable of producing a written record under conditions allowing the executing state to establish authenticity. All further official communications shall be made directly between the issuing authority and the executing authority. However, any Member State may designate a central authority or, when

---

[91] Framework Decision 2008, art 5.
[92] Framework Decision 2008, art 2(c) (definition of 'issuing authority'); see art 3(1) for notification of designations.
[93] Framework Decision 2008, art 6, which also sets out translation requirements.
[94] Framework Decision 2008, art 4.
[95] Framework Decision 2008, art 7.

its legal system so provides, more than one central authority to assist the competent authorities and, if necessary as a result of the organization of its internal judicial system, to be responsible for the administrative transmission and reception of the EEW as well as for other official correspondence relating thereto. Finally, if the issuing authority so wishes, transmission may be effected via the secure telecommunications system of the European Judicial Network.[96]

(c) Use of personal data

Personal data obtained under the Framework Decision may be used by the issuing state for the purpose of the proceedings for which the EEW may be issued and other judicial and administrative proceedings directly related to those proceedings, or to prevent an immediate and serious threat to public security. Data may not be used for any other purpose without the prior consent of the executing state, unless the issuing state has obtained the consent of the data subject. In the circumstances of a particular case, the executing state may require the Member State to which the personal data have been transferred to give information on the use made of the data.[97]

(d) Execution of warrants

Member States are obliged to execute any EEW on the basis of the principle of mutual recognition and in accordance with the provisions of the Framework Decision.[98] In the executing state, the executing authority must recognize an EEW without any further formality being required and forthwith take the necessary measures for its execution in the same way as an authority of the executing state would obtain the objects, documents, or data. This obligation is, however, subject to the grounds for non-recognition or non-execution provided for in article 13 and the grounds for postponement provided for in article 16.[99] The executing state is responsible for choosing the measures which under its national law will ensure the provision of the objects, documents, or data sought by an EEW and for deciding whether it is necessary to use coercive measures to provide that assistance. Any measures rendered necessary by the EEW must be taken in accordance with the applicable procedural rules of the executing state, but the executing authority must comply with the formalities and procedures expressly indicated by the issuing authority provided that such formalities and procedures are not contrary to the fundamental principles of law of the executing state.[100] Each Member State must ensure that any measures that would be available in a similar domestic case in the

---

[96] Framework Decision 2008, art 8.
[97] Framework Decision 2008, art 10.
[98] Framework Decision 2008, art 1(2).
[99] Framework Decision 2008, art 11(1). There are special rules which apply, or may be invoked, where the issuing authority is not a judge, a court, an investigating magistrate, or a public prosecutor: art 11(3) and (4).
[100] Framework Decision 2008, art 12.

executing state are also available for the purpose of the execution of the EEW, and that measures, including search or seizure, are available for the purpose of the execution of the EEW where it is related to any of the offences listed in article 14(2).[101]

Where search and seizure[102] is necessary to execute an EEW, verification of double criminality may be required. This is not necessary in cases involving one or more of the offences listed in article 14(2) which are punishable in the issuing state by a custodial sentence or a detention order for a maximum period of at least three years. If the EEW is not related to any of those offences and its execution would require a search or seizure, recognition or execution of the EEW may be subject to the condition of double criminality.[103]

Member States must put in place the necessary arrangements to ensure that any interested party, including bona fide third parties, have legal remedies against the recognition and execution of an EEW in order to preserve their legitimate interests. Member States may limit such legal remedies to cases in which the EEW is executed using coercive measures. The action to challenge recognition and execution is to be brought before a court in the executing state in accordance with the law of that state.[104]

Article 15 sets deadlines, which may, however, be broken where compliance is not practicable. Any decision to refuse recognition or execution must be taken 'as soon as possible' and no later than thirty days after the receipt of the EEW by the competent executing authority. The executing authority must take possession of the objects, documents, or data 'without delay' and no later than sixty days after the receipt of the EEW. Unless a legal remedy is pending or grounds for postponement exist, the executing state must 'without undue delay' transfer the objects, documents, or data obtained under the EEW to the issuing state.

---

[101] Framework Decision 2008, art 11(2). The full, and very miscellaneous, list of these offences is: 'participation in a criminal organisation, terrorism, trafficking in human beings, sexual exploitation of children and child pornography, illicit trafficking in narcotic drugs and psychotropic substances, illicit trafficking in weapons, munitions and explosives, corruption, fraud, including that affecting the financial interests of the European Communities interests, laundering of the proceeds of crime, counterfeiting currency, including of the euro, computer-related crime, environmental crime, including illicit trafficking in endangered animal species and in endangered plant species and varieties, facilitation of unauthorised entry and residence, murder, grievous bodily injury, illicit trade in human organs and tissue, kidnapping, illegal restraint and hostage-taking, racism and xenophobia, organised or armed robbery, illicit trafficking in cultural goods, including antiques and works of art, swindling, racketeering and extortion, counterfeiting and piracy of products, forgery of administrative documents and trafficking therein, forgery of means of payment, illicit trafficking in hormonal substances and other growth promoters, illicit trafficking in nuclear or radioactive materials, trafficking in stolen vehicles, rape, arson, crimes within the jurisdiction of the International Criminal Court, unlawful seizure of aircraft/ships, and sabotage.'

[102] 'Search or seizure' includes any measures under criminal procedure as a result of which a legal or natural person is required, under legal compulsion, to provide or participate in providing objects, documents, or data and which, if not complied with, may be enforceable without the consent of such a person or it may result in a sanction: Framework Decision 2008, art 2(f).

[103] Framework Decision 2008, art 14.

[104] Framework Decision 2008, art 18.

(e) Co-existence with other instruments

The Commission's original proposal would substitute the provisions of the Framework Decision for provisions in several of the existing conventions. In the event, it is to co-exist with existing legal instruments in relations between the Member States in so far as these instruments concern mutual assistance requests for evidence falling within the scope of the Framework Decision. That notwithstanding, issuing authorities must rely on the EEW when all of the objects, documents, or data required from the executing state fall within the scope of the Framework Decision. Issuing authorities may use mutual legal assistance to obtain objects, documents, or data falling within the scope of the Framework Decision if they form part of a wider request for assistance or if the issuing authority considers in the specific case that this would facilitate co-operation with the executing state.[105]

6. The Commission's suggestions for further legislation

In November 2009, the Commission published a Green Paper on obtaining evidence in criminal matters from one Member State to another and securing its admissibility.[106] After reviewing the scope and perceived limitations of the existing instruments, the Commission argues the case for the replacement of the existing legal instruments by a new single instrument. It noted that the existing rules on obtaining evidence in criminal matters in the EU were of two different kinds. On the one hand, there are instruments based on the principle of mutual assistance. The older instruments were based on mutual assistance, the newer ones (notably the Framework Decision on the European Evidence Warrant) on mutual recognition. It is argued that this duality makes the application of the rules burdensome and may cause confusion among practitioners.

So the Commission suggests the replacement of the existing legal regime on obtaining evidence in criminal matters by a single instrument based on the principle of mutual recognition and covering all types of evidence. Compared with the scope of application of the Framework Decision on the European Evidence Warrant, the new instrument would also cover evidence that—although directly available—does not already exist, such as statements from suspects or witnesses, or information obtained in real time, such as interception of communications or monitoring of bank accounts. It would also include evidence that—although already existing—is not directly available without further investigation or examination, such as analyses of existing objects, documents, or data, or obtaining bodily material, such as DNA samples or fingerprints. Many of these types of evidence raise human rights issues and are likely to be very controversial.

---

[105] Framework Decision 2008, art 21.
[106] COM(2009) 624 final, 11.11.2009. Cf W Hetzer, 'National Criminal Prosecution and European Tendering of Evidence' (2004) 12 Eur J Crime Crim L & Crim J 166, discussing, inter alia, ideas of a 'European Interview Record' to assist in the cross-border taking of evidence.

The existing instruments were seen as only approaching the issue of admissibility of evidence in an indirect manner: they do not set any common standards for gathering evidence. The Commission suggests the adoption of common standards for gathering evidence in criminal matters. Quite what this means is unclear. The harmonization of laws on criminal evidence and procedure would seem to be unduly ambitious. The House of Commons' European Scrutiny Committee shared this view:[107]

2.13 The proposals in the Green Paper are premised on assertions that cooperation between Member States in MLA under the existing instruments is not working well; not on evidence. Hence the language used is couched throughout in tentative terms. It is far from clear, for example, why the coexistence of the principles of mutual legal assistance and mutual recognition 'may hinder effective cross-border cooperation', or why the current procedures for the admissibility of evidence obtained through MLA can be described as 'indirect' because they do not set common standards for gathering evidence. Under current procedures, evidence obtained by MLA is directly admissible if lawfully obtained in the assisting EU country, and this includes evidence of telephone intercepts.

2.14 The Commission's proposals, if implemented, will reach far into the practices and procedures of domestic criminal law—at the least they should be accompanied by the evidence we are often told is an inherent part of 'better regulation' in the EU.

II. Telecommunications, computer data, and electronic surveillance

The power of state agencies such as the police or security services to intercept telecommunications between individuals, for example by 'tapping' telephones or using electronic means to overhear mobile phone calls, is very controversial in many states. In the UK, the matter is largely governed by the Regulation of Investigatory Powers Act 2000; it is significant that this Act has been repeatedly amended to enable more use of evidence obtained by such means in terrorism cases. It is therefore unsurprising that the negotiation of arrangements for international co-operation involving interception of telecommunications has proved difficult. The more modern instruments also make provision in related fields, such as those as to computer data and electronic surveillance.

1. The work of the Council of Europe

(a) Committee of Ministers Recommendations

In 1981 the Committee of Ministers of the Council of Europe established the Select Committee of Experts on the Operation of European Conventions in the Penal Field (PC-R-OC) to review the practical application of those

---

[107] Fifth Report, Session 2009–2010, chap 2.

Conventions and to suggest measures to facilitate their smooth functioning.[108] When the European Convention on Mutual Assistance in Criminal Matters was subjected to this scrutiny, there were perceived to be problems within the specific area of Letters Rogatory for the interception of telecommunications. Although the parties presumed that the Convention did in fact apply to such Letters Rogatory, there was some confusion over which provisions governed their execution and to what extent domestic law requirements could be taken into consideration.[109] As a result of the Select Committee's deliberations a Recommendation of the Committee of Ministers was produced[110] with three main aims:

(a) to facilitate mutual assistance in this area;
(b) to protect the individual against unjustified interceptions; and
(c) to provide guidance with regard to the adoption of domestic law requirements.

This particular form of action was chosen as it merely provides guidance for the Member States without creating any positive duty to act, and it leaves the method of implementation of the recommendations to the discretion of the Member States.

The Recommendation laid down rules governing Letters Rogatory for the 'interception of telecommunications', this being defined as 'the interception of messages conveyed through telephones, teleprinters, telecopiers and similar means of communication, and the transmission of records relating thereto'. It was decided that an exhaustive definition of 'telecommunications' should not be provided so that the Recommendation could apply to future developments.[111] The Recommendation only applied to Letters Rogatory within the scope of article 3 of the European Convention and therefore only to requests from 'the judicial authorities of the requesting Party for the purpose of procuring evidence or transmitting articles to be produced in evidence, records or documents'.

(b) The Convention on Cybercrime

Later Recommendations addressed a number of related issues[112] and the work culminated in the signature in Budapest on 23 November 2011 of the Convention on Cybercrime.[113] An Additional Protocol to the Convention on Cybercrime,

---

[108] *Explanatory Memorandum of Recommendation No R(85)10 on Letters Rogatory for the Interception of Telecommunications*, at p 9.
[109] *Explanatory Memorandum*, at p 10.
[110] Recommendation No R(85)10, 28 June 1985.
[111] *Explanatory Memorandum*, at p 11.
[112] Recommendations No R(87) 15 regulating the use of personal data in the police sector, R(89)9 on computer-related crime providing guidelines for national legislatures concerning the definition of certain computer crimes, R(95)4 on the protection of personal data in the area of telecommunication services, with particular reference to telephone services, and R(95)13 concerning problems of criminal procedural law connected with information technology.
[113] ETS 185. As at January 2012, there were 31 states, including the United Kingdom, which had ratified the Convention. A full Explanatory Report has been published.

concerning the criminalization of acts of a racist and xenophobic nature committed through computer systems, was adopted in January 2003.[114] Chapter II of the Convention (articles 2 to 22) contains detailed provisions as to action to be taken at the national level, including the creation of offences, and rules as to jurisdiction; for present purposes the relevant Chapter is Chapter III on International Co-operation.[115]

Article 25 of the Convention sets out a general principle: the parties are to afford one another mutual assistance to the widest extent possible for the purpose of investigations or proceedings concerning criminal offences related to computer systems[116] and data, or for the collection of evidence in electronic form of a criminal offence.[117] With certain exceptions, mutual assistance is subject to the conditions provided for by the law of the requested party or by applicable mutual assistance treaties (this includes the grounds on which the requested party may refuse co-operation), and may make mutual assistance conditional upon the existence of dual criminality.[118] For many parties, the European Convention on Mutual Assistance will be the vehicle for most requests; where no mutual assistance treaty is applicable, the provisions of articles 27 to 35 of the Convention apply, and each party is required to take such legislative and other measures as may be necessary to implement them.[119]

Each party must designate a central authority or authorities responsible for sending and answering requests for mutual assistance, the execution of such requests, or their transmission to the authorities competent for their execution.[120] The central authorities are to communicate directly with each other; however, in case of urgency, requests may be sent directly by judicial authorities of the requesting party to such authorities of the requested party or through Interpol, and an urgent request not involving coercive action may be directly transmitted by the competent authorities of the requesting party to the competent authorities of the requested party.[121]

Requests are to be executed in accordance with the procedures specified by the requesting party, except where they are incompatible with the law of the requested

---

[114] ETS 189. As at January 2012, there were 20 states, including the United Kingdom, which had ratified the Additional Protocol.

[115] It is not possible in this book to examine other aspects of cybercrime, but see *Protecting Europe against Large-scale Cyber-attacks* (House of Lords European Union Committee 5th Report of Session 2009–10, HL Paper 68), which examines the work of the European Network and Information Security Agency and the implementation of Council Directive 2008/114/EC of 8 December 2008 on the identification and designation of European critical infrastructures and the assessment of the need to improve their protection, OJ L 345/75, 23.12.2008.

[116] 'Computer system' is defined (Convention, art 1(a)) as any device or a group of interconnected or related devices, one or more of which, pursuant to a program, performs automatic processing of data.

[117] Convention, art 25(1).

[118] Convention, art 25(4).

[119] Convention, art 25(2). See also art 26 on the spontaneous provision of information to another party.

[120] Convention, art 27.

[121] Convention, art 27(9); a party may require even urgent matters to go via its central authority 'for reasons of efficiency'. For the use of 'expedited means of communication' including fax and e-mail, see art 25(3).

party.[122] Each party must designate a point of contact available on a 24-hour, seven-day-a-week basis, in order to ensure the provision of immediate assistance for the purpose of investigations or proceedings concerning criminal offences related to computer systems and data, or for the collection of evidence in electronic form of a criminal offence. Such assistance shall include facilitating, or, if permitted by its domestic law and practice, directly carrying out the provision of technical advice; the preservation of data, the collection of evidence, the provision of legal information, and the location of suspects.[123]

The Convention provides for requests for:

(a) the expedited preservation of stored computer data in respect of which the requesting party intends to submit a request for the search or similar access, seizure or similar securing, or disclosure of the data;[124]

(b) the expedited disclosure of preserved traffic data[125] where, in the course of the execution of a request for the preservation of traffic data concerning a specific communication, the requested party discovers that a service provider in another state was involved in the transmission of the communication; the requested party must expeditiously disclose to the requesting party a sufficient amount of traffic data to identify that service provider and the path through which the communication was transmitted;[126]

(c) search, access, seize or secure, and disclose, data stored by means of a computer system located within the territory of the requested party;[127]

(d) assistance in the real-time collection of traffic data associated with specified communications in their territory transmitted by means of a computer system, at least with respect to criminal offences for which real-time collection of traffic data would be available in a similar domestic case;[128] and

(e) assistance in the real-time collection or recording of content data of specified communications transmitted by means of a computer system to the extent permitted under their applicable treaties and domestic laws.[129]

---

[122] Convention, art 27(3). For grounds of refusal or postponement, see art 27(4)–(6); for provisions as to confidentiality, see arts 27(8) and 28.

[123] Convention, art 35.

[124] Convention, art 29. Dual criminality may only be relied on in certain circumstances to refuse such assistance: art 29(3)(4). For limited grounds of refusal, see art 29(5).

[125] 'Traffic data' means any computer data relating to a communication by means of a computer system, generated by a computer system that formed a part in the chain of communication, indicating the communication's origin, destination, route, time, date, size, duration, or type of underlying service: Convention, art 1(d).

[126] Convention, art 30. For limited grounds of refusal, see art 30(2).

[127] Convention, art 31. Although not really a case of mutual assistance, art 32 provides for access (without any need for the authorization of the another party) to publicly available (open source) stored computer data, regardless of where the data is located geographically; and access to and reception, through a computer system in its territory, stored computer data located in another party, if the party obtains the lawful and voluntary consent of the person who has the lawful authority to disclose the data to the party through that computer system.

[128] Convention, art 33.

[129] Convention, art 34.

2. Provisions in the EU Convention on Mutual Assistance

The subject of interception of telecommunications proved one of the most difficult in the negotiation of the EU Convention. The *Explanatory Report* contains a useful account of the technical considerations lying behind the Convention provisions. It explains that there are circumstances in which a state is not technically capable of directly intercepting telecommunications made from or received on its own territory:

Wherever the subject of the interception may be located, the interception of telecommunications made via a satellite system (and one day, undoubtedly, via other technologies) requires only one single operation by the technical installation known as the 'gateway'. The gateway makes it possible to establish the satellite link, thus enabling the use of telecommunications equipment in very large geographical areas. All of this potentially means that a State whose territory falls within the satellite's coverage area, but which does not have a gateway, would not be technically capable of directly intercepting telecommunications made from or received on its territory via a satellite telephone.

None the less, it is still possible to intercept in the following two ways: (a) for each interception it intends to carry out, the State in question may request assistance from the State on whose territory the gateway is located; or (b) the operator installs remote access to the gateway, a sort of 'remote control'. This equipment enables a country to give an interception order from a distance via a gateway situated outside its territory. It may be given to the company or companies (the 'service providers' in the Convention) which provide the satellite telecommunications service on each national territory, on condition that they carry out the orders for interceptions which are lawfully requested by the competent authorities.

It is technically possible to limit use of this remote control equipment to those telecommunications made from or received on the territory of the Member State making use of them (therefore, with the remote control equipment to which the competent authorities of a Member State have access, it will only be possible to intercept telecommunications made from or received on the territory of that Member State).

In another set of circumstances a state, may for its own purposes (or the purposes of another) be able to intercept telecommunications made from or received on the territory of another state, without having to request assistance from the latter. It was nonetheless decided to deal with this type of case in the convention, largely as a basis for any new provisions needed as technology developed.

Article 18 deals with requests for interception of telecommunications. For the purpose of a criminal investigation, a competent authority[130] in the requesting state may, in accordance with the requirements of its national law, make a request to a competent authority in the requested state for (a) the interception and immediate transmission to the requesting state of telecommunications; or (b) the interception,

---

[130] For the purpose of arts 18, 19, and 20, 'competent authority' means a judicial authority, or, where judicial authorities have no competence in the area covered by those provisions, an equivalent competent authority, specified in a statement made by a Member State under art 24(1)(e) and acting for the purpose of a criminal investigation: Convention, art 17.

recording, and subsequent transmission to the requesting state of the recording of telecommunications.[131]

Three different situations are identified:

(a) The subject of the interception is present in the requesting Member State and the requesting state needs the technical assistance of the requested Member State to intercept his or her communications.

(b) The subject of the interception is present in a third Member State which has been informed of the proposed interception[132] and the requesting Member State needs the technical assistance of the requested Member State to intercept his or her communications.

In both these types of case the requested state is to comply with a request provided it receives the standard information specified for requests,[133] and may allow the interception to proceed without further formality.

(c) The subject of the interception is present in the requested[134] Member State and his or her communications can be intercepted in that state.

In this type of case, the request must also include a summary of the facts. The requested state is to comply with a request where the requested measure would be taken by it in a similar national case; it may require further information to enable it to decide whether this would be the case.

Costs that are incurred by telecommunications operators or service providers in executing requests pursuant to article 18 are to be borne by the requesting state.[135]

Article 19 deals with interceptions of telecommunications on national territory by the use of service providers. Member States must ensure that systems of telecommunications services operated via a gateway on their territory, which for the lawful interception of the communications of a subject present in another Member State are not directly accessible on the territory of the latter, may be made directly accessible by remote control equipment for the lawful interception by that latter Member State through the intermediary of a designated service provider present on its territory.[136] In such a case the competent authorities of a Member State are entitled, for the purposes of a criminal investigation and in accordance with applicable national law, and provided that the subject of the interception is present in that Member State, to carry out the interception through the remote control equipment of a designated service provider present on its

---

[131] Convention, art 18(1). For the contents of requests, see art 18(3); for the, exceptional, cases involving recording and later transmission, see art 18(6)(7).
[132] In accordance with art 20(2)(a).
[133] In art 3.
[134] The text as published in the *Official Journal* reads 'requesting', but this is plainly an error.
[135] Convention, art 21.
[136] Convention, art 19(1).

territory without involving the Member State on whose territory the gateway is located.[137]

Article 20 establishes an obligation to inform another Member State of certain interception orders made 'in the course of criminal investigations which present the characteristics of being an investigation following the commission of a specific criminal offence, including attempts in so far as they are criminalised under national law, in order to identify and arrest, charge, prosecute or deliver judgment on those responsible'. In effect, the notified Member State has ninety-six hours in which to require that the interception be not carried out, or be discontinued. The United Kingdom made a declaration,[138] accepted by the Council, applying the article to interception warrants issued by the Secretary of State to the police or to the customs authorities where the stated purpose is the detection of serious crime, and to certain warrants issued to the Security Service.

(a) Personal data protection

Title IV of the Convention contains limited provisions on data protection. They were sharply criticized by a House of Lords' select committee, which concluded that the political will to achieve more satisfactory provisions must have been weaker than the political imperative to bring to a close the years of complex and difficult negotiations on the Convention.[139] Article 23 provides that personal data communicated or obtained otherwise under the Convention may be used by the state to which they have been transferred (a) for the purpose of proceedings to which this Convention applies; (b) for other judicial and administrative proceedings directly related to those proceedings; (c) for preventing an immediate and serious threat to public security; and (d) for any other purpose, with the prior consent of the communicating state or the consent of the data subject.

3. Provisions in the Commonwealth Scheme

As amended in 2011, the Commonwealth Scheme contains a comprehensive set of provisions, many of which were inspired by the Council of Europe's Convention on Cybercrime or the provisions in the EU Convention, but which take a different form in the Scheme.

The Scheme provides for requests for:

(a) the preservation of computer data[140] where it appears to the requesting agency or authority that there are grounds to suspect that the preserved

---

[137] Convention, art 19(2).

[138] See OJ C197, 12.7.2000, at p 23.

[139] 12th Report of the Select Committee on European Union (Session 1999–2000), para 48.

[140] Defined as the protection of computer data which already exists in a stored form from modification or deletion, or from anything that would cause its current quality or condition to change or deteriorate, 'computer data' being defined as any representation of facts, information or concepts in a form suitable for processing in a computer system, including a program suitable to cause a computer system to perform a function: Scheme, para 1(3).

computer data may contain information relevant to criminal activities in the requested country;[141]

(b) the interception of telecommunications both (i) where the subject of the interception is in the requested country, and the requesting country needs the assistance of the requested country to effect or facilitate the interception of the subject's telecommunications; and (ii) where the subject of the interception of telecommunications is in the requesting country and the requesting country needs the assistance of the requested country to effect or facilitate the interception of the subject's telecommunications;[142]

(c) the interception of transmission data;[143]

(d) the disclosure of intercept material, ie material already obtained by the interception of telecommunications under the law of the requested country otherwise than in response to a request for assistance;[144]

(e) covert electronic surveillance carried out by or with an electronic surveillance device which transmits, records, or otherwise captures audio product, visual images, or location or position information, but not covert surveillance using a device designed primarily for the interception of telecommunications;[145] and

(f) subscriber information.[146]

The Scheme is the most up to date of the various instruments, in a field where the speed of technological change is so rapid as to be a constant challenge to legislators. The improvements made to the Scheme in 2011 to accommodate recent developments vindicate the flexibility of the Scheme device.

III. United Kingdom legislation

In 1990 the United Kingdom enacted for the first time comprehensive legislation on mutual assistance in criminal matters. The Criminal Justice (International Cooperation) Act 1990 enabled the United Kingdom to comply with its moral obligations in respect of the Commonwealth Scheme and to ratify the European Convention on Mutual Assistance in Criminal Matters of 1957 and the United

---

[141] Scheme, para 21.

[142] Scheme, para 23; see para 22 for provisions applying generally to arts 23–27.

[143] Scheme, para 24. 'Transmission data' means data that relates to the telecommunication functions of dialing, routing, addressing, or signalling; is transmitted to identify, activate, or configure a device, including a computer program, in order to establish or maintain access to a telecommunication service for the purpose of enabling a communication, or is generated during the creation, transmission, or reception of a communication and identifies or purports to identify the type, direction, date, time, duration, size, origin, destination, or termination of the communication; and does not reveal the substance, meaning, or purpose of the communication: para 1(3).

[144] Scheme, para 1(3) and 25.

[145] Scheme, para 1(3), 26.

[146] Scheme, para 27. 'Subscriber information' means any information held by the service provider relating to the name, address, telephone number, e-mail address, Internet Protocol address, or any similar identifier associated with a subscriber to any telecommunications service: para 1(3).

Nations Convention against Illicit Traffic in Narcotic Drugs and Psychotropic Substances 1988, and it provided a legislative basis for the implementation of other bilateral and multilateral agreements. It was largely replaced by the Criminal Justice (International Co-operation) Act 2003, which enabled the UK to implement the 'non-borders' aspects of the Schengen agreement, the EU Convention on Mutual Assistance in Criminal Matters 2000, the evidence-freezing provisions of the 2003 Framework Decision on the execution in the European Union of orders freezing property or evidence, and the 2001 Protocol to the European Convention on requests for assistance with locating banking accounts and the provision of banking information relating to criminal investigations.

1. Requests to the United Kingdom

Provision is made under the 2003 Act for assistance to be given within the United Kingdom in response to a request received by the Secretary of State from the Government or other authority in a country or territory outside the United Kingdom. In some cases the Secretary of State will receive the request in his capacity as a 'central authority', but this is not required by the Act, which enables assistance to be given to any country that requests it, with no requirement of reciprocity. There are some special rules applying where the foreign state is a 'participating country', which means a country, other than the United Kingdom, that is an EU Member State on a day appointed for the commencement of the relevant provision in the Act, and any other country designated by an order made by the Secretary of State;[147] a number of orders have been made, each designating countries in respect of particular provisions of the Act.[148]

The Act contains no specific provisions as to the form and contents of requests, but the Home Office publishes a set of *Mutual Legal Assistance Guidelines for the United Kingdom*, which reached its ninth edition in 2011, containing information on these and other practical matters. Procedures are governed by rules of court.[149]

2. Service of process

As the *Guidelines* point out, UK domestic law permits procedural documents to be sent directly by the requesting state to the persons in the UK to whom they are addressed. So, the UK strongly encourages direct transmission of procedural documents to persons by post, unless this is not legally possible under the domestic law of the requesting state. Nonetheless, the 2003 Act contains provisions enabling the United Kingdom to respond to a request for the service of 'overseas process'. This term covers:

---

[147] Crime (International Co-operation) Act 2003, s 51(2).

[148] SI 2008/2156, SI 2009/613, SI 2009/1764, SI 2010/36, and SI 2011/229.

[149] See the Criminal Procedure Rules, Part 32 and the Magistrates' Courts (Crime (International Co-operation)) Rules 2004, SI 2004/1048.

(a) any process issued or made in the requesting country for the purposes of criminal proceedings;

(b) any document issued or made by an administrative authority in that country in administrative proceedings;

(c) any process issued or made for the purposes of any proceedings on an appeal before a court in that country against a decision in administrative proceedings; and

(d) any document issued or made by an authority in that country for the purposes of clemency proceedings.[150]

In the case of summonses or other process requiring a person to appear as defendant or attend as a witness in criminal proceedings in the requesting country, there is no question of measures of compulsion being used. The Act provides that service shall not impose any obligation under the law of any part of the United Kingdom to comply with the summons, and when the documents are served they must be accompanied by a notice to that effect, which will also suggest that the person served might seek advice on the effect of non-compliance under the law of the overseas country,[151] and pointing out that a witness attending in foreign proceedings may not enjoy the same rights and privileges as would be accorded by UK law.[152]

Service of process will normally be by post. If personal service is requested, this is arranged through the local police force.[153] The UK reserves the right not to serve process or procedural documents where to do so could place a person's safety at risk, for example, if the procedural documents reveal the address of a key witness in a murder trial.

Service abroad of process of a UK court summoning a person as a defendant or as a witness is also provided for in the Act.[154] Such process may be served by post or in some cases 'in accordance with arrangements made by the Secretary of State'.[155] Where the person to be served is in a participating country, these arrangements are only available if the correct address of the person is unknown, or it has not been possible to serve the process by post, or there are good reasons for thinking that service by post will not be effective or is inappropriate.[156] Non-compliance does not constitute contempt of court; though should it prove possible process can be

---

[150] Crime (International Co-operation) Act 2003, s 1(2).

[151] For example, if he has property there, it might be subject to seizure by way of sanction for non-appearance; or arrest for contempt of court might occur on a later visit to the country concerned.

[152] Crime (International Co-operation) Act 2003, s 2.

[153] Crime (International Co-operation) Act 2003, s 1(3). For completion of a certificate of service (or a statement where service could not be effected) see s 2(4)(5).

[154] Crime (International Co-operation) Act 2003, ss 3, 4.

[155] Crime (International Co-operation) Act 2003, s 4(1).

[156] Crime (International Co-operation) Act 2003, s 4(2)(3). Participating countries for this purpose are Albania, Austria, Belgium, Bosnia and Herzegovina, Bulgaria, Croatia, Czech Republic, Denmark, Estonia, Finland, France, Germany, Greece, Hungary, Ireland, Israel, Italy, Latvia, Lithuania, Luxembourg, Macedonia, Malta, Montenegro, Netherlands, Poland, Portugal, Romania, Serbia, Slovakia, Slovenia, Spain, Sweden, and Switzerland.

served *within* the jurisdiction and the normal consequences of non-compliance will then follow.[157]

3. Evidence for use in the United Kingdom

Chapter 2 of Part 1 of the 2003 Act contains provisions enabling evidence to be obtained overseas for use in connection with criminal investigations or proceedings in the United Kingdom; 'evidence' includes information in any form and articles, and giving evidence includes answering a question or producing any information or article.[158]

A prosecuting authority may apply to any judge or justice of the peace asking that a request be made for assistance in obtaining evidence abroad. The judge or justice must be satisfied that an offence has been committed or that there are reasonable grounds for suspecting that an offence has been committed, and that proceedings in respect of the offence have been instituted or that the offence is being investigated.[159]

A designated prosecuting authority may itself request assistance, without approaching a judge or justice, if it appears to the authority that an offence has been committed or that there are reasonable grounds for suspecting that an offence has been committed, and the authority has instituted proceedings in respect of the offence in question or it is being investigated.[160]

A request for assistance may be sent, directly or via the Secretary of State, to a court exercising jurisdiction in the place where the evidence is situated, or to any authority recognized by the government of the country in question as the appropriate authority for receiving requests of that kind.[161] In cases of urgency, assistance may be sent via Interpol or Europol.[162]

Evidence obtained by virtue of a letter of request must not, without the consent of the appropriate overseas central authority, be used for any purpose other than that specified in the letter (which in practice will mean the proceedings or investigation so specified).[163] This means that if evidence has been obtained in respect of a specified charge against the defendant, it cannot be used if fresh charges are brought; but the evidence may be made use of in civil proceedings by a party

---

[157] Crime (International Co-operation) Act 2003, s 3(6)(7).

[158] Crime (International Co-operation) Act 2003, s 51(1).

[159] Crime (International Co-operation) Act 2003, s 7(1)–(4).

[160] Crime (International Co-operation) Act 2003, s 7(5). The designated authorities in England are the Attorney General, the Financial Services Authority, the Director of Public Prosecutions, and any Crown Prosecutor; the Director of Revenue and Customs Prosecutions and any person designated under section 37(1) of the Commissioners for Revenue and Customs Act 2005; the Director of the Serious Fraud Office and any person designated under section 1(7) of the Criminal Justice Act 1987; and the Secretary of State for Trade and Industry: Crime (International Co-operation) Act 2003 (Designation of Prosecuting Authorities) Order 2004, SI 2004/1034 as amended by SI 2004/1747 and SI 2005/1130.

[161] Crime (International Co-operation) Act 2003, s 8(1)(2).

[162] Crime (International Co-operation) Act 2003, s 8(3) (which speaks of 'any body or person competent to receive it under any provisions adopted under the Treaty on European Union').

[163] Crime (International Co-operation) Act 2003, s 9(2).

who did not seek the letter of request.[164] Any document or article obtained and which is no longer required for the specified or another approved purpose must be returned to the relevant overseas authority unless that authority indicates that it need not be returned.[165]

The provisions of the Act are primarily concerned with a mechanism for obtaining evidential material; the use of the mechanism does not guarantee the admissibility of the material. This will be governed by the usual rules of evidence. It is, however, provided that in exercising its discretion to exclude evidence which would otherwise be admissible, the court is to have regard to whether it was possible to challenge the statement contained in the evidence taken in response to a letter of request by questioning the person who made it; and, in cases where proceedings have been instituted,[166] whether the law of the overseas country allowed the parties to be legally represented when the evidence was being obtained.[167]

4. Domestic freezing orders

A constable may apply under section 10 of the 2003 Act to any judge or justice of the peace for a 'domestic freezing order', an order for protecting evidence which is in a participating country[168] pending its transfer to the United Kingdom. An order may be made if the judge or justice is satisfied:

(a) that proceedings in respect of a listed offence (an offence described in article 3(2) of the Framework Decision 2003/577/JHA of 22 July 2003 on the execution in the European Union of orders freezing property or evidence, or prescribed by an order made by the Secretary of State)[169] have been instituted or that such an offence is being investigated;

(b) that there are reasonable grounds to believe that there is evidence in a participating country which is on premises specified in the application in that country; is likely to be of substantial value (whether by itself or together with other evidence) to the proceedings or investigation; is likely to be admissible in evidence at a trial for the offence; and does not consist of or include items subject to legal privilege;

(c) that a request has been made, or will be made, under the 2003 Act for the evidence to be sent to the authority making the request.

An order is sent via the Secretary of State, with the certificate required by the Framework Decision and a translation of that certificate, to a court exercising jurisdiction in the place where the evidence is situated, or an appropriate authority

---

[164] *R v Gooch (Malcolm George) (No 2)* [1999] 1 Cr App R (S) 283; *BOC Ltd v Barlow, The Times,* 10 July 2001 (CA) (both decided under the predecessor legislation).
[165] Crime (International Co-operation) Act 2003, s 9(3).
[166] In the context, this must mean that the proceedings had been instituted when the statement was taken.
[167] Crime (International Co-operation) Act 2003, s 9(4).
[168] All Member States of the EU as at 19 October 2009 (the date s 10 came into effect).
[169] Crime (International Co-operation) Act 2003, s 28(5).

in the country in question.[170] The judge or justice who made the order may vary or revoke it on an application by the person who originally applied for the order, a prosecuting authority, or any other person affected by the order.[171]

5. Evidence for use abroad

Provision is also made for the taking in the United Kingdom of evidence for use overseas, in response to requests by a court exercising criminal jurisdiction, or a prosecuting authority, in a country outside the United Kingdom; by any other authority in such a country which appears to the Secretary of State to have the function of making such requests for assistance; or by Interpol or Europol.[172]

If the request is that a court should take evidence in connection with criminal or administrative proceedings or a criminal investigation or an investigation into an act punishable in administrative proceedings, the request may be complied with only if the Secretary of State is satisfied that an offence under the law of the country in question has been committed or that there are reasonable grounds for suspecting that such an offence has been committed, and that proceedings in respect of the offence have been instituted in that country or that an investigation into the offence is being carried on there.[173] A certificate as to these matters from the appropriate authority of the overseas country will be regarded as conclusive.[174] These rules do not apply if the request relates to 'clemency proceedings'. In the case of a 'fiscal offence' (which is not defined in the Act), assistance may be given at the investigatory stage only if the request is from a Commonwealth country, or is made pursuant to a treaty binding on the United Kingdom, or if the relevant conduct would constitute an offence if it had occurred in England.[175]

The meaning of the term 'evidence' in this context was examined (in the context of the predecessor Act of 1990) in *R v Secretary of State for the Home Department, ex p Fininvest SpA*,[176] a case involving an investigation into an alleged massive fraud by, amongst others, Signor Berlusconi, who had been, and was later to become again, Prime Minister of Italy. It was argued that the letter of request identified the documents sought so widely that it was a 'fishing expedition' rather than one 'evidence'. This, as Simon Brown LJ held, is a matter not for the Home Secretary but for the court, or here the Serious Fraud Office, to which the request is referred. It was argued for those challenging the request that 'evidence' had an established meaning in the field of mutual assistance, drawn from the approach in *Rio Tinto Zinc Corp v Westinghouse Electric Corp*.[177] The court held, however, that a test

---

[170] Crime (International Co-operation) Act 2003, s 11, 28(7).
[171] Crime (International Co-operation) Act 2003, s 12.
[172] Crime (International Co-operation) Act 2003, s 13(2).
[173] Crime (International Co-operation) Act 2003, s 14(1)(2).
[174] Crime (International Co-operation) Act 2003, s 14(3).
[175] Crime (International Co-operation) Act 2003, s 14(4). These provisions enable the United Kingdom to ratify the Additional Protocol to the European Convention.
[176] [1997] 1 WLR 743 (DC).
[177] [1978] AC 547.

appropriate for civil proceedings was not readily applicable to criminal investigations. Too narrow a definition of 'evidence' would defeat the purpose of the legislation. A much broader approach was supported by the language of the 1959 Convention, which speaks[178] of 'the widest measure of mutual assistance'.

If the evidence is to be taken, the Secretary of State issues a notice nominating a court, or in an appropriate case the Serious Fraud Office, to receive such of the evidence to which the request relates as may appear to the court to be appropriate to give effect to the request.[179] The nominated court has the same powers for securing the attendance of a witness as it would have for the purpose of other proceedings before the court.[180] A witness may rely on any privilege available in criminal proceedings in England or (to the extent that the claim to privilege is conceded by the overseas court or authority) in the overseas country.[181] The powers of the English courts under the Bankers Books' Evidence Act 1879 are available in proceedings in response to letters of request.[182] The Secretary of State may, however, issue a certificate that it would be prejudicial to the security of the United Kingdom for evidence to be given, and in such a case the witness must not be compelled to give the evidence; similarly, no witness may be compelled to give evidence in his capacity as an officer or servant of the Crown.[183]

6. Evidence by television links or by telephone

Provision is made in the 2003 Act enabling the Secretary of State, in response to a request from an overseas authority, to nominate a court in which a witness may give evidence through a live television link in criminal proceedings before a court in a country outside the United Kingdom.[184] Similar provisions apply where the overseas request is for the taking of evidence by telephone, but in that case the request must come from a 'participating country'.[185]

7. Search and seizure

A request may also be made for search and seizure of property. The Secretary of State may direct that a warrant be applied for in response to a request.[186] An application for a search warrant may also be made in certain circumstances by

---

[178] Convention, Art 1.
[179] Crime (International Co-operation) Act 2003, s 15(1)(2).
[180] Crime (International Co-operation) Act 2003, Sch 1, para 1.
[181] Crime (International Co-operation) Act 2003, Sch 1, para 5.
[182] Crime (International Co-operation) Act 2003, Sch 1, para 8.
[183] Crime (International Co-operation) Act 2003, Sch 1, para 5(4)(5)(6).
[184] Crime (International Co-operation) Act 2003, s 30.
[185] Crime (International Co-operation) Act 2003, s 31. For this purpose, participating countries are Albania, Austria, Belgium, Bosnia and Herzegovina, Bulgaria, Croatia, Czech Republic, Denmark, Estonia, Finland, France, Germany, Greece, Hungary, Iceland, Ireland, Israel, Italy, Latvia, Lithuania, Luxembourg, Macedonia, Malta, Montenegro, Netherlands, Norway, Poland, Portugal, Romania, Serbia, Slovakia, Slovenia, Spain, Sweden, Switzerland, and the United States.
[186] Crime (International Co-operation) Act 2003, s 13(1)(b). For procedure see further ss 16, 17, 26, and 27.

a constable on behalf of an international joint investigation team of which he is a member.[187]

8. Surveillance by foreign officers

So far as telecommunications are concerned, section 76A of the Regulation of Investigatory Powers Act 2000[188] deals with the case in which a foreign police or customs officer is carrying out relevant surveillance outside the United Kingdom which is lawful under the law of the country or territory in which it is being carried out, but circumstances arise by virtue of which the surveillance can for the time being be carried out only in the United Kingdom. If it is not reasonably practicable in those circumstances for a UK officer to carry out the surveillance in the United Kingdom in accordance with an authorization under Part 2 of the 2000 Act (or its Scottish equivalent), the surveillance may be lawfully carried out by the foreign officer in specified and notably limited circumstances.

The crime concerned must be a crime specified in article 40(7) of the Schengen Convention or by order of the Secretary of State; the foreign officer must on arrival give notice to the UK authorities and cause an application under Part 2 of the 2000 Act to be made; the foreign officer may carry out the surveillance only in places to which members of the public have or are permitted to have access, whether on payment or otherwise, and for a maximum of five hours.

9. Overseas freezing orders

The counterpart of a domestic freezing order is an overseas freezing order, an order for protecting, pending its transfer to the overseas country, evidence which is in the United Kingdom and may be used in any proceedings or investigation in the overseas country. The provisions in the 2003 Act[189] apply when the Secretary of State receives an order made by a court exercising criminal jurisdiction, a prosecuting authority or another appropriate authority in a participating country, accompanied by the certificate required by the Framework Decision.[190] The order must relate to criminal proceedings instituted in the participating country in respect of a listed offence (an offence described in Article 3(2) of the Framework Decision 2003/577/JHA) or a criminal investigation being carried on there into such an offence. The order must be accompanied by a request for the evidence to be sent to a court or authority in the overseas authority, unless the certificate indicates when such a request is expected to be made.

The Secretary of State must by a notice nominate a court to give effect to the overseas freezing order, send a copy of the overseas freezing order to the nominated

---

[187] Crime (International Co-operation) Act 2003, s 16(2)(b).
[188] As inserted by the Crime (International Co-operation) Act 2003, s 83. See also the Regulation of Investigatory Powers (Foreign Surveillance Operations) Order 2004, SI 2004/1128.
[189] s 20 ff.
[190] All EU Member States as at 19 October 2009.

court and to the chief officer of police for the area in which the evidence is situated, and tell the chief officer which court has been nominated. The nominated court must consider the overseas freezing order on its own initiative, but before giving effect to the order, the nominated court must give the chief officer of police an opportunity to be heard. The court must give effect to the overseas order unless it considers that, if the person whose conduct is in question were charged in the overseas country with the offence to which the order relates or in the United Kingdom with a corresponding offence, he would be entitled to be discharged under any rule of law relating to previous acquittal or conviction; or that giving effect to the overseas freezing order would be incompatible with any of the Convention rights within the meaning of the Human Rights Act 1998.[191] The court may postpone giving effect to an order in respect of any evidence in order to avoid prejudicing a criminal investigation which is taking place in the United Kingdom, or if, under an order made by a court in criminal proceedings in the United Kingdom, the evidence may not be removed from the United Kingdom.[192] The court gives effect to the order by issuing a warrant or, in certain cases,[193] a production order.[194]

10. Transfer of persons in custody

Unrepealed provisions in the Criminal Justice (International Co-operation) Act 1990 enable a person in custody in the United Kingdom to be transferred to a requesting country for the purpose of giving evidence in criminal proceedings there, or of being identified in, or otherwise by his presence assisting,[195] such proceedings or the investigation of an offence.[196] The section applies not only to persons serving a sentence of imprisonment, but also to those in custody awaiting trial or sentence and persons committed to prison in default of paying a fine.[197] The consent of the person in custody is an essential pre-requisite, but a consent once given cannot be withdrawn once the Secretary of State's warrant has been issued.[198] A rather surprising provision enables the consent of a person whose physical or mental condition or youth makes it inappropriate for him to act for himself to be given by

[191] Crime (International Co-operation) Act 2003, s 21.
[192] Crime (International Co-operation) Act 2003, s 23.
[193] Where the order relates to excluded material or special procedure material in the sense of the Police and Criminal Evidence Act 1984.
[194] Crime (International Co-operation) Act 2003, s 22. For the retention and possible release of material seized, see ss 24 and 25.
[195] An example might be participation in a reconstruction of the events surrounding an alleged offence.
[196] Criminal Justice (International Co-operation) Act 1990, s 5(1).
[197] Criminal Justice (International Co-operation) Act 1990, s 5(9).
[198] Criminal Justice (International Co-operation) Act 1990, s 5(2).

some appropriate person on his behalf.[199] There are detailed provisions giving the necessary authority to the person's custodians during transit, ensuring that he remains in legal custody, and for his arrest should he escape.[200] There is no formal provision that periods of absence from the United Kingdom will count in calculating the service of a sentence; this is certainly intended, and may be handled administratively.

These provisions of the 1990 Act are supplemented by very similar provisions in the 2003 Act. Under section 47 of that Act, the Secretary of State may, pursuant to an agreement with the competent authority of a participating country,[201] issue a warrant providing for a prisoner to be transferred to that country for the purpose of assisting there in the investigation of an offence. The offence must be one which was or may have been committed in the United Kingdom.

Corresponding provisions are made in both the 1990 and 2003 Acts to enable persons in custody in other countries to be transferred to the United Kingdom.[202] The Act is silent on the question of the grant of immunity from prosecution in respect of acts taking place before the transfer. The position of the United Kingdom is that its Government will consider a grant of immunity where this is specifically requested and on a case-by-case basis; it will not grant it where to do so is judged not to be in the public interest. As a result, formal reservations or declarations have been made in respect of the immunity provisions in the European Convention,[203] the Commonwealth Scheme,[204] and the Vienna Convention.[205] The United Kingdom will not agree to the transfer through its territory of persons in custody and in transit from one state to another.[206]

11. UK bilateral treaties and agreements

In addition to the multilateral instruments providing for mutual assistance in criminal matters, there is a growing network of bilateral treaties and agreements. The United States[207] and Australia were very active in the earlier stages of the growth of this network, but the United Kingdom now has a large number of bilateral arrangements. Some are limited to drug trafficking. This is the case

---

[199] Criminal Justice (International Co-operation) Act 1990, s 5(2).

[200] Criminal Justice (International Co-operation) Act 1990, s 5(3)–(8).

[201] For this purpose, participating countries are Albania, Austria, Belgium, Bosnia and Herzegovina, Bulgaria, Croatia, Czech Republic, Denmark, Estonia, Finland, France, Germany, Greece, Hungary, Iceland, Ireland, Israel, Italy, Latvia, Lithuania, Luxembourg, Macedonia, Malta, Montenegro, Netherlands, Norway, Poland, Portugal, Romania, Serbia, Slovakia, Slovenia, Spain, Sweden, and Switzerland.

[202] Criminal Justice (International Co-operation) Act 1990, s 6; Crime (International Co-operation) Act 2003, s 48.

[203] Convention, Art 12.

[204] Scheme, para 25.

[205] Convention, Art 7(18).

[206] Cf European Convention, Art. 11(2).

[207] For a full comparison of some of the earlier texts, see A Ellis and RL Pisani, 'The United States Treaties on Mutual Assistance in Criminal Matters: A Comparative Analysis' (1985) 19 Int'l Lawyer 189.

with the agreements with Argentina,[208] the Bahamas,[209] Bahrain,[210] Barbados,[211] Bolivia,[212] Chile,[213] Colombia,[214] Ecuador,[215] Grenada,[216] Guyana,[217] Italy,[218] Malaysia,[219] Mexico,[220] Nigeria,[221] Panama,[222] Paraguay,[223] Saudi Arabia,[224] South Africa,[225]Spain,[226] and Uruguay.[227] Others, and especially the more recent, have wider effect: those with Algeria,[228] Antigua and Barbuda,[229] Australia,[230] Brazil,[231] Canada,[232] the Hong Kong SAR,[233] India,[234] Ireland,[235] Netherlands,[236] the Philippines,[237] Romania,[238] Sweden,[239] Thailand,[240] Trinidad and

[208] Cm 2592. Signed 27 August 1991; in force 1 June 1994.
[209] Cm 475. Signed 28 June 1988; in force 24 October 1990.
[210] Cm 2474. Signed 24 June 1990; in force 1 January 1992.
[211] Cm 2240. Signed 19 April 1991; in force 1 June 1993.
[212] Signed 25 August 1994, but not in force.
[213] Cm 3775. Signed 1 November 1995; in force 1 February 1996.
[214] Cm 4682. Signed, 11 February 1997; in force 5 December 1999.
[215] Cm 2162. Signed 7 May 1992; in force 1 March 1993.
[216] Cm 5940. Signed 6 February 1995; in force 1 October 2001.
[217] Cm 3523. Signed 17 July 1991; in force 24 November 1996.
[218] Cm 2853. Signed 16 May 1990; in force 8 May 1994.
[219] Cm 2883. Signed 17 October 1989; in force 1 January 1995. This agreement is to be replaced by a wider treaty, signed 21 July 2010 but not yet in force.
[220] Cm 1398. Signed 29 January 1990; entered into force on 1 October 1990. This Agreement actually contains no mutual assistance provisions in the usual sense; it provides generally for co-operation; but also requires measures to give full effect to the obligations assumed in accordance with the Vienna Convention, which do of course include the provision of mutual legal assistance. A further agreement deals with non-drugs cases: (Cm. 3378). Signed 26 February 1996; in force 1 August 1996.
[221] Cm 901. Signed 18 September 1989; in force 30 October 1993.
[222] Cm 2660. Signed 1 March 1993; in force 1 September 1994.
[223] Cm 5259. Signed 6 July 1994; in force 21 June 1998.
[224] Cm 1308. Signed 2 June 1990; in force 20 September 1991.
[225] Signed 2 September 1992; not yet in force.
[226] Cm 830. Signed 26 June 1989; in force 15 December 1990.
[227] Cm 2458. Signed, 23 January 1992; in force 19 January 1994.
[228] Cm 7922. Signed 11 July 2006; in force 27 March 2007.
[229] Cm 6336. Signed 10 March 1997; in force 1 October 2004.
[230] Cm 4760. Signed 6 February 1997; in force 10 May 2000.
[231] Cm 8087. Signed 7 April 2005; in force 13 April 2011.
[232] Cm 1326. Signed 22 June 1988; in force 4 August 1990. Originally limited to drugs cases, this was extended to other crimes by an Exchange of Notes from 17 September 1993.
[233] Cm 5199. Signed 23 January 1998; not yet in force.
[234] Cm 2957. Signed 22 September 1992; in force 1 May 1995. This deals with proceeds of crime (including crimes involving currency transfers) and terrorist funds.
[235] Cm 4306. Signed 26 November 1998; in force 1 June 2004.
[236] Cm 2655. Signed 15 September 1993; in force 2 June 1994. This is expressly designed to supplement the Council of Europe on Laundering, Search, Seizure and Confiscation of the Proceeds from Crime, 1990.
[237] Cm 7826. Signed 18 September 2009; not yet in force.
[238] Cm 5008. Signed 14 November 1995; in force 1 October 2000. This deals specifically with the proceeds of crime.
[239] Cm 1307. Signed 14 December 1989; in force from 1 April 1992. This deals specifically with the proceeds of crime.
[240] Cm 3783. Signed 12 September 1994; in force from 10 September 1997.

Tobago,[241] Ukraine[242], the United Arab Emirates,[243] the United States of America,[244] and Vietnam.[245]

In every case, reference must be made to the full text of the treaty as the content necessarily varies from case to case, depending on the nature and practice of the legal system in the country concerned.

[241] Cm 3900. Signed 5 January 1998; not yet in force.

[242] Cm 3731. Signed 18 April 1996; in force from 1 April 1997. This deals specifically with the proceeds of crime in non-drugs cases.

[243] Cm 7383. Signed 6 December 2006; in force 2 April 2008.

[244] Cm 3546. Signed 6 January 1994; in force 2 December 1996.

[245] Cm 7879. Signed 13 January 2009; in force 30 September 2009.

8

Particular Types of Criminal Activity

This chapter is concerned with international co-operation in dealing with particular types of criminal activity. In each, co-operation is particularly important, though it takes differing forms. Co-operation between law enforcement agencies is not always made the subject of express legislative provision; it takes place informally to the extent that national law allows. International treaties and conventions may deal with some topics in detail, whereas in others we find instruments which rather supplement other, more generally applicable, instruments.

I. Drug trafficking

Drug trafficking deserves a certain primacy of place in any treatment of international co-operation in criminal matters; it was one of the very first areas in which states moved decisively to a new level of co-operation in the detection and prosecution of crimes. The distribution and use of illicit drugs threatens the health not only of individuals but of societies and political systems; it has clear links to other forms of organized crime, and there is considerable political will in most countries to undertake legislative action in response. The work done in the drugs area led to similar progress in dealing with other types of crime, and with the confiscation of the proceeds of crime examined in Chapter 9.

1. The drug-trafficking problem

The following impression of the scale of the drugs problem can be seen from the following account, gleaned from the publications of the United Nations Office on Drugs and Crime (UNODC).[1]

Globally, UNODC estimates that, in 2009, between 149 and 272 million people, or 3.3 per cent to 6.1 per cent of the population aged 15–64, used illicit substances at least once in the previous year. About half are estimated to have been current drug users, having used illicit drugs at least once during the past month prior to the date of assessment. While the total number of illicit drug users has increased since the late 1990s, the prevalence rates have remained largely stable, as has the number of problem drug users (those that regularly use illicit substances and can be considered dependent, and those who inject drugs), which is estimated at between 15 and 39 million.

Cannabis is by far the most widely used illicit drug type, consumed by between 125 and 203 million people worldwide in 2009. Cannabis is followed by ATS (amphetamine-type stimulants, mainly methamphetamine, amphetamine, and ecstasy), opioids (including opium, heroin, and prescription opioids), and cocaine. While there are stable or downward trends for heroin and cocaine use in major regions of consumption, this is being offset by increases in the use of synthetic and prescription drugs. Non-medical use of prescription drugs is reportedly a growing health problem in a number of developed and developing countries. Moreover, in recent years, several new synthetic compounds have emerged in established illicit drug markets. Many of these substances are marketed as 'legal highs' and substitutes for illicit stimulant drugs such as cocaine or ecstasy.

Trafficking flows vary according to the drug type involved. Cannabis is often locally produced and thus international trafficking is limited. Cocaine and heroin are trafficked both intra- and inter-regionally. Seizures of heroin represent an annual flow of some 430 tons of heroin into the global market. Of the total,

---

[1] In particular the *World Drugs Report 2011* and the UNODC Annual Report for 2010, both of which contain much further information and analysis.

380 tons is produced from Afghan opium, almost all of which is trafficked via routes flowing into and through the countries neighbouring Afghanistan. The size of that market is estimated to total $US13 billion per year. North America accounts for more than 40 per cent of a total cocaine consumption of around 470 tons. It comes primarily from Colombia. Most ATS manufacture occurs in the region of consumption, whereas their precursor chemicals are trafficked inter-regionally.

It will be seen that the drugs problem presents different features in countries of heavy consumption, in drug-producing countries, and in transit states, for example the island states of the Caribbean lying between producer countries in South America and the profitable market in the United States.

2. Legal responses

Attempts at co-ordinated international action against drug trafficking began in 1909 with a conference in Shanghai on the trade in opium. This produced the International Opium Convention of 1912.[2] Several other Conventions and Protocols followed, dealing both with opium[3] and narcotics generally.[4] These were all consolidated in the Single Convention on Narcotic Drugs of 1961[5] and extended to man-made hallucinogenic and other substances in the Psychotropic Substances Convention 1971.[6]

These instruments have attracted much international support,[7] but, as some of their titles indicate, their emphasis is on the administrative regulation of the production and movement of the drugs themselves; they are not law enforcement conventions dealing with the conduct of those trafficking in drugs or with their profits. So, for example, the Single Convention of 1961 (as amended) assigns functions to the Commission on Narcotic Drugs of the Economic and Social Council of the United Nations and to an International Narcotics Control Board;[8] it requires states to provide annual estimates of the quantities of drugs to be used for various purposes and of stocks held, of the area of land devoted to the cultivation of the opium poppy, and of the number of establishments manufacturing synthetic drugs and of their output.[9] There are then detailed provisions as to limits upon the manufacture, production, and

---

[2] Convention relating to the Suppression of the Abuse of Opium and other Drugs, The Hague, 23 January 1912, 8 LTNS 187.

[3] See the Second International Opium Convention, Geneva, 19 February 1925, 81 LTNS 317; the Protocol Limiting and Regulating the Cultivation of the Poppy Plant, the Production of, International and Wholesale Trade in, and Use of Opium, New York, 23 June 1953, 456 UNTS 3.

[4] eg, the Convention for Limiting the Manufacture and Regulating the Distribution of Narcotic Drugs, Geneva, 16 July 1931, 139 LNTS 301, with a number of amending Protocols.

[5] New York, 30 March 1961, 520 UNTS 204, amended by a Protocol of 25 March 1972, 976 UNTS 3.

[6] Vienna, 21 February 1971, 1019 UNTS 175.

[7] As at January 2012, 184 states were party to the 1961 Convention as amended by the 1972 amending Protocol; there were 183 States Parties to the 1971 Convention.

[8] Convention, arts 5–11.

[9] Convention, art 19. See art 20 for statistical returns to be made.

importation of drugs, and as to controls on poppy straw, the coca bush and its leaves, and cannabis,[10] and the regulation of international trade.[11] The only 'penal provisions' are those in article 36, requiring States Parties to create criminal offences relating to the possession, supply, and transport of drugs, and making such offences extraditable.[12]

Many of the recognized types of mutual assistance are of value in the drugs context, as in other criminal matters; for example, summonses may need to be served, and evidence obtained. The drugs context does, however, have its own special requirements.

The evidence needed for a successful drugs prosecution will usually include scientific evidence based on an analysis of the substances with which the accused was dealing. One aspect of UNODC's work is supporting the work of drug analysis and forensic science laboratories.

Another special feature of drugs cases is the extent of joint operations between enforcement agencies in different countries. A good example is that of 'controlled delivery' under which a consignment of drugs, the existence of which has become known to the authorities, is allowed to complete the journey planned for it by the traffickers, either to discover their modus operandi or to identify the ultimate consignees and their agents along the route. It sometimes happens that some or all of the drugs are removed, an innocent substance of similar weight and appearance being substituted. Wherever any resulting prosecution is mounted, evidence will be needed from the countries along the route, especially where this type of substitution has taken place.

Finally, there is no area in which the location of assets and the forfeiture of the proceeds of crime is more important than that of drug trafficking; the amounts of money involved can be enormous, and the movement across international boundaries is inherent in the whole business.

During the 1980s there was a major effort on the part of many governments and international agencies to put in place adequate legal responses, both in domestic law and through international legal co-operation. The most significant achievement was the Vienna Convention 1988, to which states and regional organizations (such as the European Union) are actively responding.

3. The Vienna Convention

In response to a United Nations General Assembly resolution of 4 December 1984,[13] a new convention designed to cover topics, such as those in the law enforcement area, not adequately dealt with in the existing instruments, was prepared and adopted as the United Nations Convention against Illicit Traffic in

---

[10] Convention, arts 21–29.
[11] Convention, arts 30–32.
[12] See Convention, art 36(2)(b).
[13] Resolution 39/141.

Narcotic Drugs and Psychotropic Substances 1988.[14] The Convention rapidly obtained the twenty ratifications required to bring it into force[15] and duly entered into force on 11 November 1990. The United Kingdom ratified the Convention in June 1991; by January 2012 there were 185 parties.

The purpose of the Convention is stated as being the promotion of co-operation among the parties to address more effectively those aspects of drug trafficking having an international dimension.[16] Although only one article specifically addresses mutual assistance as such,[17] the whole thrust of the Convention's provisions is towards comprehensive co-operation in legal as in other aspects.

This co-operation is set firmly within the established principles of international law by the provisions of article 2, which asserts the principle of non-intervention in the domestic affairs of other states,[18] and continues by prohibiting any State Party from undertaking in the territory of another party the exercise of jurisdiction and performance of functions which are exclusively reserved for the authorities of that other party by its domestic law.[19] This outlaws the assertion and exercise of extra-territorial jurisdiction, and provides a secure base upon which to erect the structure of mutual assistance.

(a) Offences

Article 3 contains an elaborate set of provisions requiring parties to establish a range of criminal offences under domestic law. These include not only offences of production, cultivation, and possession of drugs, but also the manufacture, transport, or distribution of equipment, materials, or specified substances knowing that they are to be used for their illicit cultivation, production, or manufacture.[20] Organized drug trafficking is directly attacked by the creation of the offence of organizing, managing, or financing drugs offences,[21] and of a series of offences of participation in laundering the proceeds of such offences.[22] These offences may be committed by the drug trafficker when an attempt is made to launder the profits. The Convention goes into considerable detail as to such matters as the need for heavy penalties and a long limitations period.[23]

---

[14] Vienna, 20 December 1988. A detailed *Commentary on the United Nations Convention against Illicit Traffic in Narcotic Drugs and Psychotropic Substances 1988* (to which the present author and W C Gilmore made the major contribution) was published in 1998.

[15] Convention, art 29(1).

[16] Convention, art 2(1).

[17] Convention, art 7.

[18] Convention, art 2(2).

[19] Convention, art 2(3).

[20] Convention, art 3(1)(a)(iv) and Tables I and II.

[21] Convention, art 3(1)(a)(v).

[22] Conversion or transfer of property for the purpose of concealing or disguising its illicit origin (Convention, art 3(1)(b)(i)); concealing or disguising the true nature, source, location, disposition, movement, rights with respect to, or ownership of the proceeds of drugs offences (art 3(1)(b)(ii)); and, so far as the principles of the national legal system permit, the acquisition, possession, or use of such proceeds (art 3(1)(c)(i)).

[23] Convention, art 3(4) (sanctions reflecting 'the grave nature of these offences') and art 3(8).

(b) Extradition and jurisdiction to prosecute

The implementation of all these provisions will improve the quality of national drugs legislation, but has a further significance in the context of extradition. Any problem of double criminality will be avoided as between states each of which has enacted offences in terms of article 3, and it is further provided that such offences are not to be regarded for the purposes of extradition or mutual assistance as fiscal offences, political offences, or as politically motivated.[24]

Extradition is dealt with in article 6, which deems all offences established in accordance with article 3(1) to be extraditable offences in relation to any pre-existing extradition treaties between parties; the offences are to be included in any future extradition treaties between parties.[25] If a party needs to have an extradition treaty in place before it can act, and it receives a request from a state with whom it has no such treaty, it may consider the Vienna Convention itself as providing the necessary legal basis for extradition.[26] Article 6 contains the provision commonly found in modern extradition treaties that extradition may be refused where there are substantial grounds leading the authorities[27] of the requested state to believe that compliance would facilitate the prosecution or punishment of any person[28] on account of his or her race, religion, nationality, or political opinions, or would cause prejudice for any of those reasons to any person affected by the extradition request.[29] Parties also undertake to 'seek to conclude bilateral and multilateral agreements to carry out or to enhance the effectiveness of extradition';[30] such a positive requirement is unusual, and clearly unenforceable, but is an expression of the seriousness of purpose with which the matter of co-operation was addressed.

Article 4 specifies circumstances in which a state should itself exercise jurisdiction over Convention offences; these include cases where the offence is committed, anywhere, by a national or habitual resident of the state,[31] or was committed on board a vessel intercepted in accordance with the procedures established under the Convention.[32]

In some cases, several states will be entitled to exercise jurisdiction, though one state might prove a more convenient forum from the prosecution's point of view, for example where that state alone has jurisdiction over other persons involved in

---

[24] Convention, art 3(10).

[25] Convention, art 6(1)(2).

[26] Convention, art 6(3). After much debate the authors of the Convention used the word 'may', so that this provision is not mandatory, but also added a sentence which reads, 'The Parties which require detailed legislation in order to use this Convention as a legal basis for extradition *shall* consider enacting such legislation as may be necessary.'

[27] The text speaks of 'judicial or other competent authorities', which may in some countries mean the executive branch of government.

[28] Not necessarily the person whose extradition is sought.

[29] Convention, art 6(6).

[30] Convention, art 6(11).

[31] Convention, art 4(1)(b)(i).

[32] See Convention, art 17.

the same series of offences. It was with these considerations in mind that the authors of the Convention included a provision requiring parties to give consideration to the possibility of transferring to one another proceedings for criminal prosecution of offences established under the Convention 'in cases where such transfer is considered to be in the interests of a proper administration of criminal justice'.[33]

(c) Mutual assistance

The main provisions as to mutual assistance are to be found in article 7, which provides that 'the Parties shall afford one another, pursuant to this article, the widest measure of mutual legal assistance in investigations, prosecutions and judicial proceedings in relation to criminal offences established in accordance with Article 3(1)'.[34] A list of purposes for which mutual legal assistance may be granted is found in article 7(2), but although the list is a full one it is not intended to be exhaustive and any other forms of assistance permitted by the domestic law of the requested party may also be given.[35] The text of article 7 became fuller and more detailed as the negotiation of the Convention proceeded, and what emerged was a miniature mutual legal assistance treaty, cast in a form sufficiently flexible to accommodate the variety of procedures available, or to become available, in national legal systems.

The forms of assistance available include:

(a) taking evidence or statements from persons;[36]
(b) effecting service of judicial documents;
(c) executing searches and seizures;
(d) examining objects and sites;
(e) providing information and evidentiary items;[37]
(f) providing originals or certified copies of relevant documents and records, including bank, financial, corporate, or business records;
(g) identifying or tracing proceeds, property, instrumentalities, or other things for evidentiary purposes.

---

[33] Convention, art 8. The official *Commentary* points out that the 1990 UN Model Treaty on the Transfer of Proceedings in Criminal Matters is not fully compatible with the 1988 Convention.

[34] Convention, art 7(1).

[35] Convention, art 7(3). See also art 7(4) which deals with assisting witnesses to travel to the requesting country, including the transfer in custody of willing witnesses; this assistance is to be given 'to the extent consistent with [the requested country's] domestic law and practice'.

[36] Despite the use of the word 'statement', the paragraph is to be interpreted as including all forms of testimony by individuals, whatever procedure is used to receive that testimony: *Commentary*, para 7.9.

[37] This is intended to cover material available to the authorities of the requested party without taking action which would fall under one of the other items in para 2, eg, provision for use in proceedings in the requesting party of material already held, and perhaps already used as an exhibit in a trial in the requested party in a related matter: *Commentary*, para 7.13.

In general, a request is to be executed in accordance with the domestic law of the requested country,[38] but in one respect the Convention clearly overrides domestic law. It is provided that a party may not decline to render mutual legal assistance under article 7 on the ground of bank secrecy.[39] This is of great importance in the drugs context where the identification and location of the proceeds of crime is such a prominent feature of the necessary international co-operation.[40]

Those who drafted the Vienna Convention were well aware of the growing volume of multilateral and bilateral arrangements for mutual assistance in criminal matters, and this is reflected in a number of ways in the Convention's text. The parties are exhorted (that seeming to be the effect of the obligation to 'consider, as may be necessary, the possibility') to conclude bilateral or multilateral agreements or arrangements that would serve the purposes of, give practical effect to, or enhance the provisions of, article 7.[41] It is further declared that the provisions of article 7 do not affect the obligations under any other treaty, bilateral or multilateral, which governs or will in future govern, in whole or part, mutual legal assistance in criminal matters.[42] Although the drafting is not as clear as one might have wished, the effect appears to be that the Convention can extend but not diminish the scope of those obligations; so, for example, article 7(4) prohibiting reliance on bank secrecy in the context of the Convention would seem to prevail over a general mutual assistance treaty which did permit such reliance. A more extensive interpretation of the provision that the Convention is not to 'affect' the obligations under other treaties could rob it of all significance where the countries concerned were parties to a general mutual assistance treaty.

Where no such treaty relationship exists between the requesting and requested countries, article 7(8) to (19) apply; they set out in effect a short form of mutual assistance treaty to operate in the Convention's sphere. Provision is made for designated authorities to transmit and receive requests for assistance,[43] the form and language of the request,[44] the provision of supplementary information to assist in the execution of the request,[45] the use of information obtained and confidentiality,[46] immunities of witnesses,[47] and the grounds upon which a request may be refused. These are quite limited: apart from non-compliance with the provisions of the Convention,[48] which, it is to be hoped, will not be invoked on mere technicalities, they are likely prejudice to the sovereignty, security, *ordre public*, or other

---

[38] Convention, art 7(12).
[39] Convention, art 7(5).
[40] The actual confiscation of proceeds is dealt with in Convention, art 5.
[41] Convention, art 7(20).
[42] Convention, art 7(6).
[43] Convention, art 7(8).
[44] Convention, art 7(9)(10). The United Kingdom only accepts requests in English.
[45] Convention, art 7(11).
[46] Convention, art 7(13)(14).
[47] Convention, art 7(18). The United Kingdom will only consider granting immunity where this is specifically requested, and will not grant it if it considers that such a grant would be contrary to the public interest.
[48] Convention, art 7(15)(a).

essential interests of the requested party,[49] or impossibility of compliance having regard to prohibitions in the domestic law of the requested party or the nature of its legal system.[50] Although these provisions are in the spirit of many mutual assistance arrangements, which seek to make available to foreign authorities the facilities available to the corresponding bodies within the requested country, the danger is that sufficient weight will not be given to the intention to make a real advance in the level of co-operation in the drugs field, and that pre-existing practices and attitudes will be relied upon unthinkingly: 'It is something we have never done.'

In addition, the giving of assistance may be postponed if it would interfere with an ongoing investigation, prosecution, or proceeding in the requested country;[51] in practice good communication between the relevant authorities should ensure that this happens rarely, for the strategy for handling the case will be an agreed one.

(d) Confiscation

The confiscation of illicit profits is widely recognized as of great importance as part of any effective strategy to deal with drug trafficking. Article 5(1) requires each party to adopt measures enabling it to confiscate both the drugs and instrumentalities used in or intended for use in the crime and also the proceeds of the offence or property the value of which corresponds to that of such proceeds. This provision has a dual advantage: it ensures that the greatest possible number of states can act against the trafficker in this way, and it also removes a potential impediment to the recognition of the confiscation orders of other states by ensuring that every party has such a mechanism within its own legal system.

Each party must also adopt such measures as may be necessary to enable its competent authorities to identify, trace, and freeze or seize proceeds and instrumentalities for the purposes of eventual confiscation.[52] In relation to the tracing and confiscation of property, each party must ensure that its courts or other competent authorities may order the inspection or seizure of bank, financial, or commercial records and may not decline to do so on the ground of bank secrecy.[53] This overcomes the reluctance of some states to waive the economic advantages of bank secrecy laws, and provides a basis for the provision of information to other states that make a request for assistance in tracing property.[54]

In addition to the tracing of property, other parties may request that the property be frozen or seized and an order for confiscation be sought and enforced, or that a pre-existing order be submitted for enforcement.[55] The decisions or actions taken with regard to such requests for assistance are to be taken in accordance with the

---

[49] Convention, art 7(15)(b).
[50] Convention, art 7(15)(c), (d). In all cases, reasons for refusal must be given: art 7(16).
[51] Convention, art 7(17).
[52] Convention, art 5(2).
[53] Convention, art 5(3).
[54] ie, under Convention, art 5(4)(b).
[55] Convention, art 5(4)(a), (b).

domestic law and procedural rules of the requested party[56] and subject to any bilateral or multilateral treaty, agreement, or arrangement to which it is bound in relation to the requesting party.[57]

Despite the emphasis on the definition and implementation of the measures to be taken under article 5 by the domestic law of the requested party, the article does go into considerable detail about the scope of the measures. So, if proceeds have been transformed or converted into other property, the 'new' property must be liable to seizure and confiscation; and where proceeds have been mixed with property acquired from legitimate sources, the intermingled property is liable to confiscation up to the value of the proceeds.[58] Income or other benefits derived from proceeds, from property into which proceeds have been transformed or converted, and from property with which proceeds have been intermingled must also be made liable to seizure and confiscation.[59] The Convention permits, but does not require, the reversal of the burden of proof regarding the lawful origin of alleged proceeds,[60] and saves (without detailed provisions) the rights of bona fide third parties.

(e) Other forms of assistance

Although much of the Convention can be regarded as concerned with administrative rather than legal matters, some important improvements are made in respect of practical co-operation between investigation agencies. For example, controlled delivery of drugs[61] can be of great assistance in tracing the network involved in their movement and distribution. States have sometimes been unwilling to cooperate, perhaps because of ethical concerns about allowing drug trafficking to continue when it can be prevented. Article 11 requires parties, if permitted by the basic principles of their domestic legal systems, to take the necessary measures 'within their possibilities' to allow for controlled delivery at the international level. Arrangements, including financial arrangements, are to be made on a case-by-case basis, and it is specifically noted that these may include the interception of consignments and their being allowed to continue with the drugs intact or removed or replaced in whole or in part.

The problem of illicit traffic by sea is dealt with in some detail in article 17.[62] The jurisdiction of the flag state may be ineffective, in the sense that the ship may be far away from its port of registry; the Convention encourages procedures under which the flag state authorizes another state party to the Convention to take

---

[56] See the reiteration of this principle in Convention, art 5(9).
[57] Convention, art 5(4)(c).
[58] Convention, art 5(6)(a), (b).
[59] Convention, art 5(6)(c).
[60] Convention, art 5(7).
[61] See p 240, above.
[62] See W C Gilmore, 'Narcotics Interdiction at Sea; UK-US Co-operation' (1989) 13 Marine Policy 218; Report of the UN Commission on Narcotic Drug's Working Group on Maritime Co-operation, E/CN.7/1995/13.

appropriate measures in regard to vessels suspected of being engaged in illicit traffic. These measures may include boarding and searching the vessel; if illicit traffic is found appropriate action may then be taken with respect to the vessel and persons and cargo on board.[63] A number of safeguards are built in: the rights of coastal states are protected;[64] intervention must be carried out by a warship or military aircraft, or by a ship or aircraft clearly identifiable as being on government service;[65] and due account must be taken of the need not to endanger life at sea, the security of the vessel and the cargo, or to prejudice the commercial and legal interests of the flag state or any other interested state.[66]

Under the aegis of the Council of Europe, an Agreement on Illicit Traffic by Sea, Implementing Article 17 of the United Nations Convention against Illicit Traffic in Narcotic Drugs and Psychotropic Substances[67] was concluded in Strasbourg on 31 January 1995. However, it only came into force in 2000 and by 2012 had attracted only thirteen ratifications; the United Kingdom has not signed the Agreement.

(f) Trade in 'precursors'

Article 12 of the Vienna Convention contains a minimum set of standards to help prevent otherwise licit substances being used to create illicit narcotic drugs and psychotropic substances. 'Precursors' is the convenient term used to refer to the substances frequently used in the manufacture of drugs and psychotropic substances. Article 12 contains various measures to deal with this problem, including the very general requirement that parties take such measures as they deem appropriate to prevent the diversion of substances to illicit purposes.[68] The Convention demands that the parties introduce measures to meet five objectives:

(a) establish and maintain a system to monitor international trade in certain substances in order to facilitate the identification of suspicious transactions;

(b) provide for the seizure of those substances if there is sufficient evidence that they are for use in the illicit manufacture of a narcotic drug or psychotropic substance;

(c) notify the competent authorities and services of the Parties concerned if there is reason to believe that the import, export, or transit of a substance is destined for the illicit manufacture of narcotic drugs or psychotropic substances;

(d) require proper labelling and documentation of imports and exports; and

---

[63] Convention, art 17(4).
[64] Convention, art 17(11).
[65] Convention, art 17(10).
[66] Convention, art 17(5). For a case that illustrates the position where the flag state is not a party, see *Medvedyev v France* (App 3394/03) (2010) 51 EHRR 39 (Grand Chamber, European Ct of Human Rights).
[67] ETS No 156.
[68] Convention, art 12(1).

(e) ensure that the documents are maintained for not less than two years and are available for inspection by the competent authorities.

The parties are also required to take action that they deem appropriate to monitor the manufacture and distribution of certain substances.[69]

Work in this area was carried out by the Chemical Action Task Force created by the G7 summit in 1990 and a set of recommendations were contained in the Task Force's Final Report the following year.

4. Action within the European Union

Concern about the illicit trade in drugs has been expressed within the European institutions for some time, and the completion of the internal market, the removal of border controls in the Schengen area, and the emergence of a single European currency give greater relevance to the problem.

Concerted action within the EU was stimulated by a most influential report of a European Parliament Committee of Enquiry into the Drugs Problem in the Member States, for which Sir Jack Stewart-Clark acted as Rapporteur, and which was published in 1987.[70] It emphasized that measures to combat an international network of criminal organizations had themselves to be taken at international level, with a common strategy, and rigorously co-ordinated legal measures. The Vienna Convention was the primary instrument in the field, and the European Community (as it then was) signed the Vienna Convention and undertook, in a declaration in accordance with article 27 of the Convention, to do whatever it could to comply with its Convention obligations. This was reiterated in a Statement of June 1991, setting a target date of 31 December 1992.[71] In addition to the work leading to the Directive on Money-Laundering,[72] action has included the adoption of a European Drugs Strategy and an Action Plan on Drugs for successive periods beginning in 2000, 2005, and 2009.[73]

European action focused especially on trade in precursors: the response was two-fold. Council Regulation 3677/90[74] sought to implement article 12 of the Vienna Convention in respect of trade with third countries; Council Directive 92/109[75] dealt with intra-Community aspects. Both have been replaced, the 1990 Regulation

---

[69] Convention, art 12(8).

[70] The report is published as doc A2-114 in the *Working Documents of the European Parliament*, 1986–7.

[71] OJ L166/82, 28.6.1991.

[72] See pp 279–282.

[73] For the most recent Plan, for 2009–2012, see OJ C 326/7, 20.12.2008.

[74] Council Regulation No 3677/90 of 13 December 1990 laying down measures to be taken to discourage the diversion of certain substances to the illicit manufacture of narcotic drugs and psychotropic substances, OJ L 357/1, 20.12.1990.

[75] Council Directive 92/109/EEC of 14 December 1992 on the manufacture and the placing on the market of certain substances used in the illicit manufacture of narcotic drugs and psychotropic substances, OJ L 370/76, 19.12.1992.

by Council Regulation 111/2005,[76] and the Directive by European Parliament and Council Regulation 273/2004.[77]

Regulation 111/2005 aims to establish harmonized measures for the intra-EU control and monitoring of certain substances frequently used for the illicit manufacture of narcotic drugs or psychotropic substances with a view to preventing the diversion of such substances.[78] It provides for the licensing of operators,[79] obliges any EU operator who supplies a customer with a scheduled substance of prescribed categories to obtain a declaration from the customer which shows the specific use or uses of the scheduled substance,[80] and contains requirements as to documentation and labelling.[81] Operators are required to notify the competent authorities immediately of any circumstances, such as unusual orders or transactions involving scheduled substances to be placed on the market, which suggest that such substances might be diverted for the illicit manufacture of narcotic drugs or psychotropic substances.[82]

Regulation 273/2004 covers a wider range of matters, grouped under the headings 'monitoring',[83] 'powers of competent authorities',[84] and 'administrative co-operation'.[85] In this regulation, 'operator' is widely defined to mean 'any natural or legal person engaged in import, export of scheduled substances or intermediary activities relating thereto, including persons pursuing the activity of making customs declarations for clients on a self-employed basis, either as their principal occupation or as a secondary activity related to another occupation'.[86]

Articles 3 to 5 deal with documentation, records, and labelling as demanded by article 12(9)(d) and (e) of the Vienna Convention, exceeding the Convention requirements in that the records are to be kept for the longer period of three years from the end of the calendar year in which the operation took place.[87] The licensing of operators established in the EU is governed by articles 6 to 8. As in Regulation 111/2005, operators must notify the competent authorities of suspicious transactions.[88]

The main provisions are those dealing with export and import authorizations. Operators seeking export authorization must supply prescribed details, and a decision on the application is to be made within fifteen working days from the

---

[76] Council Regulation No 111/2005 of 22 December 2004 laying down rules for the monitoring of trade between the Community and third countries in drug precursors, OJ L 22/1, 26.1.2005.

[77] European Parliament and Council Regulation 273/2004 of 11 February 2004 on drug precursors, OJ L 47/1, 18.2.2004.

[78] Regulation, art 1.

[79] Regulation, art 3; 'operator' is defined (art 2(d)) to mean 'any natural or legal person engaged in the placing on the market of scheduled substances'.

[80] Regulation, art 4.

[81] Regulation, arts 5 and 7.

[82] Regulation, art 8.

[83] Regulation, Chapter II, arts 3–25.

[84] Regulation, Chapter III, consisting of art 26.

[85] Regulation, Chapter IV, consisting of art 27.

[86] Regulation, art 2(f).

[87] Regulation, art 4.

[88] Regulation, art 9.

date on which the file is deemed complete, though there is provision for the authorities to make further enquiries which extends the period for decision-taking.[89] The Regulation contains detailed provisions as to the granting and content of export[90] and import[91] authorizations. Competent authorities must be able to obtain information on any orders for or operations involving scheduled substances, and they must also be able to enter operators' business premises to obtain evidence of irregularities. While these powers are a basic minimum for monitoring of the movement of these substances, they do not themselves meet the requirements of the Vienna Convention,[92] which requires that the competent authorities be given the power to seize any scheduled substance if there is sufficient evidence that it is intended for the illicit manufacture of narcotic drugs or psychotropic substances.

The provision on administrative co-operation[93] simply applies Regulation 515/97 mutatis mutandis.[94]

(a) Offences and penalties

In 2004, the Council adopted a Framework Decision[95] which actually adds little to the obligations under the Vienna Convention. It requires Member States to enact as criminal offences:

(a) the production, manufacture, extraction, preparation, offering, offering for sale, distribution, sale, delivery on any terms whatsoever, brokerage, dispatch, dispatch in transit, transport, importation, or exportation of drugs;

(b) the possession or purchase of drugs with a view to conducting one of those activities;

(c) the cultivation of opium poppy, coca bush, or cannabis plant; and

(d) the manufacture, transport, or distribution of precursors, knowing that they are to be used in or for the illicit production or manufacture of drugs.[96]

But this does not apply to an act committed by its perpetrators exclusively for their own personal consumption as defined by national law.[97] Member States must set

---

[89] Regulation, art 11.

[90] Regulation, arts 12–19.

[91] Regulation, arts 20–25.

[92] Convention, art 12(9)(b).

[93] Regulation, art 27.

[94] This is Council Regulation 515/97 of 13 March 1997 on mutual assistance between the administrative authorities of the Member States and cooperation between the latter and the Commission to ensure the correct application of the law on customs and agricultural matters, OJ L 82/1, 22.3.1997, which has been much amended since its original adoption.

[95] Council Framework Decision 2004/757/JHA of 25 October 2004 laying down minimum provisions on the constituent elements of criminal acts and penalties in the field of illicit drug trafficking, OJ L 335/8, 11.11.2004.

[96] Framework Decision, art 2(1). Drugs are those specified in the 1961 Single Convention on Narcotic Drugs (as amended by the 1972 Protocol) or the 1971 Vienna Convention on Psychotropic Substances.

[97] Framework Decision, art 2(2). Incitement, aiding and abetting, and attempt are also to be covered: art 3.

'effective, proportionate and dissuasive criminal penalties', and minima are pre-scribed for particular types of offence.[98]

5. United Kingdom legislation

There is comprehensive and elaborate legislation in the United Kingdom dealing with the misuse of drugs and drug trafficking, but it is beyond the scope of this book to examine it. To list only primary legislation, implementing provisions are to be found in the much-amended Misuse of Drugs Act 1971, the Drug Trafficking Offences Act 1986, the Drug Trafficking Act 1994, and the Drugs Act 2005. Provisions related to EU instruments are also to be found in statutory instru-ments.[99]

II. Organized crime

1. The United Nations Convention of 2000

The origins of the UN Convention on Transnational Organized Crime[100] are in the work of the then UN Commission on Crime Prevention and Criminal Justice, established a few years after the signature of the Vienna Convention. At its second meeting, in 1993, the Commission recommended the convening of a World Ministerial Conference on the subject, which was held in November 1994. That conference identified a need for more effective international co-operation, particu-larly in relation to five matters:

(a) closer alignment of legislative texts concerning organized crime;

(b) strengthening international cooperation at the investigative, prosecutorial and judicial levels in operational matters;

(c) establishing modalities and basic principles for international co-operation at the regional and global levels;

(d) elaboration of international agreements on organized transnational crime; and

(e) measures and strategies to prevent and combat money laundering and to control the use of the proceeds of crime.

The conference discussed the possibility of one or more international conventions. After several rounds of consultations the General Assembly resolved[101] in

---

[98] Framework Decision, arts 4 and 5. For legal persons, see arts 6 and 7.

[99] See the Controlled Drugs (Drug Precursors) (Intra-Community Trade) Regulations 2008, SI 2008/295, the Controlled Drugs (Drug Precursors) (Community External Trade) Regulations 2008, SI 2008/296, and the Controlled Drugs (Drug Precursors) (Intra-Community Trade and Community External Trade) Regulations 2010, SI 2010/2564.

[100] See generally D McClean, *Transnational Organized Crime: A Commentary on the UN Conven-tion and its Protocols* (OUP, 2007).

[101] Resolution 53/111.

December 1998 to establish an open-ended intergovernmental ad hoc committee for the purpose of elaborating a comprehensive international convention against transnational organized crime and what became the three protocols on trafficking in persons, the smuggling of migrants, and the illicit manufacture and trafficking in firearms. All but the Firearms Protocol, which required further work, were signed in December 2000.

(a) Scope

It might be expected that such a convention would include a definition of 'transnational organized crime', but the scope of application of the UN Convention has to be gleaned from a number of articles. Article 3(1) states that the convention applies, unless otherwise stated, to the prevention, investigation, and prosecution of (a) the offences established in accordance with articles 5, 6, 8, and 23 of the Convention; and (b) serious crime as defined in the Convention where the offence is transnational in nature and involves an organized criminal group. The cited articles deal respectively with the criminalization of participation in an organized criminal group, the laundering of proceeds of crime, corruption, and obstruction of justice. 'Serious crime' means conduct constituting an offence punishable by a maximum deprivation of liberty of at least four years or a more serious penalty.[102] An offence is transnational in nature if:

(a) it is committed in more than one state;

(b) it is committed in one state but a substantial part of its preparation, planning, direction, or control takes place in another state;

(c) it is committed in one state but involves an organized criminal group that engages in criminal activities in more than one state; or

(d) it is committed in one state but has substantial effects in another state.[103]

The concept of an 'organized criminal group' requires further analysis. It is defined to mean a structured group of three or more persons, existing for a period of time and acting in concert with the aim of committing one or more serious crimes or offences established in accordance with the Convention, in order to obtain, directly or indirectly, a financial or other material benefit.[104] A 'structured group' is a group that is not randomly formed for the immediate commission of an offence and that does not need to have formally defined roles for its members, continuity of its membership, or a developed structure.[105]

---

[102] Convention, art 2(b).
[103] Convention, art 3(2). An example used in the negotiation of the Convention was where the currency of one state is counterfeited in another state and the organized criminal group has put the counterfeit currency into global circulation. States are free to criminalize offences without the transnational element: art 34(2).
[104] Convention, art 2(a).
[105] Convention, art 2(c).

(b) Extradition and jurisdiction to prosecute

The provisions as to extradition in the 2000 Convention are based on those in article 6 of the Vienna Convention, but with some additional features. So the offences created under the 2000 Convention are extraditable offences in relation to any extradition treaty existing between parties; the offences are to be included in every future extradition treaty.[106] Unlike the Vienna Convention, there is a proviso requiring double criminality, ie that the offence for which extradition is sought is punishable under the domestic law of both the requesting state and the requested state.[107] If a party that makes extradition conditional on the existence of a treaty receives a request for extradition from another party with which it has no extradition treaty, it may consider the Convention the legal basis for extradition in respect of the Convention offences.[108] Extradition remains subject to the domestic law rules of the requested state and applicable obligations in bilateral or multilateral extradition agreements, including conditions in relation to the minimum penalty requirement for extradition.[109]

A number of provisions in the 2000 Convention deal with the extradition of nationals of the requested state. If such extradition is refused solely on the nationality ground, the principle *aut dedere aut judicare*[110] applies: a prosecution should be begun in the requested state's own courts.[111] A further provision[112] deals with the case where a state is permitted under its domestic law to extradite one of its nationals only upon the condition that the person will be returned to that state to serve the sentence imposed as a result of the trial for which the extradition was sought: the two states may agree to this procedure and settle the detailed conditions. There is no obligation to extradite if the requested state has substantial grounds for believing that the request has been made for the purpose of prosecuting or punishing a person on account of that person's sex, race, religion, nationality, ethnic origin, or political opinions, or that compliance with the request would cause prejudice to that person's position for any one of these reasons.[113]

Article 15 specifies the circumstances in which a state must itself exercise jurisdiction over Convention offences. These include when the offence is committed in the territory of that state, or on board a vessel that is flying the flag of that state or an aircraft registered under the laws of that state. A state may also take jurisdiction when the offence is committed against a national of that state;[114] the

---

[106] Convention, art 16(1)–(3), (6).
[107] Convention, art 16(1), proviso.
[108] Convention, art 16(4)(5).
[109] Convention, art 16(7); the reference to minimum penalty is not found in the Vienna text.
[110] See generally M C Bassiouni and E M Wise, *Aut dedere aut judicare: the duty to extradite or prosecute in international law* (Martinus Nijhoff, 1995).
[111] Convention, art 16(10).
[112] Convention, art 16(11). Art 16(12) covers similar cases where extradition was sought only for the purpose of enforcing a sentence.
[113] Convention, art 16(14), a fuller version of art 6(6) of the Vienna Convention.
[114] No equivalent provision appears in the Vienna Convention.

offence is committed by a national of that state or a stateless person who has his or her habitual residence in its territory; or in certain cases where preliminary acts, themselves criminalized as, eg, conspiracy, take place in another state but with a view to the commission of a serious crime within the enacting state.

(c) Mutual legal assistance

Article 18 of the 2002 Convention follows the pattern, and very largely the text, of article 7 of the Vienna Convention. The forms of assistance available include:

- (a) taking evidence or statements from persons;
- (b) effecting service of judicial documents;
- (c) executing searches and seizures, and freezing;
- (d) examining objects and sites;
- (e) providing information, evidentiary items, and expert evaluations;
- (f) providing originals or certified copies of relevant documents and records, including government, bank, financial, corporate, or business records;
- (g) identifying or tracing proceeds of crime, property, instrumentalities, or other things for evidentiary purposes;
- (h) facilitating the voluntary appearance of persons in the requesting state; and
- (i) any other type of assistance that is not contrary to the domestic law of the requested state.

Article 18(7) explains the scheme of this part of the Convention. The detailed rules in article 18(9) to (29) apply to requests if the states in question are *not* bound by a treaty of mutual legal assistance.[115] If those states *are* bound by such a treaty, the corresponding provisions of that treaty apply unless the two states agree to apply the rules in article 18(9) to (29) instead; they are 'strongly encouraged' to apply these paragraphs if they facilitate co-operation. In no case may assistance be declined on the ground of bank secrecy.[116]

Other articles deal with joint investigations and special investigative techniques (such as controlled delivery and electronic surveillance);[117] the transfer of criminal proceedings;[118] the protection of witnesses[119] and victims;[120] and more generally with co-operation between law enforcement authorities.[121]

---

[115] Under art 18(9), where it applies, states may decline to render mutual legal assistance on the ground of absence of dual criminality.
[116] Convention, art 18(8).
[117] Convention, arts 19 and 20.
[118] Convention, art 21.
[119] Convention, art 24.
[120] Convention, art 25.
[121] Convention, arts 26 and 27.

III. Human trafficking

One of the Protocols to the UN Convention on Organized Crime deals with human trafficking. Trafficking in persons, and especially in women and children for purposes of sexual or labour exploitation, is a major, growing, and immensely harmful phenomenon. How many are caught up in the whole business must remain one of the 'dark numbers' of international criminal statistics, but responsible agencies suggest that up to one million persons a year may be victims of trafficking. Vivid material is included in the annual *Trafficking in Persons* reports of the United States Department of State, and there is full analysis in a United Nations Office on Drugs and Crime report.[122]

1. International action

(a) Early conventions

The first international conventions dealing with trafficking focused on trafficking in women and girls for prostitution. The International Agreement for the Suppression of the White Slave Traffic in 1904[123] was an agreement between twelve European powers; a Protocol of 1949 opened this Agreement and the 1910 Convention considered next to other states. In May 1910, an International Convention for the Suppression of White Slave Traffic was agreed. It is principally concerned with the criminalization of certain conduct and related issues such as extradition. These instruments were supplemented by two Conventions negotiated under the aegis of the League of Nations, a Convention for the Suppression of Traffic in Women and Children of 1921, and the International Convention for the Suppression of the Traffic in Women of Full Age of 1933 (each of which, amongst other things, sought to criminalize attempts and other acts of preparation). The United Nations developed a Convention for the Suppression of the Traffic in Persons and of the Exploitation of the Prostitution of Others, which came into force on 25 July 1951.[124] The Convention again concentrated on criminalization, but with articles dealing with the exchange of information, reliance on foreign convictions to establish recidivism, and extradition. Article 6 of the Convention on the Elimination of All Forms of Discrimination Against Women, which came into force on 3 September 1981, provides that States Parties must take all appropriate measures, including legislation, to suppress all forms of traffic in women and exploitation of prostitution of women.[125] Other international instruments

---

[122] *Trafficking in Persons: Global Patterns* (2006).
[123] 1 LNTS 83, signed on 18 May 1904.
[124] The United Kingdom is not a party.
[125] In May 2000 the United Nations also adopted an Optional Protocol to the Convention on the Rights of the Child dealing with the sale of children, child prostitution, and child pornography, which entered into force on 18 January 2002. See A Gallagher, 'Human Rights and the New UN Protocols on Trafficking and Migrant Smuggling: A Preliminary Analysis' (2001) 23 Human Rts Q 975.

addressed trafficking in children in particular: in 1999 the International Labour Organization adopted a Convention Concerning the Prohibition and Immediate Action for the Elimination of the Worst Forms of Child Labour, and in the following year the UN adopted the Optional Protocol to the Convention on the Right of the Child on the Sale of Children, Child Pornography and Child Prostitution.[126]

(b) The Palermo Trafficking Protocol

The latest work of the United Nations in this field is represented by the Trafficking Protocol to the Convention on Transnational Organized Crime, more formally the Protocol to Prevent, Suppress and Punish Trafficking in Persons, Especially Women and Children.[127] This attracted much support, and by January 2012 had 147 parties. As the offences established under article 5 of the Protocol are deemed to be offences established under the main Convention,[128] the provisions of the Convention dealing with jurisdiction, extradition, and mutual assistance apply equally in the context of the Protocol.

The Protocol contains definitions which have been adopted in later international instruments. So 'trafficking in human beings' is defined as:

the recruitment, transportation, transfer, harbouring or receipt of persons, by means of the threat or use of force or other forms of coercion, of abduction, of fraud, of deception, of the abuse of power or of a position of vulnerability or of the giving or receiving of payments or benefits to achieve the consent of a person having control over another person, for the purpose of exploitation. Exploitation shall include, at a minimum, the exploitation of the prostitution of others or other forms of sexual exploitation, forced labour or services, slavery or practices similar to slavery, servitude or the removal of organs.[129]

The consent of a victim of trafficking to the intended exploitation set forth in that definition is irrelevant where any of the means there stated have been used.[130] The recruitment, transportation, transfer, harbouring, or receipt of a child under eighteen for the purpose of exploitation is considered 'trafficking in human beings' even if it does not involve any of those means.[131]

---

[126] In addition to the 2005 Council of Europe Convention on Action against Trafficking in Human Beings, considered below, there are several significant regional conventions, including the Inter-American Convention on International Traffic in Minors, 1994; the South Asian Association for Regional Cooperation (SAARC) Convention on Preventing and Combating Trafficking in Women and Children for Prostitution, 2002. For the Australian Support for Victims of People Trafficking Program, see A Schloenhardt and M Loong, 'Return and Reintegration of Human Trafficking Victims from Australia' (2011) 23 Int J Refugee Law 143.

[127] See D McClean, *Transnational Organized Crime: A Commentary on the UN Convention and its Protocols* (OUP, 2007), pp 307–72.

[128] Protocol, art 1(3).

[129] Protocol, art 3(a).

[130] Protocol, art 3(b).

[131] Protocol, art 3(c), (d).

The Protocol provides for the criminalization of acts related to trafficking,[132] for the protection of victims,[133] for preventive measures,[134] and for specific types of co-operation supplementing those in the Convention.[135]

2. Work of the Council of Europe and the EU

In 2005, the Council of Europe adopted a Convention on Action against Trafficking in Human Beings,[136] which aimed, while guaranteeing gender equality, to prevent and combat trafficking in human beings; to protect the human rights of the victims of trafficking, design a comprehensive framework for the protection and assistance of victims and witnesses, and ensure effective investigation and prosecution; and to promote international co-operation on action against trafficking in human beings.[137] It applies to all forms of trafficking in human beings, whether national or transnational, whether or not connected with organized crime.[138] The definitions in the Palermo Protocol are adopted verbatim.[139]

The Convention develops the preventive and other measures in the Palermo Protocol and in Chapter VI (articles 32 to 35) deals with international co-operation and co-operation with civil society. A feature of the Convention is the monitoring mechanism elaborated in Chapter VII.

As the European Commission has pointed out,[140] several EU Member States are major destinations for trafficking in human beings from non-EU countries. In addition, there is evidence of flows of trafficking within the EU. It is reasonable to estimate from the available figures that every year several hundred thousand people are trafficked into the EU or within the EU area.

The first specific EU instrument dealing with human trafficking was Council Framework Decision 2002/629/JHA of 19 July 2002 on combating trafficking in human beings.[141] This was replaced by European Parliament and Council Directive 2011/36/EU of 5 April 2011 on preventing and combating trafficking in

---

[132] Protocol, art 5.

[133] Protocol, arts 6–8.

[134] Protocol, art 9.

[135] Protocol, arts 10–13.

[136] It has (at November 2011) 34 parties. It came into force in the United Kingdom on 1 April 2009, the Government having had doubts for some time about provisions in the Convention to give reflection periods and residence permits to those who had been trafficked. See A Harvey, 'Human Trafficking—The Road to Ratification of the Council of Europe Convention Against Trafficking in Human Beings in the UK' [2008] JIANL 218.

[137] Convention, art 1.

[138] Convention, art 2.

[139] Convention, art 4. On the definition of a 'victim' and the relevance of art 34 of the European Convention on Human Rights, especially to 'historic' victims, see A Weiss and S Chaudary, 'Assessing Victim Status under the Council of Europe Convention on Action Against Trafficking in Human Beings: the Situation of "Historical" Victims' [2011] JIANL 168.

[140] Proposal for a Directive of the European Parliament and of the Council on preventing and combating trafficking in human beings, and protecting victims, repealing Framework Decision 2002/629/JHA, COM/2010/0095 final, para 1.2

[141] OJ L 203/1, 1.8.2002. See also Council Resolution of 20 October 2003 on initiatives to combat trafficking in human beings, in particular women, OJ C 260/4, 29.10.2003.

human beings and protecting its victims.[142] This Directive builds on the Council of Europe's Convention, but is in some respects more specific. It sets precise level of penalties adapted to the severity of the offences;[143] broadens the scope of the rule on the non-application of penalties to victims for their involvement in criminal activities, whatever illicit means have been used by traffickers;[144] has a broader and more binding extraterritorial jurisdiction rule, obliging Member States to prosecute nationals and habitual residents who have committed the crime of trafficking outside the territory of the Member State;[145] provides for a higher standard of assistance to victims, especially concerning medical treatment;[146] and has special protective measures for child victims.[147]

It will be seen that international co-operation in the context of human trafficking takes the form for the most part of ensuring adequate national provisions as to jurisdiction, criminal offences, and penalties. Operational co-operation is of course essential if trafficking networks and routes are to be disrupted, but instruments and arrangements dealing more generally with operational matters can be relied upon in this field.

IV. Terrorism

The last decades of the twentieth century were marked by a growing threat of international terrorism, often financed in part by drug trafficking. The attempts to combat money laundering and organized crime generally were part of the international community's response, but specific counter-terrorism action was also taken. At first this was concentrated in those fields of activity, such as civil aviation, which were seen to be especially at risk. More general provisions followed, and the whole matter became the focus of renewed, indeed frenzied, activity after the attacks on the World Trade Center in New York and other targets in the United States in September 2001. Most of the international instruments in this field have been prepared by the United Nations or its specialized agencies.

1. International conventions

(a) Civil aviation conventions

Three conventions were negotiated under the aegis of the International Civil Aviation Organization: the Convention on Offences and Certain Other Acts Committed on Board Aircraft, signed at Tokyo on 14 September 1963; the

---

[142] OJ L 101/1, 15.4.2011. For the acceptance of this Directive by the UK, see OJ L 271/49, 18.10.2011.
[143] Directive, art 4.
[144] Directive, art 8.
[145] Directive, art 10.
[146] Directive, art 11.
[147] Directive, arts 13–15.

Convention for the Suppression of Unlawful Seizure of Aircraft, signed at The Hague on 16 December 1970; and the Convention for the Suppression of Unlawful Acts against the Safety of Civil Aviation, signed at Montreal on 23 September 1971.[148]

The Tokyo Convention 1963[149] deals with the problem of establishing jurisdiction over offences committed on board an aircraft,[150] and gives powers to the aircraft commander to restrain a person on board whom he or she has reasonable grounds to believe has committed or is about to commit an offence or an act jeopardizing safety or good order on board.[151] Every Contracting State must allow the aircraft commander to disembark such a person at any place, may take that person into custody, must make a preliminary enquiry into the facts, and keep informed the state of the person's nationality and any other concerned state. The person may be the subject of criminal proceedings in the state of embarkation, or be extradited, or be returned to the state in which the relevant journey by air began.[152] There are no specific provisions for mutual assistance.

The Hague Convention 1970[153] is directed against the hijacking of aircraft. More formally, it creates an offence committed by any person on board an aircraft in flight who unlawfully, by force or threat of force, or by any other form of intimidation, seizes, or exercises control of that aircraft, or attempts to perform any such act or is an accomplice to any such offender.[154] A Contracting State in which the alleged offender is found must either extradite the offender or, in any other case and 'without exception whatsoever', submit the case to its competent authorities for the purpose of prosecution.[155] Article 10 contains a mutual assistance provision:

Contracting States shall afford one another the greatest possible measure of assistance in connection with criminal proceedings brought in respect of the offence [created by article 1].[156]

This is in completely general terms: no particular types of assistance are specified, but there are also no grounds for refusing assistance.

The Montreal Convention 1971[157] created further offences, including various acts which endangered the safety of an aircraft in flight, ranging from the giving of false information to the placing on board of an explosive or other device. An amending Protocol, agreed in 1998, added acts directed against the personnel or

---

[148] For the text of these conventions and commentary, see *Shawcross and Beaumont on Air Law*.

[149] Effect was given to this Convention in the United Kingdom by the Tokyo Convention Act 1987 (see now the Civil Aviation Act 1982).

[150] Tokyo Convention, arts 3 and 4.

[151] Tokyo Convention, arts 5–10.

[152] See Tokyo Convention, arts 12–18.

[153] Effect was given to this Convention in the United Kingdom by the Hijacking Act 1971 (see now the Civil Aviation Act 1982).

[154] Hague Convention, art 1.

[155] Hague Convention, art 7.

[156] Hague Convention, art 10(1), which is without prejudice to any other treaty, bilateral or multilateral, in respect of mutual assistance in criminal matters: art 10(2).

[157] Effect was given to this Convention in the United Kingdom by the Protection of Aircraft Act 1973 (see now the Civil Aviation Act 1982).

facilities of airports serving civil aviation. Article 11 of this Convention is in the same form as article 10 of the Hague Convention, quoted above, so there is again a general obligation to provide mutual assistance.

(b) Maritime conventions

The Convention for the Suppression of Unlawful Acts against the Safety of Maritime Navigation,[158] agreed in Rome on 10 March 1988, draws on the material in the civil aviation conventions. The mutual assistance article[159] begins in the same general terms as the articles referred to above, but continues 'including assistance in obtaining evidence at their disposal needed for the proceedings'. It is not clear why these words were thought necessary; it may be that the differences in practice between civil and common law countries had raised doubts which needed to be put at rest. It is then provided that state shall carry out their obligations under this provision in conformity with any treaties on mutual assistance that may exist between them; in the absence of any such treaties, states are to afford each other assistance under their national law.[160] While in one sense realistic, in that states cannot do more than their national law permits, this form of words makes it clear that the Convention does not require any change in national law, and so underlines the weakness of the approach taken.

The same provisions apply in respect of the related Protocol for the Suppression of Unlawful Acts Against the Safety of Fixed Platforms Located on the Continental Shelf signed at the same time as the Convention.[161]

(c) Protection of persons

A Convention on the Prevention and Punishment of Crimes Against Internationally Protected Persons was signed in New York on 14 December 1973.[162] An 'internationally protected person' is defined[163] as meaning a Head of State, including any member of a collegial body performing the functions of a Head of State, a Head of Government, or a Minister for Foreign Affairs, whenever such a person is in a foreign state, and accompanying members of his or her family; and representatives and agents of states or international organizations entitled to protection under international law. Like the Hague Convention 1970, it requires a Contracting State in which the alleged offender is found either to extradite the offender or submit the case to its competent authorities for the purpose of prosecution.[164] The

---

[158] Effect was given to this Convention in the United Kingdom by the Aviation and Maritime Security Act 1990.

[159] Rome Convention, art 12.

[160] Rome Convention, art 12(2).

[161] The relevant provisions of the Convention are incorporated by reference: Protocol, art 1.

[162] Effect was given to this Convention in the United Kingdom by the Internationally Protected Persons Act 1978.

[163] 1973 Convention, art 1.

[164] 1973 Convention, art 7.

mutual assistance provision is an amalgam of provisions found in the texts already referred to, following the Hague text with an added reference to 'the supply of all evidence at their disposal necessary for the proceedings'.[165]

The International Convention Against the Taking of Hostages,[166] signed in New York on 18 December 1979, creates the offence of hostage taking, committed when any person seizes or detains and threatens to kill, to injure, or to continue to detain another person in order to compel a third party, namely, a state, an international intergovernmental organization, a natural or juridical person, or a group of persons, to do or abstain from doing any act as an explicit or implicit condition for the release of the hostage.[167] The mutual assistance article[168] is in the same terms as in the Internationally Protected Persons text.

(d) Material capable of terrorist use

A Convention on the Physical Protection of Nuclear Material was signed in New York and Vienna on 3 March 1980. It creates a range of offences covering the unlawful acquisition of nuclear material. The mutual assistance article[169] follows the model in the conventions just examined, with the added words 'The law of the State requested shall apply in all cases'.

The Convention on the Marking of Plastic Explosives for the Purpose of Identification signed in Montreal on 1 March 1991, while providing elaborate means of international co-operation in this technical field, creates no new offences and does not have mutual assistance provisions.

(e) Terrorist bombings

The International Convention for the Suppression of Terrorist Bombing,[170] signed in New York on 12 January 1998, does create offences. A person commits an offence under article 2 of the Convention if that person unlawfully and intentionally delivers, places, discharges, or detonates an explosive or other lethal device in, into, or against a place of public use, a state or government facility, a public transportation system, or an infrastructure facility, with the intent to cause death or serious bodily injury, or with the intent to cause extensive destruction of such a place, facility, or system, where such destruction results in or is likely to result in major economic loss. The general structure of the Convention follows that on the

---

[165] 1973 Convention, art 10(1); note the slight difference between this wording and that in the maritime conventions.
[166] Effect was given to this Convention in the United Kingdom by the Taking of Hostages Act 1982.
[167] 1979 Convention, art 1(1).
[168] 1979 Convention, art 13.
[169] 1980 Convention, art 13.
[170] Effect was given to this Convention in the United Kingdom by the Terrorism Act 2000.

maritime conventions, and the mutual assistance article[171] in particular follows that model.

(f) Financing of terrorism

A more developed set of provisions are contained in the International Convention for the Suppression of the Financing of Terrorism,[172] opened for signature in New York from 10 January 2000. Article 2 makes it an offence for any person by any means, directly or indirectly, unlawfully and wilfully, to provide or collect funds with the intention that they should be used or in the knowledge that they are to be used, in full or in part, in order to carry out (a) an act which constitutes an offence within the scope of and as defined in one of the conventions already examined; or (b) any other act intended to cause death or serious bodily injury to a civilian, or to any other person not taking an active part in the hostilities in a situation of armed conflict, when the purpose of such act, by its nature or context, is to intimidate a population, or to compel a government or an international organization to do or to abstain from doing any act.

Each State Party must take appropriate measures, in accordance with its domestic legal principles, (a) for the identification, detection, and freezing or seizure of any funds used or allocated for the purpose of committing such an offence as well as the proceeds[173] derived from such offences, for purposes of possible forfeiture; and (b) for the forfeiture of such funds and proceeds.[174] It is provided that each State Party concerned may give consideration to concluding agreements on the sharing with other States Parties, on a regular or case-by-case basis, of the funds derived from the forfeitures referred to in this article. Each State Party must consider establishing mechanisms whereby the funds derived from forfeitures are utilized to compensate the victims of Convention offences.[175] These provisions are to be implemented without prejudice to the rights of third parties acting in good faith.[176]

The mutual assistance article,[177] while drawing on the familiar provisions of earlier texts, is correspondingly more elaborate. It provides:

1. States Parties shall afford one another the greatest measure of assistance in connection with criminal investigations or criminal or extradition proceedings in respect of the offences set forth in article 2, including assistance in obtaining evidence in their possession necessary for the proceedings.
2. States Parties may not refuse a request for mutual legal assistance on the ground of bank secrecy.

---

[171] 2000 Convention, art 10.
[172] Effect was given to this Convention in the United Kingdom by the Terrorism Act 2000.
[173] 'Proceeds' means any funds derived from or obtained, directly or indirectly, through the commission of an offence under art 2: art 1(3).
[174] 2000 Convention, art 8(1), (2).
[175] 2000 Convention, art 8(3), (4).
[176] 2000 Convention, art 8(5).
[177] 2000 Convention, art 12.

3. The requesting Party shall not transmit or use information or evidence furnished by the requested Party for investigations, prosecutions or proceedings other than those stated in the request without the prior consent of the requested Party.

4. Each State Party may give consideration to establishing mechanisms to share with other States Parties information or evidence needed to establish criminal, civil or administrative liability pursuant to article 5.[178]

5. States Parties shall carry out their obligations under paragraphs 1 and 2 in conformity with any treaties or other arrangements on mutual legal assistance or information exchange that may exist between them. In the absence of such treaties or arrangements, States Parties shall afford one another assistance in accordance with their domestic law.

2. Work of the Council of Europe

(a) Convention on the Suppression of Terrorism

A European Convention on the Suppression of Terrorism[179] was prepared under the aegis of the Council of Europe and was opened for signature on 27 January 1977. Despite its rather grand title, it is actually an instrument which provides some regional enforcement to the earlier United Nations conventions. Its principal provisions are concerned with extradition. It declares that certain offences shall not be regarded as a political offence or as an offence connected with a political offence or as an offence inspired by political motives. They include offences within the scope of the Hague Convention 1970 or the Montreal Convention 1971; other serious offences involving an attack against the life, physical integrity, or liberty of internationally protected persons, including diplomatic agents; offences involving kidnapping, the taking of a hostage, or serious unlawful detention; offences involving the use of a bomb, grenade, rocket, automatic firearm, or letter or parcel bomb if this use endangers persons; and attempts and acts as an accomplice in relation to such offences.

In similar vein, the mutual assistance provision[180] provides that mutual assistance in criminal matters in connection with proceedings brought in respect of offences under the Convention may not be refused on the sole ground that it concerns a political offence or an offence connected with a political offence or an offence inspired by political motives. But nothing in the Convention is to be interpreted as imposing an obligation to afford mutual assistance if the requested state has substantial grounds for believing that the request has been made for the purpose of prosecuting or punishing a person on account of his race, religion,

---

[178] 2000 Convention, art 5 provides for the liability (criminal, civil, or administrative) of legal entities located in the territory of, or organized under the laws of, a state when the person responsible for the management or control of that legal entity has, in that capacity, committed an offence under art 2.

[179] ETS No 90. Effect was given to this Convention in the United Kingdom by the Suppression of Terrorism Act 1978.

[180] Convention, art 8.

nationality, or political opinion, or that that person's position may be prejudiced for any of these reasons.

(b) The 2003 Amending Protocol

The European Convention was amended by a Protocol agreed in 2003.[181] It added references to a number of conventions not referred to in the original text, but the other changes add little of substance.

(c) The 2005 Convention

In 2005 the Council of Europe adopted an important convention, considered more fully in the context of money laundering,[182] the Convention on Laundering, Search, Seizure and Confiscation of the Proceeds from Crime and on the Financing of Terrorism.[183] Chapter II of the Convention consists of the single article 2, which requires each party to adopt such legislative and other measures as may be necessary to enable it to apply the provisions of the Convention to the financing of terrorism. In particular, each party must ensure that it is able to search, trace, identify, freeze, seize, and confiscate property, of a licit or illicit origin, used or allocated to be used by any means, in whole or in part, for the financing of terrorism, or the proceeds of this offence, and to provide co-operation to this end 'to the widest possible extent'.

3. European Union action

Apart from powers to take specific measures against named individuals and groups, the principal EU instrument is Council Framework Decision 2002/475/JHA of 13 June 2002 on combating terrorism.[184]

This requires Member States to define certain acts as 'terrorist offences' where they are intentional acts which, given their nature or context, may seriously damage a country or an international organization where committed with the aim of seriously intimidating a population, or 'unduly compelling' a government or international organization to perform or abstain from performing any act, or seriously destabilizing or destroying the fundamental political, constitutional, economic, or social structures of a country or an international organization.[185] The listed acts are:

  (a) attacks upon a person's life which may cause death;

  (b) attacks upon the physical integrity of a person;

---

[181] CETS 190. As at January 2012 it had 31 parties, not including the UK.
[182] See p 278.
[183] CETS 198.
[184] OJ L 164/3, 22.6.2002 (as amended by Council Framework Decision 2008/919/JHA of 28 November 2008, OJ L 330/21, 9.12.2008).
[185] Framework Decision, art 1.

(c) kidnapping or hostage taking;

(d) causing extensive destruction to a government or public facility, a transport system, an infrastructure facility, including an information system, a fixed platform located on the continental shelf, a public place, or private property likely to endanger human life or result in major economic loss;

(e) seizure of aircraft, ships, or other means of public or goods transport;

(f) manufacture, possession, acquisition, transport, supply, or use of weapons, explosives, or of nuclear, biological, or chemical weapons, as well as research into, and development of, biological and chemical weapons;

(g) release of dangerous substances, or causing fires, floods, or explosions the effect of which is to endanger human life;

(h) interfering with or disrupting the supply of water, power, or any other fundamental natural resource the effect of which is to endanger human life; or

(i) threatening to commit any of these acts.

There are further provisions in respect of terrorist groups, acts involving recruitment or training for terrorism, and preliminary offences such as incitement and attempt.[186] Article 9 imposes duties in respect of jurisdiction and prosecution.

4. United Kingdom action

The Terrorism Act 2000, together with the earlier legislation giving effect to particular conventions, provides a sound basis for legislation in this area, although it has been supplemented by several later Acts, eg the Anti-Terrorism, Crime and Security Act 2001. The resulting legislation contains provisions as to offences in connection with fund-raising and money laundering in the terrorist context,[187] provides for the seizure and forfeiture of terrorist cash,[188] and terrorist finance more generally,[189] the making of account monitoring,[190] restraint and forfeiture orders,[191] freezing orders made by the Treasury by statutory instrument prohibiting persons from making funds available to or for the benefit of a person named in the order,[192] powers to restrict the disclosure of information for the purposes of overseas proceedings,[193] and gives a range of investigatory and counter-terrorism

---

[186] Framework Decision, arts 2–4 (art 3 as amended by the 2008 Framework Decision).

[187] See pp 285–286.

[188] Anti-terrorism, Crime and Security Act 2001, ss 1–2 and Sch 1 (replacing Terrorism Act 2000, ss 24–31); Magistrates' Courts (Detention and Forfeiture of Terrorist Cash) (No 2) Rules 2001, SI 2001/4013.

[189] Counter-Terrorism Act 2008, Sch 7.

[190] Terrorism Act 2000, s 38A and Sch 6 (as inserted by Anti-terrorism, Crime and Security Act 2001, s 3 and Sch 2: 'terrorist property' is defined in Sch 1).

[191] Terrorism Act 2000, s 23 and Sch 4 (as amended by Anti-terrorism, Crime and Security Act 2001, Sch 2, Part 2 and by the Crime (International Co-operation Act 2003, Sch 4).

[192] Anti-terrorism, Crime and Security Act 2001, ss 4–16 and Sch 3.

[193] Anti-terrorism, Crime and Security Act 2001, ss 17–20 and Sch 4.

powers.[194] The 2000 Act contains a definition[195] of terrorism, something on which international agreement has proved impossible. It defines terrorism as meaning the use or threat of action which:

(a) involves serious violence against a person or serious damage to property; endangers a person's life, other than that of the person committing the action; creates a serious risk to the health or safety of the public or a section of the public; or is designed seriously to interfere with or seriously to disrupt an electronic system;

(b) involves the use of firearms or explosives *or* is designed to influence the government or an international governmental organisation or to intimidate the public or a section of the public; and

(c) is made for the purpose of advancing a political, religious, racial or ideological cause.

V. Money laundering

From the point of view of the criminal, it is no use making a large profit out of criminal activity if that profit cannot be put to use. Hence the strategy, examined in Chapter 9, of legislating and devising means of international co-operation for the effective confiscation of the proceeds in an attempt to undermine the motivation behind much criminal activity.

Putting the proceeds to use is not as simple as it may sound. Although a proportion of the proceeds of crime will be kept as capital for further criminal ventures, the sophisticated offender will wish to use the rest for other purposes. In particular, he may wish to establish commercial enterprises or invest in existing enterprises, a process which may add to his power or influence and can be expected to generate for himself or his family a continuing and seemingly legitimate income. If this is to be done without running an unacceptable risk of detection, the money which represents the proceeds of the original crime must be 'laundered', ie put into a state in which it appears to have an entirely respectable provenance.[196]

Money laundering can present considerable problems to the criminal and correspondingly important opportunities for law enforcement agencies. Money-laundering devices have become increasingly sophisticated and have called for a major international effort by the law enforcement community. Various exercises have been carried out to develop and assess money-laundering typologies, most notably by the Financial Action Task Force (known by the rather unfortunate acronym FATF).[197]

---

[194] Parts IV and V (ss 32–53).

[195] s 1, as amended by the Terrorism Act 2006, s 34(a) and the Counter-Terrorism Act 2008, s 75.

[196] See generally, W C Gilmore, *Dirty Money: the Evolution of Money Laundering Countermeasures* (3rd edn, Council of Europe, 2004); G Stassen, *Money Laundering: a new International Law Enforcement Model* (CUP, 2000).

[197] In French, GAFI (*Groupe d'Action Financière sue le Blanchiment de Capitaux*). See W C Gilmore, ibid, at pp 89–158. See also Ping He, 'A Typological Study on Money Laundering' (2010) JMLC 15.

The actual business of money laundering has a number of stages. The first is the placement of the 'dirty' money into a national financial system. Despite new technologies, illegal funds are most commonly in the form of cash. The simplest process is the paying in to a bank account of the proceeds of crime, proceeds in the form of numerous and surprisingly bulky used banknotes. Some countries have withdrawn their very high-value banknotes (for example the Canadian $1000 note) specifically to combat money laundering; the introduction of the €500 note caused anxiety for related reasons. It is at this point that money laundering makes its contribution to the vocabulary of the English language in the form of the inelegant expression 'smurfing'. To smurf is to divide a large sum into small amounts and to make a series of small payments into bank accounts, perhaps using a number of different bank branches, so as to avoid drawing attention to the individual payments and keeping below the minimum amount attracting some requirement that the transaction be reported to a monitoring body. The use of ATMs avoids face-to-face contact at the bank counter, and there is increasing use of new payment methods, such as prepaid cards, mobile phone payments, and Internet payment services.[198]

Although money laundering is often discussed primarily by reference to banks, it may well be that criminals prefer some other money-handling institution, on the grounds that it is likely to be less well regulated, and its staff less well trained. Bureaux de change and gambling casinos may provide convenient alternatives.[199]

The second phase is that of distancing or layering, some transaction or series of transactions designed to make it difficult or impossible to trace the movement of the funds; an example might be the sale and re-sale of assets of high value but subject to no system of registration of title. Examples are vehicles, jewellery, antiques, and various forms of collectors' items such as rare stamps and coins. At this stage there is likely to be an international dimension, funds being transferred to 'regulatory havens', countries in which the identity of those controlling bank accounts or corporations is readily concealed.

Bearer shares, nominee holdings, and other forms of anonymous control of assets are favoured; wherever possible funds will be deliberately mixed, so that at least a part can be shown to have a legitimate source. The trust may well be preferred to a company as a device for controlling illegal funds. Typically, there is no registration of trusts and no regulatory body; it may be possible to conceal the identity of the beneficiaries (which may in any event be a set of further trusts).[200]

The final stage is the re-integration of the money, now appearing to have an entirely legitimate source, into the economy in which it is intended for use, a process which may well again include its international transfer. Frequently bogus invoices and documents of carriage are employed, creating evidence of non-existent

---

[198] See a FATF report, *Money Laundering Using New Payment Methods* (2010).
[199] See a FATF report, *Vulnerabilities of Casinos and Gaming Sector* (2009).
[200] See a FATF report, *Money Laundering Using Trust and Company Service Providers* (2010). Other FATF studies examine the use of other sectors: eg, *Money Laundering and Terrorist Financing in the Securities Sector* (2009), *Money Laundering through the Football Sector* (2009), and *Money Laundering and Terrorist Financing Through the Real Estate Sector* (2007).

or grossly over-valued imports and exports. There can be complex loan arrangements, secured on valuable assets; borrower, lender, and guarantor are all in fact the same person, but the arrangement is resolved in a way which leaves the money where it is needed as the result of what seems a standard commercial transaction.

Many money-laundering schemes require the holder of illegal funds to secure the co-operation of third parties. Some may be relatively unsophisticated people with limited awareness of the implications of their actions. One scheme involved the bringing of tourists into a country where the tourists were advised to open bank accounts, and to give the ATM cards and PINs to the launderers; the accounts were then used to launder funds. Other cases involve professional advisers, lawyers, and accountants, whose services are used to set up companies or trusts or in connection with tax and audit practices. These professionals may see only a small part of a complex scheme and suspect nothing. If they do have their suspicions, they may feel that their duty is to the client and may shelter behind professional obligations of confidentiality or legal professional privilege. The trend is for legislation to require disclosure by such professionals, much as banks have lost much of the protection of bank secrecy in cases of serious crime.

What can be done to tackle money laundering? As with any other organized criminal activity, the gathering of intelligence (and in this context especially, its sharing with other agencies and across national boundaries) is of the first importance. More specific approaches are the criminalization of any participation in the money-laundering process and the imposition on banks and other bodies duties of customer identification, record-keeping, and the reporting of certain types of transactions to a national monitoring body. As the remainder of this chapter will demonstrate, all these approaches have been developed as a result of international and national initiatives.

1. Financial Action Task Force

When what was then the 'Group of Seven', that is the leaders of the major industrial nations now increased in size and usually known as the G8, held their economic summit in Paris in July 1989, they found that the drug problem had reached 'devastating proportions'.[201] They urged the development of further bilateral and multilateral agreements, including measures to facilitate the identification, tracing, freezing, seizure, and forfeiture of the proceeds of drugs crimes. They also established a Financial Action Task Force to address the problem of money laundering and the scope for enhanced multilateral judicial assistance in that field.

The Task Force proved to be a major venture. Originally intended to be a one-off exercise, it became a semi-permanent organization based in the Organisation for Economic Co-operation and Development (OECD) offices in Paris with (by 2012) thirty-four member governments. It is described as 'semi-permanent' because its

---

[201] Economic Declaration, para 51.

existence and functions are reviewed by Finance Ministers every four years. After its initial assessment of the scale of money laundering and its methodology, the Task Force addressed issues of legal and administrative counter-measures offering Forty Recommendations. These Recommendations were revised in 1996 and again in 2003. Eight Special Recommendations on Terrorist Financing were adopted in 2001, and a ninth was added in 2004. The Recommendations provide the basis for the continuing work of FATF, which centres on securing full compliance with them, principally through mutual evaluation exercises, the third round of which was completed in 2010.

The FATF initiative has spawned a range of regional organizations pursuing a similar aim and a broadly similar methodology. The oldest established is the Caribbean Financial Action Task Force (CFATF), which dates from 1990. It has since been joined by the Asian/Pacific Group on Money-Laundering (APG), the Eastern and Southern African Anti-Money Laundering Group (ESAAMLG), a South American Financial Action Task Force (GAFISUD), the Eurasian Group on combating money laundering and financing of terrorism (EAG), the Inter Governmental Action Group against Money Laundering in West Africa (GIABA), and the Middle East and North Africa Financial Action Task Force (MENAFATF). In other parts of the world, there are comparable specialist committees of regional organizations such as the Council of Europe,[202] and the Gulf Co-operation Council. Other organizations have taken a similar detailed interest in money laundering. For example the Inter-American Drug Abuse Control Commission (CICAD) has a set of Model Regulations concerning Laundering Offences connected to Illicit Drug Trafficking and Related Offences, first adopted in 1992 and amended from time to time since then.

As the counter-measures proposed in the FATF Recommendations take effect, money launderers are increasingly likely to make use of 'havens' where those measures are not applied. Under Recommendation 21, as amended in 2003, financial institutions should give special attention to business relations and transactions with persons, including companies and financial institutions, from countries which do not or insufficiently apply the FATF Recommendations. Whenever these transactions have no apparent economic or visible lawful purpose, their background and purpose should, as far as possible, be examined, the findings established in writing, and be made available to help competent authorities. Formerly, FATF published a list of 'non-co-operative countries or territories' (NCCTs). In the early years the exercise of identifying NCCTs attracted much criticism, but the process became much more transparent and the NCCT label is no longer used. Instead FATF publishes, several times a year, lists of jurisdictions in three categories; the position in mid-2011 is indicated in the footnotes:

(a) jurisdictions subject to a FATF call on its members and other jurisdictions to apply counter-measures to protect the international financial system from

---

[202] Council of Europe Committee of Experts on the Evaluation of Anti-Money Laundering Measures and the Financing of Terrorism (MONEYVAL).

the on-going and substantial money laundering and terrorist financing risks emanating from the jurisdictions;[203]

(b) jurisdictions with strategic AML/CFT[204] deficiencies that have not made sufficient progress in addressing the deficiencies or have not committed to an action plan developed with the FATF to address the deficiencies;[205] and

(c) jurisdictions with strategic AML/CFT deficiencies that have provided a high-level political commitment to address the deficiencies through implementation of an action plan developed with the FATF.[206]

The failings identified in the listed countries typically include inadequate or no supervision of offshore banking, strict bank secrecy laws, no suspicious transaction reporting system, no requirement that the effective owners of companies be identified, and an absence of mutual legal assistance provision.

2. The role of banks and other financial institutions

At some stage in the process, money launderers must make use of the facilities of banks or similar institutions. As a result much attention has been paid to finding ways of improving banking procedures, either by self-regulation or by legal requirements, so as to combat money laundering. This involves, in particular, customer identification, the retention of transaction records, and the reporting to a specified authority of transactions which either meet certain pre-determined criteria or are for some other reason seen as suspicious.[207]

The existence of a duty of confidentiality between banker and client is of fundamental importance not only to the client but also to the state, as the extent to which the confidence is protected may affect levels of investment in a country's financial institutions and thus the general stability of its economy. The obligation is therefore a feature of every legal system, but the extent of the duty varies from country to country in terms both of its scope and the methods by which it is enforced. In some countries, including the United Kingdom, the obligation is a private one which will be enforced by the courts in a civil action. In some other countries, however, the obligation may originally have been purely contractual, but it is now protected by statute and enforced by both criminal and civil sanctions. Such a regime of 'bank secrecy', in which public policy prohibits the disclosure of information held by the institution as to its customers and their

---

[203] Iran and North Korea.

[204] ie, anti-money laundering and combating the financing of terrorism.

[205] Bolivia, Cuba, Ethiopia, Kenya, Myanmar, Sri Lanka, Syria, and Turkey.

[206] Angola, Antigua and Barbuda, Argentina, Bangladesh, Brunei Darussalam, Cambodia, Ecuador, Ghana, Honduras, Indonesia, Mongolia, Morocco, Namibia, Nepal, Nicaragua, Nigeria, Pakistan, Paraguay, Philippines, São Tomé and Príncipe, Sudan, Tajikistan, Tanzania, Thailand, Trinidad and Tobago, Turkmenistan, Ukraine, Venezuela, Vietnam, Ukraine, Yemen, and Zimbabwe.

[207] See FATF Recommendations 2003 5–11 and 13–15. Guidance on money laundering generally is issued in the UK by the Joint Money Laundering Steering Group, a private body made up of a number of associations representing banks and others active in the financial services industry; its Guidance receives Treasury approval.

accounts, has in the past been a major obstacle to international co-operation. An account is given of the approach of English law, which recognizes an obligation of confidentiality but has no bank secrecy legislation, and of the gradual elimination of bank secrecy in the context of international co-operation in criminal matters.[208]

(a) The banks' duties of confidentiality in English law

In England, and in common law jurisdictions whose approach follows that of English law in treating the duty of confidentiality as resting in contract, the classic authority is the Court of Appeal decision in *Tournier v National Provincial and Union Bank of England*.[209] In a much-cited passage, Bankes LJ examined the qualifications on the duty of confidentiality:

On principle I think that the qualifications can be classified under four heads: (a) where disclosure is under compulsion by law; (b) where there is a duty to the public to disclose; (c) where the interests of the bank require disclosure; (d) where the disclosure is made by the express or implied consent of the customer.[210]

In the present context, the key issue concerns the application of the *Tournier* principles in cases where banks or their officials are called upon to give evidence. There is no suggestion that the banker's duty of confidentiality ever protected the banker absolutely from being required to give evidence and produce accounts or other documents relevant to an issue before the courts. Before 1876 a subpoena *duces tecum* could issue and the relevant records would then have to be produced at the trial; after that date legislation, now the Bankers' Books Evidence Act 1879, enabled the court to permit a party to inspect and take copies of relevant entries, which would be admissible in evidence.[211] In effect, the Act provided a special form of discovery, subject in general to the usual rules as to discovery.[212] In 1994 the Judicial Committee of the Privy Council re-affirmed that a bank served with a subpoena could give evidence without breaching its duty of confidentiality, though it should use its best endeavours to notify the customer of the subpoena.[213] Where the bank is not itself a party to the proceedings, the limitations on the discovery powers of the court are those set in *Bankers Trust Co v Shapira*:[214] the court may act 'when there is a good ground for thinking the money in the bank is the plaintiff's money, as for instance when the customer has

---

[208] See D Chaikin, 'Adapting the Qualifications to the Banker's Common Law Duty of Confidentiality to Fight Transnational Crime' (2011) 33 Sydney L Rev 265.

[209] [1924] 1 KB 461 (CA).

[210] At 473.

[211] For the background to the Act, see *Arnott v Hayes* (1887) 36 ChD. 731 (CA); *Emmott v Star Newspaper Co Ltd* (1892) 67 LT 829 (QBD).

[212] *Parnell v Wood* [1892] P 137 (CA); *South Staffordshire Tramways Co v Ebbsmith* [1895] 2 QB 669 (CA); *Waterhouse v Barker* [1924] 2 KB 759 (CA).

[213] *Robertson v Canadian Imperial Bank of Commerce* [1995] 1 All ER 824.

[214] [1980] 1 WLR 1274 (CA).

got the money by fraud, or other wrongdoing, and paid it into his account at the bank'.[215]

An order for inspection under the Bankers' Books Evidence Act 1879 is available in criminal proceedings,[216] where the analogy of discovery is not available. In that context, the courts (including justices of the peace who have the same power as a High Court judge in this matter) recognize that an order can be a very serious interference with the liberty of the subject and is not to be made without careful consideration; but a plea that disclosure might serve to incriminate the accused account holder will not be allowed to stand in the way of the making of an order.[217]

Whatever the context, the courts have a balancing exercise to perform, weighing the public interest in preserving the confidentiality expected of bankers against the public interest either in securing a full disclosure of relevant evidence for the purposes of a trial in the English courts or, in an international context, in the English courts assisting a foreign court in obtaining evidence in England. This balancing exercise was recognized as essential by the House of Lords in *Re the State of Norway's Application (Nos 1 and 2)*.[218] In a different context it also received the blessing of the European Court of Justice in 1985. On a reference from the Hoge Raad der Nederlanden, the Court had to consider the relationship of an EC Directive concerning credit institutions[219] which required Member States to bind the relevant authorities by an obligation of professional secrecy 'except by virtue of provisions laid down by law'[220] and article 1946 of the Netherlands Civil Code, which imposed an obligation to give evidence in legal proceedings. In effect the Court held that the Code provision was not inconsistent with the Directive and that it was for the relevant national court to weigh up the conflicting interests before deciding in a particular case whether to require the witness to testify.[221]

Under English practice an order for disclosure by a bank, whatever form it takes, will be framed to have extra-territorial effect only in the most exceptional circumstances. One case in which such circumstances were held to exist is the decision of Templeman J in *London and County Securities v Caplan*,[222] where an English bank was ordered to obtain from its foreign subsidiaries documents relating to accounts connected with the defendant who was suspected of having embezzled UK £5 million from the plaintiffs. The evidence of criminal fraud, and the need for urgent and effective relief to prevent evidence and the fruits of crime disappearing, justified what the judge himself described as an 'onerous' order.

---

[215] [1980] 1 WLR 1274 at 1282; see *MacKinnon v Donaldson Lufkin & Jenrette Securities Corpn* [1986] Ch 482.

[216] Bankers' Books Evidence Act 1897, ss 7, 10.

[217] *Williams v Summerfield* [1972] 2 QB 512 (DC); *Owen v Sambrook* [1981] Crim LR 329 (DC).

[218] [1990] AC 723.

[219] Council Directive 77/780.

[220] Council Directive 77/780, art 12(1).

[221] Case 110/84 *Municipality of Hillegom v Hillenius* [1985] ECR 3947.

[222] (26 May 1978, unreported), cited without disapproval in *Bankers Trust v Shapira* [1980] 1 WLR 1274 (CA) and *MacKinnon v Donaldson Lufkin & Jenrette Securities Corpn* [1986] Ch 482.

In *R v Grossman*,[223] however, despite the need for the evidence in the context of a tax evasion prosecution, the Court of Appeal held that an order should not be made requiring an English bank (Barclays) to allow inspection under the Bankers' Books Evidence Act 1879 of an account held at its subsidiary in the Isle of Man. It was not denied that an order could be made in 'unusual circumstances', but they were not present; indeed the existence of orders of the Manx court prohibiting the disclosure of the material sought was a circumstance telling against the making of an order.

Finally, in *Mackinnon v Donaldson, Lufkin & Jenrette Securities Corpn*,[224] following the *Grossman* principles, Hoffman J set aside orders under the 1879 Act and subpoenas addressed to a New York bank (Citibank) with a branch in London which related to accounts and other documents held in the New York offices of the bank. In all the circumstances, which included the possibility that access to the material might be obtained by seeking an order from a New York court, Hoffman J refused to let stand the orders which he regarded as 'exorbitant' and an infringement of the sovereignty of the United States.

The English courts may be asked to take evidence from banks in this country for use in foreign proceedings, criminal or civil in nature. Where the assistance is sought for the purposes of a foreign criminal prosecution, the English courts will readily comply; that is to say, the 'balancing act' usually performed will generally be resolved in favour of taking the requested evidence. This was the approach of Macpherson J in *Bonalumi v Secretary of State for the Home Department*:[225] 'justice and comity' required that evidence be taken from the London branch of Banco di Roma, the Swedish Government having approached the Secretary of State who made an order under section 5 of the Extradition Act 1873[226] for the taking of the evidence.

The facts that different countries take different positions on the question of bank secrecy and that a request by one state for assistance in obtaining evidence from banks will not necessarily be acted upon in another state create real difficulties for banks which maintain branches in several different jurisdictions. The practical issues are very clearly illustrated in *X AG v A Bank*.[227]

The plaintiffs in that case were a group of associated companies marketing crude oil, mineral ores, fertilizers, and other products. Much of their business was with governments in politically sensitive areas of the world. Disclosure of these dealings

---

[223] (1981) 73 Cr App R 302 (CA). It was not recognized in *Grossman* that the Court of Appeal had no jurisdiction to entertain the appeal, as it concerned a 'criminal cause or matter': *Bonalumi v Secretary of State for the Home Dept* [1985] QB 675 (CA).

[224] [1986] Ch 482. See also *Société Eram Shipping Co Ltd v Cie Internationale de Navigation* [2004] 1 AC 260 at [22] and *United Company Rusal Plc v HSBC Bank Plc* [2011] EWHC 404 (QB) (same test applied to law firms).

[225] (16 November 1984, unreported); see [1985] QB 675 (CA) where it was held that no avenue of appeal was open from such an order.

[226] Now refealed.

[227] [1983] 2 All ER 464.

would not only damage the company commercially, by revealing its operating methods and strategies and its profit margins, but would also have serious repercussions for their customers. It might reveal stockpiling of strategic goods by particular governments, dealings by governments which were in breach either of the policies publicly declared by those same governments or of a boycott on dealing with a particular state to which they publicly adhered, or (because oil sales were the principal export of the country concerned) reveal the extent of its foreign exchange revenue. The companies' evidence was that they had made London the centre of their banking arrangements because of the stringent standards of confidentiality there prevailing.

The companies' business was carried out in United States' dollars and, perhaps for that reason, their chosen bank was the London branch of a bank with its head office in New York, and so subject to the jurisdiction of the State of New York. A New York grand jury, investigating possible tax evasion in the crude oil business, issued a subpoena requiring the production of all relevant documents and correspondence relating to the companies' London bank accounts for a given three-year period. This was subsequently confirmed by an order of a United States District Court.

The plaintiffs obtained interim injunctions in the Queen's Bench Division of the High Court restraining the bank from passing any of the relevant information or documents to its head office; in effect, the English court prohibited the bank from complying with the order of the New York court. This is an illustration of the wider problems experienced when attempts to assert extra-territorial jurisdiction meet with resistance from the governments or courts of other states.

In the particular banking context, it was recognized in *X AG v A Bank* that the ultimate decision would involve the application of the balancing exercise described in the English cases, English law being the proper law of the contract between the bank and the plaintiff companies. All that was actually decided was that the injunctions should be continued, the balance of convenience applicable at the interlocutory stage clearly favouring the plaintiffs. The court recognized the 'immediate, irreparable and incalculable' harm which disclosure would cause them, and the improbability of the banks actually facing contempt sanctions in New York. International judicial assistance must, therefore, take account of the importance of bank secrecy and of the differing approaches taken in different legal systems. The issues must, in particular, be addressed in the negotiation of mutual assistance treaties; the binding international obligations created by such treaties must either override the bank secrecy law of the requested country or preserve it in whole or in part by express provision.

(b) The retreat of bank secrecy

The FATF Recommendations, as revised in 2003, state that 'Countries should ensure that financial institution secrecy laws do not inhibit implementation of the

FATF Recommendations'.[228] Further, in a provision dating from the original 1990 set of recommendations, 'financial institutions should not keep anonymous accounts or accounts in obviously fictitious names'.[229]

Before the establishment of FATF there was a growing recognition that the aim of discovering the proceeds of crime (at least in the case of serious crime, including drug trafficking, and organized crime) was an appropriate justification for an exception to even the most stringent bank secrecy laws. The Swiss Confederation accepted this in its negotiations with the United States towards what became the first of the series of bilateral mutual assistance treaties negotiated by the United States Government. In the drugs context, the Vienna Convention of 1988[230] expressly provides that, in carrying out its Convention obligation to legislate for the identification, tracing, and seizure of proceeds of drugs offences, a party shall enable its authorities to obtain bank, financial, and commercial records, and that a party may not decline to act in that respect on the ground of bank secrecy, and similarly that mutual assistance requests may not be refused on that ground.[231] Similar provisions were included in the UN International Convention for the Suppression of the Financing of Terrorism of 1999[232] and the UN Convention against Transnational Organized Crime of 2001.[233] Within the EU, the 2001 Protocol to the EU Convention on Mutual Assistance in Criminal Matters[234] excludes bank secrecy as a reason for refusing any co-operation regarding a request for mutual assistance from another Member State.[235] The Commonwealth Scheme now contains a similar provision covering 'bank or other financial institution secrecy rules'.[236]

The FATF Recommendations contain other provisions which enhance national anti-money laundering efforts and so the potential for international co-operation.

(c) Due diligence

FATF Recommendation 5 requires financial institutions to undertake[237] customer due diligence (CDD) measures, including identifying and verifying the identity of their customers, when establishing business relations; when there is a suspicion of money laundering or terrorist financing; or when the financial institution has doubts about the veracity or adequacy of previously obtained customer identification data. Due diligence measures should also be taken when a financial institution

---

[228] Recommendation 4.

[229] Recommendation 5.

[230] Convention against Illicit Traffic in Narcotic Drugs and Psychotropic Substances, art 5(3). For the Convention, see pp 240–248.

[231] Convention, art 7(5).

[232] International Convention for the Suppression of the Financing of Terrorism, art 12(2).

[233] Convention against Transnational Organized Crime, arts 12 and 18(6).

[234] OJ C 326, 21.11.2001.

[235] Convention, art 7.

[236] Commonwealth Scheme, para 8(3).

[237] Themselves, or subject to stringent criteria set out in Recommendation 9, via intermediaries or third parties.

carries out occasional transactions of an amount greater than US$15,000,[238] and in certain cases of wire transfers.[239] Enhanced CDD measures are recommended in a number of types of case: in relation to 'politically exposed persons' and in relation to cross-border correspondent banking and other similar relationships.[240]

In this context FATF built on prior work: the importance of customer identification was stressed in a Recommendation of the Committee of Ministers of the Council of Europe of 27 June 1980[241] and in the Statement of Principles of the Basel Committee on Banking Regulations and Supervisory Practices adopted on 12 December 1988,[242] and the publication by its Working Group on Cross-Border banking of a paper on *Customer Due Diligence for Banks* in 2001.

The FATF recommendations as to due diligence and as to record-keeping (considered below) apply in specified types of situation equally to other bodies and persons: casinos, real estate agents, dealers in precious metals and in precious stones, lawyers, notaries, other independent legal professionals and accountants, trust and company service providers.[243]

(d) Record-keeping

The FATF recommendation is that financial institutions should maintain, for at least five years, records on transactions, both domestic or international, sufficient to enable them to reconstruct individual transactions so as to provide, if necessary, evidence for prosecution of criminal activity. Records of the identification data obtained through the CDD process, account files, and business correspondence should be kept for at least five years after the relevant business relationship ended.[244] Financial institutions should pay special attention to all complex, unusually large transactions, and all unusual patterns of transactions, which have no apparent economic or visible lawful purpose.[245]

(e) Reporting of suspicious transactions

Under the FATF Recommendations, if a financial institution suspects or has reasonable grounds to suspect that funds are the proceeds of a criminal activity, or are related to terrorist financing, it should be required, directly by law or

---

[238] See the Interpretative Note to Recommendations 5, 12, and 16.

[239] See FATF Special Recommendation VII and its Interpretative Note.

[240] Recommendation 7.

[241] Recommendation R(80)10, based on work done under the aegis of the European Committee on Crime Problems.

[242] For a discussion of the work of the Basel Supervisors Committee see P C Hayward, 'Prospects for International Co-operation by Bank Supervisors' (1990) 24 Int L 787. The Basel Committee was established by the governors of the central banks of the Group of Ten countries at the end of 1974. It has central bank members from 27 jurisdictions, a secretariat provided by the Bank for International Settlements in Basel, and a number of specialist working groups and task forces, and a major emphasis is on the effective supervision of all banking operations.

[243] Recommendation 12.

[244] Recommendation 10.

[245] Recommendation 11.

regulation, to report promptly its suspicions to the national financial intelligence unit (FIU).[246] Institutions and their officers and staff are to be given legal protection from criminal and civil liability which might otherwise arise if they report their suspicions in good faith to the FIU.[247] But they are also to be prohibited by law from 'tipping off' the person suspected by disclosing the fact that a suspicious transaction report is being made.[248] The institutional location of FIUs varies from country to country. Some are within the police organization, or a related body such as the UK's Serious Organised Crime Agency, but others have a judicial or administrative status. In 1995 the leading FIUs formed the 'Egmont Group'[249] on the initiative of the Belgian and US authorities to facilitate co-operation between themselves and with other bodies. By 2012 it had 127 members.

(f) Money laundering offences

A first and obvious step in combating money laundering is to ensure that it is within the reach of the criminal law. Offences of handling stolen goods, such as that created by section 22 of the Theft Act 1968 covered a small part of the ground, but were wholly inadequate in the face of sophisticated devices.

There is an emerging international consensus as to the scope of the concept of money laundering and therefore of the definition of the necessary new offences. A most influential formulation is that in article 3 of the United Nations Convention against Illicit Traffic in Narcotic Drugs and Psychotropic Substances (the Vienna Convention) of 1988.[250] The article is concerned with offences which each party must establish in its domestic law 'when committed intentionally'.[251]

In addition to offences concerning operations involving the production of drugs, these include:

the conversion or transfer of property, knowing that such property is derived from [one or more of the production-related offences], or from an act of participation in such offence or offences, for the purpose of concealing or disguising the illicit origin of the property or of assisting any person who is involved in the commission of such an offence or offences to evade the legal consequences of his actions;[252]

the concealment or disguise of the true nature, source, location, disposition, movement, rights with respect to, or ownership of property, knowing that such property is derived from

---

[246] Recommendation 13. See D Chaikin, 'How Effective are Suspicious Transaction Reporting Systems?' (2009) JMLC 238. FIUs are sometimes referred to as Financial *Information* Units.

[247] Recommendation 14(a).

[248] Recommendation 14(b).

[249] The name is derived from the Egmont Palace in Brussels where the first meeting was held.

[250] See generally, pp 241–242.

[251] Vienna Convention, art 3(1).

[252] Vienna Convention, art 3(1)(b)(i). It has been suggested that this wording could even cover the position of a lawyer receiving fees from 'laundered' funds; the experts who adopted similar language in the 1990 Council of Europe Convention (considered below) rejected that interpretation: Explanatory Memorandum to that Convention, para 33.

[one or more production-related offences] or from an act of participation in such an offence or offences;[253]

and 'subject to [the Party's] constitutional principles and the basic concepts of its legal system':

the acquisition, possession or use of property, knowing at the time of receipt, that such property was derived from [one or more of the production-related offences] or from an act of participation in such offence or offences;[254]

publicly inciting or inducing others, by any means, to commit any of [these] offences;[255] and

participation in, association or conspiracy to commit, attempts to commit and aiding, abetting, facilitating and counselling the commission of any of [these] offences.[256]

The Financial Action Task Force in its 1990 Report adopted as a working definition a description of money laundering virtually identical, though not linked to specifically drugs-related offences, to the first three paragraphs set out above.

3. Council of Europe Conventions

There are two Council of Europe Conventions in this field, both of which cover much serious criminal activity and are not limited to drug trafficking. The first Convention on Laundering, Search, Seizure and Confiscation of the Proceeds from Crime 1990[257] had forty-eight ratifications, including that of the United Kingdom, by 2012. The 1990 Convention was modernized in a new Convention on Laundering, Search, Seizure and Confiscation of the Proceeds from Crime and on the Financing of Terrorism agreed in Warsaw in May 2005,[258] and has attracted twenty-two ratifications. The new Convention had a wider scope than its predecessor, reflecting the work of FATF and other bodies in developing measures related to the prevention of money laundering, the appearance of FIUs, and work on asset-sharing and recovery. It was decided also to include provisions concerning the financing of terrorism. Many provisions of the 1990 Convention are carried over to the 2005 text, but what follows is based on the latter, more recent, version.

The Convention requires parties to establish money-laundering offences in their domestic law.[259] Article 9(1) of that Convention contains provisions corresponding to the first, second, third, and fifth paragraphs quoted above from the Vienna text, the knowledge required in each case being that the property concerned was 'proceeds'.[260] In the first three contexts, the Convention omits the reference to

---

[253] Vienna Convention, art 3(1)(b)(ii).
[254] Vienna Convention, art 3(1)(c)(i).
[255] Vienna Convention, art 3(1)(c)(iii).
[256] Vienna Convention, art 3(1)(c)(iv).
[257] ETS 141. For the confiscation aspects, see pp 296–300.
[258] CETS 198.
[259] Convention, art 9. For corporate liability, see art 10.
[260] Defined to include any economic advantage from criminal offences: Convention, art 1(a).

an 'act of participation' as being, as a matter of drafting, redundant.[261] The Convention provides additionally that it does not matter whether the predicate offence was subject to the criminal jurisdiction of the party concerned, and that it may be provided that the money laundering offences do not apply to the persons who committed the predicate offence.[262] It also allows a party to establish as offences acts meeting the description drawn from the Vienna text but where the offender did not know, but suspected or ought to have assumed, that the property was proceeds of criminal activity.[263]

Parties are required to establish FIUs,[264] and to institute 'a comprehensive domestic regulatory and supervisory or monitoring regime to prevent money laundering', taking due account of applicable international standards, including in particular the recommendations adopted by FATF.[265]

Further provisions of the Convention deal with mutual assistance in obtaining information about bank accounts and banking transactions.[266] These are based on the 2001 Protocol to the EU Convention on Mutual Assistance in Criminal Matters, examined below.[267]

4. European Union action

(a) The Money Laundering Directive

A Council Directive of 10 June 1991 on prevention of the use of the financial system for money laundering[268] took further the approaches of both the Vienna Convention and the Council of Europe's Convention; both were referred to in its preamble. While the Directive required that Member States ensured that the laundering of the proceeds of any serious crime is treated as a criminal offence and contains a definition of money laundering based on the Vienna Convention text,[269] its main purpose was to ensure that credit and financial institutions adopted a system which allows effective supervision of their customers.

The Directive was substantially amended in 2001,[270] principally by widening the scope to include predicate offences other than drug trafficking, and by extending the obligations under the 1991 Directive to certain professions and activities outside the narrower financial sector. It was replaced by the current instrument,

---

[261] Explanatory Memorandum, para 93.
[262] Convention, art 9(2).
[263] Convention, art 9(3).
[264] Convention, art 12.
[265] Convention, art 13.
[266] Convention, arts 17–19.
[267] See pp 283–284.
[268] 91/308/EEC, OJ L 166, 28.6.1991.
[269] Directive, arts 1 and 2.
[270] Directive 2001/97/EC of the European Parliament and of the Council of 4 December 2001 amending Council Directive 91/308/EEC on prevention of the use of the financial system for the purpose of money laundering, OJ L 344, 28.12.2001.

Directive 2005/60,[271] in 2005, which reflects the FATF Recommendations as revised in 2003.

Directive 2005/60 adopts a 'risk-based approach', encapsulated in two of the Recitals:

(22) It should be recognised that the risk of money laundering and terrorist financing is not the same in every case. In line with a risk-based approach, the principle should be introduced into Community legislation that simplified customer due diligence is allowed in appropriate cases.

(24) Equally, Community legislation should recognise that certain situations present a greater risk of money laundering or terrorist financing. Although the identity and business profile of all customers should be established, there are cases where particularly rigorous customer identification and verification procedures are required.

In Directive 2005/60, as in its predecessors, the definition of money laundering is taken almost verbatim from article 3(1)(b) of the Vienna Convention, but with a more general reference to 'criminal activity' substituted for that to drug offences. The definition of criminal activity, 'any kind of criminal involvement in the commission of a serious crime', means that the scope of the Directive is determined by that of 'serious crime'. In addition to some specified offences,[272] this means 'at least' all offences which are punishable by deprivation of liberty or a detention order for a maximum of more than one year or, as regards those states which have a minimum threshold for offences in their legal system, all offences punishable by deprivation of liberty or a detention order for a minimum of more than six months.[273]

The Directive applies to a wide range of people and businesses: credit institutions, financial institutions, auditors, insolvency practitioners, external accountants and tax advisers, notaries and independent legal professionals, trust or company service providers, estate agents, casinos, and other natural or legal persons trading in goods, only to the extent that payments are made in cash in an amount of €15,000 or more, whether the transaction is executed in a single operation or in several

---

[271] Directive 2005/60/EC of the European Parliament and of the Council of 26 October 2005 on the prevention of the use of the financial system for the purpose of money laundering and terrorist financing OJ L 309/15, 25.11.2005, amended by Directive 2007/64/EC of the European Parliament and of the Council of 13 November 2007, OJ L 319/1, 5.12.2007; Directive 2008/20/EC of the European Parliament and of the Council of 11 March 2008, OJ L 76/46, 19.3.2008; Directive 2009/110/EC of the European Parliament and of the Council of 16 September 2009, OJ L 267/7, 10.10.2009 and Directive 2010/78/EU of the European Parliament and of the Council of 24 November 2010, OJ L 331/120, 15.12.2010. See M van den Broek, 'The EU's Preventive AML/CFT Policy: Asymmetrical Harmonisation' (2011) JMLC 170.

[272] Acts as defined in arts 1–4 of Framework Decision 2002/475/JHA; any of the offences defined in art 3(1)(a) of the 1988 United Nations Convention against Illicit Traffic in Narcotic Drugs and Psychotropic Substances; the activities of criminal organizations as defined in art 1 of Council Joint Action 98/733/JHA of 21 December 1998 on making it a criminal offence to participate in a criminal organization in the Member States of the European Union; fraud, at least serious, as defined in arts 1(1) and 2 of the Convention on the Protection of the European Communities' Financial Interests; and corruption.

[273] Directive, art 3(5).

operations which appear to be linked.[274] Notaries and independent legal professionals are within the scope of the Directive, when they participate whether by acting on behalf of and for their client, in any financial or real estate transaction, or by assisting in the planning or execution of transactions for their client concerning: the buying and selling of real property or business entities; managing of client money, securities, or other assets; opening or management of bank, savings, or securities accounts; organization of contributions necessary for the creation, operation, or management of companies; or the creation, operation, or management of trusts, companies, or similar structures.[275]

Member States must prohibit their credit and financial institutions from keeping anonymous accounts or anonymous passbooks.[276] The whole of Chapter II of the Directive, containing articles 6 to 19, deals with customer due diligence, with special provisions concerning casinos.[277] Customer due diligence measures must be applied (a) when establishing a business relationship; (b) when carrying out occasional transactions amounting to €15,000 or more, whether the transaction is carried out in a single operation or in several operations which appear to be linked; (c) when there is a suspicion of money laundering or terrorist financing; and (d) when there are doubts about the veracity or adequacy of previously obtained customer identification data.[278] Simplified due diligence may be allowed in specific types of case.[279] Enhanced customer due diligence is to be required, on a risk-sensitive basis, in situations which by their nature can present a higher risk of money laundering or terrorist financing. This includes cases in which the customer has not been physically present for identification purposes, in respect of cross-frontier correspondent banking relationships with respondent institutions from third countries, and in respect of transactions or business relationships with politically exposed persons residing in another Member State or in a third country. Member States must also ensure that the institutions and persons covered by the Directive pay special attention to any money laundering or terrorist financing threat that may arise from products or transactions that might favour anonymity.[280]

Chapter III (articles 20 to 29) of the Directive contains provisions as to reporting obligations. The Member States are required to establish a national financial

---

[274] Directive, art 2. The last-named group is referred to as 'high-value dealers' in the UK implementing Regulations: Money Laundering Regulations 2007, SI 2007/2157, reg 3(12).

[275] Directive, art 2(3)(b). For an unsuccessful argument that the inclusion of lawyers might offend against the right to a fair trial, see Case C-305/05 *Ordre des barreaux francophones et germanophone v Conseil des ministres* [2007] ECR I-5305. It has been held (not in a money laundering context) that in EU law, legal professional privilege does not cover exchanges within a company or group with in-house lawyers: Case C-550/07 *Akzo Nobel Chemicals Ltd v European Commission* (ECJ, Grand Chamber, 14 September 2010).

[276] Directive, art 6.

[277] Directive, art 10.

[278] Directive, art 7.

[279] Directive, art 11 as amended by Directive 2009/110 and Directive 2010/78.

[280] Directive, art 13.

intelligence unit[281] in order effectively to combat money laundering and terrorist financing, and must put in place a system for the mandatory reporting of suspicious transactions.[282]

Chapter IV (comprising articles 30 to 33) contains provisions as to record-keeping. The main provision[283] obliges Member States to require the institutions and persons covered by the Directive to keep certain documents and information for use in any investigation into, or analysis of, possible money laundering or terrorist financing by the national financial intelligence unit or by other competent authorities in accordance with national law:

(a) in the case of the customer due diligence, a copy or the references of the evidence required, for a period of at least five years after the business relationship with their customer has ended;

(b) in the case of business relationships and transactions, the supporting evidence and records, consisting of the original documents or copies admissible in court proceedings under the applicable national legislation for a period of at least five years following the carrying-out of the transactions or the end of the business relationship.

Protection is afforded for those involved, in that disclosure under the terms of the Directive and made in good faith by any employee or director of an institution is not to constitute a breach of any restriction on disclosure, whether imposed by contract or by a legislative, regulatory, or administrative provision; and the Directive prevents any civil or penal responsibility of any kind attaching either to the employee or director or to the institution itself.[284]

(b) Exchange of information

The successive Directives address action to be taken within each Member State but say nothing about international co-operation. However, the Council, building on the work of the Egmont Group, had already issued a Decision concerning arrangements for co-operation between FIUs in respect of exchanging information.[285] This contains a definition of a FIU:

A central, national unit which, in order to combat money-laundering, is responsible for receiving (and to the extent permitted, requesting), analysing and disseminating to the competent authorities, disclosures of financial information which concern suspected proceeds of crime or are required by national legislation or regulation.[286]

---

[281] Directive, art 21.
[282] Directive, art 22.
[283] Directive, art 30.
[284] Directive, art 26.
[285] Council Decision of 17 October 2000 concerning arrangements for co-operation between financial intelligence units of the Member States in respect of exchanging information, OJ L 271/4, 24.10.2000.
[286] Decision, art 2(1).

Under the Decision, Member States must ensure that FIUs exchange, spontaneously or on request and in accordance either with the Decision or with existing or future Memoranda of Understanding, any available information that may be relevant to the processing or analysis of information or to investigation by the FIU regarding financial transactions relating to money laundering and the natural or legal persons involved.[287] A FIU supplying information may only refuse consent to the use of the information for the purpose of money laundering investigations or prosecutions if required to do so by its national law;[288] it may impose restrictions and conditions on the use of information for other purposes.[289] A request to supply information to another FIU may be refused where it could impair a criminal investigation already under way in the requested Member State or 'in exceptional circumstances' where divulging the information would be clearly disproportionate to the legitimate interests of a natural or legal person or the requested Member State itself or would otherwise not be in accordance with fundamental principles of its national law.[290]

(c) Mutual assistance requests for information on banking matters

A 2001 Protocol to the EU Convention on Mutual Assistance in Criminal Matters makes more extensive provision, enabling Member States to obtain much banking information from other Member States in aid of criminal investigations.

The Protocol requires each Member State to take the measures necessary to determine, in answer to a request sent by another Member State, whether a natural or legal person that is the subject of a criminal investigation holds or controls one or more accounts, of whatever nature, in any bank located in its territory and, if so, provide all the details of the identified accounts.[291] As the Explanatory Report on the Protocol[292] makes clear:

accounts that are controlled by the person under investigation include accounts of which that person is the true economic beneficiary and that this applies irrespective of whether those accounts are held by a natural person, a legal person or a body acting in the form of, or on behalf of, trust funds or other instruments for administering special purpose funds, the identity of the settlers or beneficiaries of which is unknown.

This obligation only applies if the investigation concerns an offence punishable by a penalty involving deprivation of liberty or a detention order of a maximum period of at least four years in the requesting state and at least two years in the requested state.[293] To limit the burdens on states and to prevent 'fishing expeditions', the Protocol provides that before making a request, a state must consider carefully if the

---

[287] Decision, art 1(2). Under art 1(3) a police authority acting as an FIU 'may' supply information.
[288] Decision, art 5(3).
[289] Decision, art 5(2).
[290] Decision, art 4(3).
[291] Protocol, art 1.
[292] OJ C 257/1, 24.10.2002.
[293] Protocol, art 1(3), which also refers to certain other specified offences.

information is likely to be of substantial value for the purpose of the investigation into the offence, and also to consider carefully to which Member State or States it should send the request.

A wider provision forms article 2 of the Protocol; wider in that it is not limited to specified types of offence. It obliges a requested state, on request by a requesting state, to provide the particulars of specified bank accounts and of banking operations which have been carried out during a specified period through one or more accounts specified in the request, including the particulars of any sending or recipient account. The account need not be that of a person that is the subject of a criminal investigation: the obligation applies in respect of accounts held by third persons, persons who are not themselves subject of any criminal proceedings but whose accounts are, in one way or another, linked to a criminal investigation.

Member States may make the execution of a request under either of these articles dependent on the same conditions as they apply in respect of requests for search and seizure.[294]

A further provision[295] deals with requests for the monitoring of banking transactions. Each Member State must undertake to ensure that, at the request of another Member State, it is able to monitor, during a specified period, the banking operations that are being carried out through one or more accounts specified in the request and communicate the results thereof to the requesting Member State. However, the decision to monitor is to be taken in each individual case by the competent authorities of the requested Member State, with due regard for the national law of that Member State.[296] In other words, Member States must set up the necessary mechanism but have freedom to decide whether or not it may be used in any particular case.

(d) Reporting obligations

FATF Special Recommendation 9, adopted in 2004, urges governments to take measures to detect physical cash movements, including a declaration system or other disclosure obligation. This is implemented in EU law by European Parliament and Council Regulation 1889/2005.[297] Any natural person entering or leaving the EU and carrying cash of a value of €10,000 or more must declare that sum to the competent authorities of the Member State through which he or she is entering or leaving the EU.[298]

---

[294] Protocol, arts 1(5) and 2(4).
[295] Protocol, art 3.
[296] Protocol, art 3(3).
[297] Regulation (EC) No 1889/2005 of the European Parliament and of the Council of 26 October 2005 on controls of cash entering or leaving the Community, OJ L 309/9, 25.11.2005.
[298] Regulation, art 3. For penalties under UK law for failure to make the declaration, see the Control of Cash (Penalties) Regulations 2007, SI 2007/1509.

5. UK legislation

(a) Money laundering offences

The UK legislation giving effect to the EU Directive of 2005 is principally to be found in the Money Laundering Regulations 2007.[299] The Regulations define 'money laundering' by reference to the Proceeds of Crime Act 2002.[300] So, money laundering is an act which constitutes an offence under section 327, 328, or 329 of that Act, or which constitutes an attempt, conspiracy, or incitement to commit, or which aiding, abetting, counselling, or procuring the commission of, such an offence; or which would constitute an offence under this provision if done in the United Kingdom. The offences in the 2002 Act are those of 'concealing' (where a person conceals, disguises,[301] converts, or transfers criminal property, or removes criminal property from England and Wales or from Scotland or from Northern Ireland);[302] 'arrangements' (where a person enters into or becomes concerned in an arrangement which he or she knows or suspects facilitates (by whatever means) the acquisition, retention, use or control of criminal property by or on behalf of another person);[303] and 'acquisition, use and possession' (where a person acquires, uses, or has possession of criminal property).[304] However, no offence is committed if the person concerned makes a timely disclosure of the facts to a constable, a customs officer, or a person nominated for the purpose by the person's employer (or intended to do so but had a reasonable excuse for not doing so), or where the person's actions were done in the course of (in effect) law enforcement functions.[305]

There are further offences, of failure to disclose knowledge or suspicion of money laundering;[306] and of 'tipping-off', essentially the disclosure of information

---

[299] SI 2007/2157.

[300] Regulations, reg 2(1) referring to Proceeds of Crime Act 2002, s 340(11).

[301] Concealing or disguising criminal property includes concealing or disguising its nature, source, location, disposition, movement, or ownership or any rights with respect to it: Proceeds of Crime Act 2002, s 327(3).

[302] Proceeds of Crime Act 2002, s 327. Property is criminal property if it constitutes a person's benefit from criminal conduct or it represents such a benefit (in whole or part and whether directly or indirectly), and the alleged offender knows or suspects that it constitutes or represents such a benefit. The property in question must have become criminal property as a result of some conduct which occurred prior to the act which is alleged to constitute the offence: *R v Geary* [2010] EWCA Crim 1925, [2011] 1 WLR 1634. Criminal conduct is conduct which constitutes an offence in any part of the United Kingdom, or would constitute an offence in any part of the United Kingdom if it occurred there. See Proceeds of Crime Act 2002, s 340(2)(3).

[303] Proceeds of Crime Act 2002, s 328.

[304] Proceeds of Crime Act 2002, s 329. In addition to the defences noted in the text, it is a defence here if the person concerned acquired or used or had possession of the property for adequate consideration: s 329(2)(c).

[305] Proceeds of Crime Act 2002, ss 327(2), 328(2), 329(2), 338.

[306] Proceeds of Crime Act 2002, ss 330, 331, 332. See *R v Da Silva (Hilda Gondwe)* [2006] EWCA Crim 1654, [2007] 1 WLR 303 and *Shah v HSBC Private Bank (UK) Ltd* [2010] EWCA Civ 31, [2011] 1 All ER (Comm) 67 on the meaning of 'suspicion'.

likely to prejudice an investigation or proposed investigation into money launder-ing.[307]

This latter can cause problems to banks and other institutions. In *C v S*[308] a bank had made a series of money laundering reports to the then Economic Crimes Unit of the National Criminal Intelligence Service (NICS). Later in civil proceedings an order was made that the bank disclose certain papers, and the bank feared that compliance might amount to 'tipping-off'. The NICS refused to give an assurance that it would not prosecute for that offence, and instead sought an order for the disclosure to it of the same papers. The bank faced the choice between possible prosecution and possible action for contempt of court. After an extraordinary appeal, extraordinary in that the appellant was excluded from most of the hearings, the Court of Appeal described the NICS position as 'neither sensible nor appropri-ate'. It indicated that where such conflicting pressures existed, the party required to disclose should seek a ruling from the NICS as to what material they would 'clear' for disclosure, and in the case of failure to agree the court should be asked for directions.

In *K Ltd v National Westminster Bank plc*[309] the claimant sought an injunction to compel the bank to act on his instructions to transfer money to another account. The bank suspected that the money in the customer's account was criminal property so that transferring it would be an offence. The Court of Appeal refused an injunction. Although intervention between banker and customer in the perfor-mance of the contract of mandate was a serious interference with the free flow of trade, Parliament has considered that a limited interference was to be tolerated in preference to allowing the undoubted evil of money laundering to run rife in the commercial community.

(b) Obligations of financial institutions

The European Directive, insofar it deals with the obligations of banks and other financial institutions, is also implemented in the Money Laundering Regulations 2007.[310]

The Regulations prescribe the procedures to be followed in respect of customer due diligence,[311] record-keeping,[312] registration, and supervision[313] by the super-visory authorities (the Financial Services Authority, the Office of Fair Trading, HM Revenue and Customs, and a number of professional bodies)[314] and give

---

[307] Proceeds of Crime Act 2002, s 333.
[308] [1999] 2 All ER 343 (CA). See *Governor and Company of the Bank of Scotland v A Ltd* [2001] 1 WLR 751 (CA).
[309] [2006] EWCA Civ 1039, [2007] 1 WLR 311.
[310] SI 2007/2157. For the persons and bodies to which the Regulations apply, see reg 3, which contains detailed definitions of some of the categories listed; see reg 4 for exclusions.
[311] Regulations, Part 2, regs 5–18 and Sch 2.
[312] Regulations, Part 3, regs 19–21.
[313] Regulations, Part 4, regs 22–35.
[314] Regulations, reg 23 and Sch 3.

enforcement powers.[315] Contravention of these requirements of the Regulations carries a maximum penalty, on conviction on indictment, of imprisonment for two years or a fine or both; and on summary conviction, of a fine not exceeding the statutory maximum.[316] It is a defence for the accused person to show that he or she took all reasonable steps and exercised all due diligence to avoid committing the offence.[317]

(c) Reporting obligations

In some countries, legislation may impose upon banks and similar financial institutions an obligation to report certain types of financial transaction (chosen because of their potential relevance in money laundering) as well as a more general suspicion-based duty. For example, under the Financial Transaction Reports Act 1988[318] of Australia, a 'cash dealer' is under an obligation[319] to report 'significant cash transactions' to what became the Australian Transaction Reports and Analysis Centre.[320] The term 'cash dealer' is given a very wide interpretation, including, for example, securities dealers, unit trust managers, bullion dealers, casino operators, and bookmakers; a 'significant cash transaction' is one involving the transfer of currency of not less than AU$10,000.[321] The movement of AU$10,000 in cash into or out of Australia must be reported, as must electronic funds transfers. In Canada there is a similar obligation to report the import or export of amounts over CA$10,000.[322]

However, the United Kingdom reporting rules operate in an indirect fashion. Under the Money Laundering Regulations 2007,[323] all firms (other than sole traders) carrying out relevant business must appoint a nominated officer, the money laundering reporting officer (MLRO), who is responsible for receiving internal money laundering disclosures, deciding whether these should be reported to the national financial intelligence unit, now part of the Serious Organised Crime Agency, and in appropriate cases making such a report. There are related obligations under the Proceeds of Crime Act 2002[324] and the Terrorism Act 2000.[325] Failure to make a report is an offence.[326] The MLRO is responsible for oversight of

---

[315] Regulations, Part 5, regs 36–47.

[316] Regulations, reg 45. For offences by corporate bodies, see reg 47.

[317] Regulations, reg 45(4).

[318] Originally entitled the Cash Transaction Reports Act; the Short Title was amended in 1991.

[319] Cash Transaction Reports Act 1988, s 7.

[320] See the Cash Transaction Reports Amendment Act 1991, which established the Agency under its new title.

[321] Financial Transaction Reports Act 1988, s 3(1).

[322] Cross Border Currency and Monetary Instruments Reporting Regulation, s SOR/2002-412.

[323] Regulations, reg 20(2)(d).

[324] Proceeds of Crime Act 2002, ss 337–8.

[325] Terrorism Act 2000, ss 21A and 21B, inserted by the Anti-terrorism, Crime and Security Act 2001 and as amended by the Terrorism Act 2000 and Proceeds of Crime Act 2002 (Amendment) Regulations 2007, SI 2007/3398.

[326] Proceeds of Crime Act 2002, s 330 as amended by the Proceeds of Crime Act 2002 and Money Laundering Regulations 2003 (Amendment) Order 2006, SI 2006/308 and by the Terrorism Act 2000 and Proceeds of Crime Act 2002 (Amendment) Regulations 2007, SI 2007/3398; Terrorism Act 2000, s 21A as inserted by the Anti-terrorism, Crime and Security Act 2001.

the firm's compliance with the anti-money laundering, and has to have the necessary seniority for this to be realistic. The appointment of an MLRO in the regulated sector requires the approval of the Financial Services Authority.[327]

The internal reporting procedures required by the Regulations[328] must include provisions:

(a) identifying the MLRO to receive disclosures under the Regulations;

(b) requiring anyone in the organization to whom information or other matter comes in the course of relevant business as a result of which that person knows or suspects or has reasonable grounds for knowing or suspecting that a person is engaged in money laundering must, as soon as is practicable after the information or other matter comes to him or her, disclose it to the MLRO;

(c) where a disclosure is made to the MLRO, require that officer to consider it in the light of any relevant information which is available to the firm and determine whether it gives rise to such knowledge or suspicion or such reasonable grounds for knowledge or suspicion; and

(d) where the MLRO does so determine, require him or her to disclose the matter to the national financial intelligence unit.

(d) Requests for information on banking matters

The 2001 Protocol to the EU Convention on Mutual Assistance in Criminal Matters[329] is implemented in the United Kingdom by Chapter 4 of Part I of the Criminal Justice (International Co-operation) Act 2003.

When an incoming request is received by the Secretary of State from an authority in a 'participating country',[330] the Secretary of State may direct a senior police officer or a senior customs officer to apply, or arrange for a constable or customs officer to apply, for a 'customer information order'.[331] A customer information order is an order made by a judge[332] that a financial institution specified in the application for the order must, on being required to do so by notice in writing given by the applicant for the order, provide any such customer information as it has relating to the person specified in the application.[333] The judge must be satisfied that the person specified in the application is subject to an investigation in the country in question, the investigation concerns conduct which is serious criminal

---

[327] Financial Services and Markets Act 2000, s 59.

[328] Regulations, reg 20.

[329] See pp 283–284.

[330] For this purpose, participating countries are Austria, Belgium, Bulgaria, Czech Republic, Denmark, Estonia, Finland, France, Germany, Greece, Hungary, Iceland, Ireland, Israel, Italy, Japan, Latvia, Lithuania, Luxembourg, Malta, Netherlands, Norway, Poland, Portugal, Romania, Slovakia, Slovenia, Spain, Sweden, and Switzerland.

[331] Criminal Justice (International Co-operation) Act 2003, s 32. For requests addressed to Scotland, see ss 37–41.

[332] In England and Wales, a judge entitled to exercise the jurisdiction of the Crown Court.

[333] Criminal Justice (International Co-operation) Act 2003, 32(4).

conduct, the conduct constitutes an offence in England and Wales or (as the case may be) Northern Ireland, or would do were it to occur there, and the order is sought for the purposes of the investigation.[334] A customer information order has effect in spite of any restriction on the disclosure of information (however imposed).[335] Customer information obtained in pursuance of a customer information order is passed to the Secretary of State for transmission to the foreign authority which made the request.

Similar rules govern requests for account information and the making of 'account information orders'.[336] An account monitoring order is an order made by a judge that a financial institution specified in the application for the order must, for the period stated in the order, provide account information of the description specified in the order to the applicant in the manner, and at or by the time or times, stated in the order.[337] A judge may make an account monitoring order if satisfied that there is an investigation in the country in question into criminal conduct, and that the order is sought for the purposes of the investigation.[338]

'Tipping-off', the disclosure of information about requests, is made an offence.[339]

Outgoing requests for information about a person's bank account or for monitoring banking transactions are also governed by the 2003 Act.[340]

(e) Powers of the Financial Services Authority

Under the Financial Services and Markets Act 2000, the Financial Services Authority (FSA) has the power to make rules in relation to the prevention and detection of money laundering in connection the activities it regulates.[341] The Authority has the power to carry out investigations when it finds that there are circumstances suggesting that a person may be guilty of an offence under the Money Laundering Regulations 2007,[342] and in appropriate cases to institute prosecutions.[343]

---

[334] Criminal Justice (International Co-operation) Act 2003, 33(1). For offences, see s 34.
[335] Criminal Justice (International Co-operation) Act 2003, 32(7).
[336] Criminal Justice (International Co-operation) Act 2003, s 35.
[337] Criminal Justice (International Co-operation) Act 2003, s 35(4).
[338] Criminal Justice (International Co-operation) Act 2003, s 36(1).
[339] Criminal Justice (International Co-operation) Act 2003, s 42.
[340] Criminal Justice (International Co-operation) Act 2003, ss 43–45.
[341] Financial Services and Markets Act 2000, s 146. In 2011, the FSA issued a consultation paper about a proposed guide for firms on money laundering: CPP 11/12.
[342] Financial Services and Markets Act 2000, s 168(4)(b).
[343] Financial Services and Markets Act 2000, s 402(1)(b).

9

The Proceeds of Crime

I. Introduction

Every legal system would accept as axiomatic that an offender should not be able enjoy the profits of criminal activities In earlier centuries the rule of the common law was that the entire estate of a felon was forfeit to the Crown;[1] in modern times the imposition of fines and the making of orders in favour of the victims of crime (for example a restitution order on a conviction for theft, or a compensation order in a case of criminal damage to property) go some way towards the same objective. There are, however, many highly profitable types of criminal activity—drug trafficking being a prime example—to which notions of restitution or compensation scarcely apply, because there is no readily identifiable 'victim'. A specific concept of forfeiture is clearly needed.

---

[1] The history of this and related rules is examined in the argument of counsel for the appellant (L Blom-Cooper QC) in *R v Cuthbertson* [1981] AC 470 (HL).

Its application is made more difficult by practical developments. The proceeds of crime were perhaps once typically pieces of personal property, for example stolen chattels, which could be seized or restored to their owner. Today they are more commonly represented by cash or choses in action, and subject to sophisticated money-laundering techniques. In large-scale criminal conspiracies, where many more offences will be committed than can lead to convictions being obtained, the notion of 'forfeiting the property derived by the offender from the crime for which he has been convicted' is demonstrably inadequate.

In recent years, governments in many countries have addressed this matter, and a growing body of legislation bears witness to the seriousness with which the problem is being tackled. The legislators have used a number of different techniques and concepts, and some account will be given of the development of these techniques and concepts, using examples drawn from the English experience.

1. Forbidden articles

The narrowest type of forfeiture provision concerns specific categories of forbidden articles. Where it is the policy of the law to prohibit the possession or exposure to view or offering for sale of certain types of article, forfeiture (and sometimes destruction) will commonly be found as a method of enforcement. Typical examples are those of obscene publications,[2] firearms,[3] and knives.[4] More generally, section 143(2) of the Powers of Criminal Courts (Sentencing) Act 2000 enables the court to order forfeiture where a defendant is convicted of an offence and the offence, or an offence which the court has taken into consideration in determining his sentence, consists of unlawful possession of property.

2. Forfeiture of property 'related to' a specific offence

Wider language may be used where the offence may not involve simple possession but the conduct of some transaction. In the drugs area, for example, articles such as scales and syringes may be part of the paraphernalia of the dealer. The language of section 27(1) of the Misuse of Drugs Act 1971, as amended by the Proceeds of Crime Act 2002, catches such articles and in some cases the monetary proceeds of a drugs offence. It provides that, subject to safeguards for third-party rights, the court by or before which a person is convicted of a specified drug-trafficking offence may order anything shown to the satisfaction of the court to relate to the offence to be forfeited and either destroyed or dealt with in such other manner as the court may order.

---

[2] See eg Obscene Publications Act 1964, s 1(4) (obscene articles kept for publication for gain); Protection of Children Act 1978, Sch (as substituted by the Police and Justice Act 2006, s 39) (indecent photographs of children).

[3] Firearms Act 1968, s 52.

[4] Knives Act 1997, s 6.

This has been described, by way of illustration, as covering 'the drugs involved, apparatus for making them, vehicles used for transporting them, or cash ready to be, or having just been, handed over for them'.[5] On the other hand, it has been held that a house cannot be the subject of forfeiture under this provision.[6]

Section 27 does not authorize the forfeiture of property which cannot be shown to be related to the particular offence of which the offender has been convicted.[7] It follows that money in the possession of the offender which clearly represents the proceeds of a series of drugs offences cannot be made the subject of a forfeiture order under this section unless it can be linked to the particular offences for which a conviction was obtained.[8] A fortiori, it is not possible to 'follow the assets' in seeking to forfeit property which indirectly represents the proceeds of a drugs offence.

3. Forfeiture of instrumentalities

In some contexts there are powers to confiscate property used in the commission of offences, known by the convenient if ugly phrase 'the instrumentalities of the crime'. These forfeiture powers are sometimes developed in relation to particular types of crime, an early and notable example being that of smuggling. So the Customs and Excise Management Act 1979, having provided[9] for the forfeiture of goods improperly imported, goes on to permit the forfeiture of any 'ship, aircraft, vehicle, animal, container (including any article of passengers' baggage) or other thing whatsoever which has been used for the carriage, handling, deposit or concealment of the thing so liable for forfeiture, either at a time when it is so liable or for the purpose of the commission of the offence for which it later became so liable', and also of 'any other thing mixed, packed or found with the thing so liable'.[10]

A general provision dealing with the forfeiture of instrumentalities is now contained in section 143(1) of the Powers of Criminal Courts (Sentencing) Act 2000. This enables the courts on conviction to make orders forfeiting property lawfully seized from the defendant or which was in his possession or under his control at the time when he was apprehended for the offence or when a summons in respect of it was issued, where the property was used for the purpose of committing, or facilitating the commission of, any offence, or was intended by the defendant to be used for that purpose. The property must have served (or been intended to serve) the purpose of at least facilitating an offence, though not necessarily the offence of which the offender stands convicted. A car used to

---

[5] *R v Cuthbertson* [1981] AC 47, at 484 per Lord Diplock.

[6] *R v Pearce (John Frederick)* [1996] 2 Cr App R (S) 316.

[7] *R v Cuthbertson* [1981] AC 470 (money obtained by drug-trafficking held not to relate to the offence of conspiracy, which is only an unfulfilled agreement to do something).

[8] *R v Morgan* [1977] Crim LR 488, CA; *R v Llewellyn* (1985) 7 Cr App R (S) 225; *R v Cox* (1986) 8 Cr App R (S) 384; *R v Boothe* (1987) 9 Cr App R (S) 8.

[9] s 49.

[10] Customs and Excise Management Act 1979, s 141(1).

transport prohibited drugs will fall within this provision,[11] but a car which provides the setting for an indecent assault may not.[12] The section does not apply to the proceeds of past offences, such as money gained in drug trafficking,[13] unless the court is persuaded that it was intended for use for the purpose of committing or facilitating further offences.[14]

Section 143(5) of the 2002 Act requires the court when considering whether to make a forfeiture order to have regard to the value of the property and to the likely financial and other effects on the offender, combined with the effects of any other order that the court contemplates making. This codified the principles which had already been established by case law to guide the courts when making forfeiture orders.

4. The emergence of comprehensive provision

The inadequacy of the earlier provisions, especially as exposed in the *Cuthbertson* case,[15] caused much public concern in the early years of the 1980s. The Hodgson Committee, established by the Howard League for Penal Reform, reported in 1984, and despite its unofficial status was to have a marked influence on subsequent legislation.[16] The legislation in the following years dealt piecemeal with different types of crime and it took almost two decades for a comprehensive system to emerge.

The Drug Trafficking Offences Act 1986 implemented many of the recommendations of the Hodgson Committee, and introduced a comprehensive scheme giving powers in relation to the proceeds of drug-trafficking offences extending from the initial stage of investigation to the making of a confiscation order after a conviction has been obtained. Similar principles, but with some important variations, were applied outside the drug-trafficking field by the Criminal Justice Act 1988 (for most non-drugs offences) and the Prevention of Terrorism (Temporary Provisions) Act 1989. As developed by subsequent legislation, the powers, other than those in the terrorism area, were replaced by the comprehensive provisions of the Proceeds of Crime Act 2002.[17] In the terrorism area, the Terrorism Act 2000 made fresh provision for forfeiture orders,[18] and introduced new powers for the seizure of terrorist cash at borders and ports; the last-mentioned powers were

---

[11] *R v Boothe* (1987) 9 Cr App R (S) 8 (CA).

[12] *R v Lucas* [1976] Crim LR 79 (CA). For another example, see *R v Winton* [1996] 1 Cr App R (S) 382 (charge of interception of communications; surveillance equipment correctly forfeited).

[13] *R v Slater* [1986] 1 WLR 1340 (CA); *R v Neville* (1987) 9 Cr App R (S) 222 (CA).

[14] ie applying s 43(1)(a)(ii). See *R v O'Farrell* [1988] Crim LR 387 (CA), where *Slater* and *Neville* not cited.

[15] *R v Cuthbertson* [1981] AC 470 (HL); see p 293, above.

[16] For the report of the committee, see *The Profits of Crime and Their Recovery* (Heinemann, 1984).

[17] For the background, see *Recovering the Proceeds of Crime* by the Government's Performance and Innovation Unit, *Criminal Assets* by the Working Group on the Confiscation of Assets, and the Levi Report on *Investigation, Seizing and Confiscating the Proceeds of Crime* published by the Home Office Research Unit.

[18] s 23 and Sch 4.

replaced by broader provisions in the Anti-terrorism, Crime and Security Act 2001.[19]

Provision for international co-operation is made in a number of instruments, which have been amended and developed over time as the complexities of the subject have been revealed by experience. These instruments will now be examined, and then the United Kingdom legislation implementing them.

II. International action

1. The United Nations Optional Protocol

The United Nations Model Treaty on Mutual Assistance in Criminal Matters 1990 had an Optional Protocol on the proceeds of crime. Of only six articles, the protocol left all details to bilateral agreements, but the negotiators of the Model Treaty felt that this new and important topic should be included, albeit as an Optional Protocol.

2. Provisions in the Commonwealth Scheme

The Commonwealth Scheme for Mutual Assistance in Criminal Matters, as it emerged in draft form from a meeting of Senior Officials in January 1986, contained no provisions dealing with the proceeds of crime. Some provisions were prepared in time for their inclusion in the text as adopted by Law Ministers at Harare later in the year, but they were revised, and extended to instrumentalities, in 1990.

The proceeds of crime provisions in the text of the revised Scheme agreed in 2011 are in the concise style typical of the Scheme. They may appear to lack the detail found in the European texts considered below, but it needs to be remembered that the Scheme as a whole applies to:

proceedings relating to:

    (a) the restraint or freezing of property that may be confiscated or forfeited by a court, or that may be needed to satisfy a pecuniary penalty imposed in respect of an offence;

    (b) the confiscation or forfeiture of property by a court in respect of an offence; and

    (c) the imposition or recovery of a pecuniary penalty in respect of an offence.[20]

The Scheme provides for assistance in the identification, tracing, restraining, freezing, seizure, forfeiture and confiscation of proceeds and instrumentalities of crime believed to be within the requested country.[21]

---

[19] ss 1–3 and Schs 1 and 2 (introducing provisions as to restraint orders and account monitoring orders).

[20] Scheme, para 3(3).

[21] Scheme, para 28.

Without imposing a mandatory requirement, the Scheme 'encourages' each country to take such measures as may be necessary to freeze, restrain, or seize property upon receipt (a) of a freezing, restraint or seizure order issued by a court of a requesting country, or (b) of a request that provides a basis for the requested country to believe that there are reasonable grounds for taking such actions and that the property would eventually be subject to an order of confiscation or forfeiture; and in all such cases to preserve property for confiscation or forfeiture.[22]

Similarly, each country is encouraged to take the necessary measures to give effect to an order of confiscation or forfeiture issued by a court of a requesting country; and (in a novel provision) to allow confiscation or forfeiture of such property without a criminal conviction in cases in which the offender cannot be prosecuted by reason of death, flight, or absence, or in other appropriate cases as provided by domestic law.[23]

3. The work of the Council of Europe

Much more elaborate provisions were found in the Council of Europe's Convention on Laundering, Search, Seizure, and Confiscation of Proceeds from Crime of 1990.[24] This convention had money laundering as its central concern, and it has been examined above in that context, as has the process by which it was replaced by the Council of Europe Convention on Laundering, Search, Seizure and Confiscation of the Proceeds from Crime and on the Financing of Terrorism of 2005.[25] The provisions of this latter convention dealing with the proceeds of crime are examined in the following material. It obliges parties to take certain measures affecting the content of their domestic law as well as providing for international co-operation.

(a) Domestic measures

At the national level, each party must adopt legislative or other measures enabling it to confiscate instrumentalities[26] or proceeds[27] or property the value of which corresponds to such proceeds and laundered property.[28] This obligation applies to money laundering and to a long list of offences set out in an Annex to the Convention;[29] each party may, however, make a declaration applying it only

---

[22] Scheme, para 28(3).
[23] Scheme, para 28(4).   [24] ETS 141.   [25] CETS 198.
[26] Defined as 'any property used or intended to be used, in any manner, wholly or in part, to commit a criminal offence or criminal offences': Convention, art 1(c).
[27] Defined as 'any economic advantage, derived from or obtained, directly or indirectly, from criminal offences': Convention, art 1(a).
[28] Convention, art 3(1).
[29] Participation in an organized criminal group and racketeering; terrorism, including financing of terrorism; trafficking in human beings and migrant smuggling; sexual exploitation, including sexual exploitation of children; illicit trafficking in narcotic drugs and psychotropic substances; illicit arms trafficking; illicit trafficking in stolen and other goods; corruption and bribery; fraud; counterfeiting currency; counterfeiting and piracy of products; environmental crime; murder, grievous bodily injury; kidnapping, illegal restraint and hostage-taking; robbery or theft; smuggling; extortion; forgery; piracy; and insider trading and market manipulation.

to cases in which the offence is punishable by deprivation of liberty or a detention order for a maximum of more than one year (subject to a special provision as to tax offences) and/or only to a list of specified offences.[30] Each party must adopt such legislative or other measures as may be necessary to require that, in respect of a serious offence or offences as defined by national law, an offender demonstrates the origin of alleged proceeds or other property liable to confiscation, to the extent that such a requirement is consistent with the principles of its domestic law.[31]

The 2005 Convention contains provisions as to investigation, freezing, and confiscation which are much more elaborate than those in the 1990 text. Each party must adopt such legislative and other measures as may be necessary:

(a) to enable it to identify, trace, freeze, or seize rapidly property which is liable to confiscation under article 3, in order in particular to facilitate the enforcement of a later confiscation;[32]

(b) to ensure that the measures to freeze, seize and confiscate also encompass (i) property into which the proceeds have been transformed or converted; and (ii) property acquired from legitimate sources, if proceeds have been intermingled, in whole or in part, with such property, up to the assessed value of the intermingled proceeds; and (iii) income or other benefits derived from proceeds, from property into which proceeds of crime have been transformed or converted or from property with which proceeds of crime have been intermingled, up to the assessed value of the intermingled proceeds, in the same manner and to the same extent as proceeds;[33]

(c) to ensure proper management of frozen or seized property;[34]

(d) to empower its courts or other competent authorities to order that bank, financial or commercial records be made available or be seized in order to carry out the actions required by articles 3, 4, and 5; a party may not decline to act under the provisions of this article on grounds of bank secrecy.[35] These measures must enable the party to determine whether a natural or legal person is a holder or beneficial owner of one or more accounts, of whatever nature, in any bank located in its territory and, if so, obtain all of the details of the identified accounts; to obtain the particulars of specified bank accounts and of banking operations which have been carried out during a specified period through one or more specified accounts, including the particulars of any sending or recipient account; to monitor, during a specified period, the banking operations that are being carried out through one or more identified accounts; and must ensure that banks do not disclose to the bank customer concerned or to other third persons that information has been sought or obtained, or that an investigation is being carried out. Parties are required to consider extending these measures to accounts held in non-bank financial institutions;

---

[30] Convention, art 3(2).   [31] Convention, art 3(4).   [32] Convention, art 4.
[33] Convention, art 5.   [34] Convention, art 6.   [35] Convention, art 7.

(e) to enable it to use special investigative techniques facilitating the identification and tracing of proceeds and the gathering of evidence related thereto,
such as observation, interception of telecommunications, access to computer
systems, and order to produce specific documents.[36]

(b) International co-operation

Chapter IV of the Convention, comprising articles 15 to 45, contains detailed
provisions as to international co-operation. They are all governed by the principle
that parties are to mutually co-operate with each other to the widest extent possible
for the purposes of investigations and proceedings aiming at the confiscation of
instrumentalities and proceeds.[37] The Convention makes use of a system of central
authorities,[38] and there are detailed rules as to the contents and the processing of
requests for assistance.[39]

The assistance to be given takes various forms. There is first an obligation to
provide investigative assistance, that is assistance in the identification and tracing of
instrumentalities, proceeds, and other property liable to confiscation.[40] It also
includes responding to requests for information on bank accounts and banking
transactions, and for the monitoring of such transactions.[41]

Second, there is an obligation to take provisional measures. At the request of
another party which has instituted criminal proceedings or proceedings for the
purpose of confiscation, a party must take the necessary provisional measures, such
as freezing or seizing, to prevent any dealing in, transfer, or disposal of property
which, at a later stage, may be the subject of a request for confiscation or which
might be such as to satisfy the request.[42]

Finally, there is an obligation to confiscate. A party, which has received a request
made by another party for confiscation concerning instrumentalities or proceeds,
situated in its territory, must enforce a confiscation order made by a court of a
requesting party in relation to such instrumentalities or proceeds; or submit the
request to its competent authorities for the purpose of obtaining an order of
confiscation and, if such order is granted, enforce it.[43] This also applies, mutatis
mutandis, to confiscation consisting in a requirement to pay a sum of money
corresponding to the value of proceeds, if property on which the confiscation can be
enforced is located in the requested party.[44] A provision included for the first time
in the 2005 text requires parties, to the widest extent possible under their domestic
law, to assist in the execution of measures equivalent to confiscation leading to the
deprivation of property, which are not criminal sanctions, in so far as such measures
are ordered by a judicial authority of the requesting party in relation to a criminal

---

[36] Convention, art 7(3).   [37] Convention, art 15(1).   [38] Convention, arts 33 and 34.
[39] Convention, arts 35–39.   [40] Convention, art 16.
[41] Convention, arts 17–19, largely drawn from 2001 Protocol to the EU Convention on mutual
assistance in criminal matters.
[42] Convention, art 21(1).   [43] Convention, art 23(1).   [44] Convention, art 23(3).

offence.[45] The procedures for obtaining and enforcing confiscation are governed by the law of the requested party, but a requested party is bound by certain findings of facts made in the requesting party.[46] Similarly, the disposal of confiscated property is to be in accordance with the domestic law and administrative procedures of the requested party; this is subject to priority consideration being given in certain cases to returning the confiscated property to the requesting party so that it can give compensation to the victims of the crime or return such property to their legitimate owners, and to agreement to share the property with the other party.[47]

(c) Grounds for refusing assistance

There are elaborate provisions as to the grounds on which co-operation may be refused,[48] provisions which distinguish between different types of assistance. Seven of the grounds apply to any form of assistance:

(a) the action sought would be contrary to the fundamental principles of the legal system of the requested Party;[49]

(b) the execution of the request is likely to prejudice the sovereignty, security, *ordre public* or other essential interests of the requested Party;

(c) in the opinion of the requested Party, the importance of the case to which the request relates does not justify the taking of the action sought;

(d) the offence to which the request relates is a political offence, with the exception of the financing of terrorism;

(e) the offence to which the request relates is a fiscal offence, with the exception of the financing of terrorism;

(f) the requested Party considers that compliance with the action sought would be contrary to the principle of *ne bis in idem*;

(g) the offence to which the request relates would not be an offence under the law of the requested Party if committed within its jurisdiction. However, this ground applies to co-operation under section 2 [investigative assistance] only insofar as the assistance sought involves coercive action.[50]

In the case of investigative assistance involving coercive measures, and of provisional measures, assistance may also be refused if the measures sought are unavailable in those contexts in the law of the requested party, or if the request is not authorized within the requesting party by a judge or authority acting in its criminal, as opposed to civil, jurisdiction.[51]

---

[45] Convention, art 23(5).

[46] Convention, art 24(1),(2); a party may declare that the latter obligation is subject to its constitutional principles and the basic concepts of its legal system.

[47] Convention, art 25.

[48] See Convention, art 40, as to the obligation to give reasons for any refusal of assistance.

[49] Examples discussed during the negotiation of the Convention in 1990 included contravention of the European Convention on Human Rights, and cases of exorbitant jurisdiction.

[50] Convention, art 28(1).

[51] The text is an attempt to state the effect of the tortuously drafted art 28(2)(3) of the Convention.

In respect of actual confiscation, the drafting is yet more complex. In effect, assistance may be refused if confiscation is not available under the law of the requested party because of the nature of the offence, its definition of 'proceeds' or 'instrumentalities', or its statute of limitations; in cases where confiscation has been ordered without a prior criminal conviction; where the confiscation order was not enforceable in the requesting party or was subject to ordinary means of appeal; and where the order was made in default of appearance and without the grant of 'the minimum rights of defence recognized as due to everyone against whom a criminal charge is made'.[52]

Although earlier international texts have recognized the need to protect third parties' rights, the 1990 Convention was the first to make provision for international co-operation to this end, and the 2005 text retains the provisions virtually unchanged. Article 31 provides for mutual assistance in the service of documents on third parties, those affected by provisional measures, or confiscation.[53] Article 32 provides for the recognition by a party requested to give assistance in respect of provisional measures or confiscation of judicial decisions in the requesting party regarding rights claimed by third parties. If a third party (or indeed a defendant) brings a successful claim for compensation in respect of an act or omission relating to co-operation, the parties concerned are to consult as to the apportionment of the sum due (ie, as to the contribution each should make).[54]

4. EU action

This is an area in which the Council of Europe has taken the lead, and for some time the EU contented itself with modest provisions in effect in support of the Council of Europe's work. In more recent years, the EU has adopted its own instruments, some of which, in the pursuit of legal certainty, are notably detailed.

(a) The 2001 Framework Decision

In June 2001, the Council adopted a Framework Decision on money laundering, the identification, tracing, freezing, seizing, and confiscation of instrumentalities and the proceeds of crime.[55] This was in effect supplemental to the 1990 Council of Europe Convention, providing that Member States are not to make certain reservations against that Convention.[56] So far as international co-operation is concerned, Member States were required to take the necessary steps to ensure that all requests from other Member States which relate to asset identification, tracing, freezing, or seizing and confiscation are processed with the same priority as is given to such measures in domestic proceedings.[57]

---

[52] Convention, art 28(4)(5)(6).　　　[53] It draws on the Hague Service Convention.
[54] Convention, art 35.　　　[55] 2001/500/JHA, OJ. L 182, 5.7.2001.
[56] art 1.　　　[57] art 4.

(b) The 2003 Framework Decision

A second Framework Decision[58] ensured the enforcement within the EU of freezing orders made by other Member States. A 'freezing order' was defined for this purpose as 'any measure taken by a competent judicial authority in the issuing state in order provisionally to prevent the destruction, transformation, moving, transfer or disposal of property that could be subject to confiscation or evidence'.[59] The Framework Decision applies to freezing orders issued for purposes of securing evidence, or the subsequent confiscation of property.[60] As with other Framework Decisions of this type, there is a long list of offences to which the requirement of double criminality may not be applied.[61]

The competent judicial authorities of the executing state must recognize a freezing order, duly transmitted in accordance with the Framework Decision, without any further formality being required, and must forthwith take the necessary measures for its immediate execution in the same way as for a freezing order made by an authority of the executing state, unless that authority invokes one of the grounds for non-recognition or non-execution or for postponement provided for in the Framework Decision.[62] The grounds for refusal are very limited. They are that:

(a) the certificate which must accompany the order is not produced, is incomplete or manifestly does not correspond to the freezing order;

(b) there is an immunity or privilege under the law of the executing state which makes it impossible to execute the freezing order;

(c) it is 'instantly clear' from the information provided in the certificate that rendering judicial assistance for the offence in respect of which the freezing order has been made would infringe the *ne bis in idem* principle;

(d) where applicable, there is no double criminality.[63]

The execution of a freezing order may be postponed where its execution might damage an ongoing criminal investigation, until such time as is deemed reasonable; where the property or evidence concerned have already been subjected to a freezing order in criminal proceedings, and until that freezing order is lifted; where, in the case of an order freezing property in criminal proceedings with a view to its subsequent confiscation, that property is already subject to an order made in the course of other proceedings in the executing state and until that order is lifted.[64]

---

[58] Council Framework Decision 2003/577/JHA of 22 July 2003 on the execution in the European Union of orders freezing property or evidence OJ L 196/45, 2.8.2003.
[59] Framework Decision, art 2(c).
[60] Framework Decision, art 3(1).
[61] Framework Decision, art 3(2).
[62] Framework Decision, art 5; for the duration of the freezing, see art 6.
[63] Framework Decision, art 7.
[64] Framework Decision, art 8.

(c) The 2005 Framework Decision

A third Framework Decision followed almost two years later, that of 24 February 2005 on Confiscation of Crime-Related Proceeds, Instrumentalities and Property.[65] As the Recitals explained, the existing instruments had not to a sufficient extent achieved effective cross-border co-operation with regard to confiscation, as there were still a number of Member States which were unable to confiscate the proceeds from all offences punishable by deprivation of liberty for more than one year. The aim of the new Framework Decision was to ensure that all Member States had effective rules governing the confiscation of proceeds from crime, inter alia, in relation to the onus of proof regarding the source of assets held by a person convicted of an offence related to organized crime.[66] So it was now provided that each Member State was to take the necessary measures to enable it to confiscate, either wholly or in part, instrumentalities and proceeds from criminal offences punishable by deprivation of liberty for more than one year, or property the value of which corresponds to such proceeds.[67]

Article 3 gives extended powers of confiscation in respect of many offences. Each Member State is to take the necessary measures to enable confiscation in those cases at least:

(a) where a national court based on specific facts is fully convinced that the property in question has been derived from criminal activities of the convicted person during a period prior to conviction for the offence which is deemed reasonable by the court in the circumstances of the particular case; or, alternatively,

(b) where a national court based on specific facts is fully convinced that the property in question has been derived from similar criminal activities of the convicted person during a period prior to conviction for the offence which is deemed reasonable by the court in the circumstances of the particular case; or, alternatively,

(c) where it is established that the value of the property is disproportionate to the lawful income of the convicted person and a national court based on specific facts is fully convinced that the property in question has been derived from the criminal activity of that convicted person.[68]

Each Member State may also consider adopting the necessary measures to enable it to confiscate, in accordance with those conditions and either wholly or in part, property acquired by the closest relations of the person concerned and property transferred to a legal person in respect of which the person concerned, acting either alone or in conjunction with his closest relations, has a controlling influence. The

---

[65] Council Framework Decision 2005/212/JHA of 24 February 2005 on Confiscation of Crime-Related Proceeds, Instrumentalities and Property OJ L 68/49, 15.3.2005.

[66] Recitals (9) and (10).

[67] Framework Decision, art 2(1).

[68] Framework Decision, art 3(2).

same shall apply if the person concerned receives a significant part of the legal person's income.[69] Procedures other than criminal procedures may be used to deprive the perpetrator of the property in question.[70]

(d) The 2006 Framework Decision

Finally, another Framework Decision,[71] considered alongside that last mentioned but finalized rather later, dealt with the recognition of confiscation orders. A confiscation order is defined as 'a final penalty or measure imposed by a court following proceedings in relation to a criminal offence or offences, resulting in the definitive deprivation of property'.[72] The relevant property is that identified as the proceeds of an offence, or as equivalent to either the full value or part of the value of such proceeds; or which constitutes the instrumentalities of such an offence; or is liable to confiscation resulting from the application in the issuing state of any of the extended powers of confiscation under Framework Decision 2005/212/JHA or under the law of the issuing state.[73] As with other Framework Decisions of this type, there is a long list of offences to which the requirement of double criminality may not be applied.[74]

A confiscation order is sent, with a certificate in the form prescribed by the Framework Decision to the competent authorities of the Member State in which enforcement is sought.[75] The competent authorities in the executing state must without further formality recognize a confiscation order duly transmitted and take forthwith all the necessary measures for its execution, unless they invoke one of the grounds for non-recognition or non-execution provided for in article 8, or one of the grounds for postponement of execution provided for in article 10.

The grounds for non-recognition or non-execution are both numerous and elaborate; the elaboration is a reflection of the sensitivities of Member States where criminal jurisdiction is in issue. They are that:

(a) the required certificate is not produced, is incomplete, or manifestly does not correspond to the order;

(b) execution of the confiscation order would be contrary to the principle of *ne bis in idem*;

(c) where applicable, there is no double criminality;

(d) there is immunity or privilege under the law of the executing state which would prevent the execution of a domestic confiscation order on the property concerned;

---

[69] Framework Decision, art 3(3).   [70] Framework Decision, art 3(4).

[71] Council Framework Decision 2006/783/JHA of 6 October 2006 on the application of the principle of mutual recognition to confiscation orders, OJ L 328/59, 24.11.2006.

[72] Framework Decision, art 2(c).

[73] Framework Decision, art 2(d).

[74] Framework Decision, art 6.

[75] Framework Decision, art 4. For circumstances in which an order may be sent to more than one Member State, eg where property is located in two or more Member States, see art 5.

(e) the rights of any interested party, including bona fide third parties, under the law of the executing state make it impossible to execute the confiscation order;[76]

(f) according to the certificate, the person concerned did not appear personally and was not represented by a legal counsellor in the proceedings resulting in the confiscation order, unless the certificate states that the person was informed personally, or via his representative competent according to national law, of the proceedings in accordance with the law of the issuing state, or that the person has indicated that he or she does not contest the confiscation order;

(g) the confiscation order is based on criminal proceedings in respect of criminal offences which under the law of the executing state, are regarded as having been committed wholly or partly within its territory, or were committed outside the territory of the issuing state, and the law of the executing state does not permit legal proceedings to be taken in respect of such offences where they are committed outside that state's territory;

(h) the confiscation order was issued in circumstances where confiscation of the property was ordered under extended powers of confiscation which are not those specified in the 2005 Framework Decision;

(i) the execution of a confiscation order is barred by statutory time limitations in the executing state, provided that the acts fall within the jurisdiction of that state under its own criminal law.

Execution may be postponed:

(a) if, in the case of a confiscation order concerning an amount of money, it appears that there is a risk that the total value derived from its execution may exceed the amount specified in the confiscation order because of simultaneous execution of the confiscation order in more than one Member State;

(b) where third parties are pursuing legal remedies to protect their interests;

(c) where the execution of the confiscation order might damage an ongoing criminal investigation or proceedings, until such time as it deems reasonable;

(d) where it is considered necessary to have the confiscation order or parts thereof translated at the expense of the executing state, for the time necessary to obtain its translation; and

(e) where the property is already the subject of confiscation proceedings in the executing state.

Execution of the confiscation order is governed by the law of the executing state provided that a confiscation order issued against a legal person must be executed even if the executing state does not recognize the principle of criminal liability of legal persons.[77]

---

[76] Framework Decision, art 9 gives third parties access to legal remedies.
[77] Framework Decision, art 12.

The Framework Decision is unusually specific in its provisions as to the disposal of confiscated property, which may be varied by agreement between the Member States concerned. In the case of money, if the amount obtained is below € 10,000 or its equivalent, it accrues to the executing state; in other cases, 50 per cent of the amount obtained from the execution must be passed to the issuing state. In the case of other types of property, the property may be sold, and the proceeds dealt with under the rules as to money; or it may be transferred to the issuing state; and if neither course of action is possible, it is to be disposed of under the law of the executing state.[78]

(e) Co-operation between Asset Recovery Offices

In 2004, a group of six countries (Austria, Belgium, Germany, Ireland, the Netherlands, and the United Kingdom) established the Camden Assets Recovery Inter-Agency Network (CARIN) to promote co-operation and the sharing of expertise in this field. In 2007, the EU acted to make this network part of the EU structures and required each Member State to have a designated Asset Recovery Office with an obligation to co-operate with the equivalent bodies in other Member States.[79]

III. United Kingdom provision

It is not possible here to give a full account of the powers of the English courts to order the seizure or forfeiture of the proceeds of crime.[80] An outline will be given of the powers to make the various types of order specified in the international texts and of the specific provisions for international co-operation.

1. The assets recovery function

A major innovation in the Proceeds of Crime Act 2002 was the establishment of the Assets Recovery Agency. This was, however, dissolved in 2008[81] and its work was taken over by the Serious Organised Crime Agency (SOCA), which will in turn be absorbed into a new National Crime Agency in 2013. In 2009/10 SOCA recovered assets worth £317.5 million.

---

[78] Framework Decision, art 16. There is a special rule as to cultural objects forming part of the national heritage of the executing state: art 16(3).

[79] Council Decision 2007/845/JHA of 6 December 2007 concerning cooperation between Asset Recovery Offices of the Member States in the field of tracing and identification of proceeds from, or other property related to, crime, OJ L 332/103, 18.12.2007.

[80] See T Millington and M Sutherland Williams, *The Proceeds of Crime* (3rd edn, OUP, 2010).

[81] By the Serious Crime Act 2007.

2. Interim seizure: restraint orders

Once property has been identified which is believed to represent the proceeds of crime, it is clearly of the greatest importance that it be made subject to some procedure by which its further removal or dissipation is restrained. Many countries have introduced legislation to allow for the making of some kind of 'restraint orders'. In most, such orders are to be sought *ex parte*, without notice; speed and confidentiality are of the essence. It is usually necessary to provide for a limited period of validity, so that either the order expires unless confiscation proceedings are commenced within a prescribed number of days, or it has to be renewed (or is open to challenge) in subsequent *inter partes* proceedings. If the whole of an individual's property is restrained, there must be some provision enabling him to obtain sufficient funds for reasonable living expenses and legal costs. Some countries' legislation makes fairly full provision to safeguard the interests of third parties; others leave such protection to the confiscation stage.

Under the Proceeds of Crime Act 2002, the power to make a restraint order is vested exclusively in the Crown Court. An application is made, usually by an *ex parte* application in chambers, by the prosecutor or an accredited financial investigator.[82] An order may be made if a criminal investigation or proceedings for an offence have been started in England and Wales, provided in each case that there is reasonable cause to believe that the alleged offender has benefited from his criminal conduct, and in certain other cases where applications are pending in connection with confiscation orders.[83] A restraint order prohibits any specified person[84] from dealing with any 'realisable property', subject to such exceptions as may be specified in the order. The Act contemplates exceptions to make provision for reasonable living and reasonable legal expenses, and to enable a trade, business, profession, or occupation to be carried on.[85] The court may appoint a management receiver with powers over the realizable property.[86] An order may also authorize the continued detention of assets already seized under specified legal powers.[87]

A restraint order is a serious interference with the normal rights of a person holding property, and it is provided that the order must be discharged if proposed proceedings are not instituted within such time as the court considers reasonable.[88]

---

[82] Proceeds of Crime Act 2002, s 42 as amended by the Serious Crime Act 2007, Sch 8, para 1.

[83] Proceeds of Crime Act 2002, s 40.

[84] Not just the potential defendant: see (under earlier legislation) *Re TD* [1995] COD 337, applying criteria developed in the civil case of *Arab Monetary Fund v Hashim (No 5)* [1992] 2 All ER 911.

[85] Proceeds of Crime Act 2002, s 41(3).

[86] Proceeds of Crime Act 2002, s 48.

[87] Proceeds of Crime Act 2002, s 41A, inserted by the Policing and Crime Act 2009, s 52 (not yet in force). The latter Act introduces extensive powers for the detention of property pending a court order.

[88] Proceeds of Crime Act 2002, s 42(7).

(a) Property caught by a restraint order

A restraint order may apply to all 'realisable property' held by a specified person, whether the property is described in the order or not, and all realizable property transferred to a specified person after the making of the order. 'Realisable property' means as any 'free property' held by the defendant and any free property held by the recipient of a 'tainted gift'.[89] Property is 'free' unless it is already the subject of certain other orders for forfeiture or deprivation. When these definitions are deciphered it can be seen that the consequences of a restraint order are far-reaching and that persons other than the defendant may be adversely, and quite unfairly, affected.

For example, if A (suspected of being involved in drug trafficking) has given a car to his wife B, not only the car but all of B's other property, from whatever source it came, can be restrained. The policy of the Act is to catch a large category of property pending detailed investigation as to exactly what may properly be subject to confiscation.

It is not just the recipients of gifts from the defendant who may be affected. A person may hold property in which he has only a limited interest, including possession or the right to possession. Almost inevitably an order will in practice catch all property in the possession of the named person, even that belonging to innocent third parties. Other third parties may supply goods or services to the person concerned, unaware of the fact that his assets are frozen and their bills will not be paid. The position of third parties may be eased by the possibility that a restraint order may be discharged or varied in relation to any property on the application of any person affected by the order.[90]

3. Production and disclosure orders

(a) Investigative powers

Part 8 of the Proceeds of Crime Act 2002 creates a wide range of investigative powers, in some cases generalizing powers first created in the terrorism context. They include:

(a) *production orders*, available in confiscation, money laundering, and civil recovery contexts, requiring a named person to produce or give access to material (including computer data) in that person's possession or control;

(b) *disclosure orders*, available in confiscation and civil recovery contexts, requiring a person to disclose information or documents likely to be of substantial value to the investigation;

---

[89] Proceeds of Crime Act 2002, s 83. The notion of 'tainted gift' is a complex one, but includes a gift made by the defendant of property which was obtained by the defendant as a result of or in connection with his general criminal conduct, or which (in whole or part and whether directly or indirectly) represented in the defendant's hands property obtained by him as a result of or in connection with his general criminal conduct: s 77(3).

[90] Proceeds of Crime Act 2002, s 42(3).

(c) *customer information orders*, available in confiscation, money laundering, and civil recovery contexts, requiring a financial institution to provide information about accounts and account holders; and

(d) *account monitoring orders*, available in confiscation, money laundering, and civil recovery contexts, requiring more detailed information about the operation of a specified account.[91]

4. Confiscation orders

An order for the confiscation of property, although an essential weapon in the armoury of law enforcement agencies in this field, does raise a number of legal issues of some complexity, and these may have constitutional implications. These arise out of the practical realities of the case. It is almost inevitable that funds illegally obtained will be mixed, perhaps inextricably mixed, with funds obtained by more orthodox means; it is most unlikely that clear and accurate accounts will be maintained, so that proof of the source of property will often be difficult and may need to be supported by statutory presumptions or reversal of the normal burden of proof; an assortment of third parties will have interests in the funds, some of whom will be wholly innocent of complicity in the criminal enterprise. There will be a range of degrees of independence of the third parties: some will be associates of the criminals, some family members, some corporate bodies wholly or partly controlled (perhaps through a series of nominees and holding companies) by those involved in the offences.

Such an order can be framed in two different ways. It can be an order related primarily to a *person*, making him liable to pay over to the Crown or the state the value of the proceeds of his criminal activities; this type of order is commonly called a 'confiscation order' or, especially in Australian legislation, a 'pecuniary penalty order'. Its principal disadvantage is that it is often enforceable only against the offender's assets: property which belongs to, or is in the possession of, the offender. Unless an extended meaning is given to ownership or possession for this purpose, proceeds held by an associate or relative of the offender, by a 'shell' company, or otherwise removed from his formal entitlement, will escape confiscation.

A more powerful weapon is an order related primarily to *property*, identified as being or as representing the proceeds of crime and declared to be forfeited to the Crown or the state: a 'forfeiture order'. In this case the identity of the person in whose hands the property is found is either immaterial or material only if that person's innocence is established. The range of property subject to seizure is wider, and appropriately so, but there is a corresponding need to devise procedures for the protection of innocent third parties into whose hands the property has been transferred.

A practical consideration, of great importance in considering the relevant merits of these two approaches, is the need to secure international enforcement of orders.

---

[91] For procedural aspects, see Practice Direction, Civil Recovery Proceedings, section 4.

The facility with which assets, particularly in the form of financial credits of some sort, can be passed across national boundaries means that an order enforceable only in the country of origin may be of limited value. It is undoubtedly the case that the 'confiscation order' approach, enforcing a pecuniary penalty against a convicted offender, presents fewer difficulties in this context than forfeiture.

This can be appreciated from the consideration of a case in which a forfeiture order made in State A purports to declare forfeit a corpus of property which includes property (and perhaps land) in State B. In State B legal title to the property is vested in X, a citizen of State B, who has not been the subject of any criminal proceedings. Quite apart from the entrenched approach giving primacy to the *lex situs* in matters of title to property, the attempt to enforce the order in State B and so to seize what is formally X's property will almost certainly raise constitutional arguments about the right to enjoy property, and also about due process. Even if these difficulties are absent, or can be overcome, it is not at all easy to graft procedures for the protection of innocent third parties appearing in State B on the enforcement of what purports to be a final order made in State A.

There is, however, another element in the total picture. Where a jurisdiction has created an offence of money laundering, the effect is that the practical difference between the confiscation order and the forfeiture order approaches is much reduced. The latter approach seeks to reach property held by third parties, linked in some way to the primary offender but not themselves convicted of the primary offence. If, however, such a third party can himself be convicted of money laundering, the confiscation order approach can be applied to him and to the property he controls. And if he can be convicted in State B of laundering the proceeds of a crime which took place in State A, some of the difficulties of international enforcement are circumvented.

(a) Confiscation orders under the Proceeds of Crime Act 2002

The Crown Court's power to make a confiscation order arises whenever a defendant has been convicted in that Court or committed to it for sentence or with a view to a confiscation order being considered, provided that the prosecutor has sought an order or the court has taken the view that it is appropriate to consider the matter.[92]

Once the Crown Court addresses the matter, it must select one of two methods or schemes of criminal compensation. This involves a decision as to whether or not the defendant has a 'criminal lifestyle'. If the court finds such a lifestyle, it must decide whether the defendant has benefited from '*general* criminal conduct'; in the absence of a criminal lifestyle, the focus is on benefit from '*particular* criminal conduct'.[93] In assessing benefit from *general* criminal conduct, account may be

---

[92] Proceeds of Crime Act 2002, s 6. [93] Proceeds of Crime Act 2002, s 6(4).

taken of conduct outside England and Wales which would constitute an offence if committed within England and Wales.[94]

A 'criminal lifestyle' is defined in section 75 of the Act. A defendant has a criminal lifestyle if (and only if) the offence (or any of the offences) concerned is a 'lifestyle offence' (such offences being listed in Schedule 2 and including specified offences involving drug trafficking, money laundering, terrorism, people trafficking, arms trafficking, counterfeiting, violations of intellectual property rights, prostitution, blackmail, or attempting, conspiring, or inciting the commission of any such offences); or it constitutes conduct forming part of a course of criminal activity; or it is an offence committed over a period of at least six months and the defendant has benefited from the conduct which constitutes the offence.

(b) Assumptions as to benefits of a criminal lifestyle

Where the court finds a criminal lifestyle, it must make four assumptions for the purpose of deciding (a) whether the defendant has benefited from general criminal conduct; and (b) the benefit. These assumptions are:

(a) that any property transferred to the defendant within the six years preceding the date on which proceedings were commenced was obtained as a result of general criminal conduct and at the earliest time the defendant appears to have held it;

(b) the same assumption in respect of any property held by the defendant at any time after the date of conviction;

(c) that any expenditure incurred by the defendant within the six-year period was met from general criminal conduct;

(d) for the purpose of valuing the property, that the defendant obtained it free of any other interests in it.

These assumptions, which existed in similar form in earlier legislation, are a controversial feature of the legislation.[95] The earlier legislation was subject to repeated challenges on human rights grounds, especially a suggested incompatibility with article 6.2 of the European Convention on Human Rights, which declares that everyone charged with a criminal offence must be presumed innocent until proved guilty according to law.

In a number of cases, the courts in England (and on similar legislation, Scotland) have held that article 6.2 is inapplicable as the defendant is not in the context of the confiscation aspects of the proceedings 'a person charged with a criminal offence'.

---

[94] Proceeds of Crime Act 2002, s 76(1)(b). In the case of crimes committed by several persons, a confiscation order may be made against any one offender for the full amount, without allocating fractions to individuals: *R v May* [2008] UKHL 28, [2008] 1 AC 1028.

[95] For a comparative study, see the Council of Europe's Committee on Crime Problems Best Practice Survey, *Reversal of the burden of proof in confiscation of the proceeds of crime* (PC-S-CO (2000) 8 Rev), prepared by Professor M Levi.

This has been established in a number of cases before the European Court of Human Rights[96] and affirmed by the Privy Council[97] and the House of Lords.[98]

5. Civil recovery of the proceeds of unlawful conduct

Although proceedings in connection with restraint and confiscation orders are regarded as a civil jurisdiction rather than a criminal matter,[99] Part 5 of the Proceeds of Crime Act 2002 introduced a process for the civil recovery of property obtained by unlawful means, strongly influenced by Irish and other models The new procedure was designed to fill what the Government saw as a gap in the existing provision, comprising cases where it was not possible to obtain a criminal conviction, for evidential reasons, difficulties in identifying which of a large group of individuals was actually guilty of an offence, the residence abroad of the offender in circumstances in which extradition was impossible, or the fact that the offence was committed abroad.

The Act enables the relevant enforcement authority to bring civil proceedings in the High Court (or, in Scotland, the Court of Session) to recover property that is or represents property obtained through unlawful conduct,[100] whether or not proceedings have been brought for an offence in connection with the property.[101] 'Unlawful conduct' includes conduct in the United Kingdom which is unlawful under the criminal law of the part of the United Kingdom in which it occurred; and conduct which occurs in another country and is unlawful under the criminal law of that country, and would be unlawful if it occurred in any part of the United Kingdom.[102] Property is 'obtained through unlawful conduct' if it is obtained by or in return for such conduct, for example by stealing it, or by obtaining it by means of dealing in illicit drugs, or by being paid to commit an offence, or taking a bribe to give false evidence or corruptly award a contract.[103]

Proceedings are begun by a claim form issued in the High Court.[104] A property freezing order may be made to ensure the preservation of the property,[105] as may an interim receiving order.[106] In the main proceedings, if the court finds that property

---

[96] *Phillips v United Kingdom* (1995) 20 EHRR 247; *Grayson and Barnham v United Kingdom* (2008) 48 EHRR 722.

[97] *HM Advocate v McIntosh* [2001] UKPC D1, [2003] 1 AC 1078.

[98] *R v Briggs-Price* [2009] UKHL 19, [2009] AC 1026.

[99] *Government of the United States v Montgomery* [2001] UKHL 3, [2001] 1 WLR 196; *Re O (Disclosure Order)* [1991] 2 QB 520 (CA). For procedural aspects, see Practice Direction, Civil Recovery Proceedings.

[100] Including property, movable or immovable, outside the jurisdiction: *Perry v Serious Organised Crime Agency* [2011] EWCA Civ 578, [2011] 4 All ER 470.

[101] Proceeds of Crime Act 2002, s 343.

[102] Proceeds of Crime Act 2002, s 341.

[103] Proceeds of Crime Act 2002, s 342.

[104] Proceeds of Crime Act 2002, s 343.

[105] Proceeds of Crime Act 2002, s 345A as inserted by the Serious Organised Crime and Police Act 2005, s 98. See also the Proceeds of Crime Act 2002 (Exemptions from Civil Recovery) Order 2003, SI 2003/336 and the Proceeds of Crime Act 2002 (Legal Expenses in Civil Recovery Proceedings) Regulations 2005, SI 2005/3382 as amended by SI 2008/523.

[106] Proceeds of Crime Act 2002, s 346.

is recoverable under the terms of the Act, it must make a recovery order vesting the property in a trustee for civil recovery appointed by the court.

6. Recognition and enforcement of orders

(a) Intra-UK enforcement

Part 11 of the Proceeds of Crime Act 2002 deals with co-operation between jurisdictions. Section 443 enables Orders in Council to be made for restraint orders made in one part of the United Kingdom to be enforced in other parts of the United Kingdom; for the functions of a receiver appointed in one such part to be exercisable in others; and for the authentication of orders made or warrants issued in other parts of the United Kingdom. This power has been exercised by the Proceeds of Crime Act 2002 (Enforcement in different parts of the United Kingdom) Order 2002.[107] Similar provision is made for the enforcement of production orders.[108]

So far as international co-operation is concerned, an Order in Council made under section 444 makes full provision.[109]

(b) External requests

Where an 'external request' (a request by an overseas authority to prohibit dealing with relevant property which is identified in the request)[110] made in connection with criminal investigations or proceedings in the country from which the request was made and concerning relevant property in England or Wales, the Secretary of State may refer it to the Director of Public Prosecutions or the Director of Revenue and Customs Prosecutions, or in certain cases the Director of the Serious Fraud Office to process it.[111] On application, the Crown Court,[112] if satisfied that the request meets the necessary conditions and that there is reasonable cause to believe that the alleged offender named in the request has benefited from his criminal conduct, may make a restraint order,[113] and may also appoint a managing receiver.[114]

---

[107] SI 2002/3133.

[108] Proceeds of Crime Act 2002 (Investigations in different parts of the United Kingdom) Order 2003, SI 2003/425 as amended by SI 2008/298.

[109] Proceeds of Crime Act 2002 (External Requests and Orders) Order 2005, SI 2005/3181 as amended by SI 2008/302.

[110] Proceeds of Crime Act 2002, s 447(1).

[111] Proceeds of Crime Act 2002 (External Requests and Orders) Order 2005, Art 6, as amended by SI 2008/302.

[112] Arrangements can and sometimes should be made to enable the matter to be dealt with by a High Court judge exercising the Crown Court jurisdiction: *Director of the Serious Fraud Office v Lexi Holdings plc* EWCA Crim 1443, [2009] QB 376 at [92]; *Re Stanford International Bank Ltd* [2010] EWCA Civ 137, [2011] Ch 33 at [208]ff.

[113] Proceeds of Crime Act 2002 (External Requests and Orders) Order 2005, Arts 7–9. The restraint order can apply only to property within the jurisdiction: *Serious Fraud Office v King* UKHL 17, [2008] 1 WLR 2634. See *Re Stanford International Bank Ltd* [2010] EWCA Civ 137, [2011] Ch 33 for the procedural complications where other litigation is in train. For hearsay evidence, see art 13; for appeals to the Court of Appeal and the Supreme Court, see arts 10 and 11.

[114] Proceeds of Crime Act 2002 (External Requests and Orders) Order 2005, art 15.

(c) External orders

Where an 'external order' (an order made by an overseas court where property is found or believed to have been obtained as a result of or in connection with criminal conduct, which is for the recovery of specified property or a specified sum of money)[115] has been made arising from a criminal conviction in the country from which the order was sent and concerning relevant property in England or Wales, the Secretary of State may refer it to the Director of Public Prosecutions or the Director of Revenue and Customs Prosecutions, or, in certain cases, to the Director of the Serious Fraud Office to process it.[116] An application may be made by the relevant Director to the Crown Court to give effect to the external order and to register it.[117] The Crown Court must do so if all of the following conditions are satisfied: that the external order was made consequent on the conviction of the person named in the order and no appeal is outstanding in respect of that conviction; that the external order is in force and no appeal is outstanding in respect of it; that giving effect to the external order would not be incompatible with any of the Convention rights (within the meaning of the Human Rights Act 1998) of any person affected by it; and, where the confiscation is to be of property, that property is not already subject to a charge under specified UK legislation.[118] The court may appoint an enforcement receiver.[119] Enforcement in England may be by way of proceedings for civil recovery.[120]

There is also power, not yet exercised, to enable any of the investigatory powers conferred by Part 8 of the 2002 Act to be used for the purposes of the external investigation.[121]

(d) Overseas forfeiture orders

Provision is made in the Criminal Justice (International Co-operation) Act 1990 for the enforcement in the United Kingdom of a slightly different category of order, 'overseas forfeiture orders'. These are orders made in a designated country for the forfeiture, and the destruction or other disposal, of anything in respect of which an offence that corresponds to or is similar to an offence under the law of England has been committed or which was used or intended for use in connection with the commission of such an offence, that is the instrumentalities of the crime.[122] An

---

[115] Proceeds of Crime Act 2002, s 447(2).

[116] Proceeds of Crime Act 2002 (External Requests and Orders) Order 2005, art 18, as amended by SI 2008/302.

[117] Proceeds of Crime Act 2002 (External Requests and Orders) Order 2005, art 20.

[118] Proceeds of Crime Act 2002 (External Requests and Orders) Order 2005, art 21. For registration, see art 22; for appeals to the Court of Appeal and the Supreme Court, see arts 23 and 24.

[119] Proceeds of Crime Act 2002 (External Requests and Orders) Order 2005, art 27.

[120] See Proceeds of Crime Act 2002 (External Requests and Orders) Order 2005, Part 5.

[121] Proceeds of Crime Act 2002, s 445.

[122] Criminal Justice (International Co-operation) Act 1990, s 9(1) (as amended by the Criminal Justice Act 1993, s 21(1)) and (6) (as amended by the Serious Organised Crime and Police Act 2005, s 95).

Order in Council may be made providing for the enforcement of such orders, and may require their registration in a court in the United Kingdom as a condition of that enforcement.[123] The Criminal Justice (International Co-operation) Act 1990 (Enforcement of Overseas Forfeiture Orders) Order 2005[124] sets out the detailed procedure in connection with requests for the purpose of facilitating the enforcement of an external forfeiture order which has yet to be made, and for the enforcement of forfeiture orders which have been made. The provisions are almost identical to those summarized above in connection with external requests and orders. Schedule 2 lists the designated countries to which these provisions apply.[125]

(e) Other cases

So far as terrorism is concerned, similar provision is made in the Terrorism Act 2000 (Enforcement of External Orders) Order 2001[126] in respect of external forfeiture and restraint orders from a smaller group of designated countries.[127] Finally, provision for the enforcement of forfeitures ordered by the International Criminal Court is made by the International Criminal Court Act 2001 (Enforcement of Fines, Forfeitures and Reparation Orders) Regulations 2001.[128]

---

[123] Criminal Justice (International Co-operation) Act 1990, s 9(1)(2).
[124] SI 2005/3180.
[125] Over 160 countries have been designated.
[126] SI 2001/3927.
[127] Austria, Belgium, Canada, Denmark, Finland, France, Germany, Greece, India, Ireland, Italy, Japan, Luxembourg, the Netherlands, Portugal, Spain, Sweden, and the United States.
[128] SI 2001/2379 as amended by SI 2001/822.

10

Criminal Records and the Recognition of Penalties

The growing mobility of people, especially their free movement within large geographical areas such as the European Union, inevitably means that some individuals with criminal convictions will settle in another state. Were such a person to be convicted of further offences in his or her new state of residence, it would plainly be desirable for the court to have information about all relevant previous convictions, including those obtained abroad. Similarly, convicted persons with unpaid fines or who had failed to complete custodial or non-custodial sentences (for example, of community service) or who had been disqualified from certain activities (for example, driving, or holding a gun licence) may move to a new country; the authorities there would prefer to know their history and there may be a wish on the part of the state which imposed the original penalty to see it fully enforced. This chapter examines how these issues can be addressed through mutual assistance and mutual recognition mechanisms. It also looks at another possibility, the transfer of criminal proceedings to another country.

I. Criminal records

1. The Council of Europe Convention

The pioneering European Convention on Mutual Assistance in Criminal Matters 1959[1] contains a number of relevant provisions.

(a) Judicial records

Article 13, the sole article of Chapter IV of the Convention, requires that party to communicate on request extracts from and information relating to judicial records to the judicial authorities in a Contracting Party when needed in a criminal matter. This is subject to the limitation that information may only be disclosed to the same extent that it would be made available to domestic judicial authorities in a similar case.[2]

Where the request does not fall within the terms of article 13(1) it is still to be complied with, but in such cases compliance will be governed by the domestic law, regulations, or practice of the requested state, which will tend to be more restrictive.[3] This implicitly enables requests to be made by non-judicial authorities, or by judicial authorities with no jurisdiction over criminal matters.[4] Article 13 lacks any limits on the extent of the assistance that may be requested or on the nature of the offences to which the request relates, but similarly there is no requirement as to a minimum content for the information provided.[5] This lack of specificity may prove to be a hindrance in some cases, but in others the discretion afforded may encourage co-operation.

(b) Exchange of information on judicial records

As part of the general obligation to provide mutual assistance each Contracting Party is also obliged to inform any other party of all criminal convictions and subsequent measures taken in respect of nationals of that other party which are entered in the judicial records.[6] This information is to be communicated at least

---

[1] ETS No 30. see generally pp 171–177.   [2] Convention, art 13(1).
[3] Convention, art 13(2).   [4] *Explanatory Report*, at p 19.
[5] *PPA*, at p 50.   [6] Convention, art 22.

once a year and, where a person is a national of two or more Contracting Parties, each of these shall be informed unless the person is a national of the state where he or she was convicted.[7] The term 'criminal convictions' is to be given a wide construction and 'subsequent measures' is to be taken as including, in particular, rehabilitation.[8] This obligation is potentially onerous, and is only appropriate in a regional treaty such as the European Convention, where the parties are geographically close and often contiguous.

Article 22 was further developed in the 1978 Additional Protocol. The Protocol requires that where a Contracting Party has supplied information to another party on convictions and related measures under article 22 of the Convention, a copy of the convictions and measures in question as well as any relevant information is to be provided on request in order to enable that party to consider whether any measures at national level are necessary.[9]

(c) Information in connection with proceedings

A further article of the Convention is intended to allow any party to request another to institute proceedings in its own territory against an individual, and is of particular relevance where extradition is for some reason not possible.[10] When information is laid by a Contracting Party with a view to proceedings in the courts of another party, this information is to be transmitted between the Ministers of Justice concerned unless a reservation has been made which permits states to require that information be transmitted other than via this channel.[11] When action is taken on such information the requesting party is to be informed and a copy of the record of any verdict pronounced must be provided.[12] The provisions of article 16 which deal with translation of requests and accompanying documents apply equally in this context.[13]

2. The Commonwealth Scheme

The Commonwealth Scheme contains no specific provisions as to criminal records, but a request under the Scheme may seek assistance in 'providing and producing relevant documents, records, items and other material'.[14] The Scheme avoids dealing with police-to-police co-operation, which may well be more important in this context than more formal assistance.

3. EU action

In a 2000 Communication,[15] the Commission emphasized the importance of the authorities in one Member State being aware of decisions taken in criminal matters

---

[7] Ibid.   [8] *Explanatory Report*, at p 23.   [9] Protocol, art 4.
[10] *Explanatory Report*, at p 23.   [11] Convention, art 21(1).
[12] Convention, art 21(2).   [13] Convention, art 21(3).
[14] Scheme, para 1(5)(e).   [15] COM (2000) 495 final, 26.7.2000.

in other Member States. When it came to prepare a Proposal on a European Evidence Warrant, the Commission initially decided that the same Framework Decision should also deal with records of criminal convictions.[16] The long-drawn-out negotiations on the European Evidence Warrant meant that the criminal records proposal came to be handled separately.[17]

The need to improve the quality of information exchanged on criminal records was emphasized the European Council Declaration on Combating Terrorism of March 2004. At about the same time there was considerable disquiet about some child abuse cases and a notable case involving Michel Fourniret, a Frenchman with a long criminal record who was later employed as a caretaker in a Belgian primary school.

This led to a number of actions by the Commission. In October 2004, it published a Proposal for a Council Decision on the exchange of information extracted from the criminal record.[18] In January 2005, the Commission published a more general White Paper on exchanges of information on convictions and the effect of such convictions in the European Union.[19] Finally, in December 2005 the Commission published a further Proposal on the organization and content of the exchange of information extracted from criminal records between Member States.[20]

The White Paper noted the considerable diversity in how Member States maintained records of convictions, what information was recorded, and for how long it was kept. The system created by the 1959 Convention and its Additional Protocol was seen as not operating efficiently. Although information could be requested from any other Contracting Party, it was often not possible to determine whether an individual had previous convictions without consulting all such states. The process for obtaining information, by means of a mutual assistance request, was seen as cumbersome and unfamiliar and was sometimes thought incompatible with the constraints of the domestic proceedings. It was sometimes difficult for the recipients of information to interpret it, especially as regards the sentences passed. These considerations had prompted the October 2004 Proposal, which was designed solely to make some improvements in the current mechanisms.

---

[16] Proposal for a Council Framework Decision on the European Evidence Warrant for obtaining objects, documents and data for use in criminal proceedings, COM/2003/0688 final, paras 53–5.

[17] Art 4(3) of Framework Decision 2008/978/JHA of 18 December 2008 on the European Evidence Warrant, OJ L 350/72 merely provides that 'Exchange of information on criminal convictions extracted from the criminal record shall be carried out in accordance with Council Decision 2005/876/JHA of 21 November 2005 on the exchange of information extracted from the criminal record and other relevant instruments'.

[18] COM(2004) 664 final, 13.10.2004.

[19] COM(2005) 10 final, 25.1.2005.

[20] COM(2005) 690 final, 22.12.2005.

(a) Council Decision of November 2005

The October 2004 Proposal was adopted by the Council in November 2005.[21] It introduced a system of central authorities in each Member State.[22] Each central authority was required, without delay, to inform the central authorities of the other Member States of criminal convictions and subsequent measures in respect of nationals of those Member States entered in the criminal record.[23] A central authority would also respond to requests for information; a request form was annexed to the Decision for this purpose.[24] The reply was to be sent immediately and, in any event, within a period not exceeding ten working days from the receipt of the request.[25] Requests, replies, and other relevant information could be transmitted by any means capable of producing a written record under conditions allowing the receiving Member State to establish authenticity.[26] Member States were required by the Decision to waive the right to rely among themselves on their reservations to article 13 of the 1959 Convention, but could maintain reservations made with respect to article 22 of that Convention.

(b) Framework Decision of February 2009

The December 2005 Proposal eventually emerged in February 2009 as a Council Framework Decision,[27] which subsumed and repealed the earlier Council Decision. Its declared objectives were (a) to define the ways in which a Member State where a conviction is handed down against a national of another Member State (the 'convicting Member State') transmits the information on such a conviction to the Member State of the convicted person's nationality (the 'Member State of the person's nationality'); (b) to define storage obligations for the Member State of the person's nationality and to specify the methods to be followed when replying to a request for information extracted from criminal records; and (c) to lay down the framework for a computerized system of exchange of information on convictions between Member States.[28]

The Framework Decision retains the system of central authorities,[29] and the ten-day target for replies.[30] Each Member State must take the necessary measures to

---

[21] Council Decision 2005/876/JHA of 21 November 2005 on the exchange of information extracted from the criminal record, OJ L 322/33, 9.12.2005. See J Grijpink, 'Criminal Records in the European Union' (2006) 14 Eur J Crime Crim L & Crim Just 1, examining the difficulties inherent in any system of large-scale information exchange.

[22] Council Decision, art 1.

[23] Council Decision, art 2.

[24] See Council Decision, art 5 for language requirements.

[25] Council Decision, art 3. See also art 4 for conditions on the use of personal data received.

[26] Council Decision, art 3(5).

[27] Council Framework Decision 2009/315/JHA of 26 February 2009 on the organisation and content of the exchange of information extracted from the criminal record between Member States, OJ L 93/23, 7.4.2009.

[28] Framework Decision, art 1.

[29] Framework Decision, art 3.

[30] Framework Decision, art 8.

ensure that all convictions handed down within its territory are accompanied, when provided to its criminal record, by information on the nationality or nationalities of the convicted person if he or she is a national of another Member State. The central authority of the convicting Member State must, as soon as possible, inform the central authorities of the other Member States of any convictions handed down within its territory against the nationals of such other Member States, as entered in the criminal record. Information on subsequent alteration or deletion of information contained in the criminal record must be immediately transmitted by the central authority of the convicting Member State to the central authority of the Member State of the person's nationality.[31] The Member State of nationality must store this information against the possibility of its future re-transmission to a third Member State.[32]

Under this system, the Member State of nationality should have a complete set of information. Article 6 of the Framework Decision enables requests to be made by the central authority of any Member State, or by an individual in respect of his own criminal record. The request must be made using the form annexed to the Framework Decision.[33] When information extracted from the criminal record is requested from the central authority of the Member State of the person's nationality for the purposes of criminal proceedings,[34] that central authority must transmit to the central authority of the requesting Member State information on:

(a) convictions handed down in the Member State of the person's nationality and entered in the criminal record;

(b) any convictions handed down in other Member States which were transmitted to it under the Framework Decision after 27 April 2012 (the date by which the Decision must be implemented);

(c) any convictions handed down in other Member States which were transmitted to it by 27 April 2012, and entered in the criminal record; and

(d) any convictions handed down in third countries and subsequently transmitted to it and entered in the criminal record.[35]

When information extracted from the criminal record is requested from the central authority of a Member State other than the Member State of the person's nationality, the requested Member State must transmit information on convictions handed down in the requested Member State and on convictions handed down against third country nationals and against stateless persons contained in its criminal record to the same extent as provided for in article 13 of the European Convention on Mutual Assistance in Criminal Matters of 1959.[36]

---

[31] Framework Decision, art 4.   [32] Framework Decision, art 5.

[33] Framework Decision, art 6(4).

[34] Defined to mean the pre-trial stage, the trial stage itself, and the execution of the conviction: Framework Decision, art 2(b). For restrictions on the use of information supplied for any purpose other than criminal proceedings, see art 7(2) and (3).

[35] Framework Decision, art 7(1). See arts 9 (conditions for the use of personal data) and 10 (language requirements).

[36] Framework Decision, art 7(4).

The main innovation is the detailed regulation of the format and content of information. This is set out in article 11 and in a separate but related Council Decision on the establishment of the European Criminal Records Information System.[37] The Recitals to the latter describe the European Criminal Records System as a decentralized information technology system. The criminal records data are stored solely in databases operated by Member States, with no direct online access to criminal records databases of other Member States. The common communication infrastructure of the system is initially the Trans European Services for Telematics between Administrations (S-TESTA) network. The Decision sets out reference tables of categories of offences and categories of penalties and measures using a system of codes to facilitate the mutual understanding of the information.[38]

Like its predecessor, the Framework Decision requires Member States to waive the right to rely among themselves on their reservations to article 13 of the 1959 Convention. Unlike its predecessor, it does replace as between the Member States article 22 of that Convention.[39]

(c) Making use of information: the effect of prior convictions

The 2005 White Paper on exchanges of information on convictions and the effect of such convictions in the European Union[40] asserted that 'there is no point in improving the quality of exchanges of information on convictions unless this information can actually be used'.[41] It noted a number of ways in which a conviction in one Member State might impact on the law of the other Member States: they might affect the rules governing prosecution (eg, type of procedure applicable, rules on pre-trial detention); the trial procedure (eg, choice of court); definition of the offence and choice of sentence (eg, it might be impossible to give a suspended sentence to persons with previous convictions); sentence enforcement (arrangements for early release or adjusting the conditions of imprisonment may be different for persons with previous convictions); and the possibility of sentences running concurrently.[42]

After some years of debate agreement was reached on a Council Framework Decision on the subject.[43] Its declared purpose is to determine the conditions under which, in the course of criminal proceedings in a Member State against a person, previous convictions handed down against the same person for different facts[44] in

---

[37] Council Decision 2009/316/JHA of 6 April 2009 on the establishment of the European Criminal Records Information System (ECRIS) in application of Article 11 of Framework Decision 2009/315/JHA, OJ L 93/33, 7.4.2009.

[38] Council Decision, recitals (11) and (12).

[39] Framework Decision, art 12.

[40] COM(2005) 10 final, 25.1.2005.

[41] White Paper, para 26.

[42] White Paper, paras 31 ff.

[43] Council Framework Decision 2008/675/JHA of 24 July 2008 on taking account of convictions in the Member States of the European Union in the course of new criminal proceedings, OJ L 220/32, 15.8.2008. It was to be implemented by Member States by 15 August 2010.

[44] So the principle of *ne bis in idem* which involves the same facts is not affected.

other Member States are taken into account.[45] A conviction is defined to mean any final decision of a criminal court establishing guilt of a criminal offence.[46] The essential principle is set out in article 3(1):

Each Member State shall ensure that in the course of criminal proceedings against a person, previous convictions handed down against the same person for different facts in other Member States, in respect of which information has been obtained under applicable instruments on mutual legal assistance or on the exchange of information extracted from criminal records, are taken into account to the extent previous national convictions are taken into account, and that equivalent legal effects are attached to them as to previous national convictions, in accordance with national law.

This principle is to apply at the pre-trial stage, at the trial stage itself, and at the time of execution of the conviction, in particular with regard to the applicable rules of procedure, including those relating to provisional detention, the definition of the offence, the type and level of the sentence, and the rules governing the execution of the decision.[47] Its application is not to have the effect of interfering with, revoking, or reviewing previous convictions or any decision relating to their execution by the Member State conducting the new proceedings.[48]

The Framework Decision replaces article 56 of the European Convention of 28 May 1970 on the International Validity of Criminal Judgments as between the Member States parties to that Convention.[49]

II. Recognition and enforcement of criminal penalties

The common law tradition has for centuries been opposed to any enforcement of a penal law of a foreign state.[50] The breadth of this principle was explained by Gray J in the United States Supreme Court in *Wisconsin v Pelican Insurance Co*:[51]

The rule that the courts of no country execute the law of another applies not only to prosecutions and sentences for crimes and misdemeanors, but to all suits in favour of the state for the recovery of pecuniary penalties for any violation of statutes for the protection of its revenue or other municipal laws, and to all judgments for such penalties.

This dictum was expressly approved by the Judicial Committee of the Privy Council in *Huntington v Attrill*.[52]

The position was restated by the Court of Appeal in *United States of America v Inkley*.[53] Mr Inkley, a British subject, was arrested in 1983 in the State of Florida and charged with fraud offences involving the sale of non-existent oil wells. He was given bail and entered into a bond for US$48,000, of which 10 per cent was put down as a deposit. After the death of Mr Inkley's father, he was given permission by

---

[45] Framework Decision, art 1(1).   [46] Framework Decision, art 2.
[47] Framework Decision, art 3(2).   [48] Framework Decision, art 3(3),(4).
[49] Framework Decision, art 4. See p 330, below.
[50] See Dicey Morris and Collins, *The Conflict of Laws* (14th edn, 2006), para 5–019 et seq.
[51] (1887) 127 US 265.   [52] [1893] AC 150, 157.   [53] [1989] QB 255 (CA).

a court in Florida to travel to England for the funeral. He never returned to the United States and a judgment was obtained against him in a United States District Court, sitting as a civil rather than a criminal court, for US$48,000 plus interest. Proceedings were brought in England to enforce that judgment, by way of an action upon it.

In the High Court, Gatehouse J held that the proceedings were civil proceedings and enforceable by action in the English courts. The Court of Appeal accepted the argument advanced on Mr Inkley's behalf, that the substance of the action was the enforcement of a public law remedy in the nature of a penal proceeding and, therefore, would not be enforceable in the English courts. Having reviewed the authorities, the Court set out a number of propositions:

(1) the consideration of whether the claim sought to be enforced in the English courts is one which involves the assertion of foreign sovereignty, whether it be penal, revenue or other public law, is to be determined according to the criteria of English law; (2) that regard will be had to the attitude adopted by the courts in the foreign jurisdiction which will always receive serious attention and may on occasions be decisive; (3) that the category of the right of action, ie whether public or private, will depend on the party in whose favour it is created, on the purpose of the law or enactment in the foreign state on which it is based and on the general context of the case as a whole; (4) that the fact that the right, statutory or otherwise, is penal in nature will not deprive a person, who asserts a personal claim depending thereon, from having recourse to the courts of this country; on the other hand, by whatever description it may be known if the purpose of the action is the enforcement of a sanction, power or right at the instance of the state in its sovereign capacity, it will not be entertained; (5) that the fact that in the foreign jurisdiction recourse may be had in a civil forum to enforce the right will not necessarily affect the true nature of the right being enforced in this country.

In the *Inkley* case, the bond came into existence in a criminal context; its whole purpose was to secure the attendance of the accused at a criminal trial.

This may be contrasted with a number of cases in which regulatory authorities in foreign countries seek the disgorgement of sums obtained by fraud with a view to returning the ill-gotten sums to those who had been defrauded. Even though a public body is acting, this type of case does not amount to enforcement of a foreign penal law.[54]

However, the principle of the non-enforcement of foreign penal law is now the subject of significant exceptions. Co-operation in mutual assistance in criminal matters comes close to breaching the principle. It is certainly set aside where international legal instruments require a state to recognize a foreign criminal judgment; where a prisoner is transferred to serve his or her sentence in a state other than that in which the sentence was imposed; and to some extent where criminal proceedings are transferred from one country to another.

---

[54] *United States Securities and Exchange Commission v Manterfield* [2009] EWCA Civ 27, [2010] 1 WLR 172. See also *Iran (Government of) v Barakat Galleries Ltd* [2007] EWCA Civ 1374, [2009] QB 22.

1. The work of the Council of Europe

The Additional Protocol of 1978 to the European Convention on Mutual Assistance in Criminal Matters touched on this matter. It extended the provision of mutual assistance into areas concerned with the enforcement of penalties. So, the Convention was extended to cover:

(a) the service of documents concerning the enforcement of a sentence, the recovery of a fine or the payment of costs of proceedings; and

(b) measures relating to the suspension of pronouncement of sentence or its enforcement, conditional release, deferment of the commencement of the enforcement of a sentence or the interruption of such enforcement.[55]

The measures only fall within the scope of the Convention if they are taken by judicial authorities.

2. European Convention on the Supervision of Conditionally Sentenced or Conditionally Released Offenders

Other aspects of mutual co-operation in respect of penalties had been addressed in two conventions negotiated under the auspices of the Council of Europe. The first, the European Convention on the Supervision of Conditionally Sentenced or Conditionally Released Offenders of 1964[56] had nineteen Contracting States in January 2012, not including the United Kingdom; ten were Member States of the EU and in their mutual dealings the Convention is being replaced by an EU Framework Decision considered below.[57] Under this, relatively simple, Convention the Contracting Parties undertake to grant each other the mutual assistance necessary for the social rehabilitation of the offenders to which it applies. This assistance takes the form of supervision designed to facilitate the good conduct and re-adaptation to social life of such offenders and to keep a watch on their behaviour with a view, should it become necessary, either to pronouncing sentence on them or to enforcing a sentence already pronounced.[58] The offenders to which the Convention applies include those who have 'been found guilty by a court and placed on probation without sentence having been pronounced',[59] language which does not fit those systems in which probation is seen as a sentence.

3. European Convention on the International Validity of Criminal Judgments of 1970

The second and broader convention was the European Convention on the International Validity of Criminal Judgments[60] agreed in May 1970. The original

---

[55] Additional Protocol, art 3.   [56] CETS No 51.   [57] See p 340 ff.
[58] Convention, art 1.   [59] Convention, art 2.
[60] ETS No 70. By 2012 the Convention had 22 parties, not including the United Kingdom.

impetus for the work came from a meeting of the European Committee on Crime Problems held in 1961 to discuss recidivism. The starting point was that the development of criminality in modern society and the necessity of combating it by collaboration across frontiers meant that national sovereignty should no longer be an obstacle to the recognition of the legal effects of foreign judgments in criminal matters. Those effects might be negative, where there had been an acquittal. It was early decided not to include orders for damages or restitution made in criminal proceedings and not to tackle the difficult issue of different limitation periods in national criminal law.[61] The Convention applies to sanctions involving deprivation of liberty, fines or confiscation, and disqualifications.[62]

(a) Enforcement

Where a sanction imposed in one Contracting State is enforceable in that state it may be enforced in another Contracting State after a request by the state of origin ('the sentencing state') and subject to the various conditions laid down in the Convention.[63] The sanction is not to be enforced unless under the law of the state in which enforcement is sought the act for which the sanction was imposed would be an offence[64] if committed on its territory and the person on whom the sanction was imposed would be liable to punishment if he or she had committed the act there.[65]

A request for enforcement in another Contracting State may be made only if one or more of the following conditions are fulfilled:

(a) the person sentenced is ordinarily resident in the other state;

(b) the enforcement of the sanction in the other state is likely to improve the prospects for the social rehabilitation of the person sentenced;

(c) in the case of a sanction involving deprivation of liberty, the sanction could be enforced following the enforcement of another sanction involving deprivation of liberty which the person sentenced is undergoing or is to undergo in the other state;

(d) the other state is the state of origin of the person sentenced and has declared itself willing to accept responsibility for the enforcement of that sanction;

(e) the sentencing state considers that it cannot itself enforce the sanction, even by having recourse to extradition, and that the other state can.[66]

The Convention makes detailed provision for the effect of the transfer of enforcement, including the effect on the running of limitation periods;[67] the limited capacity of the state of enforcement to commence proceedings in respect

---

[61] The history of the negotiations is fully set out in the *Explanatory Report* to the Convention.

[62] Convention, art 2. 'Disqualification' is defined (art 1) to mean any loss or suspension of a right or any prohibition or loss of legal capacity.

[63] Convention, art 3.

[64] It need not be an offence of the same name or the same scope.

[65] Convention, art 4(1).   [66] Convention, art 5.   [67] Convention, art 8.

of any offence committed before the date of the surrender of the person concerned to that state;[68] and the inability of the sentencing state to continue to enforce the sanction unless in certain circumstances the right to enforce is returned to it.[69] Provisional measures may be taken when necessary, including the arrest of the person concerned and the provisional seizure of goods.[70]

Enforcement is governed by the law of the requested state.[71] However, article 37 provides that a sanction imposed in the requesting state shall not be enforced in the requested state except by a decision of the court of the requested state. Each Contracting State may, however, empower other authorities to take such decisions if the sanction to be enforced is only a fine or a confiscation and if these decisions are susceptible of appeal to a court. Before a court takes a decision upon a request for enforcement the sentenced person must be given the opportunity to state his or her views. Upon application he or she must be heard by the court either by Letters Rogatory or in person; a hearing in person must be granted following that person's express request to that effect.[72] There must be a right of appeal to a higher court.[73]

The requested state alone is competent to take all appropriate decisions, such as those concerning conditional release.[74] The requesting state alone has the right to decide on any application for review of sentence,[75] but either state may exercise the right of amnesty or pardon.[76] If the sanction ceases to be enforceable in the sentencing state, whether because of a pardon, amnesty, or review of sentence or because a fine has been paid, enforcement in the requested state must cease.[77] Contracting States are not to claim from each other the refund of any expenses resulting from the application of the Convention.[78]

(b) Procedure for requests

Requests under the Convention are to be made in writing and sent either by the Ministry of Justice of the requesting state to the Ministry of Justice of the requested state or, if the Contracting States so agree, direct by the authorities of the requesting state to those of the requested state; in urgent cases, requests and communications may be sent through the International Criminal Police Organization (Interpol).[79] No provision is made for the offender to be consulted in any way.

---

[68] Convention, art 9.
[69] Convention, art 11.
[70] Convention, arts 31–6.
[71] See art 13 for the regime applying while a person in custody is in transit through a third Contracting State.
[72] Convention, arts 38, 39. For the matters to be considered, see art 40. The requested state is bound by the findings as to the facts in so far as they are stated in the decision or in so far as it is impliedly based on them; art 42.
[73] Convention, art 41.
[74] Convention, art 10(1).
[75] Convention, art 10(2).
[76] Convention, art 10(3).
[77] Convention, art 12.
[78] Convention, art 14.
[79] Convention, art 15. See arts 16–20 for details as to the documentation required.

(c) Grounds for refusal

The Convention sets out[80] an exclusive list of the grounds upon which enforcement may be refused, in whole or in part. These are:

   (a) where enforcement would run counter to the fundamental principles of the legal system of the requested state;

   (b) where the requested state considers the offence for which the sentence was passed to be of a political nature or a purely military one;

   (c) where the requested state considers that there are substantial grounds for believing that the sentence was brought about or aggravated by considerations of race, religion, nationality, or political opinion;

   (d) where enforcement would be contrary to the international undertakings of the requested state;

   (e) where the act is already the subject of proceedings in the requested state or where the requested state decides to institute proceedings in respect of the act;

   (f) where the competent authorities in the requested state have decided not to take proceedings or to drop proceedings already begun, in respect of the same act;

   (g) where the act was committed outside the territory of the requesting state;

   (h) where the requested state is unable to enforce the sanction;

   (i) where the request is grounded on the belief of the sentencing state that it cannot itself enforce the sanction and that the requested state can, and none of the other conditions mentioned in article 5 is fulfilled;

   (j) where the requested state considers that the requesting state is itself able to enforce the sanction;

   (k) where the age of the person sentenced at the time of the offence was such that he could not have been prosecuted in the requested state;

   (l) where under the law of the requested state the sanction imposed can no longer be enforced because of the lapse of time;[81]

   (m) where, and to the extent that, the sentence imposes a disqualification.

A request for enforcement must be refused if enforcement would run counter to the principle *ne bis in idem* as set out in articles 53 to 55 of the Convention.[82]

---

[80] Convention, art 6.

[81] The lapse of time may be relevant to the bringing of the prosecution or the enforcement of the sanction.

[82] Convention, art 7. See p 330, below.

(d) What is enforced

The enforcement of a sanction imposed under another system of law is by no means straightforward. Explanatory Report on the Convention explains the practical issues in its commentary on article 44:

The law in some of [the States of the Council of Europe] is based on a threefold division of penalties entailing deprivation of freedom (penal servitude, imprisonment and detention). Other States have only a twofold division; still other States have only one. While enforcement of a particular judgment in a State which has the same division of sanctions as the sentencing State usually raises no difficulties of adaptation, this is not so where the two States concerned have different systems.

Moreover, the legal framework in which a sanction may be imposed for a particular offence varies appreciably from one State to another; this is also true of the legal minimum and maximum length for a particular kind of sanction. It follows that a sanction imposed in the requesting State may, for example:

(a) exceed the maximum laid down for the same offence or even for the same kind of sanction in the law of the requested State;

(b) be below the minimum laid down in that law;

(c) not apply to the offence in question under that law or by reason of the nature of the sanction;

(d) even be non-existent (as a type of sanction) in the system of the requested State.

Lastly, some laws attach to certain judgments automatic effects which are unknown or merely optional in the legal systems of other States.

The Convention has, therefore, to make careful provision for the 'translation' of sanctions to fit the requirements of the requested state.

In the case of custodial sentences, the court in the requested state must impose a sanction prescribed by its own law for the same offence. This sanction may be of a nature or duration other than that imposed in the requesting state, provided that the effect is not to 'aggravate the penal situation of the person sentenced' as it results from the decision delivered in the requesting state. If the sanction originally imposed is less than the minimum which may be pronounced under the law of the requested state, the court is not bound by that minimum and must impose a sanction corresponding to the sanction imposed in the requesting state.[83] The converse case, where the original sentence exceeds the maximum prescribed in the requested state, is the subject of a possible declaration by Contracting States. The effect is that the maximum may be ignored, but only if the law of the requested state 'allows, in respect of the same offence, for the imposition of a sanction of at least the same duration as that imposed in the requesting state but which is of a more severe nature'.[84] The Explanatory Report gives the example of a requested state, the law of which provides a sanction of 'reclusion' of up to ten years for a certain offence: the declaration would allow it to enforce a foreign sanction of four

---

[83] Convention, art 44(1)(2). Time already spent in custody is taken into account: art 44(3).
[84] Convention, art 44(4).

years' imprisonment, even if according to its law the maximum *imprisonment* is two years.

Similar principles apply to monetary penalties.[85] The amount is converted into the currency of the requested state at the rate of exchange ruling at the time when the enforcement decision is taken. The resulting amount must not exceed the maximum sum fixed by the law of the requested state for the same offence, or failing such a maximum, the maximum amount customarily imposed in the requested state in respect of a similar offence.[86] If the sanction imposed in the requesting state is not available in the requested state, or exceeds the maximum set there, it may still be enforced at the original level if the law of the requested state allows for the imposition of more severe sanctions, such as imprisonment.[87] The proceeds of fines and confiscations are to be paid into the public funds of the requested state without prejudice to any rights of third parties.[88]

(e) *Judgments rendered* in absentia *and* ordonnances pénales

Those who negotiated the Convention were much concerned about the enforcement of judgments rendered *in absentia* and of *ordonnances pénales*. In neither case is the defendant directly heard. A judgment *in absentia* for the purposes of the Convention includes any judgment rendered by a court in a Contracting State after criminal proceedings at the hearing of which the sentenced person was not personally present;[89] this is a very broad definition as it includes cases where the accused is represented by counsel but excused personal attendance.

In general, the rules of the Convention apply to such judgments and *ordonnances*,[90] but there are some special provisions. Any judgment rendered *in absentia* and any *ordonnances pénales* which have not yet been the subject of appeal or opposition may, as soon as they have been rendered and even if they have not become enforceable in the sentencing state, be transmitted to the requested state for the purpose of notification and with a view to enforcement.[91] If the requested state sees fit to take action on the request to enforce a judgment rendered *in absentia* or an *ordonnance pénale*, it must cause the person sentenced to be personally notified of the decision rendered in the requesting state, informing him or her that the only remedy available is an 'opposition' under article 24 to be examined by the competent court in the requesting state or, if the person concerned so wishes, by the court in the requested state; and that, if no opposition is lodged within thirty

---

[85] For disqualifications, see arts 49–52.

[86] Convention, art 45(1). For the effect of arrangements for delayed or instalment payments, see art 45(3); for the procedure when the requested state finds it impossible to collect the fine and wishes to impose an alternative sanction, see art 48.

[87] Convention, art 45(2).

[88] Convention, art 47(1).

[89] Convention, art 21(2); see the minor exceptions in art 21(3).

[90] Convention, art 21(1).

[91] Convention, art 22.

days, the judgment will, for the entire purposes of this Convention, be considered as having been rendered after a hearing of the accused.[92]

(f) Ne bis in idem

The Convention gives effect to this principle, providing that a person in respect of whom a European criminal judgment has been rendered may for the same act neither be prosecuted nor sentenced nor subjected to enforcement of a sanction in another Contracting State if he or she was acquitted; if the sanction imposed has been completely enforced or is being enforced, or has been wholly, or with respect to the part not enforced, the subject of a pardon or an amnesty, or can no longer be enforced because of lapse of time; or if the court convicted the offender without imposing a sanction.[93] There are two exceptions both of which apply unless the Contracting State concerned had itself requested the original proceedings: a Contracting State is not obliged to recognize the effect of *ne bis in idem* if the act which gave rise to the judgment was directed against either a person or an institution or anything having public status in that state, or if the subject of the judgment had himself a public status in that state;[94] or if the act was committed in that Contracting State (or was considered as such according to the law of that state).[95]

(g) *Taking into consideration*

In many legal systems, a previous criminal record and the sentences imposed are relevant for other purposes, especially when further offences are committed and the issue arises whether the offender is to be classed as a recidivist, as an habitual offender, or does or does not qualify for concessions such as the suspension of a sentence. The Convention does little more than recognize this reality, providing merely that each Contracting State may legislate on the matter as it deems appropriate.[96]

4. EU action

(a) *Early conventions*

Two Conventions between the Member States of the European Communities addressed issues similar to those in the 1970 text.[97] The first, agreed in Brussels in May 1987, was a Convention on Double Jeopardy. It was signed but not ratified by the United Kingdom. It had to be ratified by all the then Member States: as only nine states did so, the Convention never came into force. The *ne bis in idem*

---

[92] Convention, arts 23, 24. The opposition is dealt with under the procedures set out in arts 25–30.
[93] Convention, art 53(1).   [94] Convention, art 53(2).   [95] Convention, art 53(3).
[96] Convention, arts 56, 57.   [97] Neither was published in the *Official Journal.*

principle was the subject of provisions in the Schengen Implementation Convention of 19 June 1990.[98] Articles 54 to 58 of that Convention contain provisions based upon, and often identical to, the Double Jeopardy Convention of 1987.

The second convention of this type was the Convention on the Enforcement of Foreign Criminal Sentences of 13 November 1991. It was intended in part to supplement the provisions of the 1970 Convention and facilitate its application.[99] It also remained a dead letter: ratification by all the then Member States was required to bring it into force and only three ratifications were made, the United Kingdom not even signing the Convention.

(b) After the Treaty of Amsterdam

The matter attracted renewed attention after the Council and Commission, in their Action Plan on how best to implement the provisions of the Treaty of Amsterdam on an area of freedom, security, and justice, identified the facilitation of mutual recognition of decisions and the enforcement of judgments in criminal matters as something to be addressed within two years of the entry into force of the Treaty.[100] This marked a change of focus from mutual assistance to mutual recognition. The argument was summarized in a Communication from the Commission in July 2000.[101]

Traditional judicial cooperation in criminal matters is based on a variety of international legal instruments, which are overwhelmingly characterised by what one might call the 'request'-principle: One sovereign state makes a request to another sovereign state, who then determines whether it will or will not comply with this request. Sometimes, the rules on compliance are rather strict, not leaving much of a choice; on other occasions, the requested state is quite free in its decision. In almost all cases, the requesting state must await the reply to its request before it gets what its authorities need in order to pursue a criminal case.

This traditional system is not only slow, but also cumbersome, and sometimes it is quite uncertain what results a judge or prosecutor who makes a request will get. Thus, borrowing from concepts that have worked very well in the creation of the Single Market, the idea was born that judicial cooperation might also benefit from the concept of mutual recognition, which, simply stated, means that once a certain measure, such as a decision taken by a judge in exercising his or her official powers in one Member State, has been taken, that measure—in so far as it has extra-national implications—would automatically be accepted in all other Member States, and have the same or at least similar effects there.

The Commission recognized that this was a novel area and that what might sound simple was indeed very tricky when one began to look at the details. The Tampere European Council in October 1999 had in fact already concluded that mutual recognition should become the cornerstone of judicial co-operation in both civil and criminal matters within the EU. A programme of measures to implement the

---

[98] See OJ L 239, 22.09.2000.   [99] See art 20.
[100] Action Plan, OJ C19, 23.01.1999, para 45(f).   [101] COM/2000/0495 final.

principle of mutual recognition of decisions in criminal matters was agreed by the European Council on 29 November 2000.[102] Justice issues featured in the successive programmes, the Hague Programme of 2004 and the Stockholm Programme of 2009.[103] Specific decisions took some time to negotiate.

5. The Framework Decision on financial penalties

The first of these, agreed in February 2005, was a Council Framework on the application of the principle of mutual recognition to financial penalties.[104] Although the term 'financial penalty' will in many cases be a fine imposed by a criminal court, the scope of the Framework Decision is considerably wider. It also applied to a final decision requiring a financial penalty to be paid where the decision was made (a) by an authority of the issuing state other than a court in respect of a criminal offence under the law of the issuing state, provided that the person concerned has had an opportunity to have the case tried by a court having jurisdiction in particular in criminal matters (for example, a fixed penalty notice where the recipient has the option of going to court); (b) by an authority of the issuing state other than a court in respect of acts which are punishable under the national law of the issuing state 'by virtue of being infringements of the rules of law', with the same proviso; and (c) by a court having jurisdiction in particular in criminal matters, where the decision was made regarding a decision as referred to in (b) above. Penalties imposed on legal persons are included.[105]

'Financial penalty' is also given an extensive definition. It means the obligation to pay:

(a) a sum of money on conviction of an offence imposed in a decision;

(b) compensation imposed in the same decision for the benefit of victims, where the victim may not be a civil party to the proceedings and the court is acting in the exercise of its criminal jurisdiction;

(c) a sum of money in respect of the costs of court or administrative proceedings leading to the decision; or

(d) a sum of money to a public fund or a victim support organization, imposed in the same decision.

---

[102] OJ C 12/10, 15.01.2001.

[103] See generally the Seventh Report of Session 2009–10 of the House of Commons Justice Committee, *Justice issues in Europe* (HC 162) and the Communication from the Commission 'Delivering an area of freedom, security and justice for Europe's citizens', the Action Plan Implementing the Stockholm Programme, COM/2010/0171 final, 2.12.2010.

[104] Council Framework Decision 2005/214/JHA of 24 February 2005 on the application of the principle of mutual recognition to financial penalties, OJ L 76/16, 22.3.2005. Member States were to implement the Decision by 22 March 2007, with some extensions to deal with special aspects: art 22. See a Report from the Commission on its implementation: COM(2008) 888 final, 22.12.2008.

[105] Framework Decision, art 1. A financial penalty imposed on a legal person shall be enforced even if the executing state does not recognize the principle of criminal liability of legal persons: art 9(3).

It is made clear that the term 'financial penalty' does not include orders for the confiscation of instrumentalities or proceeds of crime, and orders that have a civil nature and arise out of a claim for damages and restitution.[106]

Each Member State is required to designate the authority or authorities which are 'competent authorities' for the purposes of the Framework Decision. The default system is therefore a decentralized one. However a more centralized system may be adopted by individual Member States. A Member State may, if it is necessary as a result of the organization of its internal system, designate one or more Central Authorities to be responsible for the administrative transmission and reception of the decisions and to assist the competent authorities.[107]

The usual procedure, where a Central Authority is not used, is for a decision to be transmitted by the competent authority in the issuing state directly to the competent authority in the executing state, the state in which the natural or legal person against whom a decision has been passed has property or income, is normally resident, or, in the case of a legal person, has its registered seat. Transmission may be by any means which leaves a written record under conditions allowing the executing state to establish its authenticity. The decision must be accompanied by a Certificate in a form specified in the Annex to the Framework Decision.[108]

The contact points of the European Judicial Network may be used if there are difficulties in identifying the correct competent authority in the state of execution.[109] A special provision applying to the United Kingdom and Ireland allows those states to make a declaration requiring the decision and certificate to be sent via its central authority.[110]

Article 5 deals with the vexed issue of double criminality. In some cases, the executing state may make the recognition and execution of a decision subject to the condition that the decision is related to conduct which would constitute an offence under the law of the executing state, whatever the constituent elements or however it is described.[111] This possibility is, however, excluded for a long list of offences ranging from terrorism to breach of road traffic regulations; the list is specified in the Framework Decision but may be amended by the Council.[112]

---

[106] Enforceable under Council Regulation (EC) No 44/2001 of 22 December 2000 on jurisdiction and the recognition and enforcement of judgments in civil and commercial matters, OJ L 12/1, 16.1.2001.

[107] Framework Decision, art 2.

[108] For language requirements, see Framework Decision, art 16.

[109] Framework Decision, art 4.

[110] Framework Decision, art 4(7). Once a decision is transmitted, it may not be executed by the issuing state unless and until the executing power reverts to that state in circumstances set out in art 15.

[111] Framework Decision, art 5(3).

[112] See Framework Decision, art 5(1),(2). The prescribed list is: participation in a criminal organization; terrorism: trafficking in human beings; sexual exploitation of children and child pornography; illicit trafficking in narcotic drugs and psychotropic substances; illicit trafficking in weapons, munitions, and explosives; corruption; fraud, including that affecting the financial interests of the European Communities; laundering of the proceeds of crime; counterfeiting currency, including of the euro; computer-related crime; environmental crime, including illicit trafficking in endangered animal species and in endangered plant species and varieties; facilitation of unauthorized entry and residence; murder; grievous bodily injury; illicit trade in human organs and tissue; kidnapping, illegal restraint, and hostage-taking; racism and xenophobia; organized or armed robbery; illicit trafficking in cultural

The competent authorities in the executing state must recognize a decision duly transmitted without any further formality being required and must take 'forthwith' all the necessary measures for its execution.[113] This is subject to a limited number of grounds for non-recognition or non-execution:

(a) if the required certificate is not produced, is incomplete, or manifestly does not correspond to the decision;

(b) if it is established that a decision against the sentenced person in respect of the same acts has been delivered in the executing state or in any state other than the issuing or the executing state, and, in the latter case, that decision has been executed;

(c) in cases in which double criminality is insisted upon, the decision relates to acts which would not constitute an offence under the law of the executing state;

(d) the execution of the decision is statute-barred according to the law of the executing state and the decision relates to acts which fall within the jurisdiction of that state under its own law;

(e) the decision relates to acts which are regarded by the law of the executing state as having been committed in whole or in part in the territory of the executing state or in a place treated as such, or have been committed outside the territory of the issuing state and the law of the executing state does not allow prosecution for the same offences when committed outside its territory;

(f) there is immunity under the law of the executing state, which makes it impossible to execute the decision;

(g) the decision has been imposed on a natural person who under the law of the executing state due to his or her age could not yet have been held criminally liable for the acts in respect of which the decision was passed;

(h) the financial penalty is below €70 or its equivalent.

There was a good deal of discussion in relation to the Framework Decision and other instruments of the rules which should apply when the person concerned did not appear in person at a trial. As a Recitals in an amending Framework

---

goods, including antiques and works of art; swindling; racketeering and extortion; counterfeiting and piracy of products; forgery of administrative documents and trafficking therein; forgery of means of payment; illicit trafficking in hormonal substances and other growth promoters; illicit trafficking in nuclear or radioactive materials; trafficking in stolen vehicles; rape; arson; crimes within the jurisdiction of the International Criminal Court; unlawful seizure of aircraft or ships; sabotage; conduct which infringes road traffic regulations, including breaches of regulations pertaining to driving hours and rest periods and regulations on hazardous goods; smuggling of goods; infringements of intellectual property rights; threats and acts of violence against persons, including violence during sport events; criminal damage; theft; offences established by the issuing state and serving the purpose of implementing obligations arising from instruments adopted under the EC Treaty or under Title VI of the EU Treaty.

[113] Framework Decision, art 6.

Decision of 2009[114] explained, 'The various Framework Decisions implementing the principle of mutual recognition of final judicial decisions do not deal consistently with the issue of decisions rendered following a trial at which the person concerned did not appear in person. This diversity could complicate the work of the practitioner and hamper judicial cooperation.' New provisions were introduced which allow non-execution in these cases:

(a) according to the certificate provided, the person concerned in case of a written procedure was not, in accordance with the law of the issuing state, informed personally or via a representative, competent according to national law, of the right to contest the case and of time limits of such a legal remedy;

(b) according to the certificate provided, the person did not appear in person at the trial resulting in the decision, unless the certificate states that the person, in accordance with further procedural requirements defined in the national law of the issuing state:

   (i) in due time either was summoned in person and thereby informed of the scheduled date and place of the trial which resulted in the decision, or by other means actually received official information of the scheduled date and place of that trial in such a manner that it was unequivocally established that he or she was aware of the scheduled trial, and was informed that a decision may be handed down if he or she does not appear for the trial; or

   (ii) being aware of the scheduled trial, had given a mandate to a legal counsellor, who was either appointed by the person concerned or by the state, to defend him or her at the trial, and was indeed defended by that counsellor at the trial; or

   (iii) after being served with the decision and being expressly informed of the right to a retrial, or an appeal, in which he or she has the right to participate and which allows the merits of the case, including fresh evidence, to be re-examined, and which may lead to the original decision being reversed, expressly stated that he or she does not contest the decision, or did not request a retrial or appeal within the applicable time frame; or

(c) according to the certificate provided, the person did not appear in person, unless the certificate states that the person, having been expressly informed about the proceedings and the possibility of appearing in person in a trial, expressly waived his or her right to an oral hearing and has expressly indicated that he or she does not contest the case.[115]

---

[114] Council Framework Decision 2009/299/JHA of 26 February 2009 amending Framework Decisions 2002/584/JHA, 2005/214/JHA, 2006/783/JHA, 2008/909/JHA and 2008/947/JHA, thereby enhancing the procedural rights of persons and fostering the application of the principle of mutual recognition to decisions rendered in the absence of the person concerned at the trial, OJ L 81/24, 27.3.2009. See Recital (2).

[115] Framework Decision, art 7(2) as amended by Framework Decision 2009/299/JHA, art 3.

It is normally immaterial that the penalty is larger than that which would have been imposed in the state of execution. To that there is a limited exception: where it is established that the decision is related to acts which were not carried out within the territory of the issuing state, the executing state may decide to reduce the amount of the penalty enforced to the maximum amount provided for acts of the same kind under the national law of the executing state, when the acts fall within the jurisdiction of that state.[116]

The enforcement of a decision is to be governed by the law of the executing state in the same way as a financial penalty of that state. Where it is not possible to enforce a decision, either totally or in part, alternative sanctions, including custodial sanctions, may be applied by the executing state if its laws so provide in such cases and the issuing state has allowed for the application of such alternative sanctions in its certificate. The severity of the alternative sanction will be determined in accordance with the law of the executing state, but must not exceed any maximum level stated in the certificate transmitted by the issuing state.[117] Amnesty and pardon may be granted by the issuing state and also by the executing state, but only the issuing state may determine any application for review of the decision.[118]

Monies obtained from the enforcement of decisions shall accrue to the executing state unless otherwise agreed between the issuing and the executing state.[119] Member States cannot claim from each other the refund of costs resulting from application of the Framework Decision.[120]

6. The Framework Decision on custodial penalties

The second instrument dealt with the, potentially more difficult, issue of custodial sentences.[121] The negotiating process was undoubtedly eased by the precedent set in connection with financial penalties, but custodial sentences do give rise to additional considerations. A new Council Framework Decision[122] was agreed in November 2008. It was to be implemented by 5 December 2011 and applies to judgments transmitted after that date. It makes no provision for Central Authorities; only 'competent authorities' may be designated.[123] It is limited to final decisions or orders of a court imposing a sentence on a natural person; it applies to any custodial sentence or any measure involving deprivation of liberty imposed for a limited or unlimited period of time on account of a criminal offence on the basis of criminal proceedings.[124] Instead of merely providing for the recognition

---

[116] Framework Decision, art 8.   [117] Framework Decision, arts 9, 10.
[118] Framework Decision, art 11.   [119] Framework Decision, art 13.
[120] Framework Decision, art 17.
[121] A further instrument, agreed in 2006, and dealing with the mutual recognition of confiscation orders is dealt with in Chapter 9 in the context of the proceeds of crime.
[122] Council Framework Decision of 27 November 2008 on the application of the principle of mutual recognition to judgments in criminal matters imposing custodial sentences or measures involving deprivation of liberty for the purpose of their enforcement in the European Union, OJ L 327/27, 5.12.2008.
[123] Framework Decision, art 2.   [124] Framework Decision, art 1.

and enforcement of a sentence, it declares that is done 'with a view to facilitating the social rehabilitation of the sentenced person'.[125]

In some cases, a judgment may only be transmitted to another Member State for execution if the sentenced person gives his or her consent. However, consent is not required where the judgment is to be forwarded to the Member State of nationality in which the sentenced person lives; to the Member State to which the sentenced person will be deported once he or she is released from the enforcement of the sentence on the basis of an expulsion or deportation order included in the judgment or in a judicial or administrative decision or any other measure consequential to the judgment; or to the Member State to which the sentenced person has fled or otherwise returned in view of the criminal proceedings pending against him or her in the issuing state or following the conviction in that issuing state. In all cases where the sentenced person is still in the issuing state, he or she must be given an opportunity to state his or her opinion orally or in writing. Where the issuing state considers it necessary in view of the sentenced person's age or his or her physical or mental condition, that opportunity is to be given to his or her legal representative. The opinion of the sentenced person is to be taken into account when deciding the issue of forwarding the judgment.[126]

Before a judgment is transmitted under the Framework Decision, a number of conditions must be met:

(a) the sentenced person must be in the issuing state or in the executing state;

(b) where it is required the consent of the sentenced person must have been given; and

(c) the competent authority of the issuing state, where appropriate after consultations between the competent authorities of the issuing and the executing states, must be satisfied that the enforcement of the sentence by the executing state would serve the purpose of facilitating the social rehabilitation of the sentenced person.[127]

If these conditions are met, the judgment with a certificate in the form prescribed in the Annex to the Framework Decision may be sent to any of the following:

(a) the Member State of nationality of the sentenced person in which he or she lives;

(b) the Member State of nationality, to which, while not being the Member State where he or she lives, the sentenced person will be deported, once he or she is released from the enforcement of the sentence on the basis of an expulsion or deportation order included in the judgment or in a judicial or administrative decision or any other measure taken consequential to the judgment; or

(c) any other Member State other than a Member State, the competent authority of which consents to the forwarding of the judgment to that Member State.

---

[125] Framework Decision, art 3(1).   [126] Framework Decision, art 6.
[127] Framework Decision, art 4.

The judgment and certificate are transmitted by the competent authority of the issuing state directly to the competent authority of the executing state by any means which leaves a written record under conditions allowing the executing state to establish its authenticity.[128] In the usual case, the final decision on the recognition of the judgment and the enforcement of the sentence must be taken by the competent authority of the executing state within a period of ninety days of receipt of the judgment.[129] The executing state may, on its own initiative, request the issuing state to forward the judgment, and the sentenced person may also request the competent authorities of the issuing state or of the executing state to initiate a procedure for forwarding the judgment under the Framework Decision.[130]

The rules about double criminality are the same as those in the case of financial penalties,[131] but with a rather shorter list of offences to which the requirement does not apply.[132]

The competent authority of the executing state must recognize a judgment which has been forwarded and take forthwith all the necessary measures for the enforcement of the sentence.[133] However this obligation is subject to some special rules designed to address the fact that, unlike financial penalties, custodial sentences may differ not only in duration but also in nature: imprisonment with or without hard labour, reclusion, penal servitude, preventive detention, and so on. Where the sentence exceeds in duration the maximum penalty provided for similar offences under the national law of the executing state, the competent authority of that state may decide to adapt the sentence. The adapted sentence must not be less than the maximum penalty provided for similar offences under the law of the executing state.[134] Where the sentence is incompatible with the law of the executing state in terms of its nature, the competent authority of that state may adapt it to the punishment or measure provided for under its own law for similar offences. Such a punishment or measure is to correspond as closely as possible to the sentence imposed in the issuing state. It follows that it cannot be converted into a financial penalty.[135] In no case may an adapted sentence aggravate the sentence passed in the issuing state in terms of its nature or duration.

The obligation of the executing state is also subject to general grounds for non-recognition and non-enforcement. These correspond closely to those already noted in the case of financial penalties.[136]

---

[128] Framework Decision, art 5(1). For the languages to be used in the certificate, see art 23.

[129] Framework Decision, art 12.

[130] Framework Decision, art 4.

[131] See p 333, above.

[132] Framework Decision, art 7. The list is as that reproduced at p 333 n112 above in the context of financial penalties, down to and including sabotage. So, for example, a prison sentence for theft is not covered by the present Framework Decision.

[133] Framework Decision, art 8(1). Partial recognition and enforcement is permitted under the conditions set out in art 10, usually by agreement between the competent authorities of the issuing and the executing states.

[134] Framework Decision, art 8(2).

[135] Framework Decision, art 8(3).

[136] Framework Decision, art 9 as amended by Framework Decision 2009/299/JHA, art 5. In place of the reference to the financial penalty being below €70 or its equivalent is one that at the time the

Where the custodial sentence is to be executed under the Framework Decision, several practical issues arise. The sentenced person may be in the executing state. In such a case, the executing state may, at the request of the issuing state, before the arrival of the judgment, or before the decision to recognize the judgment and enforce the sentence, arrest the sentenced person, or take any other measure to ensure that the sentenced person remains in its territory, pending a decision to recognize the judgment and enforce the sentence.[137] The duration of the sentence must not be aggravated as a result of any period spent in custody by reason of this provision.

If the sentenced person is in the issuing state, he or she must be transferred to the executing state. This must be at a time agreed between the competent authorities of the issuing and the executing states, and no later than thirty days after the final decision of the executing state on the recognition of the judgment and enforcement of the sentence has been taken. If this deadline cannot be met due to unforeseen circumstances, the two states may set a new time limit.[138]

The enforcement of a sentence is governed by the law of the executing state, including the grounds for early or conditional release. The competent authority of the issuing state may seek information from the competent authority of the executing state as to the applicable provisions on possible early or conditional release; if these are unacceptable the issuing state may withdraw its request for the recognition and enforcement of the sentence.[139] An amnesty or pardon may be granted by the issuing state and also by the executing state.[140]

The Framework Decision contains a specialty rule. With certain exceptions, a person transferred to the executing state may not be prosecuted, sentenced, or otherwise deprived of his or her liberty for an offence committed before his or her transfer other than that for which he or she was transferred.[141]

Costs resulting from the application of the Framework Decision are borne by the executing state, except for the costs of the transfer of the sentenced person to that state and those arising exclusively in the sovereign territory of the issuing state.[142]

The Framework Decision replaces as between the Member States the European Convention on the Transfer of Sentenced Persons 1983 and its Additional Protocol; the European Convention on the International Validity of Criminal Judgments 1970; certain provisions of the Schengen *acquis*; and the Convention between the Member States of the European Communities on the Enforcement of Foreign Criminal Sentences of 1991.

---

judgment was received by the competent authority of the executing state, less than six months of the sentence remained to be served.

[137] Framework Decision, art 14. The effect must not be to aggravate the sentence; in other words, the time spent in custody under this provision will be allowed against the sentence.
[138] Framework Decision, art 15. For transit through other Member States, see art 16.
[139] Framework Decision, art 17.
[140] Framework Decision, art 19.
[141] Framework Decision, art 18.
[142] Framework Decision, art 24.

7. The Framework Decision on probation and similar measures

The third Framework Decision deals with probation and similar measures.[143] The title is misleading as the Framework Decision covers a very wide range of non-custodial sentences. One of the difficulties faced in preparing this instrument was that of defining its scope given the variety of practice in different legal systems, and the result is seen in definitions of some complexity.

The scope of the Framework Decision is initially stated to be the recognition of judgments and, where applicable, probation decisions, the transfer of responsibility for the supervision of probation measures and alternative sanctions, and decisions relating to those matters;[144] but almost all of the terms used in that statement are further defined.[145] So a 'judgment' without further definition would cover almost any court decision; in this context it means final decision or order of a court of the issuing state, establishing that a natural person has committed a criminal offence and imposing (a) a custodial sentence or measure involving deprivation of liberty, if a conditional release[146] has been granted on the basis of that judgment or by a subsequent probation decision; (b) a suspended sentence;[147] (c) a conditional sentence;[148] or (d) an alternative sanction. 'Probation measures' are obligations and instructions imposed by a competent authority on a natural person, in accordance with the national law of the issuing state, in connection with a suspended sentence, a conditional sentence, or a conditional release. An 'alternative sanction' is a sanction, other than a custodial sentence, a measure involving deprivation of liberty, or a financial penalty, imposing an obligation or instruction.

The Framework Decision further defines 'probation measures' and 'alternative sanctions' in article 4, which lists the types of requirements which must be super-vised by the executing state; an individual Member State may give notice of its willingness to supervise other types of order not included in the list. Those listed are:

(a) an obligation for the sentenced person to inform a specific authority of any change of residence or working place;

---

[143] Council Framework Decision 2008/947/JHA of 27 November 2008 on the application of the principle of mutual recognition to judgments and probation decisions with a view to the supervision of probation measures and alternative sanctions, OJ L 337/102, 16.12.2008. Implementation was required by 6 December 2011.

[144] Framework Decision, art 1(2).

[145] Framework Decision, art 2.

[146] Conditional release means a final decision of a competent authority or stemming from the national law on the early release of a sentenced person after part of the custodial sentence or measure involving deprivation of liberty has been served by imposing one or more probation measures.

[147] Defined as a custodial sentence or measure involving deprivation of liberty, the execution of which is conditionally suspended, wholly or in part, when the sentence is passed by imposing one or more probation measures included in the judgment itself or determined in a separate probation decision taken by a competent authority. A 'probation decision' is a judgment or a final decision of a competent authority of the issuing state taken on the basis of such judgment and granting a conditional release or imposing probation measures.

[148] Defined to mean a judgment in which the imposition of a sentence has been conditionally deferred by imposing one or more probation measures or in which one or more probation measures are imposed instead of a custodial sentence or measure involving deprivation of liberty, the probation measures being either included in the judgment itself or determined in a separate probation decision taken by a competent authority.

(b) an obligation not to enter certain localities, places or defined areas in the issuing or executing state;

(c) an obligation containing limitations on leaving the territory of the executing state;

(d) instructions relating to behaviour, residence, education and training, leisure activities, or containing limitations on or modalities of carrying out a professional activity;

(e) an obligation to report at specified times to a specific authority;

(f) an obligation to avoid contact with specific persons;

(g) an obligation to avoid contact with specific objects, which have been used or are likely to be used by the sentenced person with a view to committing a criminal offence;

(h) an obligation to compensate financially for the prejudice caused by the offence and/or an obligation to provide proof of compliance with such an obligation;

(i) an obligation to carry out community service;

(j) an obligation to cooperate with a probation officer or with a representative of a social service having responsibilities in respect of sentenced persons;

(k) an obligation to undergo therapeutic treatment or treatment for addiction.

The declared objective is to facilitate the social rehabilitation of sentenced persons, to improve the protection of victims and of the general public, and to facilitate the application of suitable probation measures and alternative sanctions, in case of offenders who do not live in the state of conviction.[149]

Each Member State must designate 'competent authorities' which may include non-judicial authorities, provided that in certain cases[150] a decision by a non-judicial authority may, on request of the person concerned, be reviewed by a court or by 'another independent court-like body'.[151] No central authorities can be appointed under this Framework Decision. In the usual case, the competent authority of the issuing state will forward a judgment or probation decision to the competent authority of the Member State in which the sentenced person is lawfully and ordinarily residing, where the sentenced person has returned or wants to return to that state. Exceptionally, at the request of the sentenced person, a judgment or probation decision may be forwarded to a competent authority of some other Member State if that authority has consented to such forwarding.[152] In every case, the judgment or probation decision must be accompanied by a certificate in the form in the Annex to the Framework Decision.[153]

---

[149] Framework Decision, art 1(1).

[150] Those covered by Framework Decision art 14(1)(b) and (c), principally decisions taken after non-compliance with a probation measure or alternative sanction or if the sentenced person has committed a new criminal offence.

[151] Framework Decision, art 3.

[152] Framework Decision, art 5.

[153] Framework Decision, art 6. For the languages to be used in the certificate, see art 21.

The competent authority of the executing state must recognize the judgment or probation decision and take without delay all necessary measures for the supervision of the probation measures or alternative sanctions.[154] It must take its decision as soon as possible, and, barring exceptional circumstances, within sixty days of receipt.[155]

If the nature or duration of the relevant probation measure or alternative sanction, or the duration of the probation period, is incompatible with the law of the executing state, the competent authority of that state may adapt them in line with the corresponding rules applying to equivalent offences under the law of the executing state. If such adaptation is prompted by the duration exceeding the maximum allowed under the law of the executing state, the duration as adapted must be set at that maximum level. In no case may an adapted order be more severe or of longer duration than in the original order.[156]

The obligation of the executing state is also subject to general grounds for non-recognition and non-enforcement. These correspond closely to those already noted in the case of financial penalties.[157]

The rules as to double criminality are the same as those in the Framework Decision relating to custodial sentences.[158]

The supervision and application of probation measures and alternative sanctions is governed by the law of the executing state.[159] The competent authority of that state has jurisdiction to take, in accordance with its own law, all subsequent decisions relating to a suspended sentence, conditional release, conditional sentence and alternative sanction, in particular in case of non-compliance with a probation measure or alternative sanction or if the sentenced person commits a new criminal offence. In all Member States this includes the modification of obligations or instructions contained in the probation measure or alternative sanction, or the modification of the duration of the probation period. It may also include the revocation of the suspension of the execution of the judgment or the revocation of the decision on conditional release; and the imposition of a custodial sentence or measure involving deprivation of liberty in case of an alternative sanction or conditional sentence. In these latter cases, however, a Member State may declare that it will not accept the responsibility for making some or all of such decisions; if the competent authority of the executing state believes that such a decision need to be taken it must transfer jurisdiction back to the competent authority of the issuing state.[160]

---

[154] Framework Decision, art 8(1).

[155] Framework Decision, art 12(1).

[156] Framework Decision, art 9.

[157] Framework Decision, art 11 as amended by Framework Decision 2009/299/JHA, art 5. In place of the reference to the financial penalty being below €70 or its equivalent is one that the probation measure or alternative sanction is of less than six months' duration.

[158] Framework Decision, art 10.

[159] Framework Decision, art 13.

[160] Framework Decision, art 14. Jurisdiction may also revert to the issuing state if the sentenced person absconds or no longer has a lawful and ordinary residence in the executing state, or if new criminal proceedings against the person concerned are taking place in the issuing state: art 20.

An amnesty or pardon may be granted by the issuing state and also by the executing state, but only the issuing state may decide on applications for review of the relevant judgment.[161]

Costs resulting from the application of the Framework Decision are borne by the executing state, except for costs arising exclusively within the territory of the issuing state.[162]

The Framework Decision replaces, as between Member States, the corresponding provisions of the Council of Europe Convention of 30 November 1964 on the Supervision of Conditionally Sentenced or Conditionally Released Offenders.[163]

8. Framework Decision on supervision measures as an alternative to provisional detention

In 2004 the Commission published a Green Paper[164] on another aspect of the recognition of supervision orders. This dealt with the mutual recognition of non-custodial pre-trial supervision measures. Although, at least in theory, pre-trial detention is regarded as an exceptional measure it is much used in some countries. Alternatives such as bail or its equivalent are available, but the possibility of their enforcement across borders had not previously been considered. Although some took the view that relatively few people would be affected, in 2006 the Commission produced a proposal for a 'European supervision order' for use in this context.[165] That particular idea was not accepted but there was agreement to a Framework Decision providing for mutual recognition.[166] This lays down rules according to which one Member State recognizes a decision on supervision measures issued in another Member State as an alternative to provisional detention, monitors the supervision measures, and surrenders the person concerned to the issuing state in case of breach of these measures. Its provisions are broadly similar to those in the Framework Decision on probation and similar measures. Member States are required to implement it by 1 December 2012.

9. Disqualifications

The subject of the recognition of disqualifications imposed in, or in consequence of, criminal proceedings has proved more difficult. In 2006 the Commission issued a paper addressing the issue of the recognition of disqualifications imposed in criminal proceedings.[167] This noted the range of provisions in instruments dealing

---

[161] Framework Decision, art 19.   [162] Framework Decision, art 22.
[163] Framework Decision, art 23.   [164] COM(2004) 562 final, 17.8.2004.
[165] COM(2006) 468 final, 29.8.2006.
[166] Council Framework Decision 2009/829/JHA of 23 October 2009 on the application, between Member States of the European Union, of the principle of mutual recognition to decisions on supervision measures as an alternative to provisional detention, OJ L 294/20, 11.11.2009.
[167] Communication on Disqualifications arising from criminal convictions in the European Union, COM(2006) 73 final, 21.2.2006.

with particular topics for the recognition of disqualifications.[168] At that time, the Commission favoured this 'sectoral' approach and no general Framework Decision was proposed. It has now indicated that a legislative proposal on the mutual recognition of disqualifications will be made in 2013.

III. Transfer of proceedings

In the area of civil and commercial matters, it is quite common for the courts of several states to be able to take jurisdiction to resolve a dispute. In the civil law tradition, a court cannot refuse to exercise jurisdiction properly invoked by the claimant. In the common law tradition, the defendant may ask the court, in its discretion, to stay proceedings to enable it to be tried in a more appropriate forum, the *forum conveniens*. Neither approach is entirely satisfactory; that of the civil law encourages a race to the courthouse; that of the common law may lead to protracted and expensive litigation on the preliminary issue of where to litigate, each party seeking a tactical advantage.

In criminal cases there is a quite different dynamic. The accused is in no position to argue where the trial should be held, and the prosecution is often more concerned that there should be a conviction than which court should pronounce it. So there may well be agreement between the prosecuting authorities of two states that one or the other should host the criminal proceedings. International texts can provide a framework within which this can take place.

1. European Convention on the Transfer of Proceedings in Criminal Matters

A European Convention on the Transfer of Proceedings in Criminal Matters[169] was signed on 15 May 1972 and came into force on 30 March 1978; its aim was to supplement the work which the Member States of the Council of Europe had already done in the field of criminal law by addressing the disadvantages resulting from conflicts of jurisdiction.[170] As at December 2011 there were twenty-five states that had become parties to the Convention, but they do not include the United Kingdom.

The Convention operates by permitting the transfer of proceedings between Contracting States when the requested state appears to be in a better position to bring those proceedings to a successful conclusion. It offers, therefore, an interesting alternative to the more conventional types of mutual assistance in criminal matters, which contemplate trial in the requesting state.

---

[168] eg, Framework Decision 2004/68/JHA on combating the sexual exploitation of children and child pornography, OJ L 13/44, 20.1.2004 (prevention from exercising professional activities related to the supervision of children).

[169] ETS No 73.

[170] Convention, preamble.

The various grounds permitting transfer are set out in article 8, which is broadly drawn. A request may be made in any of these cases:

(a) if the suspected person is ordinarily resident in the requested state;

(b) if the suspected person is a national of the requested state or if that state is his state of origin;

(c) if the suspected person is undergoing or is to undergo a sentence involving deprivation of liberty in the requested state;

(d) if proceedings for the same or other offences are being taken against the suspected person in the requested state;

(e) if it (ie, the requesting state) considers that transfer of the proceedings is warranted in the interests of arriving at the truth and in particular that the most important items of evidence are located in the requested state;

(f) if it considers that the enforcement in the requested state of a sentence if one were passed is likely to improve the prospects for the social rehabilitation of the person sentenced;

(g) if it considers that the presence of the suspected person cannot be ensured at the hearing of proceedings in the requesting state and that his presence in person at the hearing of proceedings in the requested state can be ensured;

(h) if it considers that it could not itself enforce a sentence if one were passed, even by having recourse to extradition, and that the requested state could do so.

The transfer of proceedings is made competent by article 2, which simply states that any Contracting State shall have competence to prosecute under its own criminal law any offence to which the law of another Contracting State is applicable. This competence is to be exercised solely pursuant to a request for proceedings presented by another Contracting State.

The transfer of proceedings is also to be considered where a state is aware of proceedings in another Contracting State for the same offence.[171] The two states are to evaluate the circumstances found in article 8 and determine which of them should alone continue the proceedings,[172] as article 3 gives states the power to waive or desist from proceedings against a suspect who is being or will be prosecuted for the same offence by another Contracting State. Proceedings should also be continued in a single state when two or more Contracting States have jurisdiction over several offences which are materially distinct but ascribed either to a single person or several persons acting in unison; or where a single offence is ascribed to several persons so acting.[173] Where a state waives its proceedings in favour of another state, it is to be deemed to have transferred its proceedings.[174]

---

[171] Convention, art 30 (in Part IV of the Convention dealing with 'Plurality of Criminal Proceedings').

[172] Convention, art 31.   [173] Convention, art 32.   [174] Convention, art 33.

While the Convention itself is a detailed document, the procedure for transferring proceedings is relatively simple. When a person is suspected of having committed an offence under the law of a Contracting State that state may request another Contracting State to take action on its behalf in accordance with the Convention.[175] Requests are to be transmitted between the Ministries of Justice and, in cases of urgency, through Interpol, although states may also reserve the right to use other channels.[176] There are various other procedural requirements, most notably that if the competence of the requested state is grounded solely on article 2 then the suspect must be informed of the request with a view to allowing him or her to present views on the matter before a decision on the request is taken.[177] It should also be noted that parties may not claim the refund of any expenses resulting from the application of the Convention.[178]

The Convention does not permit the requested state to take any action unless dual criminality is present and sanctions could have been imposed on the suspect in the requested state in those particular circumstances.[179] Once this has been established, the requested state decides in accordance with its own law what action should be taken on a request for assistance,[180] although the grounds on which a request may be refused are limited by article 11. The grounds given in article 11 are numerous, ranging from procedural requirements to permitting refusal where the offence was purely military or fiscal or of a political nature. Assistance may also be refused where proceedings would be contrary to the fundamental principles of the legal system of the requested state. A request may not be granted under the Convention if the case is time-barred in the requesting state, or when action is prevented by the application of the double jeopardy principle (*ne bis in idem*), as stated in article 35.[181] Article 35 provides that a person in respect of whom a final and enforceable criminal judgment has been rendered may neither be prosecuted nor sentenced nor subjected to enforcement of a sanction in another Contracting State for the same act, where he or she was acquitted; or the sanction imposed has been completely enforced or is being enforced, or has been wholly or partly the subject of a pardon or amnesty, or can no longer be enforced through lapse of time; or if the court did not impose a sanction on conviction. This is not to prevent the application of wider domestic provisions relating to the effect of *ne bis in idem* attached to foreign criminal judgments.[182] Where the act in question was committed in a Contracting State or was considered by the law of that state to have been committed there, that state is not bound to accept the effect of *ne bis in idem* unless it has itself requested the proceedings.[183]

Where the suspect has been finally sentenced in a Contracting State the transfer of proceedings may only be requested where the state cannot itself enforce the sentence even by having recourse to extradition and the other state does not accept

---

[175] Convention, art 6. [176] Convention, art 13. [177] Convention, art 17.
[178] Convention, art 20. [179] Convention, art 7(1). [180] Convention, art 9.
[181] Convention, art 10. [182] Convention, art 37. [183] Convention, art 35(3).

enforcement of a foreign judgment as a matter of principle or refuses to enforce such sentence.[184]

Once a state has made a request for assistance it can no longer prosecute the suspect in respect of the requested offence or enforce a judgment which has previously been pronounced against him or her. However, until the requested state makes a decision on the request, the requesting state may continue to take all the steps in a prosecution up to bringing the case to trial. The right to prosecute may revive in certain circumstances.[185]

Provisional powers are granted to the requested state where an intention to transmit a request has been announced and the requested state's jurisdiction is based solely on article 2. If the law of the requested state authorizes remand in custody for the offence in question and there are reasons to fear that the suspect will abscond or cause evidence to be suppressed, the requested state may provisionally arrest the suspect on the application of the requesting state.[186] Detention must in no circumstances be for longer than forty days.[187] In addition, the requested state has jurisdiction to apply all such provisional measures, including remand in custody and seizure of property, as would have been available had the offence been committed in its territory.[188]

Making a request for assistance also has the important effect of delaying the time limit for proceedings in the requesting and requested states for six months; in the case of the requested state this is subject to the requirement that jurisdiction be founded solely on article 2.[189] Where something has been done in the requesting state which validly interrupts the limitation period, this has the same effect in the requested state and vice versa.[190] Punishment for the offence cannot be any more severe than that which could have been imposed by the requesting state unless jurisdiction is not founded on article 2. Where it is not so founded, the sanction is to be that prescribed by the law of the requested state unless that law provides otherwise.[191]

2. Model Treaty on the Transfer of Proceedings in Criminal Matters

The United Nations has also prepared a Model Treaty dealing with the transfer of proceedings in criminal matters. Unlike the Council of Europe Convention, which is intended to provide comprehensive regulation of requests for assistance between its Contracting Parties, the United Nations Model is designed only to provide a guide in negotiations.

The provisions of the Model Treaty are simple. Where a person is suspected of having committed an offence, the state whose laws were violated may, if the proper interests of justice so require, request that another state take proceedings in respect of that offence and all Contracting Parties are to make legislative

---

[184] Convention, art 8(2).   [185] Convention, art 21.   [186] Convention, art 27.
[187] Convention, art 29.   [188] Convention, art 28.   [189] Convention, arts 22 and 23.
[190] Convention, art 26(2).   [191] Convention, art 25.

provision extending their criminal jurisdiction to enable proceedings to be taken, despite their necessarily extra-territorial nature.[192]

Requests for such transfers of proceedings are to be made in writing and transmitted either through diplomatic channels, between the respective Ministries of Justice, or via any other authorities that the parties may designate.[193] The costs of executing a request are not to be refunded unless otherwise agreed between the two states.[194]

Where proceedings are pending in two or more states against the same person for the same offence, the states are to decide which one of them is to continue with the prosecution. Such a decision is to have the same consequences as follow under the Model Treaty from a request for the transfer of proceedings.[195]

On receipt of a request the competent authorities of the requested state are to determine what action they can take under their own law in order to comply as fully as possible with the request.[196] However, the request may only be complied with if there is dual criminality.[197] Assistance may be refused on four grounds:

(a) if the suspect is not a national of or ordinarily resident in the requested state;

(b) if the act is an offence under military law but not also under the ordinary criminal law;

(c) if the offence is connected with taxes, duties, customs, or exchange matters; or

(d) if the offence is regarded by the requested state as being of a political nature.[198]

When the requesting state announces its intention to transmit a request, it may seek the application of such provisional measures, including detention and seizure, as would be applied under the law of the requested state if the offence had been committed in its own territory.[199]

The Model Treaty makes provision for the rights both of the suspect and the victim of the crime. An 'interest' may be expressed in the transfer by the suspect, or by his close relatives or his legal representatives. Before the request is made, the requesting state is, if practicable, to allow the suspect to express views on the alleged offence and the transfer, unless the suspect has absconded or otherwise obstructed the course of justice;[200] the text is silent as to what is to be done with these views, there being no obligation to communicate them to the requested state. The rights of the victim of the crime, in particular those relating to restitution or compensation, are not to be affected by the transfer of proceedings. If there has been no settlement prior to the transfer, the requested state is to permit the representation of the claim in the transferred proceedings if this is permitted by its law; this is a

---

[192] UN Model Treaty, art 1.
[193] UN Model Treaty, art 2. For the documentation required, see arts 3 and 4.
[194] UN Model Treaty, art 14.   [195] UN Model Treaty, art 13.
[196] UN Model Treaty, art 5.   [197] UN Model Treaty, art 6.
[198] UN Model Treaty, art 7.   [199] UN Model Treaty, art 12.
[200] UN Model Treaty, art 8.

reference to procedures akin to the intervention of a *partie civile* in French criminal cases. If the victim of the crime has died, this right is to be extended to any dependants.[201]

While the Model Treaty does not attempt to deal with the finer points of procedure, it has to cover those procedural matters which are of especial importance. These include the effects of the transfer on the requesting state. When the request is accepted the requesting state must provisionally discontinue the prosecution, to avoid double jeopardy, except to the extent that it is necessary to continue investigation and provide judicial assistance for the benefit of the requested state. The discontinuance becomes final when the requesting state is informed that the case has been finally disposed of in the requested state.[202]

The Treaty also deals with the effects of the transfer of proceedings on the requested state. The proceedings are to be governed by the law of the requested state, but where that state only has jurisdiction by virtue of the extended jurisdiction created by the Model Treaty,[203] the sentence imposed must not more severe than that which might be imposed in the requesting state.[204] This could, of course, raise difficult questions: is a suspended sentence of imprisonment, with no immediate penalty, more severe than a very heavy fine? As far as possible, any acts which were performed in the requesting state with a view to proceedings or procedural requirements and in accordance with its law are to have the same validity in the requested state as if they had been performed by its authorities.[205]

3. EU action

This is a matter which the European Union Member States have examined, with as yet no clear result. An agreement between the Member States on the transfer of proceedings in criminal matters was signed in 1990, before the Third Pillar came into being. That agreement never entered into force due to a lack of ratifications.

In 2009, a group of Member States proposed a Council Framework Decision on Transfer of Proceedings in Criminal Matters, but it has made little progress. The UK was opposed to some of its provisions, notably that in article 5(1), that for the purpose of applying the Framework Decision, any Member State would have competence to prosecute, under its national law, any offence to which the law of another Member State was applicable.[206]

---

[201] UN Model Treaty, art 9.
[202] UN Model Treaty, art 10.
[203] ie, jurisdiction is based on art 1(2).
[204] UN Model Treaty, art 11(1).
[205] UN Model Treaty, art 11(2).
[206] See the 27th report of the House of Commons European Scrutiny Committee for Session 2008–9.

Index